ARTIFICIAL INTELLIGENCE

A Systems Approach

ARTIFICIAL INTELLIGENCE

A Systems Approach

M. TIM JONES

JONES AND BARTLETT PUBLISHERS
Sudbury, Massachusetts
BOSTON   TORONTO   LONDON   SINGAPORE

World Headquarters

Jones and Bartlett Publishers
40 Tall Pine Drive
Sudbury, MA 01776
978-443-5000
info@jbpub.com
www.jbpub.com

Jones and Bartlett Publishers
Canada
6339 Ormindale Way
Mississauga, Ontario L5V 1J2
Canada

Jones and Bartlett Publishers
International
Barb House, Barb Mews
London W6 7PA
United Kingdom

Jones and Bartlett's books and products are available through most bookstores and online booksellers. To contact Jones and Bartlett Publishers directly, call 800-832-0034, fax 978-443-8000, or visit our website www.jbpub.com.

Substantial discounts on bulk quantities of Jones and Bartlett's publications are available to corporations, professional associations, and other qualified organizations. For details and specific discount information, contact the special sales department at Jones and Bartlett via the above contact information or send an email to specialsales@jbpub.com.

ISBN 978-0-7637-7337-3

Cover Design: Tyler Creative

Library of Congress Cataloging-in-Publication Data
JONES, M. TIM.
  Artificial intelligence : a systems approach / M. Tim Jones.
    p. cm.
  Includes index.
    ISBN-13: 978-0-9778582-3-1 (hardcover with cd-rom : alk. paper)
  1. Artificial intelligence—Data processing. 2. Artificial intelligence—Mathematical models. I. Title.
    Q336.J68 2008
    006.3—dc22

                                                                                2007045869

6048
Printed in the United States of America
12 11 10 09 08   10 9 8 7 6 5 4 3 2 1

DEDICATION

This book is dedicated to my wonderful wife, Jill, without whom this book would not be possible. I'm also indebted to my parents Maury and Celeta, who instilled in me a desire to learn and wonder.

ACKNOWLEDGMENTS

At the time of this writing, AI is celebrating its 50th anniversary. It was August of 1956 when researchers met at the Dartmouth Summer Research Project on Artificial Intelligence with the agenda of creating intelligent machines. In the 50 years that followed, AI has become a genuine field of study, but the road has not been without its bumps.

Acknowledging all those who've contributed to AI would fill a book much larger than this. But I'd like to personally recognize John McCarthy for introducing AI in 1955 (at the Dartmouth Summer Project) and for having created the wonderful Lisp programming language.

TABLE OF CONTENTS

1 THE HISTORY OF AI

The history of AI is interesting all by itself. It's a modern-day drama, filled with excitement and anticipation, discovery, and disappointment. From over-promises of early (and later) AI research, to fears of the unknown from the general public, AI's history is worthy of study by itself. In this chapter, we'll explore AI's tumultuous history and also provide a summary introduction to each of the chapters of this book.

WHAT IS INTELLIGENCE?

To build software that is deemed intelligent, it's helpful to begin with a definition of intelligence. Intelligence can be simply defined as a set of properties of the mind. These properties include the ability to plan, solve problems, and in general, reason. A simpler definition could be that intelligence is the ability to make the right decision given a set of inputs and a variety of possible actions.

Using this simple definition of intelligence (making the right decision), we can apply this not only to humans, but also to animals that exhibit rational behavior. But the intelligence that is exhibited by human beings is much more complex than that of animals. For example, humans have the ability to communicate with language, but so do some animals. Humans can also solve problems, but the same can be said of some animals. One difference then is that humans embody many aspects of intelligence (the ability to communicate, solve problems, learn and adapt) where animals typically embody a small number of intelligent characteristics, and usually at a much lower level than humans.

We can use the same analogy on AI applied to computer systems. For example, it's possible to build an application that plays a world-class game of Chess, but this program knows nothing of the game of Checkers, nor how to make a good cup of tea. A data mining application can help identify fraud, but can't navigate a complex environment. From this perspective, the most complex and intelligent applications can be deemed intelligent from one perspective, but lack even the simplest intelligence that can be seen in the least intelligent of animals.

NOTE ▶ *Famed author Isaac Asimov once wrote about his experience with aptitude tests in the army. In the army, he scored well above the norm. But what he realized was that he could score well on tests that were developed by others that shared his academic bents. He opined that if the tests were developed by people involved in auto repair, he would have scored very poorly. The issue being that tests are developed around a core of expertise, and scoring poorly on one doesn't necessarily indicate a lack of intelligence.*

THE SEARCH FOR MECHANICAL INTELLIGENCE

History is filled with stories of the creation of intelligent machines. In the 800s BC, the Iliad described the winged Talos, a bronze automaton forged by Hephaestus to protect Crete. The inner workings of Talos weren't described, except that he was bronze, and filled with ichor (or a Greek god's blood). A more recent example is Mary Shelley's Frankenstein, in which the scientist recreates life from old. In 1921, Karel Capek's play "Rossum's Universal Robots" introduced the concept of cheap labor through robotics.

But one of the most interesting applications of artificial intelligence, in a non-robitic form, was that of the HAL 9000 introduced by Arthur C. Clark in his his novel "2001: A Space Odyssey." HAL was a sentient artificial intelligence that occupied the Discovery spaceship (en route to Jupiter). HAL had no physical form, but instead managed the spaceship's systems, visually watched the human occupants through a network of cameras, and communicated with them in a normal human voice. The moral behind the story of HAL was one of modern-day programming. Software does exactly what one tells it to do, and can make incorrect decisions trying to focus on a single important goal. HAL obviously was not created with Isaac Asimov's three laws of robotics in mind.

THE VERY EARLY DAYS (THE EARLY 1950s)

While the term artificial intelligence had not yet been conceived, the 1950s were the very early days of AI. Early computer systems were being built, and the ideas of building intelligent machines were beginning to form.

Alan Turing

In 1950 it was Alan Turing who asked whether a machine could think. Turing not long before had introduced the concept of his universal abstract machine (called the *Turing Machine*) that was simple and could solve any mathematical problem (albiet with some complexity). Building on this idea, Turing wondered that if a computer's response were indistinguishable from a human, then the computer could be considered a thinking machine. The result of this experiment is called the *Turing Test*.

In the Turing test, if the machine could fool a human into thinking that it was also human, then it passed the intelligence test. One way to think of the Turing test is by communicating to the other agent through a keyboard. Questions are asked of the peer through written text, and responses are provided through the terminal. This test provides a way to determine if intelligence was created. Considering the task at hand, not only must the intelligent peer contain the necessary knowledge to have an intelligent conversation, it must be able to parse and understand natural language and generate natural language responses. The questions may involve reasoning skills (such as problem solving), so mimicking humans would be a feat!

An important realization of Turing during this period was the need to start small and grow intelligence, rather than expecting it to materialize. Turing proposed what he called the *Child Machine* in which a lesser intelligent agent would be created and then subjected to a course of education. Rather than assume that we could build an adult intelligence, we would build a child intelligence first and then inject it with knowledge. This idea of starting small and at lower levels corresponds with later ideas of so-called "scruffy" thinkers. The human brain is complex and not fully understood, instead of striving to imitate this, why not start smaller at the child (or even smaller organism) and work our way up? Turing called this the *blank sheets* argument. A child is like a notebook that's full of blank sheets, but is a mechanism by which knowledge is stored.

Alan Turing's life ended at a young age, but he's considered the founder of the field of AI (even though the moniker would not be applied for another six years).

AI, Problem Solving, and Games

Some of the earliest applications of AI focused on games and general problem solving. At this time, creating an intelligent machine was based on the belief that the machine would be intelligent if it could do something that people do (and perhaps find difficult).

NOTE▶ *In 1950, Claude Shannon proposed that the game of Chess was fundamentaly a search problem. In fact, he was correct, but brute force search isn't truly practical for the search space that exists with Chess. Search, heuristics, and a catalog of opening and ending moves provides a faster and more efficient way to play Chess. Shannon's seminal paper on computer Chess produced what is called the Shannon number, or 10^{120}, which represents the lower bound of the game tree complexity of Chess. [Shannon 1950]*

The first AI program written for a computer was called "The Logic Theorist." It was developed in 1956 by Allen Newell, Herbert Simon, and J. C. Shaw to find proofs for equations. [Newell 1956] What was most unique about this program is that it found a better proof than had existed before for a given equation. In 1957, Simon and Newell built on this work to develop the General Problem Solver (GPS). The GPS used means-end analysis to solve problems, but in general was restricted to toy problems.

Like complex math, early AI researchers believed that if a computer could solve problems that they thought were complex, then they could build intelligent machines. Similarly, games provided an interesting testbed for the development of algorithms and techniques for intelligent decision making.

In the UK at Oxford University in the early 1950s, researchers developed game-playing programs for two complex games. Christopher Strachey developed a Checkers playing program on the Ferranti Mark I. By 1952, his program could play a reasonable game of Checkers. Dietrich Prinz developed a program, again for the Ferranti Mark I, that could play Chess (mate-in-two variety). His program could search a thousand possible moves, but on this early computer, it required significant time and played very slowly.

In 1952, Arthur Samuel raised the bar for AI programs. His Checkers playing program, which ran on the IBM 701, included learning and generalization. What Samuel did with his learning Checkers program was unique in that he allowed two copies of his program to play one another, and therefore learn from each other. The result was a program that could defeat its creator. By 1962, Samuel's Checkers program defeated the former Connecticut Checkers champion.

 Samuel's program, and his approach of playing copies against one another, is one of the first examples of computing survival of the fittest and the field which came to be called evolutionary computation.

ARTIFICIAL INTELLIGENCE EMERGES AS A FIELD

By the mid 1950s, AI began to solidify as a field of study. At this point in AI's life, much of the focus was on what is called *Strong AI* Strong AI is focused on building AI that mimics the mind. The result is a sapient entity with human-like intelligence, self-awareness, and consciousness.

The Dartmouth AI Summer Research Project

In 1956, the Dartmouth AI Conference brought about those involved in research in AI: John McCarthy (Dartmouth), Marvin Minsky (Harvard), Nathaniel Rochester (IBM), and Claude Shannon (Bell Telephone Laboratories) brought together researchers in computers, natural language processing, and neuron nets to Dartmouth College for a month-long session of AI discussions and research. The Summer research project on AI began:

> We propose that a 2 month, 10 man study of artificial intelligence be carried out during the summer of 1956 at Dartmouth College in Hanover, New Hampshire. The study is to proceed on the basis of the conjecture that every aspect of learning or any other feature of intelligence can in principle be so precisely described that a machine can be made to simulate it. An attempt will be made to find how to make machines use language, form abstractions and concepts, solve kinds of problems now reserved for humans, and improve themselves. We think that a significant advance can be made in one or more of these problems if a carefully selected group of scientists work on it together for a summer.

Since then, many AI conferences have been held around the world, and on a variety of disciplines studied under the AI moniker. In 2006, Dartmouth held the "Dartmouth Artificial Intelligence Conference: The Next Fifty Years" (informally known as AI@50). The conference was well attended (even from a few that attended the first conference 50 years prior), and analyzed AI's progress and how its challenges relate to those of other fields of study.

Building Tools for AI

In addition to coining the term artificial intelligence, and bringing together major researchers in AI in his 1956 Dartmouth conference, John McCarthy designed the first AI programming language. LISP was first described by McCarthy in his paper titled "Recursive Functions of Symbolic Expressions and their Computation by Machine, Part I." The first LISP compiler was also implemented in LISP, by Tim Hart and Mike Levin at MIT in 1962 for the IBM 704.

This compiler introduced many advanced features, such as incremental compilation. [LISP 2007] McCarthy's LISP also pioneered many advanced concepts now familiar in computer science, such as trees (data structures), dynamic typing, object-oriented programming, and compiler self-hosting.

LISP was used in a number of early AI systems, demonstrating its usefulness as an AI language. One such program, called SHRDLU, provides a natural language interface to a table-top world of objects. The program can understand queries about the table-top "world," reason about the state of things in the world, plan actions, and perform some rudimentary learning. SHRDLU was designed and implemented by Terry Winograd at the MIT AI Lab on a PDP-6 computer.

LISP, and the many dialects that evolved from it, are still in wide use today. Chapter 13 provides an introduction to the languages of AI, including LISP.

The Focus on Strong AI

Recall that the focus of early AI was in Strong AI. Solving math or logic problems, or engaging in dialogue, was viewed as intelligent, while activities such as walking freely in unstable environments (which we do every day) were not.

In 1966, Joseph Weizenbaum of MIT developed a program that parodied a psychologist and could hold an interesting dialogue with a *patient*. The design of Eliza would be considered simple by today's standards, but its pattern-matching abilities, which provided reasonable responses to patient statements was real to many people. This quality of the program was troubling to Weizenbaum who later became a critic of AI because of its lack of compassion.

Constrained Applications

While much of early AI was Strong-focused, there were numerous applications that focused on solving practical problems. One such application was called the "Dendral Project," emerging in 1965 at Stanford University. Dendral was developed to help organic chemists understand the organization of unknown organic molecules. It used as its inputs mass spectrometry graphs and a knowledge base of chemistry, making it the first known expert system.

Other constrained applications in this era include Macsyma, a computer algebra system developed at MIT by Carl Engelman, William Martin, and Joel Moses. Macsyma was written in MacLisp, a dialect of LISP developed at MIT. This early mathematical expert system demonstrated solving integration problems with symbolic reasoning. The ideas demonstrated in Macsyma eventually made their way into commercial math applications.

Bottom-Up Approaches Emerge

Early AI focused on a top-down approach to AI, attempting to simulate or mimic the higher level concepts of the brain (planning, reasoning, language understanding, etc.). But bottom-up approaches began to gain favor in the 1960s, primarily modeling lower-level concepts, such as neurons and learning at a much lower level. In 1949, Donald Hebb introduced his rule that describes how neurons can associate with one another if they are repeatedly active at the same time. The contribution of one cell's firing to enable another will increase over time with persistent firing, leading to a strong relationship between the two (a causal relationship).

But in 1957, the perceptron was created by Frank Rosenblatt at the Cornell Aeronautical Laboratory. The perceptron is a simple linear classifier that can classify data into two classes using an unsupervised learning algorithm. The perceptron created considerable interest in neural network architectures, but change was not far away.

NOTE ► *Hebbian learning, perceptrons, and more advanced neural network architectures and learning algorithms are covered in the neural network Chapters 8 and 9.*

AI'S WINTER

Prior to the 1970s, AI had generated considerable interest, and also considerable hype from the research community. Many interesting systems had been developed, but these fell quite short of the predictions made by some in the community. But new techniques such as neural networks breathed new life into this evolving field, providing additional ways for classification and learning. But the excitement of neural networks came to an end in 1969 with the publication of the mongraph titled "Perceptrons." This monograph was written by Marvin Minsky and Seymour Papert, strong advocates of Strong (or top-down) AI. The authors rightly demonstrated that single-layer perceptrons were limited, particularly when confronted with problems that are not linearly separable (such as the XOR problem). The result was a steep decline of funding into neural network research, and in general, research in AI as a field. Subsequent research would find that the multi-layer networks solved the linear separation problem, but too late for the damage done to AI.

Hardware built for AI, such as the LISP machines, also suffered a loss of interest. While the machines gave way to more general systems (not necessarily programmed in LISP), the functional languages like LISP continued to attract attention. Popular editors such as EMACS (developed during this period) still support a large user community with a scripting shell based on LISP.

Results-Oriented Applications

While there was a reduction in focus and spending in AI research in the 1970s, AI development continued but in a more focused arena. Applications that showed promise, such as expert systems, rose as one of the key developments in this era.

One of the first expert systems to demonstrate the power of rules-based architectures was called MYCIN, and was developed by Ted Shortliffe following his dissertation on the subject while at Stanford (1974). MYCIN operated in the field of medical diagnosis, and demonstrated knowledge representation and inference. Later in this decade, another dissertation at Stanford by Bill VanMelles built on the MYCIN architecture and serves as a model for the expert system shell (still in use today). In Chapter 5 we'll provide an introduction to the representation of knowledge and inference with logic.

Other results-oriented applications included those focused on natural language understanding. The goal of systems in this era was in the development of intelligent question answering systems. To understand a question stated in natural language, the question must first be parsed into its fundamental parts. Bill Woods introduced the idea of the Augmented Transition Network (or ATN) that represents formal languages as augmented graphs. From Eliza in the 1960s to ATNs in the 1970s, Natural Language Processing (NLP) and Natural Language Understanding (NLU) continues today in the form of chatterbots.

Additional AI Tools Emerge

John McCarthy introduced the idea of AI-focused tools in the 1950s with the development of the LISP language. Expert systems and their shells continued the trend with tools for AI, but another interesting development that in a way combined the two ideas resulted from the Prolog language. Prolog was a language built for AI, and was also a shell (for which expert systems could be developed). Prolog was created in 1972 by Alain Colmeraur and Phillipe Roussel based on the idea of Horn clauses. Prolog is a declarative high-level language based on formal logic. Programs written in Prolog consist of facts and rules that reason over those facts. You can find more information on Prolog in Chapter 5 Knowledge Representation and Chapter 13, The Languages of AI.

Neat vs Scruffy Approaches

A split in AI, its focus, and basic approaches was also seen during this period. Traditional, or top-down AI (also called Good-Old-Fashioned-AI, or GOFAI for short) continued during this period but new approaches began to emerge that looked at AI from the bottom-up. These approaches were also labeled *Neat* and *Scruffy* approaches segregating them into their representative camps. Those in the neat camp favored formal approaches to AI that were pure and provable. But those in the scruffy camp used methods less provable but still yielding useful and significant results. A number of scruffy approaches to AI that became popular during this period included genetic algorithms (modeling natural selection for optimization) and neural networks (modeling brain behavior from the neuron up).

Genetic algorithms became popularized in the 1970s due to the work of John Holland and his students at the University of Michigan. Holland's book on the topic continues to be a useful resource. Neural networks, while stagnant for a time after the publication of "Perceptrons," were revived with Paul John Werbos' creation of the backpropagation algorithm. This algorithm remains the most widely used supervised learning algorithm for training feedforward neural networks. You can learn more about genetic algorithms and evolutionary computation in Chapter 3 and neural networks in Chapters 8, and 9.

AI RE-EMERGES

Just as spring always follows the winter, AI's winter would eventually end and bring new life into the field (starting in the mid to late 1980s). The re-emergence of AI had significant differences from the early days. Firstly, the wild predictions of creating intelligent machines were for the most part over. Instead, researchers and AI practitioners focused on specific goals primarily in the *weak* aspects of AI (as opposed to *Strong* AI). Weak AI focused on solving specific problems, compared to Strong AI, whose goal was to emulate the full range of human cognitive capabilities. Secondly, the field of AI broadened to include many new types of approaches, for example, the biologically inspired approaches such as Ant Colony Optimization (ACO).

The Silent Return

An interesting aspect of AI's return was that it occurred silently. Instead of the typical claims of Strong AI, weak algorithms found use in a variety of settings. Fuzzy logic and fuzzy control systems were used in a number of settings, including camera auto-focus, antilock braking systems as well as playing a part in medical diagnosis. Collaborative filtering algorithms found their way into product recommendation at a popular online bookseller, and popular Internet search engines use AI algorithms to cluster search results to help make finding what you need easier.

The silent return follows what Rodney Brooks calls the "AI effect." AI algorithms and methods transition from being "AI" to standard algorithms and methods once they become practically useful. The methods described above are one example, another is speech recognition. The algorithms behind recognizing the sounds of speech and translating them into symbols were once described within the confines of AI. Now these algorithms are commonplace, and the AI moniker has long since passed. Therefore, the AI effect has a way of diminishing AI research, as the heritage of AI research becomes lost in the practical application of the methods.

Messy and Scruffy Approaches Take Hold

With AI's resurgence came different views and approaches to AI and problem solving with AI algorithms. In particular, the scruffy approaches became more widespread and the algorithms became more applicable to real-world problems. Neural networks continued to be researched and applied, and new algorithms and architectures resulted. Neural networks and genetic algorithms combined to provide new ways to create neural network architectures that not only solved problems, but did so in the most efficient ways. This is because the survival of the fittest features of the genetic algorithm drove neural network architectures to minimize for the smallest network to solve the given problem at hand. The use of genetic algorithms also grew in a number of other areas including optimization (symbolic and numerical), scheduling, modeling and many others. Genetic algorithms and neural networks (supervised and unsupervised) are covered in Chapters 7, 8, and 9.

Other bottom-up and biologically inspired approaches followed in the 1990s and beyond. In early 1992, for example, Marco Dorigo introduced the idea of using stigmergy (indirect communication in an environment, in this case, pheromones). Dorigo's use of stigmergy was applied to a variety of problems. Ant Colony Optimization (or ACO) is demonstrated with the traveling salesman problem in Chapter 12.

Also emerging out of the messy approaches to AI was a new field called Artificial Life. Artificial Life research studies the processes of life and systems related to life through a variety of simulations and models. In addition to modeling singular life, ALife also simulates populations of lifeforms to help understand not only evolution, but also the evolution of characteristics such as language. Swarm intelligence is another aspect of this that grew from ALife research. ALife is interesting in the context of AI because it can use a number of AI methods such as neural networks (as the neuro-controller of the individuals in the population) as well as the genetic algorithm to provide the basis for evolution. This book provides a number of demonstrations of ALife both in the context of genetic algorithms and neural networks.

NOTE

One of the earliest simulation environments that demonstrated artificial life was the "game of life" created by John Conway. This was an example of a cellular automaton, and is explored later.

Another bottom-up approach that evolved during AI's re-emergence used the human immune system as inspiration. Artificial Immune Systems (or AIS) use principles of the immune system and the characteristics that it exhibits for problem solving in the domains of optimization, pattern recognition, and data mining. A very novel application of AIS is in computational security. The human body reacts to the presence of infections through the release of antibodies which destroy those infectious substances. Networks of computers can perform the same function, for example, in the domain of network security. If a software virus is found on a computer within a given network, other "antibody" programs can be dispatched to contain and destroy those viruses. Biology continues to be a major source of inspiration for solutions to many types of problems.

Agent Systems

Agents, which are also referred to as intelligent agents or software agents, are a very important element of modern-day AI. In many ways, agents are not an independent aspect of but instead a vehicle for AI applications. Agents are applications that exhibit characteristics of intelligent behavior (such as learning or classification), but are not in themselves AI techniques. There also exists other agent-based methods such as agent-oriented computing and multi-agent systems. These apply the agent metaphor for solving a variety of problems.

One of the most popular forms of intelligent agents is "agency" applications. The word agency is used because the agent represents a user for some task that it performs for the user. An example includes a scheduling application. Agents representing users intelligently negotiate with one another to schedule activities given a set of constraints for each user.

The concept of agents has even been applied to the operation of a deepspace spacecraft. In 1999 NASA integrated what was called the "Remote Agent" into the Deep Space 1 spacecraft. Deep Space 1's goal was to test a number of high-risk technologies, one of which was an agent that was used to provide autonomy to the spacecraft for limited durations of time. The Remote Agent employed planning techniques to autonomously schedule experiments based on goals defined by ground operators. Under constrained conditions, the Remote Agent succeeded in proving that an intelligent agent could be used to autonomously manage a complicated probe and satisfy predefined objectives.

Today you'll find agents in a number of areas, including distributed systems. Mobile agents are independent agents that include autonomy and the ability to travel amongst nodes of a network in order to perform their processing. Instead of the agent communicating with another agent remotely, the mobile agent can travel to the other agent's location and communicate with it directly. In disconnected network situations, this can be very beneficial. You can learn more about intelligent agents (including mobile agents) in Chapter 11.

AI INTER-DISCIPLINARY R&D

In many cases, AI research tends to be fringe research, particularly when it's focused on Strong AI. But what's notable about research in AI is that the algorithms tend to find uses in many other disciplines beyond that of

AI. AI research is by no means pure research, but its applications grow well beyond the original intent of the research. Neural networks, data mining, fuzzy logic, and Artificial Life (for example) have found uses in many other fields. Artificial Life is an interesting example because the algorithms and techniques that have resulted from research and development have found their way into the entertainment industry (from the use of swarming in animated motion pictures to the use of AI in video games).

Rodney Brook's has called this the AI effect, suggesting that another definition for AI is "almost implemented." This is because once an AI algorithm finds a more common use, it's no longer viewed as an AI algorithm but instead just an algorithm that's useful in a given problem domain.

SYSTEMS APPROACH

In this book, the majority of the algorithms and techniques are studied from the perspective of the systems approach. This simply means that the algorithm is explored in the context of inputs and outputs. No algorithm is useful in isolation, but instead from the perspective of how it interacts with its environment (data sampling, filtering, and reduction) and also how it manipulates or alters its environment. Therefore, the algorithm depends on an understanding of the environment and also a way to manipulate the environment. This systems approach illustrates the practical side of artificial intelligence algorithms and techniques and identifies how to ground the method in the real world (see Figure 1.1).

As an example, one of the most interesting uses of AI today can be found in game systems. Strategy games, for example, commonly occupy a map with two or more opponents. Each opponent competes for resources in the environment in order to gain the upper hand over the other. While collecting resources, each opponent can schedule the development of assets to be used to defeat the other. When multiple assets exist for an opponent (such as a military unit), they can be applied in unison, or separately to lay siege on another opponent.

Where strategy games depend on a higher-level view of the environment (such as would be viewed from a general), first-person shooter games (FPS) take a lower-level view (from that of a soldier). An agent in an FPS depends most often on its view of the battlefield. The FPS agent's view of the environment is at a much lower level, understanding cover, objectives, and local enemy positions. The environment is manipulated by the FPS agent through its own movement, attacking or defending from enemies (through finding cover), and possibly communicating with other agents.

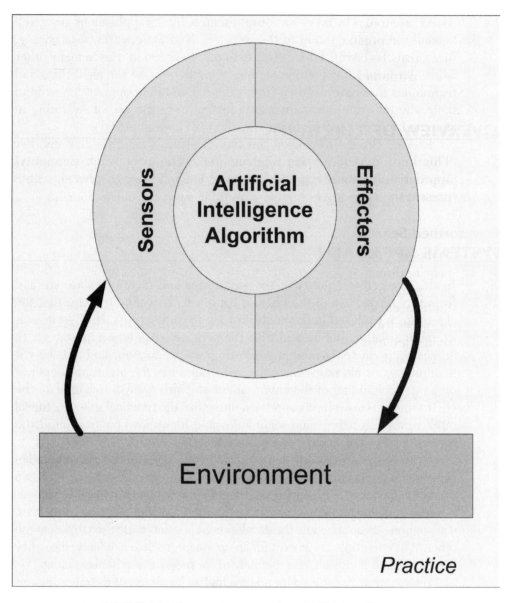

FIGURE 1.1 **The systems approach to Artificial Intelligence.**

An obvious example of the systems approach is in the field of robotics. Mobile robots, for example, utilize an array of sensors and effects that make up the physical robot. At the core of the robot is one or more algorithms that yield rational behavior.

In each case, the AI algorithm that's chosen is the core of an agent's sensors (inputs) and effectors (outputs). For this reason, the algorithm can't truly be useful or understood unless it's considered from its place in the environment.

OVERVIEW OF THIS BOOK

This book covers a wide range of AI techniques, each segmented appropriately into their particular genre. The following chapter summaries present the ideas and methods that are explored.

Uninformed Search

In the early days of AI, AI was a search, whether search involved looking for a plan, or through the various moves that are possible (and subsequent moves) in a game of Checkers. In this chapter on uninformed (or blind) search, the concept of search in various spaces is introduced, the representation of spaces for search, and then the various popular algorithms used in blind search are explored. This includes depth-first, breadth-first, uniform-cost-search, and others.

Informed Search

Informed search is an evolution of search that applies heuristics to the search algorithm, given the problem space, to make the algorithm more efficient. This chapter covers best-first, a star, hill climbing, simulated annealing, tabu search, and constraint satisfaction.

AI and Games

One of the earliest uses of blind and informed search was in the application to games. Games such as Checkers and Chess were believed to be an intelligent activity, and if a computer could be endowed with the ability to play a game and win against a human opponent, it could be considered intelligent. Samuel's Checkers program demonstrated a program that could defeat its creator, and while a feat, this experiment did not produce an intelligent computer except within the domain of Checkers. This chapter explores two-player games and the core of many game-playing systems, the minimax algorithm. A variety of games are then discussed, from the classical games such as Chess, Checkers, and Go to video game AI, exploring movement, behavior, team, and real-time strategy AI.

Knowledge Representation

Knowledge representation has a long history in AI, particularly in Strong AI research. The goal behind knowledge representation is to find abstractions for knowledge that result in a base of knowledge that's useful to a given application. For example, knowledge must be represented in a way that makes it easy for a computer to reason with it and understand the relationships between elements of the knowledge base. This chapter will provide an introduction to a number of fundamental knowledge representation techniques as well as introduce the ideas behind predicate and first-order logic to reason with knowledge.

Machine Learning

Machine learning is best described as learning from example. Machine learning incorporates a variety of methods such as supervised and unsupervised learning. In supervised learning, a teacher is available to define correct or incorrect responses. Unsupervised learning differs in that no teacher is present. (Instead, unsupervised learning learns from the data itself by identifying its) relationships. This chapter provides an introduction to machine learning, and then explores a number of machine learning algorithms such as decision trees and nearest neighbor learning.

Evolutionary Computation

Evolutionary computation introduced the idea of scruffy approaches to AI. Instead of focusing on the high level, trying to imitate the behavior of the human brain, scruffy approaches start at a lower level trying to recreate the more fundamental concepts of life and intelligence using biological metaphors. This chapter covers a number of the evolutionary methods including genetic algorithms, genetic programming, evolutionary strategies, differential evolution, and particle swarm optimization.

Neural Networks I

While neural networks are one of the earliest (and more controversial) techniques, they remain one of the most useful. The attack on neural networks severely impacted AI funding and research, but neural networks re-emerged from AI's winter as a standard for classification and learning. This chapter introduces the basics of neural networks, and then explores the supervised neural network algorithms (least-mean-squares, backpropagation, probabilistic neural networks, and others). The chapter ends with a discussion of neural network characteristics and ways to tune them given the problem domain.

Neural Networks II

Where the previous chapter explored supervised neural network algorithms, this chapter provides an introduction to the unsupervised variants. Unsupervised algorithms use the data itself to learn without the need for a "teacher." This chapter explores unsupervised learning algorithms, including Hebbian learning, Simple Competitive Learning, k-Means Clustering, Adaptive Resonance Theory, and the Hopfield auto-associative model.

Intelligent Agents

Intelligent (or Software) Agents are one of newest techniques in the AI arsenal. In one major definition, agents are applications that include the concept of "agency." This means that those applications represent a user and satisfy the goals of the task autonomously without further direction from the user. This chapter on intelligent agents will introduce the major concepts behind intelligent agents, their architectures and applications.

Biologically Inspired and Hybrid Models

AI is filled with examples of the use of biological metaphors, from early work in neural networks to modern-day work in artificial immune systems. Nature has proven to be a very worthy teacher for complex problem solving. This chapter presents a number of techniques that are both biologically inspired as well as hybrid (or mixed) models of AI. Methods such as artificial immune systems, simulated evolution, Lindenmayer systems, fuzzy logic, genetically evolved neural networks, and ant colony optimization are explored, to name a few.

Languages of AI

While most people think of LISP when considering the languages of AI, there have been a large number of languages developed specifically for AI application development. In this chapter, a taxonomy of computer languages is presented followed by short examples (and advantages) of each. Then a number of AI-specific languages are investigated, exploring their history and use through examples. Languages explored include LISP, Scheme, POP-11, and Prolog.

CHAPTER SUMMARY

The history of AI is a modern-day drama. It's filled with interesting characters, cooperation, competition, and even deception. But outside of the drama, there has been exceptional research and in recent history an application of AI's ideas in a number of different settings. AI has finally left the perception of fringe research and entered the realm of accepted research and practical development.

REFERENCES

[LISP 2007] Wikipedia "Lisp (programming language)", 2007.
Available online at http://en.wikipedia.org/wiki/Lisp_%28programming_ language%29
[Newell 1956] Newell, A., Shaw, J.C., Simon, H.A "Emperical Explorations of the Logic Theory Machine: A Case Study in Heuristics," in Proceedings of the Western Joint Computer Conference, 1956.
[Shannon 1950] Shannon, Claude, "Programming a Computer for Playing Chess," *Philisophical Magazine* 41, 1950.

RESOURCES

Rayman, Marc D., et al "Results from the Deep Space 1 Technology Validation Mission," 50th International Astronomical Congress, Amsterdam, The Netherlands, 1999.
de castr, Leandro N., Timmis, Jonathan Artificial Immune Systems: A New Computational Intelligence Approach Springer, 2002.
Holland, John Adaptation in Natural and Artificial Systems. University of Michigan Press, Ann Arbor, 1975.
McCarthy, John "Recursive Functions of Symbolic Expressions and their Computation by Machine (Part I)," Communications of the ACM, April 1960.
Shortliffe, E.H. "Rule-based Exper Systems: The Mycin Experiments of the Stanford Heuristic Programming Project," Addison-Wesley, 1984.
Winograd, Terry "Procedures as a Representation for Data in a Computer Program for Understanding Natural Language," MIT AI Technical Report 235, February 1971.
Woods, William A. "Transition Network Grammars for Natural Language Analysis," Communications of the ACM 13:10, 1970.

EXERCISES

1. In your own words, define intelligence and why intelligence tests can hide the real measure of intelligence.
2. What was the Turing test, and what was it intended to accomplish?
3. Why were games the early test-bed for AI methods? How do you think AI and games are viewed today?
4. How did Arthur Samuel set the bar for learning programs in the 1950s?
5. What was the first language developed specifically for AI? What language followed in the 1970s, developed also for AI?
6. Define Strong AI.
7. What event is most commonly attributed to leading to AI's winter?
8. What is meant by Scruffy and Neat approaches to AI?
9. After AI's winter, what was most unique about AI's re-emergence?
10. This book explores AI from the systems approach. Define the systems approach and how this perspective is used to explore AI.

Chapter **2**

UNINFORMED SEARCH

U ninformed search, also called blind search and naïve search, is a class of general purpose search algorithms that operate in a brute-force way. These algorithms can be applied to a variety of search problems, but since they don't take into account the target problem, are inefficient. In contrast, informed search methods (discussed in Chapter 3) use a heuristic to guide the search for the problem at hand and are therefore much more efficient. In this chapter, general state space search is explored and then a variety of uninformed search algorithms will be discussed and compared using a set of common metrics.

SEARCH AND AI

Search is an important aspect of AI because in many ways, problem solving in AI is fundamentally a search. Search can be defined as a problem-solving technique that enumerates a problem space from an initial position in search of a goal position (or solution). The manner in which the problem space is searched is defined by the search algorithm or strategy. As search strategies offer different ways to enumerate the search space, how well a strategy works is based on the problem at hand. Ideally, the search algorithm selected is one whose characteristics match that of the problem at hand.

CLASSES OF SEARCH

Four classes of search will be explored here. In this chapter, we'll review uninformed search, and in Chapter 3, informed search will be discussed. Chapter 3 will also review constraint satisfaction, which tries to find a set of values for a set of variables. Finally, in Chapter 4, we'll discuss adversarial search, which is used in games to find effective strategies to play and win two-player games.

GENERAL STATE SPACE SEARCH

Let's begin our discussion of search by first understanding what is meant by a search space. When solving a problem, it's convenient to think about the solution space in terms of a number of actions that we can take, and the new state of the environment as we perform those actions. As we take one of multiple possible actions (each have their own cost), our environment changes and opens up alternatives for new actions. As is the case with many kinds of problem solving, some paths lead to dead-ends where others lead to solutions. And there may also be multiple solutions, some better than others. The problem of search is to find a sequence of operators that transition from the start to goal state. That sequence of operators is the solution.

How we avoid dead-ends and then select the best solution available is a product of our particular search strategy. Let's now look at state space representations for three problem domains.

Search in a Physical Space

Let's consider a simple search problem in physical space (Figure 2.1). Our initial position is 'A' from which there are three possible actions that lead to position 'B,' 'C,' or 'D.' Places, or states, are marked by letters. At each place, there's an opportunity for a decision, or action. The action (also called an operator) is simply a legal move between one place and another. Implied in this exercise is a goal state, or a physical location that we're seeking.

This search space (shown in Figure 2.1) can be reduced to a tree structure as illustrated in Figure 2.2. The search space has been minimized here to the necessary places on the physical map (states) and the transitions that are possible between the states (application of operators). Each node in the tree is a physical location and the arcs between nodes are the legal moves. The depth of the tree is the distance from the initial position.

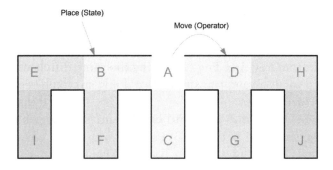

FIGURE 2.1: A search problem represented as a physical space.

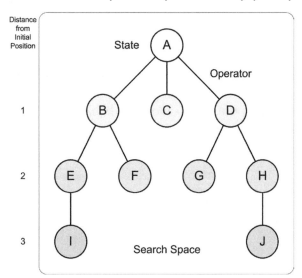

FIGURE 2.2: Representing the physical space problem in Figure 2.1 as a tree.

Search in a Puzzle Space

The "Towers of Hanoi" puzzle is an interesting example of a state space for solving a puzzle problem. The object of this puzzle is to move a number of disks from one peg to another (one at a time), with a number of constraints that must be met. Each disk is of a unique size and it's not legal for a larger disk to sit on top of a smaller disk. The initial state of the puzzle is such that all disks begin on one peg in increasing size order (see Figure 2.2). Our goal (the solution) is to move all disks to the last peg.

As in many state spaces, there are potential transitions that are not legal. For example, we can only move a peg that has no object above it. Further, we can't move a large disk onto a smaller disk (though we can move any disk to an empty peg). The space of possible operators is therefore constrained only to legal moves. The state space can also be constrained to moves that have not yet been performed for a given subtree. For example, if we move a small disk from Peg A to Peg C, moving the same disk back to Peg A could be defined as an invalid transition. Not doing so would result in loops and an infinitely deep tree.

Consider our initial position from Figure 2.3. The only disk that may move is the small disk at the top of Peg A. For this disk, only two legal moves are possible, from Peg A to Peg B or C. From this state, there are three potential moves:

1. Move the small disk from Peg C to Peg B.
2. Move the small disk from Peg C to Peg A.
3. Move the medium disk from Peg A to Peg B.

The first move (small disk from Peg C to Peg B), while valid is not a potential move, as we just moved this disk to Peg C (an empty peg). Moving it a second time serves no purpose (as this move could have been done during the prior transition), so there's no value in doing this now (a heuristic). The second move is also not useful (another heuristic), because it's the reverse of the

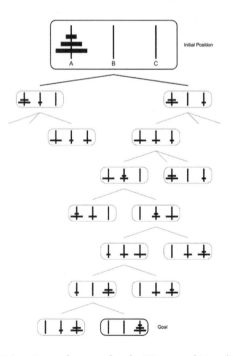

FIGURE 2.3:   A search space for the "Tower of Hanoi" puzzle.

previous move. This leaves one valid move, the medium disk from Peg A to Peg B. The possible moves from this state become more complicated, because valid moves are possible that move us farther away from the solution.

> *TIP* *A heuristic is a simple or efficient rule for solving a given problem or making a decision.*

When our sequence of moves brings us from the initial position to the goal, we have a solution. The goal state in itself is not interesting, but instead what's interesting is the sequence of moves that brought us to the goal state. The collection of moves (or solution), done in the proper order, is in essence a *plan* for reaching the goal. The plan for this configuration of the puzzle can be identified by starting from the goal position and *backtracking* to the initial position.

Search in an Adversarial Game Space

An interesting use of search spaces is in games. Also known as game trees, these structures enumerate the possible moves by each player allowing the search algorithm to find an effective strategy for playing and winning the game.

> *NOTE* *The topic of adversarial search in game trees is explored in Chapter 4.*

Consider a game tree for the game of Chess. Each possible move is provided for each possible configuration (placement of pieces) of the Chess board. But since there are 10^{120} possible configurations of a Chess board, a game tree to document the search space would not be feasible. Heuristic search, which must be applied here, will be discussed in Chapter 3.

Let's now look at a much simpler game that can be more easily represented in a game tree. The game of Nim is a two-player game where each player takes turns removing objects from one or more piles. The player required to take the last object loses the game.

Nim has been studied mathematically and solved in many different variations. For this reason, the player who will win can be calculated based upon the number of objects, piles, and who plays first in an optimally played game.

> *NOTE* *The game of Nim is said to have originated in China, but can be traced to Germany as the word nimm can be translated as take. A complete mathematical theory of Nim was created by Charles Bouton in 1901. [Bouton 1901]*

Let's walk through an example to see how Nim is played. We'll begin with a single small pile to limit the number of moves that are required. Figure 2.4 illustrates a short game with a pile of six objects. Each player may take one, two, or three objects from the pile. In this example, Player-1 starts the game, but ends the game with a loss (is required to take the last object which results in a loss in the misère form of the game). Had Player-1 taken 3 in its second move, Player-2 would have been left with one resulting in a win for Player-1.

A game tree makes this information visible, as illustrated in Figure 2.5. Note in the tree that Player-1 must remove one from the pile to continue the game. If Player-1 removes two or three from the pile, Player-2 can win if playing optimally. The shaded nodes in the tree illustrate losing positions for the player that must choose next (and in all cases, the only choice left is to take the only remaining object).

Note that the depth of the tree determines the length of the game (number of moves). It's implied in the tree that the shaded node is the final move to be made, and the player that makes this move loses the game. Also note the size of the tree. In this example, using six objects, a total of 28 nodes is required. If we increase our tree to illustrate a pile of seven objects, the tree increases to 42 nodes. With eight objects, three balloons to 100 nodes. Fortunately, the tree can be optimized by removing duplicate subtrees, resulting in a much smaller tree.

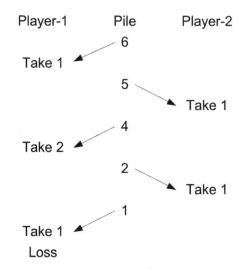

FIGURE 2.4: A sample game of Nim with a pile of six objects.

TREES, GRAPHS, AND REPRESENTATION

A short tour of trees and graphs and their terminology is in order before exploring the various uninformed search methods.

A graph is a finite set of *vertices* (or *nodes*) that are connected by *edges* (or *arcs*). A *loop* (or *cycle*) may exist in a graph, where an arc (or edge) may lead back to the original node. Graphs may be *undirected* where arcs do not imply a direction, or they may be *directed* (called a *digraph*) where a direction is implicit in the arc. An arc can also carry a weight, where a cost can be associated with a path.

Each of these graphs also demonstrates the property of connectivity. Both graphs are *connected* because every pair of nodes is connected by a path. If every node is connected to every node by an arc, the graph is *complete*. One special *connected* graph is called a *tree*, but it must contain no *cycles*.

Building a representation of a graph is simple and one of the most common representations is the *adjacency matrix*. This structure is simply

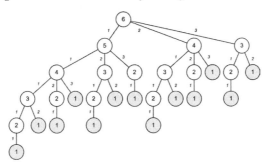

FIGURE 2.5: **A complete Nim game tree for six objects in one pile.**

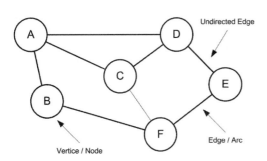

FIGURE 2.6: **An example of an undirected graph containing six nodes and eight arcs.**

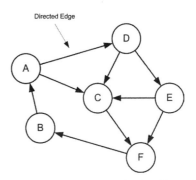

FIGURE 2.7: **An example of a directed graph containing six edges and nine arcs.**

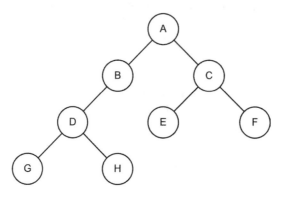

FIGURE 2.8: A connected graph with no cycles (otherwise known as a tree).

an N by N matrix (where N is the number of nodes in the graph). Each element of the matrix defines a connectivity (or adjacency) between the node referenced as the row and the node referenced as the column.

Recall the undirected graph in Figure 2.6. This graph contains six nodes and eight arcs. The *adjacency matrix* for this undirected graph is shown in Figure 2.9. The two dimensions of the graph identify the source (row) and destination nodes (column) of the graph. From Figure 2.6, we know that node A is adjacent to nodes B, C, and D. This is noted in the adjacency matrix with a value of one in each of the B, C, and D columns for row A. Since this is an undirected graph, we note symmetry in the adjacency matrix. Node A connects to node B (as identified in row A), but also node B connects to node A (as shown in row B).

For a directed graph (as shown in Figure 2.7), the associated adjacency matrix is illustrated in Figure 2.10. Since the graph is directed, no symmetry can be found. Instead, the direction of the arcs is noted in the matrix. For example, node B connects to node A, but node A has no associated connection to node B.

An interesting property of the adjacency matrix can be found by reviewing the rows and columns in isolation. For example, if we review a single row, we can identify the nodes to which it connects. For example, row C shows only a connection to node F (as indicated by the one in that cell). But if we review the column for node C, we find the nodes that have arcs connecting to node C. In this case, we see nodes A, D, and E (as illustrated graphically in Figure 2.7). We can also find whether a graph is complete. If the entire matrix is non-zero, then the graph is complete. It's also simple to find a disconnected graph (a node whose row and column contain zero values). Loops in a graph can also be algorithmically discovered by enumerating the matrix (recursively

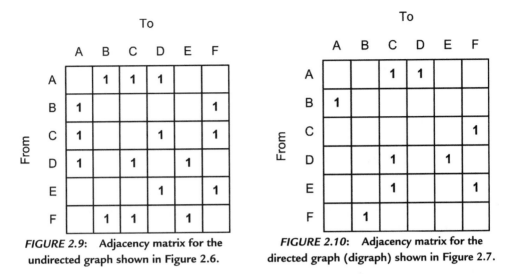

FIGURE 2.9: Adjacency matrix for the undirected graph shown in Figure 2.6.

FIGURE 2.10: Adjacency matrix for the directed graph (digraph) shown in Figure 2.7.

following all paths looking for the initial node).

In the simple case, the values of the adjacency matrix simply define the connectivity of nodes in the graph. In weighted graphs, where arcs may not all be equal, the value in a cell can identify the weight (cost, or distance). We'll explore examples of this technique in the review of neural network construction (Chapter 11).

Adjacency lists are also a popular structure where each node contains a list of the nodes to which it connects. If the graph is sparse, this representation can require less space.

UNINFORMED SEARCH

The uninformed search methods offer a variety of techniques for graph search, each with its own advantages and disadvantages. These methods are explored here with discussion of their characteristics and complexities.

Big-O notation will be used to compare the algorithms. This notation defines the asymptotic upper bound of the algorithm given the depth (d) of the tree and the branching factor, or the average number of branches (b) from each node. There are a number of common complexities that exist for search algorithms. These are shown in Table 2.1.

Table 2.1: Common orders of search functions.

O-Notation   Order

O(1)   Constant (regardless of the number of nodes)

O(n)   Linear (consistent with the number of nodes)

O(log n)   Logarithmic

O(n²)   Quadratic

O(cⁿ)   Geometric

O(n!)   Combinatorial

Big-O notation provides a worst-case measure of the complexity of a search algorithm and is a common comparison tool for algorithms. We'll compare the search algorithms using *space complexity* (measure of the memory required during the search) and *time complexity* (worst-case time required to find a solution). We'll also review the algorithm for *completeness* (can the algorithm find a path to a goal node if it's present in the graph) and *optimality* (finds the lowest cost solution available).

Helper APIs

A number of helper APIs will be used in the source code used to demonstrate the search functions. These are shown below in Listing 2.1.

LISTING 2.1:   Helper APIs for the search functions.

```
/* Graph API */
graph_t  *createGraph (int nodes );
void      destroyGraph (graph_t *g_p );
void      addEdge (graph_t *g_p, int from, int to, int value );
int       getEdge (graph_t *g_p, int from, int to );
/* Stack API */
stack_t  *createStack (int depth );
void      destroyStack (stack_t *s_p );
void      pushStack (stack_t *s_p, int value );
int       popStack (stack_t *s_p );
int       isEmptyStack (stack_t *s_p );
/* Queue API */
queue_t  *createQueue (int depth );
void      destroyQueue (queue_t *q_p );
void      enQueue (queue_t *q_p, int value );
int       deQueue (queue_t *q_p );
int       isEmptyQueue (queue_t *q_p );
/* Priority Queue API */
pqueue_t *createPQueue (int depth );
```

```
void      destroyPQueue (pqueue_t *q_p );
void      enPQueue (pqueue_t *q_p, int value, int cost );
void      dePQueue (pqueue_t *q_p, int *value, int *cost );
int       isEmptyPQueue (pqueue_t *q_p );
int       isFullPQueue (pqueue_t *q_p );
```

The helper functions can be found on the CD-ROM at ./software/ common.

General Search Paradigms

Before we discuss some of the uninformed search methods, let's look at two simple general uninformed search methods.

The first is called '*Generate and Test.*' In this method, we generate a potential solution and then check it against the solution. If we've found the solution, we're done, otherwise, we repeat by trying another potential solution. This is called '*Generate and Test*' because we generate a potential solution, and then test it. Without a proper solution, we try again. Note here that we don't keep track of what we've tried before; we just plow ahead with potential solutions, which is a true blind search.

Another option is called '*Random Search*' which randomly selects a new state from the current state (by selecting a given valid operator and applying it). If we reach the goal state, then we're done. Otherwise, we randomly select another operator (leading to a new state) and continue.

Random search and the '*Generate and Test*' method are truly blind methods of search. They can get lost, get caught in loops, and potentially never find a solution even though one exists within the search space.

Let's now look at some search methods that while blind, can find a solution (if one exists) even if it takes a long period of time.

Depth-First Search (DFS)

The Depth-First Search (DFS) algorithm is a technique for searching a graph that begins at the root node, and exhaustively searches each branch to its greatest depth before backtracking to previously unexplored branches (Figure 2.11 illustrates this search order). Nodes found but yet to be reviewed are stored in a LIFO queue (also known as a *stack*).

 A stack is a LIFO (Last-In-First-Out) container of objects. Similar to a stack of paper, the last item placed on the top is the first item to be removed.

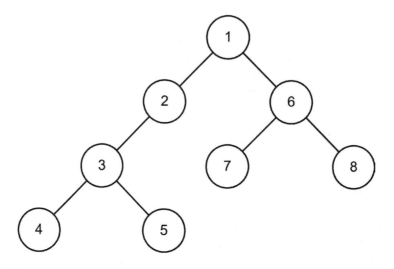

FIGURE 2.11:   Search order of the DFS algorithm over a small tree.

The space complexity for DFS is O(bd) where the time complexity is geometric (O(b^d)). This can be very problematic on deep branching graphs, as the algorithm will continue to the maximum depth of the graph. If loops are present in the graph, then DFS will follow these cycles indefinitely. For this reason, the DFS algorithm is not complete, as cycles can prohibit the algorithm from finding the goal. If cycles are not present in the graph, then the algorithm is complete (will always find the goal node). The DFS algorithm is also not optimal, but can be made optimal using path checking (to ensure the shortest path to the goal is found).

> *The DFS implementation can be found on the CD-ROM at ./software/ ch2/dfs.c.*

Graph algorithms can be implemented either recursively or using a stack to maintain the list of nodes that must be enumerated. In Listing 2.2, the DFS algorithm is implemented using a LIFO stack.

Listing 2.2:   The depth-first search algorithm.

```
#include <stdio.h>
#include "graph.h"
#include "stack.h"
#define A        0
#define B        1
```

```
#define C      2
#define D      3
#define E      4
#define F      5
#define G      6
#define H      7
int init_graph( graph_t *g_p )
{
  addEdge( g_p, A, B, 1 );
  addEdge( g_p, A, C, 1 );
  addEdge( g_p, B, D, 1 );
  addEdge( g_p, C, E, 1 );
  addEdge( g_p, C, F, 1 );
  addEdge( g_p, D, G, 1 );
  addEdge( g_p, D, H, 1 );
  return 0;
}
void dfs( graph_t *g_p, int root, int goal )
{
  int node;
  int to;
  stack_t *s_p;
  s_p = createStack( 10 );
  pushStack( s_p, root );
  while ( !isEmptyStack(s_p) ) {
   node = popStack( s_p );
   printf("%d\n", node);
   if (node == goal) break;
   for (to = g_p->nodes-1 ; to > 0 ; to--) {
    if (getEdge( g_p, node, to ) ) {
     pushStack( s_p, to );
    }
   }
  }
  destroyStack( s_p );
  return;
}
int main()
{
  graph_t *g_p;
```

```
g_p = createGraph( 8 );
init_graph( g_p );
dfs( g_p, 0, 5 );
destroyGraph( g_p );
return 0;
}
```

A search algorithm is characterized as exhaustive when it can search every node in the graph in search of the goal. If the goal is not present in the graph, the algorithm will terminate, but will search each and every node in a systematic way.

Depth-Limited Search (DLS)

Depth-Limited Search (DLS) is a modification of depth-first search that minimizes the depth that the search algorithm may go. In addition to starting with a root and goal node, a depth is provided that the algorithm will not descend below (see Listing 2.3). Any nodes below that depth are omitted from the search. This modification keeps the algorithm from indefinitely cycling by halting the search after the pre-imposed depth. Figure 2.12 illustrates this search with a depth of two (no nodes deeper than level two are searched).

The DLS implementation can be found on the CD-ROM at ./software/ch2/dls.c.

Listing 2.3:   The depth-limited search algorithm.

```c
#include <stdio.h>
#include "graph.h"
#include "stack.h"
#define A       0
#define B       1
#define C       2
#define D       3
#define E       4
#define F       5
#define G       6
#define H       7
int init_graph( graph_t *g_p )
{
```

```
      addEdge( g_p, A, B, 1 );
      addEdge( g_p, A, C, 1 );
      addEdge( g_p, B, D, 1 );
      addEdge( g_p, C, E, 1 );
      addEdge( g_p, C, F, 1 );
      addEdge( g_p, D, G, 1 );
      addEdge( g_p, D, H, 1 );
      return 0;
}
void dls( graph_t *g_p, int root, int goal, int limit )
{
  int node, depth, to;
  stack_t *s_p, *sd_p;
  s_p = createStack( 10 );
  sd_p = createStack( 10 );
  pushStack( s_p, root );
  pushStack( sd_p, 0 );
  while ( !isEmptyStack(s_p) ) {
    node = popStack( s_p );
    depth = popStack( sd_p );
    printf("%d (depth %d)\n", node, depth);
    if (node == goal) break;
    if (depth < limit) {
      for (to = g_p->nodes-1 ; to > 0 ; to--) {
        if (getEdge( g_p, node, to ) ) {
          pushStack( s_p, to );
          pushStack( sd_p, depth+1 );
        }
      }
    }
  }
  destroyStack( s_p );
  destroyStack( sd_p );
  return;
}
int main()
{
  graph_t *g_p;
  g_p = createGraph( 8 );
  init_graph( g_p );
```

```
dls( g_p, 0, 5, 2 );
destroyGraph( g_p );
return 0;
}
```

While the algorithm does remove the possibility of infinitely looping in the graph, it also reduces the scope of the search. If the goal node had been one of the nodes marked 'X', it would not have been found, making the search algorithm incomplete. The algorithm can be complete if the search depth is that of the tree itself (in this case d is three). The technique is also not optimal since the first path may be found to the goal instead of the shortest path.

The time and space complexity of depth-limited search is similar to DFS, from which this algorithm is derived. Space complexity is O(bd) and time complexity is O(b^d), but d in this case is the imposed depth of the search and not the maximum depth of the graph.

Iterative Deepening Search (IDS)

Iterative Deepening Search (IDS) is a derivative of DLS and combines the features of depth-first search with that of breadth-first search. IDS operates by performing DLS searches with increased depths until the goal is found.

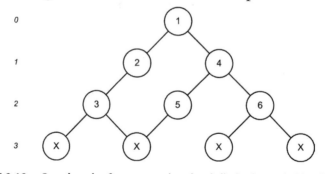

FIGURE 2.12: **Search order for a tree using depth-limited search (depth = two).**

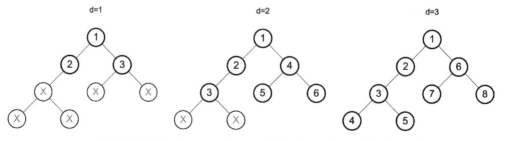

FIGURE 2.13: **Iterating increased depth searches with IDS.**

The depth begins at one, and increases until the goal is found, or no further nodes can be enumerated (see Figure 2.13).

As shown in Figure 2.13, IDS combines depth-first search with breadth-first search. By minimizing the depth of the search, we force the algorithm to also search the breadth of the graph. If the goal is not found, the depth that the algorithm is permitted to search is increased and the algorithm is started again. The algorithm, shown in Listing 2.4, begins with a depth of one.

LISTING 2.4:   The iterative deepening-search algorithm.

```
#include <stdio.h>
#include "graph.h"
#include "stack.h"
#define A        0
#define B        1
#define C        2
#define D        3
#define E        4
#define F        5
#define G        6
#define H        7
int init_graph( graph_t *g_p )
{
  addEdge( g_p, A, B, 1 );
  addEdge( g_p, A, C, 1 );
  addEdge( g_p, B, D, 1 );
  addEdge( g_p, C, E, 1 );
  addEdge( g_p, C, F, 1 );
  addEdge( g_p, D, G, 1 );
  addEdge( g_p, D, H, 1 );
  return 0;
}
int dls( graph_t *g_p, int root, int goal, int limit )
{
  int node, depth;
  int to;
  stack_t *s_p, *sd_p;
  s_p = createStack( 10 );
  sd_p = createStack( 10 );
  pushStack( s_p, root );
```

```
    pushStack( sd_p, 0 );
    while ( !isEmptyStack(s_p) ) {
      node = popStack( s_p );
      depth = popStack( sd_p );
      printf("%d (depth %d)\n", node, depth);
      if (node == goal) return 1;
      if (depth < limit) {
        for (to = g_p->nodes-1 ; to > 0 ; to--) {
          if (getEdge( g_p, node, to ) ) {
            pushStack( s_p, to );
            pushStack( sd_p, depth+1 );
          }
        }
      }
    }
    destroyStack( s_p );
    destroyStack( sd_p );
    return 0;
  }
  int main()
  {
    graph_t *g_p;
    int    status, depth;
    g_p = createGraph( 8 );
    init_graph( g_p );
    depth = 1;
    while (1) {
      status = dls( g_p, 0, 5, depth );
      if (status == 1) break;
      else depth++;
    }
    destroyGraph( g_p );
    return 0;
  }
```

The IDS implementation can be found on the CD-ROM at ./software/ch2/ids.c.

IDS is advantageous because it's not susceptible to cycles (a characteristic of DLS, upon which it's based). It also finds the goal nearest to the root node,

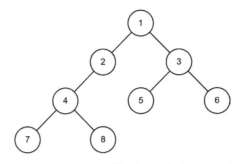

FIGURE 2.14: Search order of the breadth-first search algorithm.

as does the BFS algorithm (which will be detailed next). For this reason, it's a preferred algorithm when the depth of the solution is not known.

The time complexity for IDS is identical to that of DFS and DLS, $O(b^d)$. Space complexity of IDS is $O(bd)$.

Unlike DFS and DLS, IDS is will always find the best solution and therefore, it is both complete and optimal.

Breadth-First Search (BFS)

In Breadth-First Search (BFS), we search the graph from the root node in order of the distance from the root. Because the order search is nearest the root, BFS is guaranteed to find the best possible solution (shallowest) in a non-weighted graph, and is therefore also complete. Rather than digging deep down into the graph, progressing further and further from the root (as is the case with DFS), BFS checks each node nearest the root before descending to the next level (see Figure 2.14).

The implementation of BFS uses a FIFO (first-in-first-out) queue, differing from the stack (LIFO) implementation for DFS. As new nodes are found to be searched, these nodes are checked against the goal, and if the goal is not found, the new nodes are added to the queue. To continue the search, the oldest node is dequeued (FIFO order). Using FIFO order for new node search, we always check the oldest nodes first, resulting in breadth-first review (see Listing 2.5).

LISTING 2.5: The breadth-first search algorithm.

```
#include <stdio.h>
#include "graph.h"
#include "queue.h"
#define A        0
```

```
#define B       1
#define C       2
#define D       3
#define E       4
#define F       5
#define G       6
#define H       7
int init_graph( graph_t *g_p )
{
  addEdge( g_p, A, B, 1 );
  addEdge( g_p, A, C, 1 );
  addEdge( g_p, B, D, 1 );
  addEdge( g_p, C, E, 1 );
  addEdge( g_p, C, F, 1 );
  addEdge( g_p, D, G, 1 );
  addEdge( g_p, D, H, 1 );
  return 0;
}
void bfs( graph_t *g_p, int root, int goal )
{
  int node;
  int to;
  queue_t *q_p;
  q_p = createQueue( 10 );
  enQueue( q_p, root );
  while ( !isEmptyQueue(q_p) ) {
    node = deQueue( q_p );
    printf("%d\n", node);
    if (node == goal) break;
    for (to = g_p->nodes-1 ; to > 0 ; to--) {
      if (getEdge( g_p, node, to ) ) {
        enQueue( q_p, to );
      }
    }
  }
  destroyQueue( q_p );
  return;
}
int main()
{
```

```
graph_t *g_p;
g_p = createGraph( 8 );
init_graph( g_p );
bfs( g_p, 0, 7 );
destroyGraph( g_p );
return 0;
}
```

The BFS implementation can be found on the CD-ROM at ./software/ch2/bfs.c.

The disadvantage of BFS is that each node that is searched is required to be stored (space complexity is $O(b^d)$). The entire depth of the tree does not have to be searched, so d in this context is the depth of the solution, and not the maximum depth of the tree. Time complexity is also $O(b^d)$.

In practical implementations of BFS, and other search algorithms, a closed list is maintained that contains those nodes in the graph that have been visited. This allows the algorithm to efficiently search the graph without re-visiting nodes. In implementations where the graph is weighted, keeping a closed list is not possible.

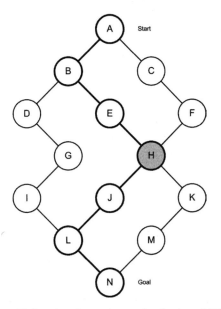

FIGURE 2.15: **Bidirectional search meeting in the middle at node H.**

Bidirectional Search

The Bidirectional Search algorithm is a derivative of BFS that operates by performing two breadth-first searches simultaneously, one beginning from the root node and the other from the goal node. When the two searches meet in the middle, a path can be reconstructed from the root to the goal. The searches meeting is determined when a common node is found (a node visited by both searches, see Figure 2.15). This is accomplished by keeping a closed list of the nodes visited.

Bidirectional search is an interesting idea, but requires that we know the goal that we're seeking in the graph. This isn't always practical, which limits the application of the algorithm. When it can be determined, the algorithm has useful characteristics. The time and space complexity for bidirectional search is O(bd/2), since we're only required to search half of the depth of the tree. Since it is based on BFS, bidirectional search is both complete and optimal.

Uniform-Cost Search (UCS)

One advantage of BFS is that it always finds the shallowest solution. But consider the edge having a cost associated with it. The shallowest solution may not be the best, and a deeper solution with a reduced path cost would be better (for example, see Figure 2.16). Uniform -Cost Search (UCS) can be applied to find the least-cost path through a graph by maintaining an ordered list of nodes in order of descending cost. This allows us to evaluate the least cost path first

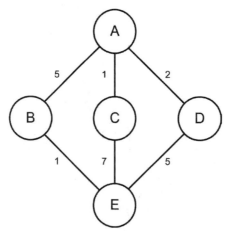

FIGURE 2.16: An example graph where choosing the lowest cost path for the first node (A->C) may not result in the best overall path through the graph (A->B->E).

> *Uniform-cost search is an uninformed search method because no heuristic is actually used. The algorithm measures the actual cost of the path without attempting to estimate it.*

The algorithm for UCS uses the accumulated path cost and a priority queue to determine the path to evaluate (see Listing 2.6). The priority queue (sorted from least cost to greatest) contains the nodes to be evaluated. As node children are evaluated, we add their cost to the node with the aggregate sum of the current path. This node is then added to the queue, and when all children have been evaluated, the queue is sorted in order of ascending cost. When the first element in the priority queue is the goal node, then the best solution has been found.

LISTING 2.6: The uniform-cost search algorithm.

```c
#include <stdio.h>
#include "graph.h"
#include "pqueue.h"
#define A       0
#define B       1
#define C       2
#define D       3
#define E       4
int init_graph( graph_t *g_p )
{
  addEdge( g_p, A, B, 5 );
  addEdge( g_p, A, C, 1 );
  addEdge( g_p, A, D, 2 );
  addEdge( g_p, B, E, 1 );
  addEdge( g_p, C, E, 7 );
  addEdge( g_p, D, E, 5 );
  return 0;
}
void ucs( graph_t *g_p, int root, int goal )
{
  int node, cost, child_cost;
  int to;
  pqueue_t *q_p;
  q_p = createPQueue( 7 );
  enPQueue( q_p, root, 0 );
  while ( !isEmptyPQueue(q_p) ) {
```

```
  dePQueue( q_p, &node, &cost );
  if (node == goal) {
    printf("cost %d\n", cost);
    return;
  }
  for (to = g_p->nodes-1 ; to > 0 ; to--) {
    child_cost = getEdge( g_p, node, to );
    if (child_cost) {
      enPQueue( q_p, to, (child_cost+cost) );
    }
  }
}
destroyPQueue( q_p );
return;
}
int main()
{
  graph_t *g_p;
  g_p = createGraph( 6 );
  init_graph( g_p );
  ucs( g_p, A, E );
  destroyGraph( g_p );
  return 0;
}
```

Step	Investigating Node	Priority Queue		
1		A(0)		
2	A	C(1)	D(2)	B(5)
		A(0)	A(0)	A(0)
3	C	D(2)	B(5)	E(8)
		A(0)	A(0)	C(1)
				A(0)
4	D	B(5)	E(7)	E(8)
		A(0)	D(2)	C(1)
			A(0)	A(0)
5	B	E(6)	E(7)	E(8)
		B(5)	D(2)	C(1)
		A(0)	A(0)	A(0)

FIGURE 2.17:   Node evaluations and the state of the priority queue.

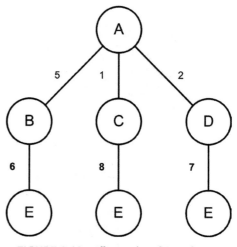

FIGURE 2.18:   Illustrating the path cost through the graph.

The UCS implementation can be found on the CD-ROM at ./software/ ch2/ucs.c.

The UCS algorithm is easily demonstrated using our example graph in Figure 2.16. Figure 2.17 shows the state of the priority queue as the nodes are evaluated. At step one, the initial node has been added to the priority queue, with a cost of zero. At step two, each of the three connected nodes are evaluated and added to the priority queue. When no further children are available to evaluate, the priority queue is sorted to place them in ascending cost order.

At step three, children of node C are evaluated. In this case, we find the desired goal (E), but since its accumulated path cost is eight, it ends up at the end of the queue. For step four, we evaluate node D and again find the goal node. The path cost results in seven, which is still greater than our B node in the queue. Finally, at step five, node B is evaluated. The goal node is found again, with a resulting path cost of six. The priority queue now contains the goal node at the top, which means at the next iteration of the loop, the algorithm will exit with a path of A->B->E (working backwards from the goal node to the initial node).

To limit the size of the priority queue, it's possible to prune entries that are redundant. For example, at step 4 in Figure 2.17, the entry for E(8) could have been safely removed, as another path exists that has a reduced cost (E(7)).

The search of the graph is shown in Figure 2.18, which identifies the path cost at each edge of the graph. The path cost shown above the goal node (E) makes it easy to see the least-cost path through the graph, even when it's not apparent from the initial node.

UCS is optimal and can be complete, but only if the edge costs are non-negative (the summed path cost always increases). Time and space complexity are the same as BFS, $O(b^d)$ for each, as it's possible for the entire tree to be evaluated.

IMPROVEMENTS

One of the basic problems with traditional DFS and BFS is that they lack a visited list (a list of nodes that have already been evaluated). This modification makes the algorithms complete, by ignoring cycles and only following paths that have not yet been followed. For BFS, keeping a visited list can reduce the search time, but for DFS, the algorithm can be made complete.

ALGORITHM ADVANTAGES

Each of the algorithms has advantages and disadvantages based on the graph to be searched. For example, if the branching factor of the graph is small, then BFS is the best choice. If the tree is deep, but a solution is known to be shallow in the graph, then IDS is a good choice. If the graph is weighted, then UCS should be used as it will always find the best solution where DFS and BFS will not.

CHAPTER SUMMARY

Uninformed search algorithms are a class of graph search algorithms that exhaustively search for a node without the use of a heuristic to guide the search. Search algorithms are of interest in AI because many problems can be reduced to simple search problems in a state space. The state space consists of states (nodes) and operators (edges), allowing the state space to be represented as a graph. Examples range from graphs of physical spaces to massive game trees such as are possible with the game of Chess.

The depth-first search algorithm operates by evaluating branches to their maximum depth, and then backtracking to follow unvisited branches. Depth-limited search (DLS) is based on DFS, but restricts the depth of the search. Iterative-deepening search (IDS) uses DLS, but continually increases the search depth until the solution is found.

The breadth-first search (BFS) algorithm searches with increasing depth from the root (searches all nodes with depth one, then all nodes with depth two, etc.). A special derivative algorithm of BFS, bidirectional search (BIDI), performs two simultaneous searches. Starting at the root node and the goal node, BIDI performs two BFS searches in search of the middle. Once a common node is found in the middle, a path exists between the root and goal nodes.

The uniform-cost search (UCS) algorithm is ideal for weight graphs (graphs whose edges have costs associated with them). UCS evaluates a graph using a priority queue that is ordered in path cost to the particular node. It's based on the BFS algorithm and is both complete and optimal.

ALGORITHMS SUMMARY

Table 2.2: Summary of the uninformed algorithms and their characteristics.

Algorithm	Time	Space	Optimal	Complete	Derivative
DFS	$O(b^m)$	$O(bm)$	No	No	
DLS	$O(b^l)$	$O(bl)$	No	No	DFS
IDS	$O(b^d)$	$O(bd)$	Yes	No	DLS
BFS	$O(b^d)$	$O(b^d)$	Yes	Yes	
BIDI	$O(b^{d/2})$	$O(b^{d/2})$	Yes	Yes	BFS
UCS	$O(b^d)$	$O(b^d)$	Yes	Yes	BFS

b, branching factor

d, tree depth of the solution

m, tree depth

l, search depth limit

REFERENCES

[Bouton 1901] "Nim, a game with a complete mathematical theory," Ann, Math, Princeton 3, 35-39, 1901-1902.

EXERCISES

1. What is uninformed (or blind) search and how does it differ from informed (or heuristic) search?
2. The graph structure is ideal for general state space representation. Explain why and define the individual components.
3. Define the queuing structures used in DFS and BFS and explain why each uses their particular style.
4. What is the definition of tree depth?
5. What is the definition of the branching factor?
6. What are time and space complexity and why are they useful as metrics for graph search?
7. If an algorithm always finds a solution in a graph, what is this property called? If it always finds the best solution, what is this characteristic?
8. Considering DFS and BFS, which algorithm will always find the best solution for a non-weighted graph?
9. Use the DFS and BFS algorithms to solve the Towers of Hanoi problem. Which performs better and why?
10. Provide the search order for the nodes shown in Figure 2.19 for DFS, BFS, DLS (d=2), IDS (start depth = 1), and BIDI (start node A, goal node I).

11. In general, IDS is better than DFS. Draw a graph where this is not the case.
12. In general, IDS is not complete. Why?
13. Identify a major disadvantage of bidirectional search.
14. Using the UCS algorithm, find the shortest path from A to F in Figure 2.20.

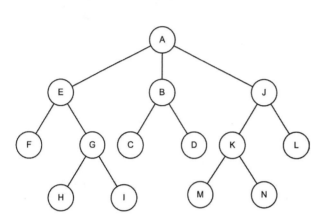

FIGURE 2.19: Example graph.

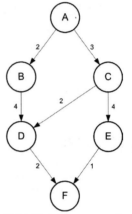

FIGURE 2.20: Example weighted graph.

Chapter **3** **INFORMED SEARCH**

I n Chapter 2, we explored the uninformed search methods such as depth-first and breadth-first search. These methods operate in a brute-force fashion and are subsequently inefficient. In contrast, this chapter will present the informed search methods. These methods incorporate a heuristic, which is used to determine the quality of any state in the search space. In a graph search, this results in a strategy for node expansion (which node should be evaluated next). A variety of informed search methods will be investigated and, as with uninformed methods, compared using a common set of metrics.

NOTE ► *A heuristic is a rule of thumb that may help solve a given problem. Heuristics take problem knowledge into consideration to help guide the search within the domain.*

INFORMED SEARCH

In this chapter, we'll explore a number of informed search methods, including best-first search, a-star search, iterative improvement algorithms such as hill climbing and simulated annealing, and finally, constraint satisfaction. We'll demonstrate each with a sample problem and illustrate the heuristics used.

BEST-FIRST SEARCH (BEST-FS)

In Best-First search, the search space is evaluated according to a heuristic function. Nodes yet to be evaluated are kept on an OPEN list and those that have already been evaluated are stored on a CLOSED list. The OPEN list is represented as a priority queue, such that unvisited nodes can be dequeued in order of their evaluation function (recall the priority queue from Chapter 2 for the Uniform-Cost Search).

The evaluation function $f(n)$ is made up of two parts. These are the heuristic function ($h(n)$) and the estimated cost ($g(n)$), where (see Eq 3.1):

$$f(n) = g(n) + h(n) \qquad \text{(Eq 3.1)}$$

We can think of the estimated cost as a value measurable from our search space, and the heuristic function as an educated guess. The OPEN list is then built in order of $f(n)$. This makes best-first search fundamentally *greedy* because it always chooses the best local opportunity in the search *frontier*.

NOTE ▶ *The search frontier is defined as the set of node opportunities that can be searched next. In Best-First search, the frontier is a priority queue sorted in $f(n)$ order. Given the strict order of $f(n)$, the selection of the node to evaluate from the priority queue is greedy.*

The complexity of best-first is $O(b^m)$ for both time and space (all nodes are saved in memory). By maintaining a CLOSED list (to avoid revisiting nodes and therefore avoiding loops) best-first search is complete, but it is not optimal, as a solution can be found in a longer path (higher $h(n)$ with a lower $g(n)$ value.

TIP ▶ *Best-First search is a combination of evaluation functions, $h(n)$ and $g(n)$. Note that Breadth-First search is a special case of Best-First search where $f(n) = h(n)$, and Uniform-Cost search is a special case of Best-First search where $f(n) = g(n)$.*

Best-First Search and the N-Queens Problem

Let's now discuss the best-first search algorithm in the context of a large search space. The N-queens problem is a search problem where the desired result is an N by N board with N queens such that no queen threatens another (see Figure 3.1). For this board, in each of the horizontal, vertical, and diagonal rows, no queen is able to capture another.

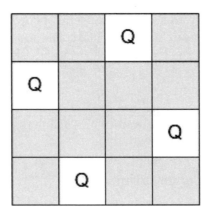

FIGURE 3.1: Sample N-Queens board (where N=4).

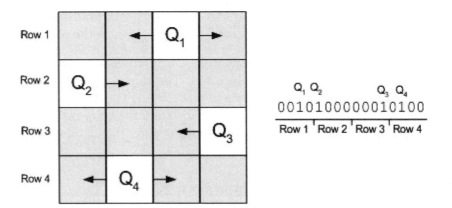

FIGURE 3.2: Board representation for the N-Queens problem (where N=4).

An important aspect of problem solving and search is representation. For this example, we'll choose a simple representation that fits the solution space well and makes it simple to enumerate. Each board position is represented by a single bit and if the bit is zero, then the position is vacant, otherwise, it is occupied by a queen. We'll simplify the problem by assigning a queen to each row on the board. Enumerating the search space is then defined as looking at the possible moves of queens horizontally. For example, the queen at the top of Figure 3.1 can move left or right, but the queen in the second row can only move right (see Figure 3.1). Figure 3.2 also shows the board representation as a 16-bit value (unsigned short, in the case of C).

Given a state (the board configuration), we can identify the child states for this board by creating a new board for each of the possible queen position changes, given horizontal movement only. For Figure 3.2, this board configuration can result in six new child states (a single queen change position in each). Note that since we maintain a closed list, board configurations that have already been evaluated are not generated, resulting in a small tree and more efficient search.

For the heuristic, we'll use the node's depth in the tree for $h(n)$, and the number of conflicts (number of queens that could capture another) for $g(n)$.

Best-First Search Implementation

Let's now look at a simple implementation of Best-First search in the C language. We'll present the two major functions that make up this search algorithm; the first is best_fs, which is the main loop of the algorithm. The second function, generateChildNodes, builds out the possible states (board configurations) given the current state.

Our main function (best_fs) is the OPEN list enumerator and solution tester. Prior to calling this function, our OPEN list (priority queue) and CLOSED list have been created. The root node, our initial board configuration, has been placed on the OPEN list. The best_fs function (see Listing 3.1) then dequeues the next node from the open list (best f(n)) If this node has a g(n) (number of conflicts) of zero, then a solution has been found, and we exit.

LISTING 3.1:   The Best-Search first main function.

```
void best_fs ( pqueue_t *open_pq_p, queue_t *closed_q_p )
{
  node_t *node_p;
  int   cost;
  /* Enumerate the Open list */
  while ( !isEmptyPQueue (open_pq_p) ) {
    dePQueue ( open_pq_p, (int *)&node_p, &cost );
    /* Solution found? */
    if (node_p->g == 0) {
      printf("Found Solution (depth %d):\n", node_p->h);
      emitBoard ( node_p );
      break;
    }
    generateChildNodes( open_pq_p, closed_q_p, node_p );
```

```
      }
      return;
   }
```

Note in Listing 3.1 that while cost is the $f(n)$, we check $g(n)$ to determine whether a solution is found. This is because $f(n)$ may be non-zero since it includes the depth of the solution ($h(n)$).

The BestFS implementation can be found on the CD-ROM at ./software/ ch3/bestfs.c.

The next function, generateChildNodes, takes the current board configuration and enumerates all possible child configurations by potentially moving each queen one position. The moves array defines the possible moves for each position on the board (-1 means only right, 2 means both left and right, and 1 means only left). The board is then enumerated, and whenever a queen is found, the moves array is checked for the legal moves, and new child nodes are created and loaded onto the OPEN list.

Note that we check the CLOSED list here to avoid creating a board configuration that we've seen before. Once all positions on the current board have been checked, and new child nodes are created, the function returns to best_fs.

When a new board configuration is found, the createNode function is called to allocate a new node structure and places this new node on the OPEN list (and CLOSED list). Note here that the one plus the depth (h(n)) is passed in to identify the level of the solution in the tree.

LISTING 3.2:   The generateChildNodes function to enumerate the child nodes.

```
void generateChildNodes( pqueue_t *pq_p,
               queue_t *closed_q_p, node_t *node_p )
{
   int i;
   unsigned short cboard1, cboard2;
   const int moves[16]={ -1, 2, 2, 1,
               -1, 2, 2, 1,
               -1, 2, 2, 1,
               -1, 2, 2, 1 };
/* Generate the child nodes for the current node by
 * shuffling the pieces on the board.
```

```
        */
      for (i = 0 ; i < 16 ; i++) {
        /* Is there a queen at this position? */
        if (checkPiece( node_p->board, i )) {
          /* Remove current queen from the board */
          cboard1 = cboard2 = ( node_p->board & ~(1 << (15-i) ) );
          if (moves[i] == -1) {
            /* Can only move right */
            cboard1 |= ( 1 << (15-(i+1)) );
            if (!searchQueue( closed_q_p, cboard1)) {
              (void)createNode( pq_p, closed_q_p, cboard1, node_p->h+1 );
            }
          } else if (moves[i] == 2) {
            /* Can move left or right */
            cboard1 |= ( 1 << (15-(i+1)) );
            if (!searchQueue( closed_q_p, cboard1)) {
              (void)createNode( pq_p, closed_q_p, cboard1, node_p->h+1 );
            }
            cboard2 |= ( 1 << (15-(i-1)) );
            if (!searchQueue( closed_q_p, cboard2)) {
              (void)createNode( pq_p, closed_q_p, cboard2, node_p->h+1 );
            }
          } else if (moves[i] == 1) {
            /* Can only move left */
            cboard2 |= ( 1 << (15-(i-1)) );
            if (!searchQueue( closed_q_p, cboard2)) {
              (void)createNode( pq_p, closed_q_p, cboard2, node_p->h+1 );
            }
          }
        }
      }
      return;
    }
```

Let's now watch the algorithm in action. Once invoked, a random root node is enqueued and then the possible child configurations are enumerated and loaded onto the OPEN list (see Listing 3.3). The demonstration here shows a shallow tree of three configurations checked, the root node, one at level one, and the solution found at depth two. A condensed version of this run is shown in Figure 3.3.

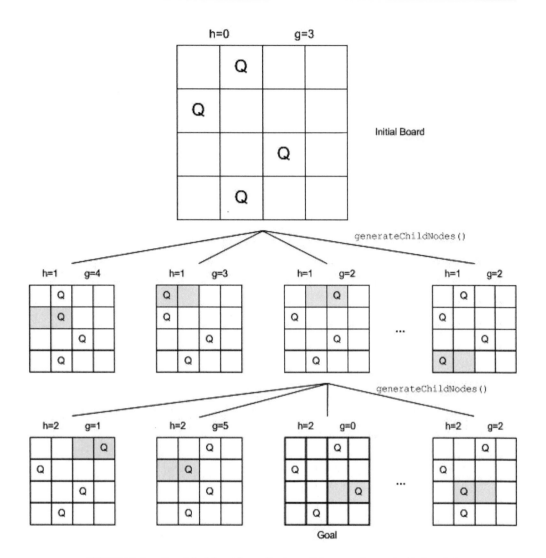

FIGURE 3.3: Graphical (condensed) view of the search tree in Listing 3.3.

LISTING 3.3:   Best-First Search for the N-Queens problem (N=4).

```
        New node: evaluateBoard 4824 = (h 0, g 3)
        Initial Board:
        board is 0x4824
        0 1 0 0
        1 0 0 0
```

```
0 0 1 0
0 1 0 0
```
Checking board 0x4824 (h 0 g 3)
  New node: evaluateBoard 2824 = (h 1, g 2)
  New node: evaluateBoard 8824 = (h 1, g 3)
  New node: evaluateBoard 4424 = (h 1, g 4)
  New node: evaluateBoard 4814 = (h 1, g 3)
  New node: evaluateBoard 4844 = (h 1, g 4)
  New node: evaluateBoard 4822 = (h 1, g 3)
  New node: evaluateBoard 4828 = (h 1, g 2)
Checking board 0x2824 (h 1 g 2)
  New node: evaluateBoard 1824 = (h 2, g 1)
  New node: evaluateBoard 2424 = (h 2, g 5)
  New node: evaluateBoard 2814 = (h 2, g 0)
  New node: evaluateBoard 2844 = (h 2, g 2)
  New node: evaluateBoard 2822 = (h 2, g 3)
  New node: evaluateBoard 2828 = (h 2, g 2)
Checking board 0x2814 (h 2 g 0)
Found Solution (h 2 g 0):
board is 0x2814

```
0 0 1 0
1 0 0 0
0 0 0 1
0 1 0 0
```

Variants of Best-First Search

One interesting variant of best-first search is called *greedy best-first search*. In this variant, $f(n) = h(n)$, and the OPEN list is ordered in f order. Since h is the only factor used to determine which node to select next (identified as the closeness to the goal), it's defined as greedy. Because of this, greedy best-first is not complete as the heuristic is not *admissible* (because it can overestimate the path to the goal). We'll discuss admissibility in more detail in the discussion of A-star search.

Another variant of best-first search is *beam-search*, like greedy best-first search, it uses the heuristic $f(n) = h(n)$. The difference with beam-search is that it keeps only a set of the best candidate nodes for expansion and simply throws the rest way. This makes beam-search much more memory efficient than greedy best-first search, but suffers in that nodes can be discarded which could result in the optimal path. For this reason, beam-search is neither optimal or complete.

A* SEARCH

A* search, like best-first search, evaluates a search space using a heuristic function. But A* uses both the cost of getting from the initial state to the current state $(g(n))$, as well as an estimated cost (heuristic) of the path from the current node to the goal $(h(n))$. These are summed to the cost function $f(n)$ (See Eq 3.1). The A* search, unlike best-first, is both optimal and complete.

The OPEN and CLOSED lists are used again to identify the frontier for search (OPEN list) and the nodes evaluated thus far (CLOSED). The OPEN list is implemented as a priority queue ordered in lowest $f(n)$ order. What makes A* interesting is that it continually re-evaluates the cost function for nodes as it re-encounters them. This allows A* to efficiently find the minimal path from the initial state to the goal state.

Let's now look at A* at a high level and then we'll dig further and apply it to a well-known problem. Listing 3.4 provides the high level flow for A*.

LISTING 3.4: High-level flow for the A* search algorithm.

```
Initialize OPEN list (priority queue)
Initialize CLOSED list
Place start node on the OPEN list
Loop while the OPEN list is not empty
        Get best node (parent) from OPEN list (least f(n))
        if parent is the goal node, done
        Place parent on the CLOSED list
        Expand parent to all adjacent nodes (adj_node)
                if adj_node is on the CLOSED list
                        discard adj_node and continue
                else if adj_node is on the OPEN list
                        if adj_node's g value is better than
                                the OPEN.adj_node's g value
                                discard OPEN.cur_node
                                calculate adj_node's g, h and f values
                                set adj_node predecessor to parent
                                add adj_node to OPEN list
                                continue
                end
        else
                calculate adj_node's g, h and f values
                set adj_node predecessor to parent
```

```
                              add adj_node to OPEN list
                    end
          end
end loop
```

Note in the flow from Listing 3.4 that once we find the best node from the OPEN list, we expand all of the child nodes (legal states possible from the best node). If the new legal states are not found on either the OPEN or CLOSED lists, they are added as new nodes (setting the predecessor to the best node, or parent). If the new node is on the CLOSED list, we discard it and continue. Finally, if the new node is on the OPEN list, but the new node has a better g value, we discard the node on the OPEN list and add the new node to the OPEN list (otherwise, the new node is discarded, if its g value is worse). By re-evaluating the nodes on the OPEN list, and replacing them when cost functions permit, we allow better paths to emerge from the state space.

As we've defined already, A* is complete, as long as the memory supports the depth and branching factor of the tree. A* is also optimal, but this characteristic depends on the use of an *admissible* heuristic. Because A* must keep track of the nodes evaluated so far (and also the discovered nodes to be evaluated), the time and space complexity are both $O(b^d)$.

> NOTE ▶ *The heuristic is defined as admissible if it accurately estimates the path cost to the goal, or underestimates it (remains optimistic). This requires that the heuristic be monotonic, which means that the cost never decreases over the path, and instead monotonically increases. This means that $g(n)$ (path cost from the initial node to the current node) monotonically increases, while $h(n)$ (path cost from the current node to the goal node) monotonically decreases.*

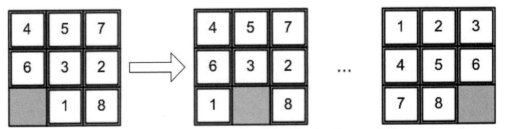

FIGURE 3.4: The Eight Puzzle and a demonstration of moving from an initial configuration to the goal configuration (does not include all steps).

A* Search and the Eight Puzzle

While A* has been applied successfully to problem domains such as path-finding, we'll apply it here to what's called the Eight Puzzle (also known as the N by M, or n^2-1 tile puzzle). This particular variation of the puzzle consists of eight tiles in a 3 by 3 grid. One location contains no tile, which can be used to move other tiles to migrate from one configuration to another (see Figure 3.4).

Note in Figure 3.4 that there are two legal moves that are possible. The '1' tile can move left, and the '6' tile can move down. The final goal configuration is shown at the right. Note that this is one variation of the goal, and the one that we'll use here.

The Eight Puzzle is interesting because it's a difficult problem to solve, but one that's been studied at length and is therefore very well understood. [Archer 1999] For example, the number of possible board configurations of the Eight Puzzle is $(n*n)!$, but only half of these are legal configurations.

TIP

During the 1870s, the Fifteen Puzzle (4 by 4 variant of the N by M puzzle) became a puzzle craze much like the Rubik's cube of the 1970s and 1980s.

On average, 22 moves are required to solve the 3 by 3 variant of the puzzle. But considering 22 as the average depth of the tree, with an average branching factor of 2.67, 2.4 trillion non-unique tile configurations can be evaluated.

Eight-Puzzle Representation

We'll use a common representation for the Eight Puzzle, a linear vector containing the tile placement from left to right, top to bottom (see Figure 3.5). This particular figure shows the moves possible from the initial puzzle configuration to depth two of this particular state space tree.

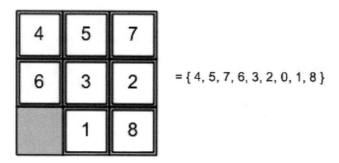

= { 4, 5, 7, 6, 3, 2, 0, 1, 8 }

FIGURE 3.5: **Eight Puzzle configuration using a simple vector.**

For our heuristic, we'll use the depth of the tree as the cost from the root to the current node (otherwise known as $g(n)$), and the number of misplaced tiles ($h(n)$) as the estimated cost to the goal node (excluding the blank). The path cost ($f(n)$) then becomes the cost of the path to the current node ($g(n)$) plus the estimated cost to the goal node ($h(n)$). You can see these heuristics in the tree in Figure 3.6. From the root node, only two moves are possible, but from these two moves, three new moves (states) open up. At the bottom of this tree, you can see that the cost function has decreased, indicating that these board configurations are likely candidates to explore next.

NOTE ▶ *There are two popular heuristics for the N-puzzle problem. The first is simply the number of tiles out of place, which in general decreases as the goal is approached. The other heuristic is the Manhattan distance of*

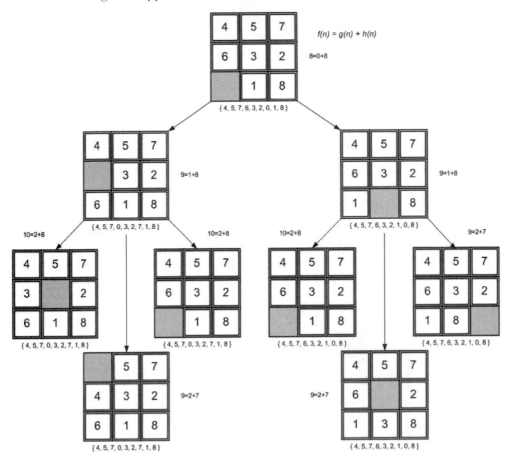

FIGURE 3.6:   Eight Puzzle tree ending at depth two, illustrating the cost functions.

tiles which sums the tile distance of each out of place tile to its correct location. For this implementation, we'll demonstrate the simple, but effective, tiles-out-of-place heuristic.

TIP

While there are (3*3)! board configurations possible, there are only (3*3)!/2 valid configurations. The other half of the configurations are unsolvable. We'll not dwell on this here, but in the source implementation you'll see the test in initPuzzle using the concept of inversions to validate the configuration of the board. This concept can be further explored in [KGong 2005].

A* Search Implementation

The core the of A-star algorithm is implemented in the function astar(). This function implements A-star as shown in Listing 3.4. We'll also present the evaluation function, which implements the 'tiles-out-of-place' metric. The list and other support functions are not presented here, but are available on the CD-ROM for review.

NOTE

The A* implementation can be found on the CD-ROM at ./software/ch3/ astar.c.

Let's start with the evaluation function which calculates the estimated cost from the current node to the goal (as the number of tiles out of place), see Listing 3.6. The function simply enumerates the 3 by 3 board as a one-dimensional vector, incrementing a score value whenever a tile is present in a position it should not be in. This score is then returned to the caller.

LISTING 3.6:   The Eight Puzzle h(n) estimated cost metric.

```
double evaluateBoard( board_t *board_p )
{
  int i;
  const int test[MAX_BOARD-1]={1, 2, 3, 4, 5, 6, 7, 8 };
  int  score=0;
  for (i = 0 ; i < MAX_BOARD-1 ; i++) {
   score += (board_p->array[i] != test[i]);
  }
  return (double)score;
}
```

The astar function is shown in Listing 3.7. Prior to calling this function, we've selected a random board configuration and placed it onto the OPEN list. We then work through the OPEN list, retrieving the best node (with the least f value using getListBest) and immediately place it on the CLOSED list. We check to see if this node is the solution, and if so, we emit the path from the initial node to the goal (which illustrates the moves that were made). To minimize searching too deeply in the tree, we halt enumerating nodes past a given depth (we search them no further).

The next step is to enumerate the possible moves from this state, which will be a maximum of four. The getChildBoard function is used to return an adjacent node (using the index passed in to determine which possible move to make). If a move isn't possible, then a NULL is returned and it's ignored.

With a new child node, we first check to see if it's already been evaluated (if it's on the CLOSED list). If it is, then we're to destroy this node and continue (to get the child node for the current board configuration). If we've not seen this particular board configuration before, we calculate the heuristics for the node. First, we initialize the node's depth in the tree as the parent's depth plus one. Next, we call evaluateBoard to get the *tiles-out-of-place* metric, which will act as our h value (cost from the root node to this node). The g value is set to the current depth, and the f value is initialized with Eq 3.1.

$$f_n = \alpha g_n + {}^{*}\beta h_n \qquad \text{(Eq 3.1)}$$

We include an *alpha* and *beta* parameter here to give different weights to the g and h values. In this implementation, *alpha* is 1.0 and *beta* is 2.0. This means that more weight is given to the h value, and subsequently the closer a node is to the goal is weighed higher than its depth in the state space tree.

With the f value calculated, we check to see if the node is on the OPEN list. If it is, we compare their f values. If the node on the OPEN list has a worse f value, the node on the OPEN list is discarded and the new child node takes its place (setting the predecessor link to the parent, so we know how we got to this node). If the node on the OPEN list has a better f value, then the node on the OPEN list remains on the open list and the new child is discarded.

Finally, if the new child node exists on neither the CLOSED or OPEN list, it's a new node that we've yet to see. It's simply added to the OPEN list, and the process continues.

This algorithm continues until either one of two events occur. If the OPEN list becomes empty, then no solution was found and the algorithm exits. If the solution is found, then showSolution is called, and the nodes linked together via the predecessor links are enumerated to show the solution from the initial node to the goal node.

LISTING 3.7:   The A* algorithm.

```
void astar( void )
{
  board_t *cur_board_p, *child_p, *temp;
  int i;
  /* While items are on the open list */
  while ( listCount(&openList_p) ) {
    /* Get the current best board on the open list */
    cur_board_p = getListBest( &openList_p );
    putList( &closedList_p, cur_board_p );
    /* Do we have a solution? */
    if (cur_board_p->h == (double)0.0) {
      showSolution( cur_board_p );
      return;
    } else {
      /* Heuristic - average number of steps is 22 for a 3x3, so
       * don't go too deep.
       */
      if (cur_board_p->depth > MAX_DEPTH) continue;
      /* Enumerate adjacent states */
      for (i = 0 ; i < 4 ; i++) {
        child_p = getChildBoard( cur_board_p, i );
        if (child_p != (board_t *)0) {
          if ( onList(&closedList_p, child_p->array, NULL) ) {
            nodeFree( child_p );
            continue;
          }
          child_p->depth = cur_board_p->depth + 1;
          child_p->h = evaluateBoard( child_p );
          child_p->g = (double)child_p->depth;
          child_p->f = (child_p->g * ALPHA) + (child_p->h * BETA);
          /* New child board on the open list? */
          if ( onList(&openList_p, child_p->array, NULL) ) {
            temp = getList(&openList_p, child_p->array);
            if (temp->g < child_p->g) {
```

```
          nodeFree(child_p);
          putList(&openList_p, temp);
          continue;
        }
        nodeFree( temp );
      } else {
        /* Child board either doesn't exist, or is better than a
         * previous board.  Hook it to the parent and place on the
         * open list.
         */
        child_p->pred = cur_board_p;
        putList( &openList_p, child_p );
      }
     }
    }
   }
  }
 }
 return;
}
```

Eight Puzzle Demonstration with A*

In the implementation, the tiles are labeled A-H with a space used to denote the blank tile. Upon execution, once the solution is found, the path taken from the initial board to the goal is enumerated. This is shown below in Listing 3.8, minimized for space.

LISTING 3.8:   A sample run of the A* program to solve the Eight Puzzle.

```
$./astar
GBD
FCH
 EA
BGD
FCH
E A
BGD
FCH
EA
GBD
FC
```

EAH

...

ABC
 DF
GEH

ABC
D F
GEH

ABC
DEF
G H

ABC
DEF
GH

A* Variants

The popularity of A* has spawned a number of variants that offer different characteristics. The *Iterative-Deepening A** algorithm backtracks to other nodes when the cost of the current branch exceeds a threshold. To minimize the memory requirements of A*, the *Simplified Memory-Bounded A** algorithm (SMA*) was created. SMA* uses the memory made available to it, and when it runs out of memory, the algorithm drops the least promising node to make room for new search nodes from the frontier.

Applications of A* Search

A* search is a popular technique and has seen use as a path-finding algorithm for computer strategy games. For better performance, many games employ simpler shortcut methods for path-finding by limiting the space of their movement (using a much sparser graph over the landscape), or by pre-calculating routes for in-game use.

HILL-CLIMBING SEARCH

Hill climbing is an iterative improvement algorithm that is similar to greedy best-first search, except that backtracking is not permitted. At each step in the search, a single node is chosen to follow. The criterion for the node to follow is that it's the best state for the current state. Since the frontier for the search is a single node, the algorithm is also similar to beam search using a beam width of one (our OPEN list can contain exactly one node).

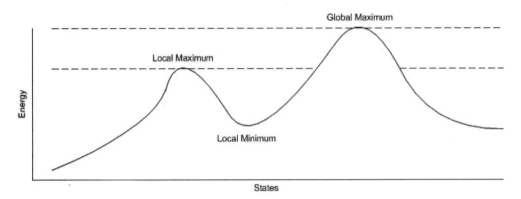

FIGURE 3.7:   **State space illustrating the problem with hill climbing.**

The problem with hill climbing is that the best node to enumerate locally may not be the best node globally. For this reason, hill climbing can lead to local optimums, but not necessarily the global optimum (the best solution available). Consider the function in Figure 3.7. There exists a local optimum and a global optimum. The goal should be to maximize the function, but if we begin at the far left and work our way toward the global optimum, we get stuck at the local optimum.

SIMULATED ANNEALING (SA)

Simulated Annealing (SA) is another iterative improvement algorithm in which randomness is incorporated to expand the search space and avoid becoming trapped in local minimum. As the name implies, the algorithm simulates the process of annealing.

Annealing is a technique in metal-casting where molten metal is heated and then cooled in a gradual manner to evenly distribute the molecules into a crystalline structure. If the metal is cooled too quickly, a crystalline structure does not result, and the metal solid is weak and brittle (having been filled with bubbles and cracks). If cooled in a gradual and controlled way, a crystalline structure forms at a molecular level resulting in great structural integrity.

The basic algorithm for simulated annealing is shown in Listing 3.9. We start with an initial solution candidate and the loop while the temperature is greater than zero. In this loop, we create an adjacent candidate solution by perturbing our current solution. This changes the solution to a neighboring solution, but at random. We then calculate the delta energy between the new (adjacent) solution, and our current solution. If this delta energy is less than zero, then our new solution is better than the old, and we accept it (we move the new adjacent solution to our current solution).

LISTING 3.9:   Simulated annealing algorithm.

```
simulated_annealing()
{
 cur_solution = random()
 computeE( cur_solution )
 while (Temperature > 0)
 adj_solution = perturb_solution( cur_solution )
 computeE( adj_solution )
 deltaE = adj_solution.energy – cur_solution.energy
 /* Is new solution better, then take it */
 if (deltaE < 0)
  cur_solution = adj_solution
 else
  p = exp( -deltaE / Temperature )
  /* Randomly accept worse solution */
  if ( p > RANDOM(0..1) )
    cur_solution = adj_solution
  end
 end
  reduce Temperature
 end
end simulated_annealing
```

If our new solution was not better than the old, then we accept it with a probability proportional to the current temperature and the delta energy. The lower the temperature, the less likely we'll accept a worse solution. But the better the delta energy, the more likely we'll accept it. This probability is calculated as shown in Eq 3.2.

$$p = \exp\left(\frac{\Delta E}{T}\right) \qquad \text{(Eq 3.2)}$$

Since our temperature decreases over time, it's less likely that a worse solution will be accepted. Early on when the temperature is high, worse solutions can be accepted allowing the search to move away from local maximum in search of the global maximum. As the temperature decreases, it becomes more difficult to accept a worse solution, which means that the algorithm settles on a solution and simply fine-tunes it (if possible).

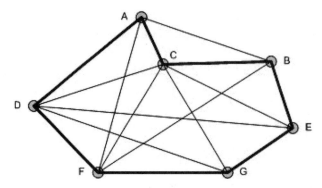

FIGURE 3.8: A Sample TSP tour through a small graph.

The classical simulated annealing algorithm also includes *monte carlo* cycles where a number of trials are performed before decreasing the temperature.

The Traveling Salesman Problem (TSP)

To demonstrate the simulated annealing algorithm, we'll use the classic Traveling Salesman Problem (or TSP). In the TSP, we're given a set of cities and a relative cost for traveling between each city to each other. The goal is to find a path through all cities where we visit all cities once, and find the shortest overall tour. We'll start at one city, visit each other city, and then end at the initial city.

Consider the graph shown in Figure 3.8. Many cities are connected to one another, but an optimal path exists that tours each city only once.

The TSP is both interesting and important because it has practical implications. Consider transportation problems where deliveries are required and fuel and time are to be minimized. Another interesting application is that of drilling holes in a circuit board. A number of holes must be drilled quickly on a single board, and in order to do this, an optimal path is needed to minimize the movement of the drill (which will be slow). Solutions to the TSP can therefore be very useful.

TSP Tour Representation

To represent a set of cities and the tour between them, we'll use an implicit *adjacency list*. Each city will be contained in the list, and cities that are next to one another are implied as connected in the tour. Recall our sample TSP in Figure 3.8 where seven cities make up the world. This will be represented as shown in Figure 3.9.

City	X coord	Y coord
A	A_x	A_y
C	C_x	C_y
B	B_x	B_y
E	E_x	E_y
G	G_x	G_y
F	F_x	F_y
D	D_x	D_y

FIGURE 3.9: Adjacency list for the TSP tour shown in Figure 3.8.

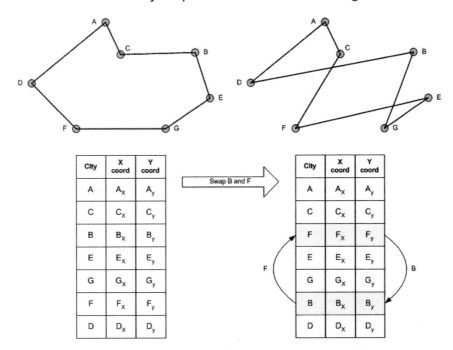

FIGURE 3.10: Demonstration of row swapping to perturb the tour.

Note that the list shown in Figure 3.9 is a single list in tour order. When we reach the end of the list, we wrap to the first element, completing the tour. To perturb the tour we take two random rows from the list and swap them. This is demonstrated in Figure 3.10. Note how by simply swapping two elements, the tour is greatly perturbed and results in a worse tour length.

Simulated Annealing Implementation

The implementation of simulated annealing is actually quite simple in the C language. We'll review three of the functions that make up the simulated annealing implementation, the main simulated annealing algorithm, perturbing a tour, and computing the length of the tour. The remaining functions are available on the CD-ROM.

LISTING 3.10:   Structures for the TSP solution.

```
typedef struct {
 int x, y;
} city_t;
typedef struct {
city_t cities[MAX_CITIES];
double tour_length;
} solution_t;
```

The Euclidean distance of the tour is calculated with compute_tour. This function walks through the tour, accumulating the segments between each city (see Listing 3.11). It ends by wrapping around the list, and adding in the distance from the last city back to the first.

LISTING 3.11:   Calculating the Euclidean tour with `compute_tour`.

```
void compute_tour( solution_t *sol )
{
 int i;
 double tour_length = (double)0.0;
 for (i = 0 ; i < MAX_CITIES-1 ; i++) {
  tour_length +=
    euclidean_distance(
          sol->cities[i].x, sol->cities[i].y,
          sol->cities[i+1].x, sol->cities[i+1].y );
```

```
    }
  tour_length +=
     euclidean_distance(
                  sol->cities[MAX_CITIES-1].x,
                  sol->cities[MAX_CITIES-1].y,
                  sol->cities[0].x, sol->cities[0].y );
   sol->tour_length = tour_length;
   return;
  }
```

Given a solution, we can create an adjacent solution using the function perturb_tour. In this function, we randomly select two cities in the tour, and swap them. A loop exists to ensure that we've selected two unique random points (so that we don't swap a single city with itself). Once selected, the x and y coordinates are swapped and the function is complete.

LISTING 3.12:   Perturbing the tour by creating an adjacent solution.

```
  void perturb_tour( solution_t *sol )
  {
   int p1, p2, x, y;
   do {
     p1 = RANDMAX(MAX_CITIES);
     p2 = RANDMAX(MAX_CITIES);
   } while (p1 == p2);
   x = sol->cities[p1].x;
   y = sol->cities[p1].y;
   sol->cities[p1].x = sol->cities[p2].x;
   sol->cities[p1].y = sol->cities[p2].y;
   sol->cities[p2].x = x;
   sol->cities[p2].y = y;
   return;
  }
```

Finally, the simulated_annealing function implements the core of the simulated annealing algorithm. The algorithm loops around the temperature, constantly reducing until it reaches a value near zero. The initial solution has been initialized prior to this function. We take the current solution and perturb it (randomly alter it) for a number of iterations (the Monte Carlo step). If the new solution is better, we accept it by copying it into the current solution. If the new solution is worse, then we accept it with a probability defined by Eq 3.2. The worse the new solution and the lower the temperature, the less likely we are to accept the new solution. When the Monte Carlo step is complete, the temperature is reduced and the process continues. When the algorithm completes, we emit the city tour.

LISTING 3.13:   The simulated annealing main function implementation.

```
int simulated_annealing( void )
{
  double temperature = INITIAL_TEMP, delta_e;
  solution_t tempSolution;
  int iteration;
  while( temperature > 0.0001 ) {
   /* Copy the current solution to a temp */
   memcpy( (char *)&tempSolution,
       (char *)&curSolution, sizeof(solution_t) );
   /* Monte Carlo Iterations */
   for (iteration = 0 ;
      iteration < NUM_ITERATIONS ; iteration++) {
    perturb_tour( &tempSolution );
    compute_tour( &tempSolution );
    delta_e = tempSolution.tour_length –
        curSolution.tour_length;
    /* Is the new solution better than the old? */
    if (delta_e < 0.0) {
     /* Accept the new, better, solution */
     memcpy( (char *)&curSolution,
         (char *)&tempSolution, sizeof(solution_t) );
    } else {
     /* Probabilistically accept a worse solution */
     if ( exp( (-delta_e / temperature) ) > RANDOM()) {
      memcpy( (char *)&curSolution,
          (char *)&tempSolution, sizeof(solution_t) );
     }
    }
   }
   /* Decrease the temperature */
```

```
    temperature *= ALPHA;
  }
  return 0;
}
```

Simulated annealing permits a random walk through a state space, greedily following the best path. But simulated annealing also probabilistically allows following worse paths in an effort to escape local maximums in search of the global maximum. This makes simulated annealing a random search, but heuristically driven. For all of its advantages, simulated annealing is incomplete and suboptimal.

Simulated Annealing Demonstration

Let's now look at the simulated annealing algorithm in action. We'll look at the algorithm from a variety of perspectives, from the temperature schedule, to a sample solution to TSP for 25 cities.

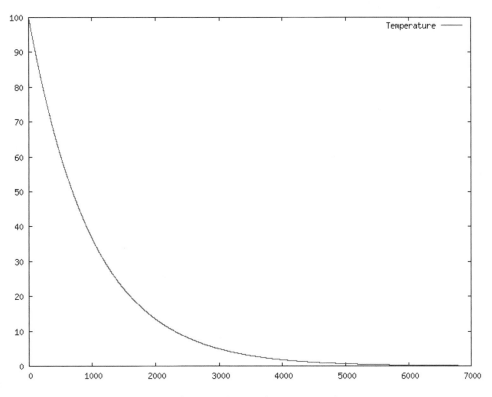

FIGURE 3.11: **The temperature decay curve using Eq 3.3.**

The temperature schedule is a factor in the probability for accepting a worse solution. In this implementation, we'll use a geometric decay for the temperature, as shown in Eq 3.3.

$$T = aT \qquad \text{(Eq 3.3)}$$

In this case, we use an alpha of 0.999. The temperature decay using this equation is shown in Figure 3.11.

The relative fitness of the solution over a run is shown in Figure 3.12. This graph shows the length of the tour during the decrease in temperature. Note at the left-hand side of the graph that the relative fitness is very erratic. This is due to the high temperature accepting a number of poorer solutions. As the temperature decreases (moving to the right of the graph), poorer solutions are not accepted as readily. At the left-hand side of the graph, the algorithm permits exploration of the state space, where at the right-hand of the graph, the solution is fine-tuned.

A sample TSP tour is shown finally in Figure 3.13. This particular solution was for a 25 city tour.

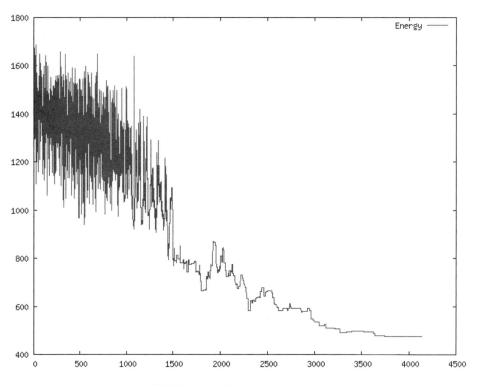

FIGURE 3.12: **The relative fitness.**

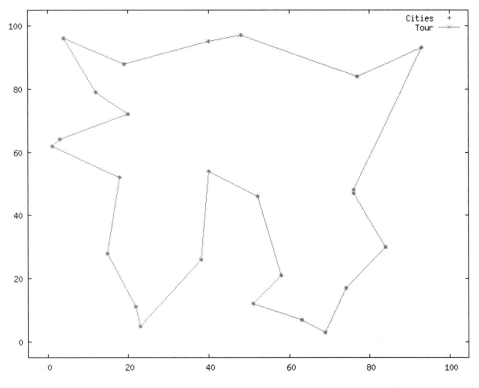

FIGURE 3.13: **Sample TSP tour optimized by simulated annealing.**

TABU SEARCH

Tabu search is a very simple search algorithm that is easy to implement and can be very effective. The basic idea behind Tabu search is neighborhood search with a *Tabu* list of nodes that is made up of nodes previously evaluated. Therefore, the search may deteriorate, but this allows the algorithm to widen the search to avoid becoming stuck in local maxima. During each iteration of the algorithm, the current search candidate is compared against the best solution found so far so that the best node is saved for later. After some search criteria has been met (a solution found, or a maximum number of iterations) the algorithm exits.

The Tabu list can be of finite size so that the oldest nodes can be dropped making room for new Tabu nodes. The nodes on the Tabu list can also be timed, such that a node can only be Tabu for some period of time. Either case allows the algorithm to reuse the Tabu list and minimize the amount of memory needed.

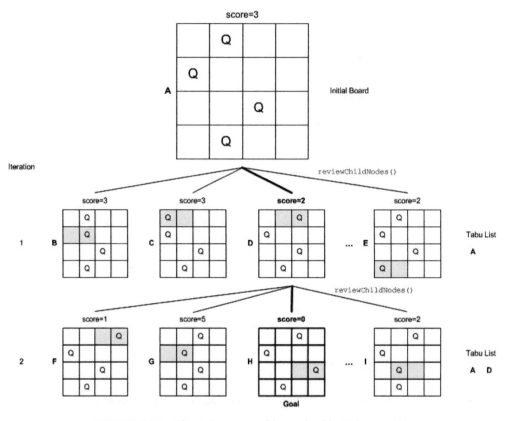

FIGURE 3.14:   **The 4-Queens problem solved by Tabu search.**

Monitoring Tabu search through the state space of the 4-Queens problem is shown in Figure 3.14. The initial position is the root, which has a score of three (three conflicts). The goal is to minimize the score, where zero is a solution (goal node). At the first iteration, the neighbor nodes are evaluated, and the best selected. Note also here that our initial node has been placed on the Tabu list. At iteration two, the neighbors are evaluated for the current node and the best is chosen to move forward. The Tabu list now contains the previous two best nodes. In this iteration, we've found a node with a score of zero, which indicates a goal node and the algorithm terminates.

The basic flow for Tabu search is shown in Listing 3.14. Given an initial position (shown here as a initial random position), the search space is enumerated by taking the best neighbor node that is not Tabu. If it's better than our best saved solution, it becomes the best solution. The process then continues with the last solution until a termination criteria is met.

LISTING 3.14:   The basic flow of the Tabu search algorithm.

```
tabu_search()
{
cur_solution = random()
evaluate_position( cur_solution )
best = cur_solution
  tabu( cur_solution )
  while (!termination_critera) {

    /* Get the best neighbor, not on the tabu list */
    cur_solution = best_non_tabu_neighbor( cur_solution )
    evaluate_position( cur_solution )

    tabu( cur_solution )
    if (cur_solution.f < best.f) {
      best = cur_solution

    }
}
  return best
}
```

To illustrate the Tabu search algorithm, we'll use the N-Queens problem as demonstrated with the best-first search algorithm. (See Figure 3.1 for a recap of the problem and desired solution.) After discussing the basic Tabu search implementation, we'll explore some of the variants that improve the algorithm.

Tabu Search Implementation

The Tabu search algorithm is very simple and can be illustrated in a single function (see Listing 3.15, function `tabu_s`). This function is the core of the Tabu search algorithm. The supporting functions are not shown here, but are available on the CD-ROM.

The C source language implementation of Tabu search can be found on the CD-ROM at ./software/ch3/tabus.c.

The implementation begins with a seeding of the random function (RANDINIT) followed by the creation of the Tabu queue. This queue represents our Tabu list, or those elements that will not be evaluated further if rediscovered. The initial solution is then created, and copied to the best solution (via initBoard to create the solution, and evaluateBoard to evaluate the value of the solution). The current solution is then loaded onto the Tabu list so that it's not evaluated again.

The loop then begins, for which we'll operate forever, or until a solution is found. For this simple problem, we'll always find a solution in some number of iterations. The call to reviewChildNodes evaluates the neighbor solutions, and picks the best one that is not on the Tabu list. This solution is returned (by reference) and then loaded onto the Tabu list. Note here that we first check to see if it's already on the Tabu list. If not, we check the state of the Tabu list. If full, we need the oldest element to make room for the new node, and then add it to the queue.

Recall that queues are FIFO in nature. Therefore, removing a node from the queue automatically removes the oldest node, satisfying the policy for the algorithm (remove the oldest node first, if the Tabu list is full).

Finally, we check the value of the solution, and if zero, we have the goal node. This can now be emitted using the emitBoard function.

LISTING 3.15: Basic Tabu search algorithm implementation in C.

```
void tabu_s()
{
  unsigned short best_sol, cur_sol;
  int best_f, cur_f;
  RANDINIT();
  tabu_q = createQueue(MAX_ELEMENTS);
  /* Get initial board */
  cur_sol = best_sol = initBoard();
  cur_f = best_f = evaluateBoard( best_sol );
  enQueue( tabu_q, best_sol );
  while( 1 ) {
    printf("Iteration for %x\n", cur_sol);
    /* Return (by reference) the best non-tabu neighbor */
    reviewChildNodes( &cur_sol, &cur_f );
    /* Add the current best solution to the tabu list (remove
     * the oldest if needed).
     */
    if (!searchQueue( tabu_q, cur_sol )) {
      if (isFullQueue( tabu_q )) {
```

```
      (void)deQueue( tabu_q );
    }
    enQueue( tabu_q, cur_sol );
  }
  /* Save the best solution so far */
  if (cur_f <= best_f) {
    best_sol = cur_sol;
    best_f = cur_f;
  }
  /* Solution found? */
  if (best_f == 0 ) {
    emitBoard( best_sol );
    break;
  }
}
destroyQueue( tabu_q );
return;
}
```

Tabu Search Demonstration

The Tabu search application efficiently finds the solution to this problem (a state space of 256 unique nodes). The first evaluateBoard is the initial node (see Listing 3.16), followed by four iterations of the algorithm. Note that while the initial node had a cost of two, subsequent nodes evaluated were worse, but eventually led to the goal. Tabu search permits the evaluation away from local minimum to find the global minimum, as demonstrated here.

LISTING 3.16:   Sample execution of Tabu search for the 4-Queens problem.

```
evaluateBoard 1281 = (f 2)
Iteration for 1281
 evaluateBoard 2281 = (f 2)
 evaluateBoard 2181 = (f 3)
 evaluateBoard 2481 = (f 3)
 evaluateBoard 2241 = (f 2)
 evaluateBoard 2221 = (f 3)
 evaluateBoard 2281 = (f 2)
 evaluateBoard 2282 = (f 3)
Iteration for 2281
 evaluateBoard 4281 = (f 1)
```

```
evaluateBoard 4181 = (f 1)
evaluateBoard 4481 = (f 3)
evaluateBoard 4281 = (f 1)
evaluateBoard 4241 = (f 3)
evaluateBoard 4282 = (f 2)
Iteration for 4281
evaluateBoard 8281 = (f 2)
evaluateBoard 8181 = (f 3)
evaluateBoard 8481 = (f 4)
evaluateBoard 8241 = (f 2)
evaluateBoard 8221 = (f 3)
evaluateBoard 8281 = (f 2)
evaluateBoard 8282 = (f 2)
Iteration for 8282
evaluateBoard 4282 = (f 2)
evaluateBoard 2282 = (f 3)
evaluateBoard 4182 = (f 0)
evaluateBoard 4482 = (f 2)
evaluateBoard 4282 = (f 2)
evaluateBoard 4142 = (f 2)
evaluateBoard 4181 = (f 1)
evaluateBoard 4184 = (f 3)
solution is 0x4182
0 1 0 0
0 0 0 1
1 0 0 0
0 0 1 0
```

Tabu Search Variants

In order to make Tabu search more effective for very difficult search problems, a number of modifications exist. The first of these is called *intensification* and essentially intensifies the search around a given point (such as the best known solution). The idea is that we take a promising node, and intensify the search around this point. This is implemented using an intermediate memory, which contains the neighbor nodes to dig into further.

One issue that comes up in local search algorithms is that they can get stuck in local optimums. Tabu search introduces the concept of *diversification* to allow the algorithm to search nodes that have been previously unexplored to expand the space of search.

When we follow the best solutions, it's very possible to get stuck in local optimums for difficult problems. Another interesting variant is called *constraint relaxation*, which relaxes the neighborhood selection algorithm to accept lower quality nodes in the search space. This permits the algorithm to expand its search to descend into lower quality solutions in search of higher quality solutions. [Gendreau 2002]

CONSTRAINT SATISFACTION PROBLEMS (CSP)

In many search problems, we're interested not just in the goal, but how we got from the initial state to the goal state (take for example, the eight puzzle). As we'll learn later, planning systems rely on this aspect of search as a plan is nothing more than a sequence of steps to get from a given state to a goal state. For some problems, we're not interested in the path to the goal, but instead just the goal state (for example, the N-Queens problem). Problems of this type are called Constraint Satisfaction Problems (CSP).

Formally, we can think about CSP in terms of a set of *variables* with a *domain* of possible values, and a set of *constraints* that specify the allowable combinations of variable values. Consider the following simple example. We wish to find values for the set of variables x and y each having a domain of {1-9}, such that Eq 3.4 (the constraint) is satisfied.

$$x + y = x * y \qquad \text{(Eq 3.4)}$$

Without much work, we know that assigning the value of two for both x and y satisfies the constraint defined by the equation.

Graph Coloring as a CSP

One of the more popular CSPs is called Graph Coloring. Given a graph, and a set of colors, the problem is to color the nodes such that an edge does not directly connect to a node of the same color. Consider the map shown in Figure 3.15. We can see a set of objects that are adjacent to one another. Object A is adjacent to objects B and C, while object D is adjacent only to object B. The graph portion of Figure 3.14 illustrates the graph of the map. From this graph, we can see edges which define the adjacency of the objects (nodes) of the graph.

Now consider the problem of coloring the map given the constraints that each object can be one color and no colored objects should be adjacent to one another. Can the graph be colored using three colors (red, green, and blue)?

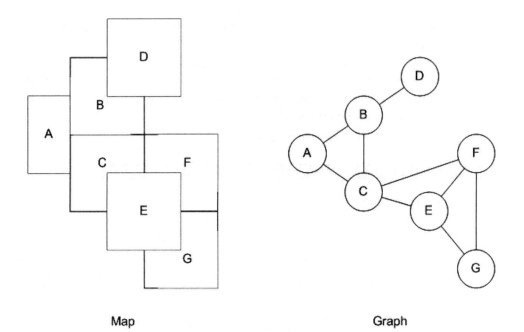

Map Graph

FIGURE 3.15: **The classical graph coloring CSP.**

Using trial and error, we can very easily color this simple graph by iterating through the nodes of the graph and assigning a color so that our constraint remains satisfied. Let's start with node A, color it, and then step to each remaining node, coloring as we go. In Listing 3.17, we see the coloring process. Each node is followed by a constraint, with the color finally chosen in parentheses.

Node A – Pick any color (Red)
Node B – Pick a color other than Red (Blue)
Node C – Pick a color other than Red and Blue (Green)
Node D – Pick a color other than Blue (Red)
Node E – Pick a color other than Green (Red)
Node F – Pick a color other than Green or Red (Blue)
Node G – Pick a color other than Red or Blue (Green)

LISTING 3.17:   Graph coloring through trial and error.

Through a simple process of elimination, we've been able to color the graph using the constraints of previously colored nodes to determine the color to paint adjacent nodes (final result shown in Figure 3.17).

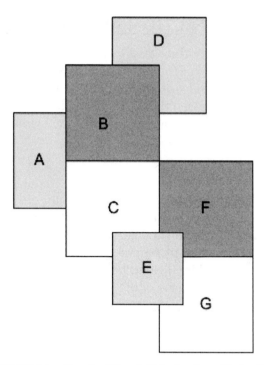

FIGURE 3.16: **Result of Graph Coloring from Listing 3.17.**

> *The famous Four Color Theorem (to prove that only four colors are required to color any planar map) dates back to the mid 1800s. There were numerous failed attempts to prove the theorem and it remained conjecture until 1976, when Appel and Haken created a formal proof.*

Scheduling as a CSP

One of the most practical applications of constraint satisfaction is to the problem of scheduling. Numerous types of scheduling problems exist, from airline timetables to the scheduling of manufacturing processes. The scheduling problem comes down to allocating *resources* to *activities* in *time* preserving a set of constraints. For example, in a manufacturing problem, a resource can be processed through a variety of activities each requiring a specific amount of time. In addition, activities have precedence that must be maintained (a resource must be processed by Activity A before Activity B). The goal of the CSP in this problem is to identify an optimal schedule of resources through the activities such that the end product can be optimally produced.

CONSTRAINT-SATISFACTION ALGORITHMS

A large number of algorithms exist to solve CSPs from the simple *Generate and Test* algorithm to constraint-propagation and consistency. We'll explore a few of the available algorithms that can be used. Note that some of the algorithms we've discussed thus far (such as depth-first search investigated in Chapter 2, and simulated annealing and Tabu search from Chapter 3) can be used effectively to solve CSPs.

Generate and Test

Generate and Test is the simplest of the algorithms to identify a solution for a CSP. In this algorithm, each of the possible solutions is attempted (each value enumerated for each variable) and then tested for the solution. Since testing each combination of variable within the domain of each value can be extremely slow and inefficient, heuristics can be applied to avoid those combinations that are outside of the solution space.

Backtracking

The *backtracking* algorithm operates with a simple uninformed search algorithm, such as depth-first search. At each node, a variable is instantiated with a value and the constraint violations are checked. If the values are legal, search is permitted to continue, otherwise, the current branch is abandoned and the next node from the OPEN list is evaluated.

To increase the efficiency of the backtracking algorithm, the *most constrained variable* is instantiated first. Take for example, node C from Figure 3.14. In this case, the node has four neighbors (the most of any node in the graph).

> Both Generate and Test and backtracking are common systematic search algorithms, as they systematically assign values to variables in search of a solution. Generate and Test is highly inefficient, while backtracking suffers from trashing, or the repeated failure to find a solution for the same reason (for example, a single variable remaining constant).

Forward Checking and Look Ahead

Forward checking is similar to backtracking, except that when a particular node is evaluated for the current variable (called arc consistency), only those valid nodes are considered for the OPEN list to evaluate in the future. Nodes that can be detected as invalid are immediately ignored, resulting only in the most promising branches for further search. This can minimize a number of nodes generated for search, but tends to involve more work when evaluating a single node (for forward checking of constraints).

A variation on forward checking is called *look ahead*. In this algorithm, instead of simply evaluating child nodes based on the currently instantiated value, all subsequent to be instantiated variables are instantiated given the currently instantiated values. This results in very flat search trees. (See Figure 3.17 for a graphical view of backtracking, forward checking, and look ahead.)

Forward checking is commonly more effective than backtracking as the number of nodes to be evaluated is reduced.

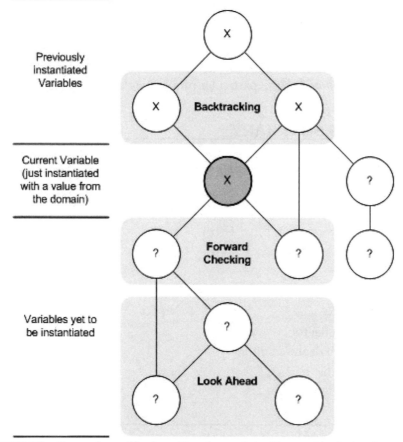

FIGURE 3.17: Comparison of backtracking, forward checking, and look ahead constraint propagation algorithms.

Min-Conflicts Search

An interesting *heuristic repair* algorithm is the Min-Conflicts heuristic. This algorithm begins by choosing the variable that violates the fewest number of constraints and then systematically improves the solution through using an algorithm such as hill climbing or A* with the heuristic function $h(n)$ defined as the total number of constraints violated.

CHAPTER SUMMARY

Informed search methods, unlike the uninformed (or blind) methods, use a heuristic to determine the quality of any state in the search space. This allows the algorithm to guide the search and choose the next node to expand. In this chapter, a number of informed search methods were explored, including best-first search, A* search, hill-climbing search, simulated annealing, Tabu search, and finally algorithms for constraint satisfaction. Understanding the informed methods of search is important because much of problem solving in AI can be refined to search methods. The key is choosing the algorithm that is best suited to the particular problem at hand.

ALGORITHMS SUMMARY

Table 3.1:   Summary of the uninformed algorithms and their characteristics.

Algorithm	Time	Space	Optimal	Complete	Derivative
Best-First Search	$O(bm)$	$O(bm)$	No	Yes	BFS/UCS
A* Search	$O(2^N)$	$O(b^d)$	Yes	Yes	BestFS
IDA*	$O(2^N)$	$O(d)$	Yes	Yes	A*
SMA*					
SimAnneal	-	-	No	No	
Tabu	-	-	No	No	

b, branching factor
d, tree depth of the solution
m, tree depth

REFERENCES

[Archer 1999] Archer, A.F. "A Modern Treatment of the 15 Puzzle," *American Math*. Monthly 106, 793-799, 1999.

[KGong 2005] Gong, Kevin. "A Mathematical Analysis of the Sixteen Puzzle." Last updated 12/2005.
Available online at http://www.kevingong.com/Math/SixteenPuzzle.html

[Gendreau 2002] Gendreau, Michel. "An Introduction to Tabu Search," Universite de Montreal. July 2002. Available online at http://www.ifi.uio.no/infheur/Bakgrunn/Intro_to_TS_Gendreau.htm

RESOURCES

[Glover 1990] Glover, Fred. "Tabu Search: A Tutorial," Interfaces, 20 (4): 74-94, 1990.

EXERCISES

1. Best-first search uses a combined heuristic to choose the best path to follow in the state space. Define the two heuristics used ($h(n)$ and $g(n)$).
2. Best-first search uses both an OPEN list and a CLOSED list. Describe the purpose of each for the best-first algorithm.
3. Describe the differences between best-first search and greedy best-first search.
4. Describe the differences between best-first search and beam search.
5. What are the advantages of beam search over best-first search?
6. A* search uses a combined heurstic to select the best path to follow through the state space toward the goal. Define the two heuristics used ($h(n)$ and $g(n)$).
7. Briefly describe A* search and the problems to which it can be applied.
8. What is meant by an admissible heuristic?
9. How do the alpha and beta parameters tune the heuristics for A* search?
10. Briefly explain the difference between A* search and SMA*. What advantage does SMA have over A*?
11. Hill climbing is a standard iterative improvement algorithm similar to greedy best-first search. What are the primary problems with hill climbing?
12. Describe Simulated annealing and if it combines iterative improvement with stochastic search.
13. Describe the algorithm and how it differs from random search.

14. What is the purpose of the Monte Carlo step in the simulated annealing algorithm?
15. Briefly describe the Tabu search algorithm.
16. The Tabu list can be sized for the problem at hand. What effect does changing the size of the Tabu list have on the search algorithm?
17. Describe the intensification and diversification modifications of Tabu search.
18. Describe the essence of a constraint satisfaction problem.
19. What are some of the major applications of constraint satisfaction search?
20. Compare and contrast the CSP algorithms of backtracking, forward checking, and look ahead.

4   AI AND GAMES

A I has a long history in the genre of games. From the first intelligent Checkers player, to the team AI developed for first-person-shooters, AI is at the core. This chapter will cover aspects of game AI from traditional game playing of Checkers, Chess, Othello, and Go to more recent video games including first-person-shooters, strategy games, and others. We'll introduce the minimax algorithm and alpha-beta pruning, which are central to traditional two-player games. We'll then explore other algorithms that can be found in modern game systems.

TWO-PLAYER GAMES

Two-player games are games in which two players compete against each other. These are also known as zero-sum games. The goal then in playing a two-player game is choosing a move that maximizes the score of the player and/or minimizes the score of the competing player.

NOTE   *A zero-sum game is one in which the gain of one player is balanced exactly by the loss of the other player. Zero sum games have been studied extensively by John von Neumann and Oskar Morgenstern and then later by John Nash. Chess is an example of a zero-sum game. In contrast, non-zero-sum games are those in which two players attempt to get rewards from a banker by cooperating or betraying the other player. The prisoner's dilemma is a classic example of a non-zero-sum game. Both zero and non-zero-sum games are types of games within the field of game theory. Game theory has a range of uses from parlor games such as Poker, to the study of economic phenomena from auctions to social networks.*

Consider the two-player game Tic-Tac-Toe. Players alternate moves, and as each move is made, the possible moves are constrained (see the partial Tic-Tac-Toe game tree in Figure 4.1). In this simple game, a move can be selected based on the move leading to a win by traversing all moves that are constrained by this move. Also, by traversing the tree for a given move, we can choose the move that leads to the win in the shallowest depth (minimal number of moves).

Tic-Tac-Toe is an interesting case because the maximum number of moves is tiny when compared to more complex games such as Checkers or

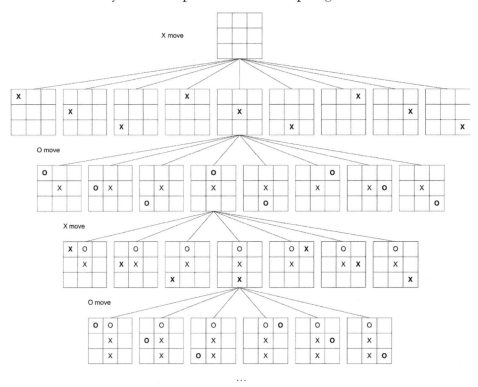

FIGURE 4.1:   Partial game tree for the two-player game of Tic-Tac-Toe.

Chess. Tic-Tac-Toe is also open to numerous optimizations. Consider, for example, the first X move in Figure 4.1. If the board is rotated, only three unique moves are actually possible. Without optimization, there exist 362,880 nodes within the complete game tree.

NOTE *Two-player games are useful as a test-bed for validating competitive algorithms. Also of interest are one-player games (also known as puzzles). Examples of useful one-player games include the n-disk Towers of Hanoi puzzle and the N-puzzle (see Chapters 2 and 3).*

At each node in the tree (a possible move) a value defining the *goodness* of the move toward the player winning the game can be provided. So at a given node, the child nodes (possible moves from this state in the game) each have an attribute defining the relative goodness of the move. It's an easy task then to choose the best move given the current state. But given the alternating nature of two-player games, the next player makes a move that benefits himself (and in zero-sum games, results in a deficit for the alternate player).

A static evaluation function (that measure the *goodness* of a move) is used to determine the value of a given move from a given game state. The evaluation function identifies the relative value of a successor move from the list of possible moves as a measure of the move quality toward winning the game. Consider the partial game tree in Figure 4.2.

The static evaluation function is defined as the number of possible win positions not blocked by the opponent minus the number of possible win positions (row, column, and diagonal) for the opponent not blocked by the current player:

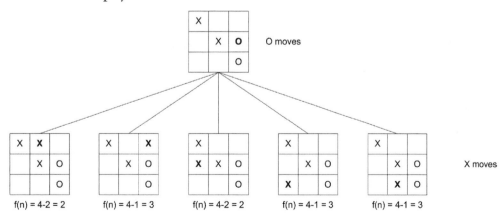

FIGURE 4.2: **Tic-Tac-Toe game tree with static evaluation function.**

$$f(n) = win\_positions\text{-}lose\_positions \qquad (\text{Eq } 4.1)$$

Using this evaluation function, we identify the goodness of the board configuration given a move for X in Figure 4.2. The higher the result of the static evaluation function, the closer the move brings the player toward a win. Three moves result in the evaluation function equaling three, but only one move can lead to a win for X as the other two lead to a subsequent win for O. Therefore, while the static evaluation function is useful, another heuristic is necessary to pick the move with the highest static evaluation while protecting against a loss in the next move.

Let's now look at an algorithm that provides a means to select a move that brings the player closer to a win while moving the opponent further from a win.

THE MINIMAX ALGORITHM

In simple games, algorithms exist that can search the game trees to determine the best move to make from the current state. The most well known is called the Minimax algorithm. The minimax algorithm is a useful method for simple two-player games. It is a method for selecting the best move given an alternating game where each player opposes the other working toward a mutually exclusive goal. Each player knows the moves that are possible given a current game state, so for each move, all subsequent moves can be discovered.

At each node in the tree (possible move) a value defining the *goodness* of the move toward the player winning the game can be provided. So at a given node, the child nodes (possible moves from this state in the game) each have an attribute defining the relative goodness of the move. It's an easy task then to choose the best move given the current state. But given the alternating nature of two-player games, the next player makes a move that benefits them (and in zero-sum games, results in a deficit for the alternate player).

NOTE ▶ *The ply of a node is defined as the number of moves needed to reach the current state (game configuration). The ply of a game tree is then the maximum of the plies of all nodes.*

Minimax can use one of two basic strategies. In the first, the entire game tree is searched to the leaf nodes (end-games), and in the second, the tree is searched only to a predefined depth and then evaluated. Let's now explore the minimax algorithm in greater detail.

NOTE▶ *When we employ a strategy to restrict the search depth to a maximum number of nodes (do not search beyond N levels of the tree), the look ahead is restricted and we suffer from what is called the horizon effect. When we can't see beyond the horizon, it becomes easier to make a move that looks good now, but leads to problems later as we move further into this subtree.*

Minimax is a depth-first search algorithm that maintains a minimum or a maximum value for successor nodes at each node that has children. Upon reaching a leaf node (or the max depth supported), the value of the node is calculated using an evaluation (or utility) function. Upon calculating a node's utility, we propagate these values up to the parent node based on whose move is to take place. For our move, we'll use the maximum value as our determiner for the best move to make. For our opponent, the minimum value is used. At each layer of the tree, the child nodes area is scanned and depending on whose move is to come, the maximum value is kept (in the case of our move), or the minimum value is kept (in the case of the opponent's move). Since these values are propagated up in an alternating fashion, we maximize the minimum, or minimize the maximum. In other words, we assume that each player makes the move next that benefits them the most. The basic algorithm for minimax is shown in Listing 4.1.

LISTING 4.1:   Basic algorithm for minimax game tree search.

```
minimax( player, board )
        if game_won( player, board ) return win
        for each successor board
                if (player == X) return maximum of successor boards
                if (player == O) return minimum of successor boards
        end
end
```

To demonstrate this approach, Figure 4.3 shows the end-game for a particular Tic-Tac-Toe board configuration. Both X and O have played three turns, and now it's X's turn. We traverse this tree in depth-first order, and upon reaching either a win/lose or draw position, we set the score for the board. We'll use a simple representation here, -1 representing a loss, 0 for a draw, and 1 for a win. The boards with bold lines define the win/loss/ draw boards where the score is evaluated. When all leaf nodes have been evaluated, the node values can be propagated up based on the current player.

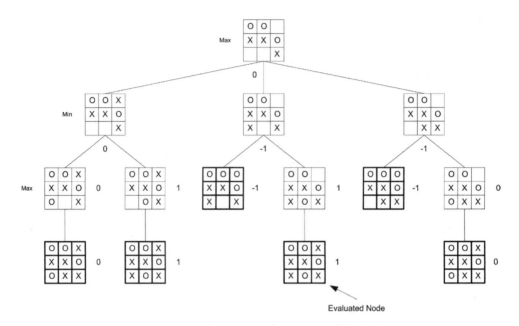

FIGURE 4.3:   End-game tree for a game of Tic-Tac-Toe.

At layer 2 in the game tree, it's O's turn, so we minimize the children and score the parent with the smallest value. At the far left portion of the game tree, the values 0 and 1 are present, so 0 is kept (the minimum) and stored in the parent. At layer 1 in the tree, we're looking at the maximum, so out of node scores 0, -1, and -1, we keep 0 and store this at the parent (the root node of our game tree).

With the scores having been propagated to the root, we can now make the best move possible. Since it's our move, we're maximizing, so we look for the node with the largest score (the left-most node with a value of 0), and we take this position. Our opponent (who is minimizing) then chooses the minimum node value (left-most node in tree depth 2). This leaves us with our final move, resulting in a draw.

Note that in a game where perfect information is available to each player, and no mistakes are made, the end-result will always be a draw. We'll build a program to play Tic-Tac-Toe to illustrate how this algorithm can be constructed. Like any tree algorithm, it can be built simply and efficiently using recursion.

An alternative to building the entire search tree is to reduce the depth of the search, which implies that we may not encounter leaf nodes. This is also known as an imperfect information game and can result in sub-optimal strategies of play. The advantage of reducing the search tree is that game play can occur much more quickly and minimax can be used for games of higher complexity (such as Chess or Checkers).

Recursively searching an entire game tree can be a time (and space) consuming process. This means that minimax can be used on simple games such as Tic-Tac-Toe, but games such as Chess are far too complex to build an entire search tree. The number of board configurations for Tic-Tac-Toe is around 24,683. Chess is estimated to have on the order of 10^{100} board configurations – a truly massive number.

Minimax and Tic-Tac-Toe

Let's now look at an implementation of the minimax algorithm that uses recursion between two functions. We'll first explore the representation of the problem, which can be very important to be able to store large numbers of board configurations for game tree search.

The Tic-Tac-Toe board requires nine positions where each position can take one of three values (an 'X,' 'O,' or empty). Bitwise, we can represent our values in two bits, which gives us four unique identifies. With nine positions on the Tic-Tac-Toe board, requiring two bits each, we can use a 32-bit value to represent the entire board with numerous bits left over (see Figure 4.4 for the Tic-Tac-Toe board representation).

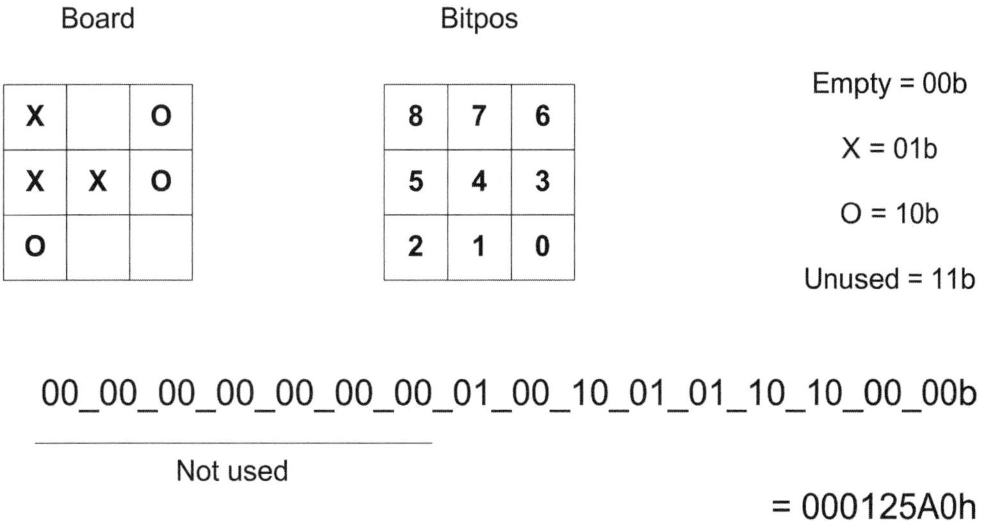

Board   Bitpos

X		O
X	X	O
O		

8	7	6
5	4	3
2	1	0

Empty = 00b

X = 01b

O = 10b

Unused = 11b

00_00_00_00_00_00_00_01_00_10_01_01_10_10_00_00b

Not used

= 000125A0h

FIGURE 4.4:   Representing a Tic-Tac-Toe board in a packed 32-bit value.

TIP

> *From Figure 4.4, we can see that the Tic-Tac-Toe board fits easily within a 32-bit type, including room to spare. Using a 32-bit value is also important for efficiency as most modern computer systems use this type internally for atomic memory access register storage.*

The minimax algorithm is easily implemented as a recursive algorithm. For this implementation, we'll use two functions that recursively call each other. Each function plays the game in the context of a specific player (see Listing 4.2).

LISTING 4.2:   Recursive algorithm for minimax game tree search.

```
play_O ( board )
        if end_game( board ) return eval( board )
        for each empty slot in board
                new_board = board
                mark empty cell with O in new_board
                value = play_X( new_board )
                if value < min
                        value = min
                end
        return value
end
play_X ( board )
        if end_game( board ) return eval( board )
        for each empty slot in board
                new_board = board
                mark empty cell with X in new_board
                value = play_O( new_board )
                if value > max
                        value = max
                end
        end
        return value
end
```

A call to play_X begins the construction of the game tree with a specific board. Each function begins with a call to end-game, which determines if the game has ended (no cells available to place a piece, or the game has been won). If the end-game has been detected, the board is evaluated and a score returned. We'll use a very simple scoring method for the Tic-Tac-Toe board. If the game has been won by the X player, a '1' is returned. If the game has been won by the O player, a '-1' is returned. Finally, if a draw results, the value 0 is returned.

If the end-game has not occurred, the current board is iterated, looking for empty locations. For each empty location, the function places its value (in a new board, to avoid corrupting the current board that will be used multiple times). The new board is then passed to the alternate function to continue

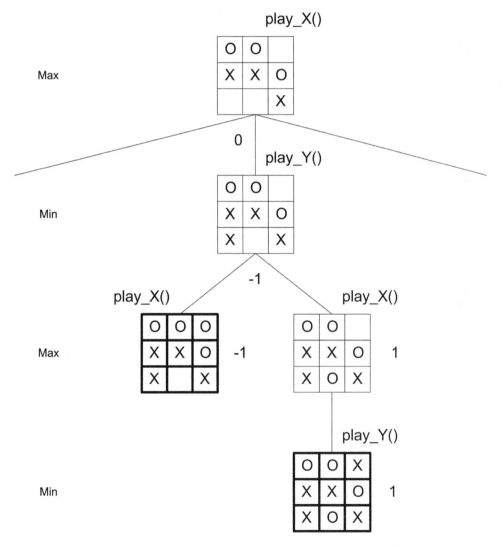

FIGURE 4.5: Demonstrating the two recursive functions in a partial game tree.

building the game tree for the opposing player. As the play_ function returns its value, it's compared to the current min or max value depending on the current role of the player (X is maximizing, O is minimizing).

We could have implemented this using one function, but two functions makes it a bit easier to understand as we know when we're in play_X, that we're maximizing and when we're in play_Y, we're minimizing. The relationships of the two functions and their roles are shown in Figure 4.5.

Minimax Implementation for Tic-Tac-Toe

As shown in Listing 4.3, we'll use two functions to implement the recursive game-tree search. We'll discuss these two functions in particular, but not the entire implementation, which can be found on the CD-ROM.

The source code for the minimax Tic-Tac-Toe game player can be found on the CD-ROM at ./software/ch4/minimax.c.

Once the human player's move has been accepted and placed on the board, a call is made to evaluateComputerMove (with the new game board, and a depth of 0, since we're at the root of the tree). We'll discuss the implementation for both functions now, as they fundamentally are the same, except for the minimum and maximum checking.

Upon entry to the function, we immediately check for a win by the opposing player (since this call is done when the opposing player has made a move). If the prior player executed a play that won the game, the score is returned (MIN_INFINITY for evaluateComputerMove, MAX_INFINITY for evaluateHumanMove). This may seem opposite, but we're maximizing for the computer player, and we check for this in the opposing function, evaluateHumanMove. We then walk through all available open board positions, place our token in the space, and then call the opposing function for evaluation. Upon return, we store the min or max, depending on the function's role (max for computer player that is maximizing, min for human player that is minimizing). If no empty spaces were found, then by default the game is a draw and we return this score.

One important point to note in evaluateComputerMove is that as we store a new max value, which identifies the current best move, we check the depth of this particular board configuration. As computer_move is a global (identifying the best move so far), we only want to store this for the board configuration containing our possible next move, not every board in the tree to the depths of the ultimate solution. This can be identified as the tree depth, which will be 0.

LISTING 4.3:   Recursive algorithm Implementation for minimax game tree search.

```
short evaluateHumanMove( unsigned int board, int depth )
{
 int i, value;
 unsigned int new_board;
 short min = MAX_INFINITY+1;
  short evaluateComputerMove( unsigned int, int );
  /* The computer (max) just made a move, so we evaluate that move here
*/
  if (checkPlayerWin(O_PLAYER, board)) return MAX_INFINITY;
  for (i = 0 ; i < MAX_CHILD_NODES ; i++) {
   if (getCell(i, board) == EMPTY) {
    new_board = board;
    putCell( X_PLAYER, i, &new_board );
    value = evaluateComputerMove( new_board, depth+1 );
    if (value <= min) {
     min = value;
    }
   }
  }
  /* No move is possible -- draw */
  if (min == MAX_INFINITY+1) {
   return DRAW;
  }
  return min;
}
int computer_move;
short evaluateComputerMove( unsigned int board, int depth )
{
 int i, value;
 unsigned int new_board;
 short max = MIN_INFINITY-1;
  /* The human (min) just made a move, so we evaluate that move here */
  if (checkPlayerWin(X_PLAYER, board)) return MIN_INFINITY;
  for (i = 0 ; i < MAX_CHILD_NODES ; i++) {
   if (getCell(i, board) == EMPTY) {
    new_board = board;
    putCell( O_PLAYER, i, &new_board );
    value = evaluateHumanMove( new_board, depth+1 );
```

```
        if (value >= max) {
          max = value;
          if (depth == 0) computer_move = i;
          }
        }
      }
      /* No move is possible -- draw */
      if (max == MIN_INFINITY-1) {
        return DRAW;
      }
      return max;
    }
```

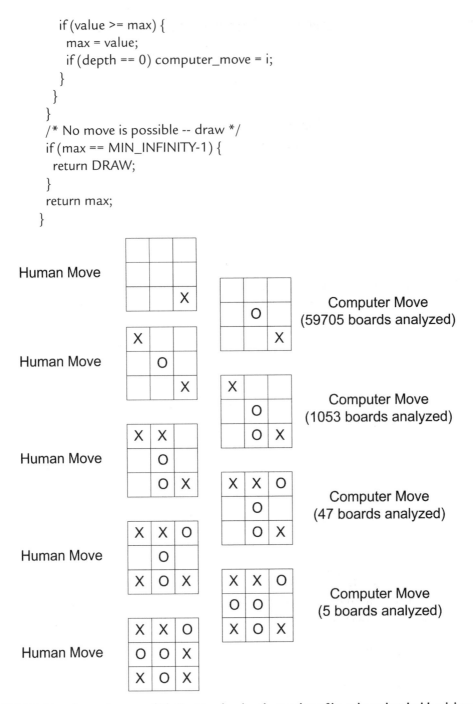

FIGURE 4.6: A sample game of Tic-Tac-Toe showing the number of boards analyzed with minimax.

Minimax is a great algorithm for small depth and branching factors, but it can consume quite a bit of storage for more complex problems. Figure 4.6 shows a sample game played using the minimax algorithm. The computer plays four moves, chosen by minimax. For each of those four moves, a total of 60,810 configurations are evaluated.

While there are 3^9 unique Tic-Tac-Toe boards, there are actually many fewer valid boards as an early win (prior to filling up the board) makes all successor boards invalid.

What's needed is a way to avoid searching branches of the game tree that are obviously bad. One way to achieve this is through a pruning algorithm called Alpha-Beta that's used in conjunction with the minimax algorithm.

Minimax with Alpha-Beta Pruning

Alpha-beta pruning is a simple algorithm that minimizes the game-tree search for moves that are obviously bad. Consider a Tic-Tac-Toe board where the opposing player would win on the next move. Rather than going on the offensive with another move, the best move is the one that defends the board from a win on the next move.

Chess is a classic example of this problem. Consider moving the king so that it's in immediate danger. It's an invalid move, and therefore the game tree that followed this move could be pruned (not evaluated) to reduce the search space.

This is the basic idea of alpha-beta pruning. Identify moves that are not beneficial, and remove them from the game tree. The higher in the game tree that branches are pruned the greater effect in minimizing the search space of the tree. Let's now explore the algorithm behind alpha-beta pruning.

During the depth-first search of the game tree, we calculate and maintain two variables called *alpha* and *beta*. The alpha variable defines the best move that can be made to maximize (our best move) and the beta variable defines the best move that can be made to minimize (the opposing best move). While we traverse the game tree, if alpha is ever greater than or equal to beta, then the opponent's move forces us into a worse position (than our current best move). In this case, we avoid evaluating this branch any further.

Let's look at an example game tree to demonstrate the operation of alpha-beta pruning. We'll use the simple game tree shown in Figure 4.7. The algorithm begins by setting alpha to -INFINITY and beta to +INFINITY, and then makes a call to the minimizing routine. The minimizer iterates through the successor nodes and finds the smallest utility of three. This

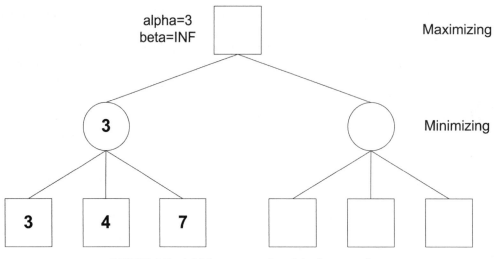

FIGURE 4.7: Initial game tree for alpha-beta pruning.

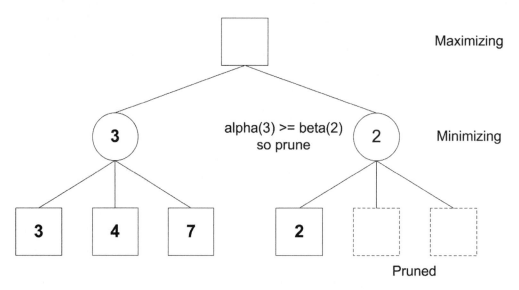

FIGURE 4.8: Pruned game tree at the minimizer level.

becomes the beta variable in the minimizer, but is returned to the maximizer function to become the alpha variable.

The current alpha and beta variables are then passed to the minimizer again for check of the right-hand subtree (see Figure 4.8). Once the first node is evaluated (from left to right), we find its utility to be two. Since this value is less than our beta (currently +INFINITY), beta becomes two. We then check to see if alpha >= beta. It is, and therefore we can conclude the remaining nodes will be minimized to two or less (since the parent node is a minimizer), which is less than the utility of the left-hand subtree, and available for pruning.

The idea behind alpha-beta pruning is that if we're evaluating moves, and find a move that's worse than the move we've discovered so far, we ignore it and move on (don't dig any deeper into that subtree).

The source code for minimax with alpha-beta pruning can be found on the CD-ROM at ./software/ch4/alphabeta.c.

The implementation for alpha-beta pruning is quite simple as the only necessity is to maintain the alpha and beta variables and determine when pruning should occur. Listing 4.4 provides the alpha-beta implementation, as amended from our original minimax functions from Listing 4.3.

Listing 4.4:   Updated minimax implementation for alpha-beta pruning.

```
short evaluateHumanMove( unsigned int board, int depth,
              int alpha, int beta )
{
 int i, value;
 unsigned int new_board;
 short min = MAX_INFINITY+1;
 short evaluateComputerMove( unsigned int, int, int, int );
 /* The computer (max) just made a move, so we evaluate that move here
*/
 if (checkPlayerWin(O_PLAYER, board)) return MAX_INFINITY;
 for (i = 0 ; i < MAX_CHILD_NODES ; i++) {
  if (getCell(i, board) == EMPTY) {
   new_board = board;
   putCell( X_PLAYER, i, &new_board );
   value = evaluateComputerMove( new_board, depth+1, alpha, beta );
   if (value < min) {
    min = value;
   }
   if (value < beta) beta = value;
   /* Prune this subtree by not checking any further successors */
   if (alpha >= beta) return beta;
  }
```

```
}
/* No move is possible -- draw */
if (min == MAX_INFINITY+1) {
  return DRAW;
}
return min;
}
short evaluateComputerMove( unsigned int board, int depth,
                int alpha, int beta )
{
  int i, value;
  unsigned int new_board;
  short max = MIN_INFINITY-1;
  /* The human (min) just made a move, so we evaluate that move here */
  if (checkPlayerWin(X_PLAYER, board)) return MIN_INFINITY;
  for (i = 0 ; i < MAX_CHILD_NODES ; i++) {
    if (getCell(i, board) == EMPTY) {
      new_board = board;
      putCell( O_PLAYER, i, &new_board );
      value = evaluateHumanMove( new_board, depth+1, alpha, beta );
      if (value > max) {
        max = value;
        if (depth == 0) computer_move = i;
      }
      if (value > alpha) alpha = value;
      /* Prune this subtree by not checking any further successors */
      if (alpha >= beta) return alpha;
    }
  }
  /* No move is possible -- draw */
  if (max == MIN_INFINITY-1) {
    return DRAW;
  }
  return max;
}
```

In both functions, the alpha (upper-bound) and beta (lower-bound) variables are maintained from the current node's utility. Recall that upon first call, alpha is –INFINITY and beta is +INFINITY. For each node, the alpha is compared to the beta, and if greater-than or equal, the remaining

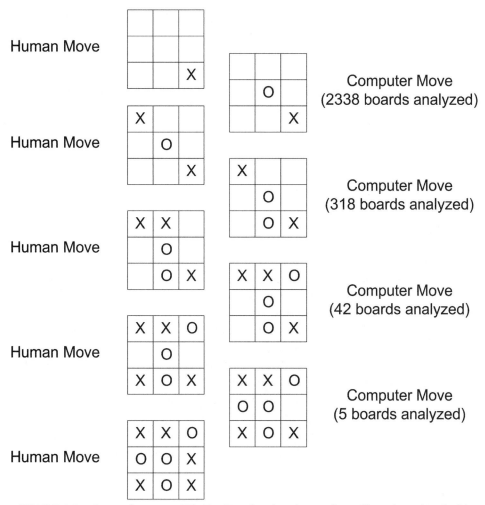

FIGURE 4.9: A sample game of Tic-Tac-Toe showing the number of boards analyzed with alpha-beta pruning.

successor nodes are pruned (by simply returning at this point, with the current alpha value).

So how does alpha-beta pruning help to optimize the basic minimax algorithm? Let's review a sample game played using alpha-beta, and the number of boards evaluated at each step (see Figure 4.9). The computer's first move with alpha-beta scanned a total of 2,338 Tic-Tac-Toe boards. Recall from Figure 4.6 that the first move for the minimax algorithm scanned 59,705 Tic-Tac-Toe boards. Quite a difference, making it possible to do game-tree search for more complex games, such as Chess or Checkers.

When alpha-beta pruning is used, the number of nodes on average that need to be scanned is $O(b^{d/2})$. This compared to minimax, which will scan on average $O(b^d)$ nodes. The branching factor can also be reduced in the best case from b, for minimax, to $b^{1/2}$ for alpha-beta pruning. When the effective branching factor of a game tree is reduced, the possibilities for search can extend deeper into a game tree or make more complex game trees searchable.

The average branching factor for Chess is 38, while the average branching factor for Checkers is 8 (for non-capture positions). [Lu 1993]

CLASSICAL GAME AI

Let's now explore the application of AI and search that's used in classical games such as Chess, Go, Backgammon, and even Bridge and Poker. The application of AI to games is one of search, knowledge, and heuristics. Understanding AI and games is important because it provides a sandbox to test the efficacy of search algorithms. It's also a means to understand the complexity of games. For example, while building a worthy AI algorithm for the game of Go is elusive, Bridge-playing AI algorithms regularly win at the highest level of Bridge championships.

In this section, we'll review some of the more popular games that have found use of AI and the technologies they employ. As we'll soon discover, minimax with alpha-beta pruning is a popular technique among intelligent game-playing programs, but heuristics also play a big part in building faster and more efficient players.

Checkers

We'll begin our exploration of AI in classical games with a quick review of AI's application in Checkers. Arthur Samuel, an early pioneer in AI and machine learning, did some of the earliest work in giving computers the ability to learn from experience. In addition to programming a computer to play Checkers on the IBM 701 computer, he pioneered the idea of letting the program learn by competing against itself. The resulting Checkers program competed and defeated the fourth ranked player in the nation. [Samuel 1959] Arthur Samuel's work on the checkers program was so important in non-numerical computation, that he influenced the designers of IBM's early computers to include new logical instructions. [McCarthy 1990]

NOTE *The Checkers program built at the University of Alberta, Canada, is the first program to win vs a human in the machine world championship competition. [Chinnok]*

Samuel's work remains of interest in the world of Checkers AI, but more recently, neural networks have been employed. In the Anaconda Checkers player, enough knowledge was provided for an understanding of the legal moves in the game, and then the "player" was adapted using an evolutionary strategy (genetic algorithms evolving the weights of the neural network). The result was a Checkers player that beat a commercially available Checkers program 6-0. [Chellapilla, Fogel 2000].

TIP *The topic of genetically evolved neural networks is covered in Chapter 8.*

Checkers is much simpler than Chess in both the types of pieces at play (two for Checkers, six for Chess) and the rules that are used during play. Further, in Checkers, each player has half the board to play (32 squares instead of the full 64). But while simpler than Chess, Checkers is complex in its own right. Let's now review how Checker's AI represents the board and plays an intelligent game.

Checker-Board Representation

The data structure representation of a Checkers board is important because it is a strong determiner in the efficiency of the search and evaluation aspects of the program (as well as the amount of overall memory used by the search game tree, opening book, and endgame database).

A common representation is a simple 8 by 8 matrix that contains one of six values (empty, red, black, red-king, and black-king). An optimization of the 8 by 8 is the 10 by 10 model, which includes a border of one cell around the entire board (with these cells containing the static value offboard). This simplifies the move generator in identifying illegal moves.

Other representations exist to pack the board into a smaller space, but commonly rely on a particular CPU architecture and the instructions to interrogate and manipulate the individual bits.

Techniques Employed by Checkers Programs

Checkers programs have some similarities with other types of AI players such as Chess in that they have unique opening and ending game phases. For this reason, we'll see similarities between Checkers and Chess programs.

Opening Books

Since Checkers has been widely studied from a theoretical perspective, there is a large amount of work in investigating opening moves that can lead to beneficial board configurations. Commonly, a database of opening moves for a given strategy is interrogated to select the first set of moves before the evaluation and search functions are used to drive piece movement.

Static Evaluation Function

The board evaluator is commonly a weighted numeric feature vector. Particular features include the number of red pieces, number of black pieces, disparity of pieces (number of red pieces minus the number of black pieces), the number of red kings, etc. The weights are commonly tuned by a human expert, but can also be tuned automatically (meaning the evaluation function is no longer static).

> NOTE *Chinook includes 22 weighted features that define the evaluation function. The feature weights are typically hand-tuned (in some cases for a specific competition).*

Search Algorithm

As with most classical games, minimax with alpha-beta pruning is used as the means to search the game tree. Checkers has an average branching factor of 10, which is less than Chess, but large enough to make searching the entire tree infeasible.

While alpha-beta pruning does a great job of minimizing the search tree, there are other techniques that can be applied heuristically to further reduce the game tree's search space.

A number of search enhancements exist such as *windowing*, where the alpha and beta bounds are a window of the previously computed values and can result in faster searching of the game tree. Other modifications include *Principal Variation Search* (PVS), which applies windowing to each node in the game tree.

Move History

To speed up the search, a hash-table is constructed during play that maintains board configurations and their characteristics. Since particular boards can show up frequently during a game, they can be stored (with their associated alpha and beta parameters from the minimax tree) to minimize searching the particular subtree. The hashtable permits a fast lookup of the board configuration to see if it has been seen before. If so, its alpha and beta parameters are returned, which are then used by the alpha-beta search.

TIP

> *A common hash function used in Checkers hash-tables is called Zobrist hashing. This hash function creates an XOR of the checker board, which results in uniquely different hash results for different board configurations (which is necessary for fast hash store and lookup to ensure a hit).*

End-game Database

An end-game database contains a relation between board configurations where a few pieces remain, and the strategy that will lead to a win. These (typically compressed) databases encode the board in a compact way and then use an index function to quickly identify the strategy to be used.

NOTE

> *The Chinook end-game database includes all eight piece board configurations (almost 444 billion configurations). The database is compressed using a run-length encoding of the end-game representation.*

Chess

Chess is an interesting test-bed for intelligent applications because the game is rich and complex with a massive search space. For this reason, traditional search algorithms are woefully inadequate to play a reasonably intelligent game.

Chess is a game of perfect information, unlike games such as Poker, where not all of the information is known to each player. Both players see the same Chess board and know all moves that are possible for both players.

Early Chess computers operated in a brute-force way, as the speed of the computer was viewed as its greatest asset. Understanding the complexity of the game of Chess, it's now known that more is required (but computational speed doesn't hurt).

NOTE

> *Early in the days of Chess automation, limited depth search minimax was used to determine the best move to make. With limited CPU power and memory, minimax operated in very shallow trees, so the horizon effect minimized the intelligence of the moves. With the advent of minimax variations, you'll still find minimax as the core algorithm in modern Chess systems today.*

Chess programs are commonly made up of three modules. The first is a move generator which analyzes the current board and identifies the legal moves that can be made. The second module is the evaluation function, which computes a relative utility for a given board configuration (how good a given board is compared to others for a given board configuration). The final module is the search algorithm which must efficiently iterate through the available board configurations, given a move, and decide which path to take through the tree to select the next move to make.

In the 1990s IBM's Deep Blue successfully defeated Gary Kasparov, who at the time was the world Chess champion.

Chess-Board Representation

A simple representation for a Chess board is an 8 by 8 two Dimensional array with each cell containing an identifier representing the state of the cell. For example, 0 would represent an empty cell, 1 for a white pawn, -1 for a black pawn, etc.

An improved representation added a two cell board to the entire board, which was filled with a known character signifying an illegal move. This made it easier to identify illegal moves as would be possible with knights, and optimized the bounds checking aspect of the Chess program.

Today, a common representation for Chess programs is the bitboard. Using a 64-bit word (available on many computers), each cell on the Chess board can be represented by a bit in the 64-bit word. Each bit simply determines if a piece is in the cell (1) or if the cell is empty (0). But instead of having a single bitboard for the entire Chess board, there's a bitboard for every type of piece on the Chess board (one each for the white and black piece types). A pawn bitboard would represent the placement of white pawns on the board. A bishop bitboard would contain bits for the black bishops. The advantage of the bitboard is that the computers that support the 64-bit type can very easily represent and query the state of the boards through bit masking operations, which are extremely efficient.

Another advantage of the bitboard is the efficiency in selecting a legal move. By bitwise or-ing (combining) the bitboards, you can see which cells are taken on the board and therefore, which moves are legal. It's a simple operation that's efficient for move generation.

Techniques Used in Chess programs

Let's now look at some of the major techniques and algorithms that are employed by Chess programs.

Opening Book Database

The first few moves in a Chess game are important to help establish good board position. For this reason, many Chess systems employ a database of opening moves for a given strategy that can be linearly searched.

Minimax Search with Alpha-Beta Pruning

Chess systems typically use a modified version of game-tree search by performing only a shallow search of the game tree using minimax with alpha-beta pruning. While not intuitive, moves that result in smaller scores (gain or loss) are sometimes chosen that can improve the overall board position rather than a short-term gain.

> *The typical branching factor for Chess is around 35, but with alpha-beta pruning, this can be reduced to an effective branching factor of 25. Still large, but this reduction can help greatly to allow deeper searches into the game tree.*

Other search algorithms have been devised for Chess such as aspiration search, which sets the bound of the alpha and beta parameters to some heuristically defined value instead of +INFINITY and -INFINITY. This narrows the search to nodes with a particular characteristic. There's also quiescence search, which tries to evaluate positions that are "relatively quiescent," or dead. [Shannon 1950]

> *Another mechanism to minimize the search space is called null move forward pruning. The basic idea here is if you do nothing (no move), can the opponent do anything to change the board configuration to their benefit? If the answer is no, then opponent moves could be safely pruned from the tree. Hashed transposition tables are also employed to identify subtrees that have already been evaluated to avoid repetitive search. The hash is used to quickly identify the identical board configuration.*

Static Board Evaluation

It should be clear that unless we're near the end-game, our search of the game tree will not encounter any leaf nodes. Therefore, we'll need to have a good utility function that helps us decide which move to make given our nearby horizon. The utility function for Chess defines whether a given board configuration is good or bad for the player, and it can decide this based on a large number of factors. For example, is our king or an important piece in jeopardy, or is the opponent in jeopardy for the current board? Is a piece lost in the board, and if it is, what's the cost of the piece (pawn being the least, followed by the bishop, knight, rook, and queen in increasing value). Some of the other evaluations that can take place include the space available for pieces to move to and then the number of current threats (for or against). [AI Chess]

While the minimax algorithm with alpha-beta pruning provides the means to search the game tree, the evaluation function helps us to decide which path is best based on a number of independent utility functions.

Othello

The game of Othello (also known as Reversi) is another game for which many algorithms of AI have been applied. Examples of AI algorithms that have been implemented in Othello players include basic heuristics, minimax with alpha-beta pruning, neural networks, genetic algorithms, and others.

Othello has some common aspects that are similar to other two-player zero-sum games. For example, like Chess, Othello has an opening game, a mid-game, and an end-game. During these phases of the game, the algorithms may differ for how moves are searched and selected (we'll explore some of these shortly).

AI for Othello programs, like Chess and Checkers, regularly beat human champions of the game. For example, in 1997, the Othello program Logistello defeated the world champion Takeshi Murakami six games to zero. This program retired the following year from tournament play.

Techniques Used in Othello Programs

Opening Knowledge

Like many game-playing systems, opening moves are a good indicator for later strong board positions. For this reason, knowledge of strong initial board positions is collected and used by many Othello-playing programs. In some cases, the data is collected automatically through self-play.

Static Evaluation Function

The most important aspect of all Othello programs is the evaluation function. It's also one of the most difficult parts to program, as there are a number of variations that can be applied. Three particular variations are *disk-square tables*, *mobility-based evaluation*, and *pattern-based evaluation*. [Anderson 2005]

Disk-square tables evaluate the board from the perspective that different cells have different values. For example, the corner cell evaluates to a high score, where the cells next to corners evaluate to low scores.

In *mobility-based evaluation*, moves that maximize mobility (defined as the number of moves available) are scored higher than those that minimize mobility.

Finally, *pattern-based evaluation* functions attempt to pattern match local configurations to determine the utility of a move. This is commonly done by evaluating each row, column, diagonal, and corner configuration independently and then summing them, potentially with weights for different features.

Additionally, there are a number of heuristics that can be used in evaluating potential moves. This includes avoiding edge moves (as they can create opportunities for the opponent), as well as maintaining access to regions of the board (as can be the case when all edge disks in a region are for the current player).

Search Algorithm

In the mid-and end-game phases of Othello, minimax game-tree search with alpha-beta pruning is used. Alpha-beta pruning is especially significant in Othello as searching nine plies with minimax alone evaluates about a billion nodes. Using alpha-beta pruning, the number of nodes to evaluate reduces to a million nodes and sometimes less. The Logistello Othello player makes use of minimax with alpha-beta, among other specialized algorithms for Othello.

In addition to minimax with alpha-beta pruning, selective search can be used effectively. Selective search is similar to iterative deepening (see Chapter 2). In selective search, we search to a shallow depth, and then take paths that lead to the best moves, and search them to a much deeper depth. This allows us to search deeper into the game tree by focusing our search to moves that provide the greatest benefit. Using this method with statistics to understand the relationship between the shallow search and the deeper search is called *Multi-Prob-Cut*, or MPC. This was created by Michael Buro and is formalized to cut-pairs (for example, the shallow search of four levels to the deep search of 12 levels is called a cut pair of 4/12).

End-games

As the game nears the end, the number of available moves decreases and allows a much deeper search of the game tree. As in the mid-game, minimax search with alpha-beta pruning works well, but variations such as MPC are also used.

Other Algorithms

While minimax and alpha-beta are common, and used in varying stages of the game, other algorithms have also found application in Othello. The Othello program Hannibal makes use of multi-layer neural networks for move determination. In order to train the neural network, a random multi-layer neural network is created and then plays against itself. The moves that led to a win are reinforced in the network through a backpropagation algorithm.

Conversely, the moves that resulted in a loss are negatively reinforced to weaken their selection in the future. After many games and associated backpropagation a reasonable Othello player results.

Go

We'll end our discussion of perfect information games with the game of Go. Go is one of the current AI challenges as the scope and complexity of the game is quite large. Consider, for example, the game tree branching factor which is a great determiner of game complexity. In the game of Chess, the average branching factor is 35. But in Go, the typical branching factor is 300. This order of magnitude difference means that game-tree search with minimax, even when applying alpha-beta pruning, results in shallow tree searches. Even then, considerable memory and time are required.

To give a concrete example, four moves in Chess can evaluate 35^4 board configurations (or roughly 1.5 million). In Go, four moves would evaluate 200^4 board configurations (or 1.6 trillion).

While considerable development continues for building an intelligent Go player, the results have not been promising. Chess, even with its massive game trees is now viewed as simple in comparison to Go. For this reason, some believe that when a Go program is able to play at the championship level, AI will have matured to a new level. [Johnson 1997]

Go-Board Representation
Representing a Go board can be a little different than in other game board's representation. In addition to the simple board representation (19 by 19 board with values indicating empty, black stone, or white stone), other attributes are maintained to support analysis of the board and subsequent move generation. Attributes include groups of connected stones, eye information (patterns of stones), and life-and-death status (which stones are in danger of capture, and which can be kept alive).

Techniques Used in Go Programs
Go has some similarities with other game playing AI, and also some differences. It's interesting to note that building algorithms for computer Go has ranged from game-tree search, rules systems, evolutionary algorithms, and cognitive science. But given the complexity of Go, new algorithms are likely necessary to deal with the breadth and depth found in the game.

Opening Moves

Like most other game AI, the opening moves are important to establish a good board configuration. For this reason, almost all Go programs use what's known as Joseki libraries. These libraries contain sequences of moves that can be used prior to using the evaluation function for move generation.

Move Generation

Given the large branching factor of Go, simply taking each legal move and generating a game tree to a certain depth is not feasible. Instead, heuristics are applied to identify which legal moves are good candidates for review. For this set of moves, evaluation is invoked to determine which to take. This differs from Chess, for example, where search determines the move to take. In Go, move candidates are generated, and then these are evaluated to determine which is best.

Some of the heuristics that can be applied to Go move generation include shape or group generation (attempting to match patterns in a pattern library), keeping groups alive, or trying to kill opponents groups, and also expanding or defending territories on the board. Heuristics can also be applied for global moves, or those that focus on local regions of the board.

NOTE ▶ *Relating to move generation, some Go programs implement Goal Generation. This provides a higher-level view of the strategy and tactics to be used for lower-level move generation.*

Evaluation

Once a set of candidate moves are identified, the moves are ordered to evaluate them based on their relative importance. The importance could be based on the current goal (as dictated by a higher-level goal generator), capturing a string, or making an eye, among others.

Evaluating the candidate moves can now be performed using game-tree search (such as minimax with alpha-beta pruning). But Go differs quite a bit in how the search is performed. For example, the Go Intellect program uses heuristics within the search to determine when to cut off a search based on a pre-determined target value, or to associate an urgency value with a move and to consider this when evaluating the position. Other programs can restrict moves to a region of the board and perform local tree search.

Other algorithms have been used in evaluating Go board configurations, such as And-Or graphs, neural networks, Temporal Difference (TD) learning, and Proof-Number Search. By far the most important characteristic of Go programs lies in heuristics and rules developed by strong Go players or through retrograde analysis.

End-game

The use of the end-game database finds successful use in Go, like many other complex games. These databases can be automatically generated from board configurations and applying rules to determine the best move to make, and then after determining the final outcome, attributing the move with win/loss/draw.

Backgammon

Let's now leave the world of perfect information games and explore a number of imperfect information games (or stochastic games). Recall that in a perfect information game, each player has access to all available information about the game (nothing is hidden). Backgammon introduces the element of chance, where dice are rolled to determine the legal moves that are possible.

What makes Backgammon so interesting in the domain of AI is that it is extremely complex. Recall that in Chess, the average branching factor is 35, and in Go, the branching factor can be as high as 300. In Backgammon, the branching factor reaches 400, making it infeasible as a candidate for game-tree search. Simple lookup of moves based on a given board configuration is also infeasible due to the enormous number of states in Backgammon (estimated at over 10^20).

Luckily, there are some other AI techniques that have been successfully applied to Backgammon, and play at the same level as human champions.

Techniques Used in Backgammon Programs

While other complex games such as Chess, Checkers, and Othello have successfully used game-tree search for move evaluation and generation, the high branching ratio of Backgammon makes it infeasible. Two approaches that have been applied to Backgammon are both based on multi-layer neural networks with self-learning.

Neurogammon

The Neurogammon player (created by Gerald Tesauro) used a multi-layer neural network and the backpropagation algorithm for training. The raw board configuration was used as the MLP network input, and the output defined the move to make. Neurogammon was trained using supervised learning (backpropagation) and a database of games recorded from expert Backgammon players. The result was a strong Backgammon player, but due to its dependence on a finite database of recorded games, played below the level of expert players.

TD-Gammon

The subsequent Backgammon program, also built by Tesauro, called TD-Gammon, used a multi-layer neural network knowledge structure, but a different technique for training as well as an improved learning algorithm.

First, TD-Gammon makes use of the Temporal Difference, or TD, learning algorithm (covered in Chapter 8). For each play, the virtual dice were rolled, and each of the potential 20 moves were evaluated. The move with the highest estimated value was used as the expected value. The board configuration was then applied to the neural network and then fed-forward

Board Configurations

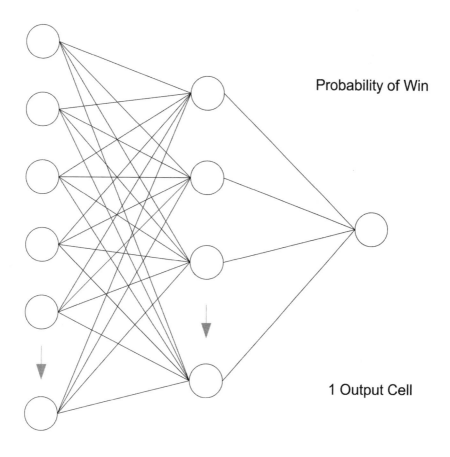

198 Input Cells   160 Hidden Cells

FIGURE 4.10: **TD-Gammon MLP neural network representation.**

through the network. A delta error was then computed given the resulting value and the move with the highest expected value, and the error applied to the weights of the network.

Interestingly, no expert games were applied to the network, but instead the neural network was used to select moves for the player and the opponent. In this way, the neural network played against itself, and after many games, a neural network resulted that could play (and win) at the expert level.

> *The ability for TD-Gammon to learn the game of Backgammon with zero initial knowledge of the game is a testament to the work of Arther Samuel's Checkers player that introduced the idea of self-play as a means to build a program that learned without the need for supervision.*

Additionally, Tesauro updated the inputs to the neural network to include not only the configuration of the Backgammon board, but also some specialized inputs that characterized features of the current board.

When not learning, the TD-Gammon program used the generated neural network as the means for move generation. For each of the possible moves from a given board configuration, each possible new board (after the move is made) is applied to the neural network. The result of the network is the probability of a win, given the last move (see Figure 4.10). The process then is simply to evaluate each of the possible moves (using a move generator) and select the new board configuration, which yields the highest probability for win (the output cell of the neural network).

Tesauro's TD-Gammon has evolved since the initial version. The initial TD-Gammon (0.0) utilized 40 hidden nodes within the neural network and 300K training games to tie for best using other Backgammon programs (such as Neurogammon). Later versions of TD-Gammon increased the hidden nodes to 160 and also increased the number of training games to well above one million. The result was a strong Backgammon player that operates at the same level as the best human players in the world. [Sutton/Barto 1998]

In addition to having zero knowledge of the game, the neural network has learned the best opening positions that differed from those thought to be the best at the time by human players. In fact, human players now use the opening positions found by TD-Gammon.

Poker

Poker is a very interesting game that doubles as an ideal test-bed for AI algorithms. It's also a game of many aspects that can utilize different AI techniques. As Poker is a game of imperfect information (not all information is available to all players in terms of their cards), a Poker program must include the ability to model the likely card the opponent has.

What makes Poker most interesting is that Poker is a game of deception. In addition to modeling the opponent and their strategy, the Poker program must be able to see through deceptive tactics of the opponent in terms of bluffing (attempting to make another player believe that their hand is better than it actually is). Of equal importance is the requirement to avoid predictable play. Professional Poker players can easily exploit any predictable feature or pattern of a Poker player, and therefore some element of randomness is necessary.

From a practical perspective, a number of characteristics are necessary to build a strong Poker program. The first is the ability to evaluate the given hand (as compared to the invisible hands of the opponents) and determine whether the hand could win. The likelihood would be measured as a probability, but given the need to avoid predictability of the player, bluffing must be incorporated to make use of weak hands. The betting strategy is also an important characteristic. While this could be based solely on hand strength, it should also include data from the opponent model, payoff from the pot, etc. The opponent model is another important element which is used to understand the player's hidden cards based on their behavior (betting strategy, past experience, etc.).

Loki - A Learning Poker Player

The Loki Poker player is a learning program that incorporates opponent modeling with play that can be difficult to predict. The simplified basic architecture of Loki is shown in Figure 4.11. The primary elements of this architecture are the Tripler Generator, Hand Evaluator, Opponent Modeler, and finally the Action Selector.

The fundamental element of the architecture is what's called the *triple*. A triple is a set of three probabilities that represent the probability of folding, raising, and calling. Using the public game state, the opponent's behavior is modeled by maintaining triples for the various game states. As the opponent makes decisions, the triples are updated to maintain a constant picture of what the opponent does given a certain scenario.

Using the model of the opponent, we can then identify what we should do given our current hand and the probability of the opponent's move. From this, we generate a triple. The action selector can then randomly pick one of the actions based on the probabilities in the triple. Using probabilities in this way makes it much more difficult for the opponent to predict what we will do, since fundamentally it can be random.

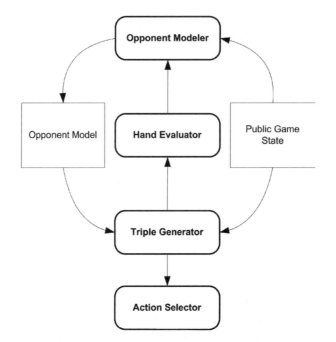

FIGURE 4.11:   **Basic architecture of the Loki Poker player (Adapted from [Loki 2003]).**

The betting strategy is based on an internal simulation given a scenario and the expected payout. The simulation makes use of game-tree search to identify the possible outcomes, but the search is selective to avoid the large state space that could be enumerated.

Loki has also made use of self-play as a means to learn the game of Poker and self-optimization. The variance in play with Loki (using probability triples) allowed it to play numerous versions of itself, while adapting to the play. The opponent modeling and simulation allow Loki to play reasonably strong Poker.

Scrabble

For our final classical game, we'll explore the game of Scrabble. The interesting ideas behind building a Scrabble player are also ones that we've seen thus far in other classical game players.

The Maven Scrabble player (created by Brian Sheppard) divides its play into three separate phases. These are the mid-game (which lasts until there are nine or fewer tiles left in the bag), pre-end-game phase (which begins when nine tiles are left) and finally, the end-game phase (when no tiles remain).

In the mid-game phase, Maven uses a simulation-based approach to determine which move to make. The evaluation function for choosing the move is based simply on that move which leads to the maximum number of points. Given the available tiles to the player, the computer identifies the words that are possible (using the board, which determines the legal moves that can be made). These words (potential moves) are then ordered by quality (score). Some of these potential moves are then simulated by random drawing of tiles (such as with Poker AI), with play continuing some number of turns (typically two to four ply search in a game tree). During the simulation, the points scored are evaluated and associated with the given potential move. Performing thousands of random drawings allows the program to understand the best move to make (word to place on the board).

The pre-end-game phase operates similarly to the mid-game, but this phase works toward setting up a good situation for the end-game.

Finally, the end-game phase begins once no tiles are left in the bag. At this stage in the game, no tiles are left in the bag, and each player can deduce the remaining tiles on the opposing player's racks (as all tiles are on the board or in the racks). At this point, the game changes from a game of imperfect information to one of perfect information. The B* algorithm is then applied at this stage for a deep search of the word possibilities.

For fast word lookup, a lexicon of words is stored in a tree. This permits fast lookup of related words where the root is the first letter of the word, and the leaf contains the last letter for a given word. For example, the word 'exam' and 'example' would exist from the same root of letter 'e.'

Maven shares a number of techniques that we've explored thus far in classical game playing AI. Recall that many games, such as Chess, split the game up into a number of phases. Each phase may differ in game complexity and therefore incorporate different algorithms, or strategies, for play. Also of interest is the use of simulation to identify the directions of game play that can occur (as Scrabble is a game of chance and imperfect information). Recall that Poker used simulation to identify the different paths of play given hidden (or hole) cards. Similarly, Maven uses simulation to better understand the effects or word selection from the perspective of opponent tiles and also tiles that still remain in the bag.

VIDEO GAME AI

While classical games have concentrated on building optimal players using AI, video games such as first-person-shooters (FPS) or strategy games focus more on building AI that is both challenging and enjoyable to play. As challenging is relative to the player's ability, the AI ideally should be adaptive and increase in difficulty as the player's ability increases.

Much of the development of AI for classical games focused on brute-force search relying on high-performance computing. Video game AI differs greatly in that little of the CPU is available for the AI (as little as 10%, since the majority of the CPU is tied up with the physics and graphics engines). Therefore, novel algorithms are necessary to synthesize believable characters and behaviors in video games that consume little of the CPU.

TIP

> *While AI is the term commonly used to describe the opponent's behavior in a variety of video games, this is a misnomer. Most video game AI is simplistic in nature and rarely rises above the level of finite state machines.*

Applications of AI Algorithms in Video Games

Let's now review some of the techniques used in video game AI. We'll take a cross-section of the domains in which AI can be applied, and then explore some of the algorithms that have been used there.

NOTE

> *The following sections define some of the commonly used elements for AI, but not necessarily the state of the art. See the references section for more information on where video game AI is going today.*

The application of AI into video games is a rich area for research on a number of levels. Video game environments (such as can be found in real-time strategy games or first-person-shooters) provide a useful test-bed for the application and visualization of AI techniques. Games themselves have become a huge industry (it's estimated that games gross more than movies), so the development of AI techniques with the associated constraints that can be found in games (such as minimal CPU allotment) can be very beneficial. It's also possible to allow different algorithms and techniques to compete against one another in these environments to understand their subtle differences and advantages.

In addition to the entertainment value of video games, the techniques for building believable characters also finds value (and research funding) in military applications. For example, flight combat simulators that mimic the strategy and tactics of veteran pilots, or the hierarchical and disciplined behavior of troops on the ground in battle management simulators. Each of these applications requires intelligent algorithms that may differ in embodiment, but evolve from the same set of techniques.

NOTE *The physical embodiment of many of these ideas and algorithms in the field of robotics will be explored in Chapter 10.*

Movement and Path-finding

The object of path-finding in many games from first or third-person-shooters, to real-time strategy games is identifying a path from point A to point B. In most cases, multiple paths exist from point A to point B, so constraints may exist such as shortest path, or least cost. Consider, for example, two points separated by a hill. It may in fact be faster to go around the hill, than going over it, but going up the hill could give some advantage to the player (say an archer with an enemy opponent on the opposite down-slope).

In some cases, path-finding is search. The landscape upon which we're to plot a route is a graph of nodes representing waypoints. Each edge of the graph has a given cost (for example, plains could have an edge cost of one, where inclines could have an edge cost consistent with its slope). Considering path-finding as search through a graph of nodes with weighted edges, the A* search algorithm (explored in Chapter 3) is ideal for this application. It is optimal compared to DFS and BFS, and can give us the optimal path.

The problem with A* is that it's a very compute-intensive algorithm. Considering the number of agents in a real-time strategy game that need to move around the map, the amount of time taken by A* would be multiplied. As the AI in a real-time strategy game would also need to support high-level goal planning and economic strategy, path-finding is but one element that should be optimized.

Luckily, there are some other options to simplify the operation of determining which move to make in a map. We'll start with a simple example that demonstrates offensive and defensive movement using a graph and lookup table, and then explore some of the other techniques used.

Table Lookup with Offensive and Defensive Strategy

Any map can be reduced to a graph, where the nodes are the places that can be visited, and the edges are the paths between the nodes. Reducing a map in this way does a couple of things. First, it potentially reduces a map with an infinite number of points into a graph with fewer points. The edges, or the paths between nodes in the graph, define the various ways that we can travel around our graph (and our map).

Consider the simple map of a room in Figure 4.12. In this map, the human player enters at the bottom. Our Non-Player-Character (or, NPC) enters at the top. There are many locations on the map that the player and NPC could go, but very few of them are important. Note that this is a simplistic example, and a real system would include many more map points.

Consider that we're developing an AI for an FPS. The object is for the player and NPC to fight one another, but this implies that we must instill in our NPC the ability to attack the player by moving to his location. Additionally, if our NPC is injured, we want to avoid the player to regain our strength. To make it simpler for our NPC agent, we'll encode the map as a simple graph. This graph contains the defensive positions that will be important to our NPC (see Figure 4.13).

In Figure 4.13, our simple map has been reduced to an even simpler graph. This contains the seven positions that our NPC agent may exist. Additionally, the edges of the graph show the legal moves that our NPC

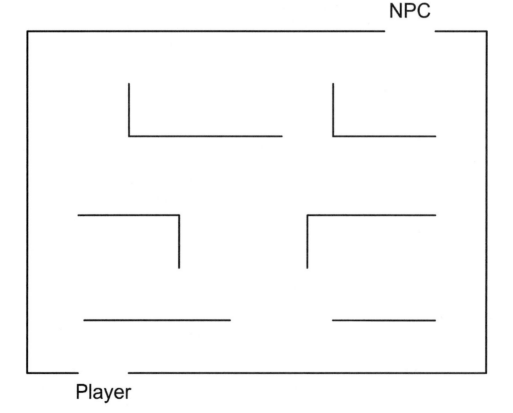

FIGURE 4.12:   **Simple map for a NPC AI.**

agent may make. Note that since the player may exist at any location in the map (not restricted to the graph), we define rectangles for the player. If the player is in the rectangle, we'll simplify his position to the node contained in the rectangle. The purpose of this will become clear shortly.

NOTE ▶ *We'll assume here, for the sake of simplicity, that the NPC always sees the player. In a more complicated system, the player would need to be in the NPC's field-of-view (FOV) in order for the NPC to identify the player's presence.*

We now have a simple graph for our NPC. The next step is to define what our NPC agent should do depending on its strategy. For simplicity, we'll implement two basic strategies. If our NPC is healthy, we'll take an offensive strategy to attack the player. If the NPC is not healthy, then we'll take a defensive strategy.

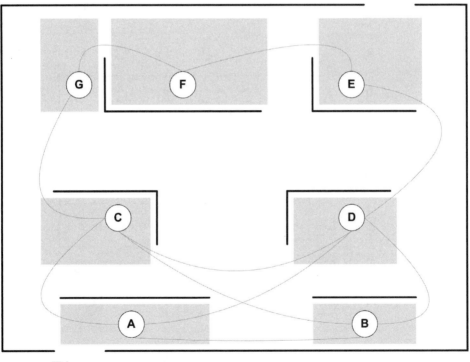

NPC

Player

FIGURE 4.13: Simple map reduced to an even simpler graph.

Let's begin with the offensive strategy (shown in Figure 4.14). The strategy is implemented as a simple graph connectivity matrix with two dimensions. The rows represent the current location of our NPC, while the columns represent the current location of the player. Recall that our player can exist anywhere in the map. If the player is in a rectangle, we'll use the node contained in the rectangle to identify the player's current position. If the player is not in a rectangle, we'll simply define this as unknown.

The strategy defined in Table 4.14 is one of following the player to his position in the map. For example, if the NPC is at node E, and the player is around node A, then the NPC will use the offensive strategy table and move to node D. If the player then moves from node A to node C, we use the table again for the NPC at node D, and the player at node C, which results in the NPC moving to node C (on the attack).

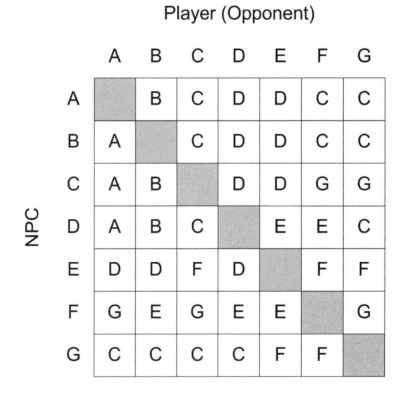

FIGURE 4.14: Lookup table for the NPC agent offensive strategy.

TIP

The lookup table provides for reactive behaviors, as our NPC simply reacts to the movement of the player. Note that it's also stateless, no state is kept between lookups, and the NPC simply uses its position and the player's position to determine the next move.

The defensive strategy is shown in Table 4.15. This strategy is one of taking some time to heal by avoiding the player. Take, for example, the NPC at node D and the player again around node A. The lookup table returns a move from node D to node E, essentially putting distance between us and the player. If the player then moved to node D, the lookup table would return node F, moving away from an eventual move by the player to node E. Note that in some cases, the best move is to not move at all. If the NPC was at node G and the player at node B, the return value from the table is '-' indicating to simply stay put.

Player (Opponent)

NPC \	A	B	C	D	E	F	G
A		C	D	C	-	B	B
B	D		G	C	A	-	-
C	D	G		G	A	B	D
D	E	E	E		A	B	B
E	-	F	-	F		D	D
F	E	G	E	G	G		E
G	F	-	F	-	C	C	

Defensive Strategy

FIGURE 4.15: Lookup table for the NPC agent defensive strategy.

While simple, this method gives us an efficient way to build offensive and defensive strategies for an NPC. No search is involved, simply table lookup. To add some level of unpredictability in the offensive strategy, the move could be selected randomly with some probability, rather than simply taking the lookup value.

> NOTE *Consider also the offensive strategy in Figure 4.14 as a path-finder to a given node. If we need to get from node G to node B, the lookup table takes us from node G to node C and then finally to node B. The lookup table in this way gives us a simple and efficient algorithm to get from point A to point B. This works well in static environments, but tends to fall apart if the environment changes over time.*

In large environments, it can also be possible to segregate a map into multiple connected maps, each having funnel points for which an NPC may travel. Figure 4.16 shows a map of three zones. Rather than including a single lookup table for all points, three separate lookup tables would exist. If our NPC agent was in the left room, it could use the lookup table to determine which path to take to a given node. If the destination were outside of the room, it would by default move to node A, and from there, the external lookup table would take over for routing the NPC to its destination. If the

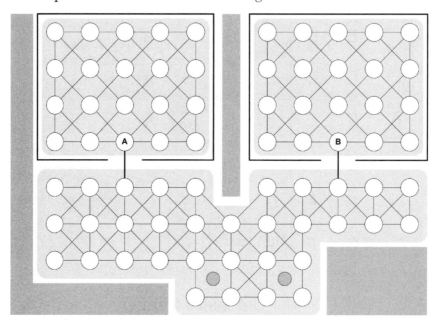

FIGURE 4.16:   **Segregating a map into separate zones to simplify path-finding.**

destination were to the room on the right-hand side, the NPC would be directed to node B, and upon reaching node B, use its lookup table to get the rest of the way.

It's also very common for these algorithms to time-slice their processing. This permits the work to be done over a number of iterations, without tying up the CPU on a single operation.

NPC Behavior

In the last section, we gave our NPC the ability to traverse a map using strategies based on the NPC's health (using intentional offensive and defensive strategies). Let's now explore some options for giving our NPC the ability to behave intelligently in its environment.

The behavior of an NPC can't be considered in isolation, because behavior is ultimately grounded in the environment. The NPC must be able to *perceive* its environment (see, hear, etc.). With the information perceived from the environment (as well as internal state information such as motivation), the NPC can *reason* about what should be done. The result of reasoning is potentially an intentional act, which is performed as an *action* (see Figure 4.17). This action (and subsequent actions) is what we externally view as the agent's behavior.

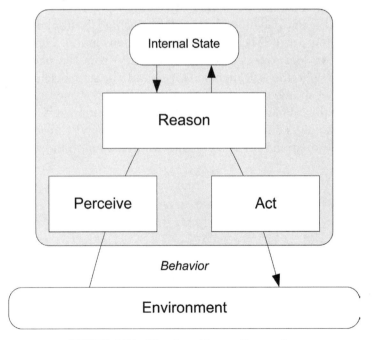

FIGURE 4.17: **The closed Loop of reasoning.**

The NPC will be equipped with a set of sensors that allow it to sense, or perceive, its environment. These sensors could indicate objects (such as the player) in its field-of-view in terms of sight, or direction of an object using localization of sound. With a set of sensors as input, the NPC can now reason about what to do. The internal state is also kept to indicate a higher-level set of goals that are to be achieved, or to indicate the health of the NPC (which could change its strategy). Given the state of the environment and the internal state of the NPC, an action can be selected. This can alter the environment, change the NPC's internal state, and result in a change in what the NPC will do next. An NPC's action could be moving to a new location (as described in the previous section), communicating with other NPCs (possibly about the location of the player), changing its weapon, or changing its stance (going from an upright to a prone position).

Let's now review a few of the options that can give our NPC some basic reasoning abilities.

Static State Machines

One of the simplest methods, and also one of the most common, is the state machine. State machines consist of a set of states, and arcs, between the states that define the conditions necessary for transition. Consider the simple game AI state machine in Figure 4.18.

Our NPC sentry defined by the state machine (better known as a Finite State Machine, or FSM) has two basic functions in life. The NPC marches between two locations, guarding some entry from the player. When the player is in sight, the NPC fights to the death. The state machine implements this as three simple states (one can think of them as *mental states*). In the first state, the NPC marches to the location identified as X. It continues to march to X unless one of two things happen. If the NPC reaches location X, it's at its destination for the state, and we transition to the alternate march

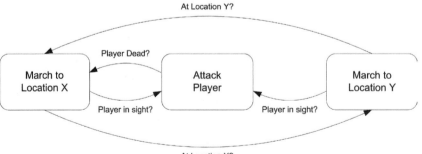

FIGURE 4.18: State machine for a simple game AI.

state. If the NPC sees the player, it attacks. If neither of these events occurs, the NPC continues marching.

When the NPC sees the player, by entering its field-of-view, the FSM transitions to the attack state. In this state, the NPC fights to the death. If the NPC dies, then the state machine is no longer active (the NPC lies lifeless in the environment). If the NPC defeats the player, it begins marching again toward location X.

There's not much to the FSM, but they are simple and easy to debug. They are also very predictable, but it's possible to add transition probabilities to give the NPC a small element of randomness.

Layered Behavior Architectures

Our previous FSM defined a very simple agent that had two things on its mind, marching and attacking. What was most important to the NPC was attacking, but while no player was in its field-of-view, it was quite happy to march back and forth. But what happens if our NPC has more things to worry about. If the NPC's health is low, it should head to the infirmary. If the NPC is low on ammo, it should head to the armory to reload. If more than one player appears to attack, should it fight, or rush to the guard house to pull the alarm? These aren't entirely complex, but the NPC now needs to engage in some thought to determine the most appropriate action for the given scenario.

One way to handle this conflict in action selection is Rodney Brooks' *subsumption architecture*. This architecture confines responsibilities to isolated layers, but allows the layers to subsume one another if the need arises. Let's look at our simple NPC again to see how we might map the new refined behaviors into subsumption (see Figure 4.19).

FIGURE 4.19: Behavior layers for the simple NPC.

Figure 4.19 illustrates one example of our NPC's requirements to a layered architecture. These levels should be viewed in relative importance. At level one, our NPC performs his guard duty, dutifully marching along his route. If the player comes into view, the NPC switches to the attack layer to rid the environment of the pesky player. From Brookes' architecture, the *Attack* layer subsumed (took priority over) the *March* layer. If no players are in the field-of-view, and the NPC needs to be healed or replenish his ammunition, the *sustain* layer takes over to perform those actions. Finally, the NPC will turn to the *survive* layer if more than one player is seen in the field-of-view. As the constraints are met within the layers, the NPC will default to the lowest layer. Therefore, once the player is disposed of, and the ammo and health are returned, the NPC will return to the march in level one.

Within each of these layers, individual FSMs can be used to implement the relevant behavior. In this way, entirely new state machines are consulted based on the current behavior layer for the NPC.

NOTE ▶ *An interesting analogy to NPCs in video games is the field of Intelligent Agents. We'll explore the field of Intelligent Software Agents in Chapter 11.*

Other Action-Selection Mechanisms

We'll discuss other relevant algorithms that could be used to select an action for an NPC in the following chapters. Neural networks are an interesting example of behavior selection (classification), as are planning algorithms and numerous other machine-learning algorithms (reinforcement learning, to name one). The machine-learning algorithms are of particular interest as they can instill the ability for the NPC to learn and behave in new ways given previous encounters with the player.

NOTE ▶ *In a typical game, a game engine provides the base platform for graphics and fundamental game-play. The NPC behaviors are commonly implemented using high-level scripts, with a script interpreter implemented within the game engine. This provides a great amount of flexibility, where the game engine is implemented in a high-level language such as C or C++ for efficiency, and the NPC behaviors are implemented in a scripting language for flexibility.*

Team AI

In many games, there's not just a single NPC soldier that we're fighting against, but an entire army that must work together in harmony with a single or handful of goals in mind. The control can exist at a number of levels within a hierarchy (see Figure 4.20), from the squad leader directing troops to flank an enemy in the field using real-time battlefield information, to the general managing his entire army to implement the higher-level military strategies.

Managing an overall army can entail a large number of problems, from scheduling and production, to resource allocation, to the overall strategy and tactics of the force in the field.

The problem here can be simplified greatly by minimizing the number of levels or organization. First, the individual soldiers simply follow orders, and unless they are routed, can fight to the death. These individual units can be programmed using finite state machines, or other simple mechanisms for behavior.

TIP

> *Following orders is a requirement, but there's also something to be said for autonomy at the soldier level, taking advantage of a local situation to improve the chances of a global win.*

The problem to solve then is the higher-level control of the entire force. This can be subdivided as well, especially when forces are split for independent goals. At the highest level is the Strategic AI. This layer of the AI has the

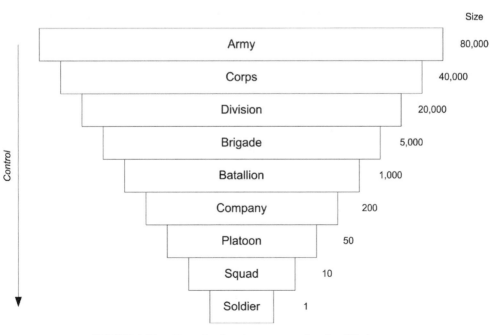

FIGURE 4.20: Organizational structure of a simplified army.

global view of the battlefield, troop strengths, available resources, etc. Next is the Tactical AI whose job is to implement the strategy provided from above. At the lowest rung is the individual soldier, on whose collective shoulders that overall strategy relies.

> *For this discussion, we'll focus on Team AI that opposes a human player, but much of this can also be applied to Team AI that cooperatively supports the player, though this can be considerably more difficult. For example, working cooperatively with the player requires that the NPC help, but also stay out of the player's way.*

Goals and Plans

An interesting mechanism for high-level control over a hierarchy of military units is in defining a goal, and then creating a plan to reach that goal. Also necessary is the need to reformulate a plan, when it eventually fails.

Let's first discuss the planning vernacular and then explore how it can be applied to team AI. First, there's the *goal*. A goal can be an end-goal (for the end of the game) or an intermediate goal that moves us closer to an end-game situation. Formally, a goal is a condition that is desired to be satisfied. Example goals include taking an enemy position, destroying a bridge, flanking an enemy, etc. To reach a goal, we must perform a series of

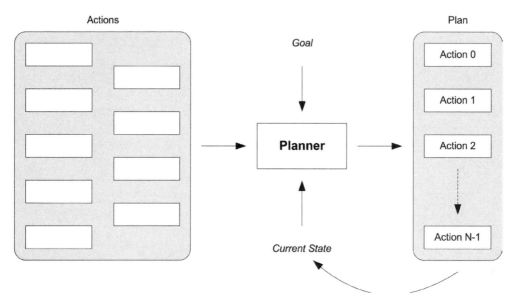

FIGURE 4.21: The plan and its elements.

actions, which are independent steps within a plan. Each action potentially has a prerequisite that must be met in order for the action to be performed. Example actions include moving a set of NPC units to a location, attacking the enemy, planting a charge, etc. The *plan*, then, is a set of actions that when performed in the given order, achieve a goal (see Figure 4.21). The method by which a plan is formulated is through the use of a *planner*.

As an example, let's say we have two NPCs that desire to attack a player that is firing from a covered position. An effective attack is for one NPC to provide covering fire at the player, while the other NPC moves to a flanking position to be in a better position to attack the player. This could be represented simply as shown in Figure 4.22.

The goal of the plan is to eliminate the player that's in a covered position (meaning the player is shielded from fire from the NPC's current position). To eliminate the player, one NPC provides covering fire on the player so that another NPC can move to a flanking position to attack the player. Once this NPC is in a position to fire, the other NPC rushes the player's position. Implicit in the plan is cooperation, and through a strict ordering of the

Goal: Eliminate(Player)

Prerequisites:

Covered_Position(Player)

Alive(Player)

Plan:

Action-1: Identify_Flanking_Position(NPC_1)

Action-2: Covering_Fire(NPC_2)

Action-3: Move_to_Flanking_Position(NPC_1)

Action-4: Fire_at_Player(NPC_1)

Action-5: Rush_Player_Position(NPC_2)

FIGURE 4.22:   **Sample plan to eliminate a player in a covered Position.**

actions, coordination. Later, we'll see how planning is achieved (and like much of AI, it's fundamentally a search problem).

> NOTE ▶ *Implicit in planning are preconditions (or prerequisites) that must be met in order for the plan to be valid. Consider the plan in Figure 4.22 if only one NPC is present. What happens if NPC_1 is eliminated while on the move to its flanking position? Preconditions must be met for a plan to be valid, and if at any time actions in a plan cannot be performed, the plan cannot continue. Therefore, in dynamic environments, planning and replanning go hand-in-hand.*

Real-Time Strategy AI

A final interesting use of AI is in the development of real-time strategy games. Real-Time Strategy AI differs from Team AI in that we will deal not only with the militaristic aspects of the game, but also the economic aspects. For example, in a real-time strategy game, elements of the civilization must engage in resource gathering as part of a higher-level goal of building an army to defeat an opponent.

For example, in the beginning of a real-time strategy game, the focus is societal and military buildup. This involves creating new citizens to build the economy. Once the economy reaches a certain level, a military buildup can occur to attack and defeat an enemy.

The conditions described could be embedded within the game engine itself, but for flexibility, could be implemented separately permitting ease of modification without having to rebuild the game engine. One possibility that's been used in the past is Rule-Based Systems (or RBS).

Rule-Based Programming

Rule-based systems are an effective way to encode expert knowledge about game play into a strategy game. Rule-based systems are so interesting that a standards committee has been formed to study their use in games. [IGDA 2005]

> NOTE ▶ *We'll explore rule-based programming as part of the review of knowledge representation in Chapter 6.*

A rule-based system is made up of two memories, one that holds facts, and another that holds a set of rules that exist to determine the behavior. A rule-matching algorithm is applied to the facts, and those rules that match facts are saved into the conflict-set. This set of rules is then reviewed and one rule picked to fire in a process called conflict resolution. The rule is then applied and the working memory is updated.

 Selecting a rule to fire from a list of rules that have matched can use a number of algorithms. One could select at random, the last rule to match, or the rule that's most specific (had the largest number of conditions).

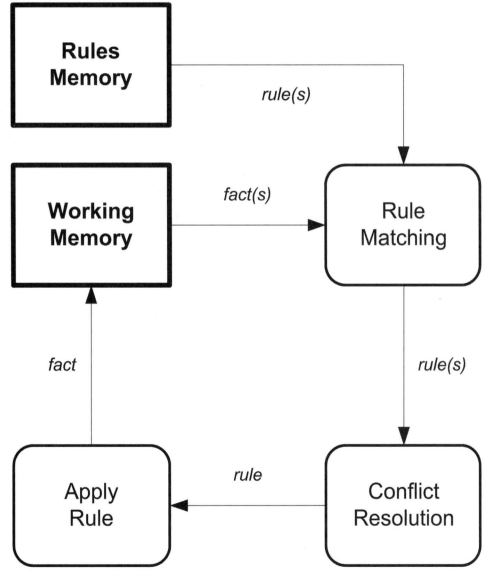

FIGURE 4.23: Typical flow of a rule-based system.

Now that we've explored the process, let's look at the anatomy of facts and rules. A fact is an atomic element of knowledge that can be used in conjunction with other facts to reason using rules. Facts can take on a variety of forms; one of the most common is the S-expression (or Symbolic Expression), which simply is a way of structuring the data. Consider the following four facts in our simple knowledge base:

```
(opponent-1 size large)
(opponent-2 size small)
(army size large)
```

Regarding our game world, these facts tell us that the first opponent is large in size, the second opponent is small, and our army is also considered large. Before looking at some rules given our small knowledge base, let's review the structure of a rule.

Rules are made up of two things, antecedents and consequents. If you think about a rule as an if/then construct, then the 'if' is the antecedent, and the 'then' is the consequent. Consider the following simple comparison:

```
if ((opponent.size <= SMALL_SIZE) &&
    (army.size >= LARGE_SIZE)) {
attack_opponent();
    }
```

This conditional simply says that if the opponent's military size is small, and ours is large, we'll attack them. A simple rule that encodes this behavior could be implemented as follows:

```
(rule "Attack Opponent Based Upon Size"
        (?opponent size small)
        (army size large)
        ==>
        (army attack ?opponent) )
```

Note that the '?opponent' element will match any opponent in the working memory, and when it matches one, we'll use this same opponent when attacking. Once this rule fires, our working memory will exist as:

```
(opponent-1 size large)
(opponent-2 size small)
(army size large)
(army attack opponent-1)
```

This new fact would drive behavior within the game engine to formulate a plan to attack the enemy. The RBS could also remove facts as driven by consequents to reflect the dynamic environment of the game.

TIP

> *To deal with sizes, the RBS can 'fuzzify' values from ranges to distinct sets. For example, the size used in the previous examples could identify the range [0..4999] as small, [5000..9999] as medium, and [10000..50000] as large. This reduces the complexity of the inputs and simplifies the rules base.*

An RBS is a useful method for encoding knowledge into a game that can be used to drive behaviors, especially high-level behaviors in matters of strategy. It's also advantageous because it allows the strategy element to be decoupled from the game engine and permits later tweaking by game developers.

CHAPTER SUMMARY

This chapter provided a broad spectrum of techniques used in game AI, from classical games, to modern video games. In classical games such as Chess and Checkers, and even information imperfect games such as Poker, the minimax game-tree search algorithm with alpha-beta pruning can be found. In these games, the goal of developers is to build an opponent that can defeat world-class players. In contrast, the goal in video games is to build opponents that are challenging to play, but not perfect. Even with this limitation in mind, various AI technologies can be found in modern games, from neural networks, to rule-based systems and decision trees, to embed game opponents that are both challenging and adaptive to the human's level of play.

REFERENCES

[AI Horizon] Available online at:
http://www.aihorizon.com/essays/chessai/boardrep.htm
[AI Chess] Available online at:
http://www.cs.cornell.edu/boom/2004sp/ProjectArch/Chess/algorithms. html
[Archer 1999] Archer, A.F. "A Modern Treatment of the 15 Puzzle," *American Math.* 106:, 793-799, 1999.

[Anderson 2005] Anderson, Gunnar. "Writing an Othello program," Available online at:
http://www.radagast.se/othello.

[Chellapilla, Fogel 2000] Chellapilla, Kumar and Fogel, David B. "Anaconda Defeats Hoyle 6-0: A Case Study Competing an Evolved Checkers Program against Commercially Available Software (2000)." Proceedings of the 2000 Congress on Evolutionary Computation CEC00.

[IGDA 2005] "Working Group on Rule-based Systems," AI Interface Standards Committee, The 2005 AIISC Report, 2005. Available online at:
http://www.igda.org/ai/report-2005/rbs.html

[Johnson 1997] Johnson, George. "To Test a Powerful Computer, Play an Ancient Game." Introduction to Computation and Cognition. Available online at:
http://www.rci.rutgers.edu/%7Ecfs/472_html/Intro/NYT_Intro/ChessMatch/ToTest.html

[Loki 2003] Jonathan Schaeffer, Darse Billings, Lourdes Pena, Duane Szafron. "Learning to Play Strong Poker." 2003.

[Lu 1993] Lu, Chien-Ping Paul. "Parallel Search of Narrow Game Trees." Master's thesis, University of Alberta, Department of Computing Science, Edmonton, Canada, 1993.

[McCarthy 1990] Available online at:
http://www-db.stanford.edu/pub/voy/museum/samuel.html

[Samuel 1959] Samuel, A. L. "Some Studies in Machine Learning using the Game of Checkers," IBM Journal of Research and Development, 1959.

[Shannon 1950] J. Schaeffer "1989 World Computer Chess Championship," *Computers, Chess and Cognition*, Springer-Verlag, New York, 1990.

[Sutton/Barto 1998] Sutton, Richard S., and Barto, Andrew G. "Reinforcement Learning: An Introduction." MIT Press, 1998.

RESOURCES

Bruce Moreland's Chess Programming Topics. Available online at:
http://www.seanet.com/~brucemo/topics/topics.htm

[Chinook] Available online at:
http://www.cs.ualberta.ca/%7Echinook/

The Intelligent Go Foundation. Available online at:
http://intelligentgo.org/en/computer-go/overview.html

Bouzy, Bruno and Cazenave, Tristan. "Computer Go: an AI Oriented Survey." Universite Paris.

Brooks, Rodney. "A Robust Layered Control System for A Mobile Robot," *IEEE Journal of Robotics and Automation* RA-2, April 1986.

Tesauro, Gerald. "Temporal Difference Learning and TD-Gammon." Available online at:

http://www.research.ibm.com/massive/tdl.html

TD-learning, Neural Networks, and Backgammon. Available online at:

http://www.cs.cornell.edu/boom/2001sp/Tsinteris/gammon.htm

[Sheppard 2002] Sheppard, Brian. "World-championship-caliber Scrabble,"

Artificial Intelligence 134: (2002), 241-275.

EXERCISES

1. What is meant by adversarial search, and how does it differ from traditional tree search?
2. What is ply in game-tree search?
3. Given the game tree shown in Figure 4.24, what is the value at the root node?
4. Minimax can search to the leaves of the tree, or to a predefined depth. What are the consequences of ending a search at a predefined depth?

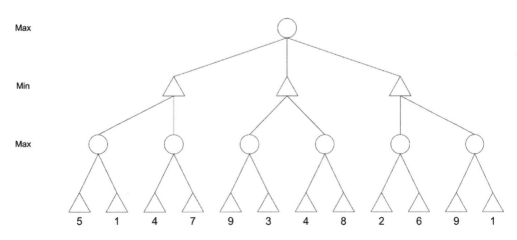

FIGURE 4.24: Sample game tree for minimax search.

5. Given the game tree shown in Figure 4.25, what is the value at the root node and which nodes are pruned from the search?
6. What was the first successful game-playing program that used self-play to learn an effective strategy?
7. Explain what is meant by perfect-information and imperfect-information games. Give a few examples of each, and define which type they are.
8. Define some of the similarities and differences for building a game-playing AI for Checkers and Chess.
9. What are some of the major differences between building AI for classical games and video games?

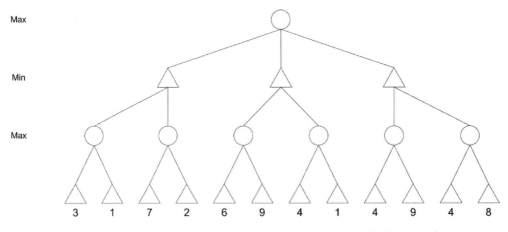

FIGURE 4.25: Sample game tree for minimax search with alpha-beta pruning.

5 KNOWLEDGE REPRESENTATION

K nowledge Representation (KR), as the name implies, is the theory and practice of representing knowledge for computer systems. By that we mean concise representations for knowledge in a form that's directly manipulatable by software. This is an important distinction because representing knowledge is only useful if there's some way to manipulate the knowledge and infer from it.

INTRODUCTION

From the perspective of Strong AI, KR is concerned with the cognitive science behind representing knowledge. How, for example, do people store and manipulate information? Many of the early representation schemes resulted from this research, such as frames and semantic networks.

This chapter will explore the various schemes for the representation of knowledge, from the early representation methods to present-day methods such as the Semantic Web. We'll also explore some of the mechanisms for the communication of knowledge, as would be used in multi-agent systems.

TYPES OF KNOWLEDGE

While a large taxonomy of the varying types of knowledge, could be created we'll focus on two of the most important, *declarative* and *procedural*.

Declarative (or descriptive) knowledge is the type of knowledge that is expressed as declarations of propositions (or factual knowledge). On the other hand, procedural knowledge is expressed as the knowledge of achieving some goal (for example, how to perform a given task). Procedural knowledge is commonly represented using productions, and is very easy to use but difficult to manipulate. Declarative knowledge can be represented as logic, and is simpler to manipulate, but is more flexible and has the potential to be used in ways beyond the original intent.

NOTE ► *In Chapter 11, we'll investigate intelligent agent architectures, some of which operate on declarative knowledge (such as Prodigy), where others utilize procedural knowledge (such as the Procedural Reasoning System).*

Other types of knowledge exist, for example, analogous knowledge (associations between knowledge) and meta-knowledge (knowledge about knowledge). We'll explore these types of knowledge as well.

THE ROLE OF KNOWLEDGE

From the context of AI, representing knowledge is focused on using that knowledge to solve problems, and the implication that knowledge is more than just factual information. Therefore, the manner in which the knowledge is stored is important. For example, we can store knowledge in a human readable form and use it (such as this book), but knowledge stored in this form is not readily useful by AI. Therefore, the knowledge must be stored in a way that makes it possible for AI to search it, and if necessary, infer new knowledge from it.

The primary goal of knowledge representation is to enable an intelligent entity (program) with a knowledge base to allow it to make intelligent decisions about its environment. This could embody an embodied agent to know that fire is hot (and it should be avoided), or that water in certain cases can be used to douse a fire to make it passable. It could also be used to reason that repeated attempts to log in to a secure address is potentially an attempt to hack a device, and that the peer address associated with this activity could be monitored on other activities.

SEMANTIC NETWORKS

Semantic networks are a useful way to describe relationships between a numbers of objects. This is similar to an important feature of human memory, where there exists a large number of relations. Consider the concept of free association. This technique was developed by Sigmund Freud, where the patient continually relates concepts given a starting seed concept. The technique assumed that memories are arranged in an associative network, which is why thinking of one concept can lead to many others. The idea behind free association is that during the process, the patient will eventually stumble across an important memory.

Consider the example shown in Figure 5.1. This simple semantic network contains a number of facts and relationships between that knowledge. Typical semantic networks use the "IS_A" and "AKO" (A Kind Of) relation to link knowledge. As shown here, we've updated the relationships to provide more meaning to the network. The rectangles in the network represent objects, and the arcs represent relationships. Here we can see that two capital cities are shown, and are capitals on the same continent. One capital is of a state of the United States, while another is of Venezuela. Simple relations also show that two cities of New Mexico are Albuquerque and Santa Fe.

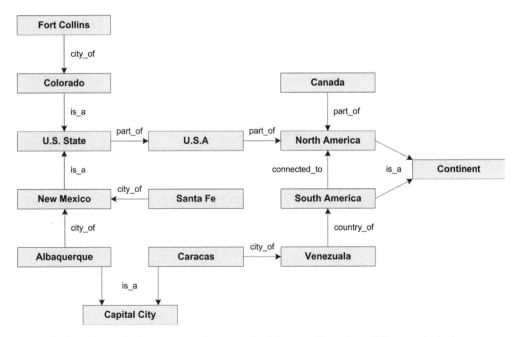

FIGURE 5.1: **A simple semantic network with a small number of facts and relations.**

The interesting characteristic of semantic networks is that they have the ability to represent a large number of relationships between a large numbers of objects. They can also be formed in a variety of ways, with varying types of relationships. The construction of the semantic network is driven by the particular application.

An interesting example of a semantic network is the Unified Modeling Language, or UML. UML is a specification for object modeling in a graphical notation. It's a useful mechanism to visualize relationships of large and complex systems, and includes the ability to translate from a graphical form (abstract model) to a software form.

FRAMES

Frames, as introduced by Marvin Minsky, are another representation technique that evolved from semantic networks (frames can be thought of as an implementation of semantic networks). But compared to semantic networks, frames are structured and follow a more object-oriented abstraction with greater structure. The frame-based knowledge representation is based around the concept of a frame, which represents a collection of slots that can be filled by values or links to other frames (see Figure 5.2).

An example use of frames is shown in Figure 5.3. This example includes a number of different frames, and different types of frames. The frames that are colored gray in Figure 5.3 are what are called *generic* frames. These frames are frames that describe a class of objects. The single frame which is not colored is called an *instance* frame. This frame is an instance of a generic frame. Note also the use of inheritance in this example. The Archer generic frame defines a number of slots that are inherited by generic frames of its class. For example, the Longbowman generic frame inherits the slots of the Archer generic frame. Therefore, while the weapon slot is not defined in the Longbowman frame, it inherits this slot and value from the Archer frame.

Similarly, 'john' is an instance of the Longbowman frame, and inherits the 'weapon' slot and value as well. Note also the redefinition fo the 'defense' slot value. While a frame may define a default value for this slot, it may be overridden by the instance frame.

```
<frame-name
    <slot1-name slot1-value>
    <slot2-name slot2-value>
    ...
>
```

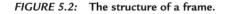

FIGURE 5.2:   **The structure of a frame.**

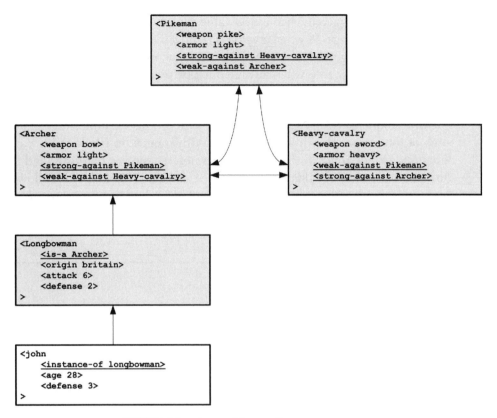

FIGURE 5.3:   **A set of frames for a strategy game.**

Finally, in this example, we also relate generic frames through comparison. We define that an instance of an Archer is strong against an instance of the Pikeman frame.

What makes frames different than semantic networks are the active components that cause side effects to occur when frames are created, manipulated, or removed. There are even elements that control actions for slot-level manipulations. These can be thought of as triggers, but are also referred to as *Demons*. Adding triggers to a frame representation language is called *procedural attachement* and is a way to include inferential capabilities into the frame representation (see Table 5.1).

TABLE 5.1:   Procedural attachments for use in frames.

Demon	Action
if_new	Triggered when a new frame is added.

if_added	Triggered when a new value is placed into a slot.
if_removed	Triggered when a value is removed from a slot.
if_replaced	Triggered when a value is replaced in a slot.
if_needed	Triggered when a value must be present in an instance frame.

An example of this is shown in Listing 5.1. In this example, we define some of the frames shown in Figure 5.3. With frames (in iProlog), we can define ranges for some of the needed parameters (such as defense), and if the value falls outside of this range, indicate this issue to console. This allows the frames to not only include their own metadata, but also their own self-checking to ensure that the frames are correct and consistent.

LISTING 5.1:   Frame examples with iProlog.

```
Archer ako object with
        weapon: bow;
        armor: light;
        strong-against: Pikeman;
        weak-against: Heavy-cavalry;

Longbowman ako Archer with
        origin: britain;
        attack: 6;
                range           0..9
        defense: 2;
                range           0..9
                help            if new value > 9 then
                                        printf(new value, "defense too large."
john isa Longbowman with
        if_removed              print("No longer...")!
        age: 28;
                range           1..70
        defense 3;
```

An extension of the frame concept is what are called *scripts*. A script is a type of frame that is used to describe a timeline. For example, a script can be used to describe the elements of a task that require multiple steps to be performed in a certain order.

PROPOSITIONAL LOGIC

Propositional Logic, also known as sentential logic, is a formal system in which knowledge is represented as propositions. Further, these propositions can be joined in various ways using logical operators. These expressions can then be interpreted as truth-preserving inference rules that can be used to derive new knowledge from the old, or test the existing knowledge.

First, let's introduce the proposition. A *proposition* is a statement, or a simple declarative sentence. For example, "lobster is expensive" is a proposition. Note that a definition of truth is not assigned to this proposition; it can be either true or false. In terms of binary logic, this

proposition could be false in Massachusetts, but true in Colorado. But a proposition always has a truth value. So, for any proposition, we can define the true-value based on a truth table (see Figure 5.4). This simply says that for any given proposition, it can be either true or false.

We can also negate our proposition to transform it into the opposite truth value. For example, if P (our proposition) is "lobster is expensive," then ~P is "lobster is not expensive." This is represented in a truth table as shown in Figure 5.5.

Propositions can also be combined to create compound propositions. The first, called a *conjunction*, is true only if both of the conjuncts are true (P and Q). The second called a *disjunction*, is true if at least one of the disjuncts are true (P or Q). The truth tables for these are shown in Figure 5.6. These are obviously the AND and OR truth tables from Boolean logic.

The power of propositional logic comes into play using the conditional forms. The two most basic forms are called *Modus Ponens* and *Modus Tollens*. Modus Ponens is defined as:

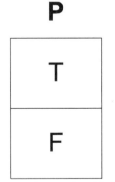

FIGURE 5.4: Truth table for a proposition.

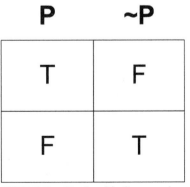

FIGURE 5.5: Truth table for negation of a proposition.

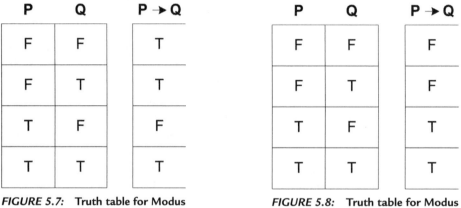

FIGURE 5.6: **True table for conjunction and disjunction of two propositions.**

P	Q	P → Q
F	F	T
F	T	T
T	F	F
T	T	T

P	Q	P → Q
F	F	F
F	T	F
T	F	T
T	T	T

FIGURE 5.7: **Truth table for Modus Ponens.**   *FIGURE 5.8:* **Truth table for Modus Tollens.**

P, (P->Q), infer Q

which simply means that given two propositions (P and Q), if P is true then Q is true. In English, let's say that P is the proposition "the light is on" and Q is the proposition "the switch is on." The conditional here can be defined as:

if "the light is on" then "the switch is on"

So, if "the light is on" is true, the implication is that "the light is on." Note here that the inverse is not true. Just because "the switch is on," doesn't mean that "the light is on." This is a piece of knowledge that gives us some insight into the state of the switch of which we know the state of the light.

In other words, using this rule, we have a way to syntactically obtain new knowledge from the old.

NOTE   *In these examples, we can think of P as the antecedent, and Q as the consequent. Using the if/then form, the conditional portion of the claim is the antecedent and the claim following the 'then' is the consequent.*

The truth table for Modus Ponens is shown in Figure 5.7.

Modus Tollens takes the contradictory approach of Modus Ponens. With Modus Tollens, we assume that Q is false and then infer that the P must be false. Modus Tollens is defined as:

P, (P->Q), not Q, therefore not P.

Returning to our switch and light example, we can say "the switch is not on," therefore "the light is not on." The formal name for this method is proof by contrapositive. The truth table for Modus Tollens is provided in Figure 5.8.

> *To help make sense of the names, Modus Ponens is Latin for "mode that affirms," while Modus Tollens is Latin for the "mode that denies."*

A famous inference rule from propositional logic is the hypothetical syllogism. This has the form:

((P->Q) ^ (Q->R), therefore (P->R)

In this example, P is the major premise, Q is the minor premise. Both P and Q have one common term with the conclusion, P->R. The most famous use of this rule, and the ideal illustration, is provided below:

Major Premise (P):   All men are mortal.
Minor Premise (Q):   Socrates is a man.
Conclusion: Socrates is mortal.

Note in this example that both P and Q share a common term (men/man) and the Conclusion shares a term from each (Socrates from Q, and mortal from P).

Propositional logic includes a number of additional inference rules (beyond Modus Ponens and Modus Tollens). These inferences rules can be used to infer knowledge from existing knowledge (or deduce conclusions from an existing set of true premises).

Deductive Reasoning with Propositional Logic

In deductive reasoning, the conclusion is reached from a previously known set of premises. If the premises are true, then the conclusion must also be true.

Let's now explore a couple of examples of deductive reasoning using propositional logic. As deductive reasoning is dependent on the set of premises, let's investigate these first.

1) If it's raining, the ground is wet.

2) If the ground is wet, the ground is slippery.

The two facts (knowledge about the environment) are Premise 1 and Premise 2. These are also inference rules that will be used in deduction. Now we introduce another premise that it is raining.

3) It's raining.

Now, let's prove that it's slippery. First, using Modus Ponens with Premise 1 and Premise 3, we can deduce that the ground is wet:

4) The ground is wet.   (Modus Ponens: Premise 1, Premise 3)

Again, using Modus Ponens with Premise 3 and 4, we can prove that it's slippery:

5) The ground is slippery. (Modus Ponens: Premise 3, Premise 4)

Note that in this example, the hypothetical syllogism would work as well, proving that the ground is slippery in a single step.

Limitations of Propositional Logic

While propositional logic is useful, it cannot represent general-purpose logic in a compact and succinct way. For example, a formula with N variables has 2**N different interpretations. It also doesn't support changes in the knowledge base easily.

Truth values of propositions can also be problematic, for example; consider the compound proposition below. This is considered true (using Modus Ponens where P -> Q is true when P is false and Q is false, see Figure 5.7).

If dogs can fly, then cats can fly.

Both statements are obviously false, and further, there's no connection between the two. But from the standpoint of propositional logic, they are syntactically correct. A major problem with propositional logic is that entire propositions are represented as a single symbol. In the next section, we'll look at another logic representation that permits finer control and a more accurate representation of an environment.

FIRST-ORDER LOGIC (PREDICATE LOGIC)

In the previous section, propositional logic was explored. One issue with this type of logic is that it's not very expressive. For example, when we declare a proposition such as:

The ground is wet.

it's not clear which ground we're referring to. Nor can we determine what liquid is making the ground wet. Propositional logic lacks the ability to talk about specifics.

In this section, we'll explore predicate calculus (otherwise known as First-Order Logic, or FOL). Using FOL, we can use both predicates and variables to add greater expressiveness as well as more generalization to our knowledge.

In FOL, knowledge is built up from constants (the objects of the knowledge), a set of predicates (relationships between the knowledge), and some number of functions (indirect references to other knowledge).

Atomic Sentences

A constant refers to a single object in our domain. A sample set of constants include:

marc, elise, bicycle, scooter, the-stranger, colorado

A predicate expresses a relationship between objects, or defines properties of those objects. A few examples of relationships and properties are defined below:

owns, rides, knows,

person, sunny, book, two-wheeled

With our constants and predicates defined, we can now use the predicates to define relationships and properties of the constants (also called Atomic sentences). First, we define that both Marc and Elise are 'Persons.' The 'Person' is a property for the objects (Marc and Elise).

Person(marc)

Person(elise)

The above may appear as a function, with Person as the function and Marc or Elise as the argument. But in this context, Person(x) is a unary relation that simply means that Marc and Elise fall under the category of Person. Now we define that Marc and Elise both know each other. We use the *knows* predicate to define this relationship. Note that predicates have *arity*, which refers to the number of arguments. The 'Person' predicate has an arity if one where the predicate 'knows' has an arity of two.

Knows(marc, elise)

Knows(elise, marc)

We can then extend our domain with a number of other atomic sentences, shown and defined below:

Rides(marc, bicycle)	- Marc rides a bicycle.
Rides(elise, scooter)	- Elise rides a scooter.
Two-Wheeled(bicycle)	- A Bicycle is two-wheeled.
Book(the-stranger)	- The-Stranger is a book.
Owns(elise, Book(the-stranger))	- Elise owns a book called The Stranger.

Finally, a function allows us to transform a constant into another constant. For example, the sister_of function is demonstrated below:

Knows(marc, sister_of(sean))   -Marc knows Sean's sister.

Compound Sentences

Recall from propositional logic that we can apply Boolean operators to build more complex sentences. In this way, we can take two or more atomic sentences and with connectives, build a compound sentence. A sample set of connectives is shown below:

∧   AND
∨   OR
¬   NOT
⇒   Logical Conditional (then)
⇔   Logical Biconditional

Examples of compound sentences are shown below:

Knows(marc, elise) ∧ Knows(elise, marc)
- Marc and Elise know one another.

Knows(marc, elise) ∧ ¬Knows(elise, marc)
- Marc knows Elise, and Elise does not know Marc.

Rides(marc, scooter) ∨ Rides(marc, bicycle)
- Marc rides a scooter or Marc rides a bicycle.

We can also build conditionals using the logical conditional connective, for example:

Knows(marc, elise) ⇒ Knows(elise, marc)
- If Marc knows Elise, then Elise knows Marc.

This can also be written as a biconditional, which changes the meaning slightly. The biconditional, a ⇔ b simply means "b if a and a if b," or "b implies a and a implies b."

Knows(marc, elise) ⇔ Knows(elise, marc)
- Marc knows Elise if Elise knows Marc.

> NOTE ▶ *Another way to think about the biconditional is from the construction of two conditionals in the form of a conjunction, or:*
>
> $$(a \Rightarrow b) \wedge (b \Rightarrow a)$$
>
> *This implies that both are true or both are false.*

Variables

So far, we've explored sentences where all of the information was present, but to be useful, we need the ability to construct abstract sentences that don't specify specific objects. This can be done using *variables*. For example:

Knows(x, elise) ⇒ Person(x)
- If x Knows Elise, then x is a Person.

If we also knew that: 'Knows(marc, elise)' then we could deduce that Marc is a person (Person(marc)).

Quantifiers

Let's now bring it together with quantifiers. A *quantifier* is used to determine the *quantity* of a variable. In first-order logic, there are two quantifiers, the universal quantifier ($\forall$) and the existential quantifier ($\exists$). The universal quantifier is used to indicate that a sentence should hold when anything is substituted for the variable. The existential quantifier indicates that there is something that can be substituted for the variable such that the sentence holds. Let's look at an example of each.

$\exists$ x. Person(x)
- There exists x, that is a Person.

$\forall$ x. $\exists$ x. Person(x) $\land$ (Knows(x, elise) $\lor$ Knows (x, marc))
- For all people, there exists someone that Knows Marc or Elise.

$\forall$ x. $\exists$ x. Knows(x, elise) $\Rightarrow$ Person(x)
- For any x, if there is someone x that Knows Elise, then x is a Person.

Now that we have a basic understanding of first-order logic, let's explore FOL further with Prolog.

TIP

Chapter 13 provides an introduction to the languages of AI, including Prolog.

First-Order Logic and Prolog

Prolog is actually based on a version of FOL with some subtle differences that we'll explore. Prolog is in essence a language for the representation of knowledge. It allows the definition of facts (or clauses) and also rules (which are also clauses, but have bodies). Let's begin with a quick introduction to Prolog and follow with a few examples to demonstrate both its knowledge representation and reasoning abilities.

TIP

A Prolog environment is made up of a number of elements, but three of the important items are the knowledge base (rules and facts), the inference engine, and the interpreter (the interface to the inference engine and knowledge base).

Simple Example

Let's start with an example that was first explored with propositional logic. Consider the argument:

All men are mortal.
Socrates is a man.
Therefore, Socrates is mortal.

We can translate everything but the conclusion into predicate logic as follows:

$\forall$ x Man(x) $\Rightarrow$ Mortal(x)
Man(Socrates)

So for all X where X is a Man, then X is also a Mortal. We've provided the predicate indicating that Socrates is a Man, therefore Socrates is also Mortal. Now let's see how this is translated into Prolog. First, we'll define the rule:

mortal(X) :-
man(X).

Note that in Prolog, the rule is defined differently than the FOL argument (as a Horn clause). To the Prolog theorem prover, this can be read as "to show mortal(X), solve man(X)." The rule can also be read "mortal(X) if man(X)." Note the period at the end of the rule indicates the end of the sentence.

Next, we provide our fact (Socrates is a man):

man(socrates).

Note that this is identical to defining a rule for a fact, which could be specified as:
man(Socrates) :- true.

All of the information has now been defined. A query can now be issued to Prolog to test the conclusion. Two methods are shown below. The first simply tests the conclusion, and the second is a query for those objects that satisfy the predicate:

| ?- mortal(Socrates).
yes
| ?- mortal(X)
X = socrates
yes

Note in the second example that we've requested that Prolog match for the predicate (for what objects does the expression evaluate to true?). It returns with the X variable instantiated to Socrates (the expected result).

NOTE ▼

In the early 1980s, Japan began the Fifth Generation Computer Systems project. The goal of this project was the development of a "fifth generation" super-computer built for massive parallelism with AI as its primary application. The core language for the computer was Prolog, but as Prolog at the time did not support concurrency, other languages were developed in its place. While the project was under development, technology around the world evolved in different directions (microprocessors and software). The project did not meet with success, but did produce five parallel machines and a variety of applications. [Feigenbaum 1983]

Information Retrieval and KR

Prolog is often viewed as a way to intelligently store and retrieve information, but can do so in a way that makes it more useful than what is commonly available in a traditional relational database system. Let's begin with an example of using Prolog to represent a small amount of knowledge and then explore a few rules to make sense of the knowledge.

The first step is to define the domain of knowledge, or the facts for which the later rules will utilize. This example will use a set of simple facts about the Solar System, beginning with those planets that orbit the sun. A common predicate will be used called orbits, which will be used not only to describe the planets (objects that orbit the sun) but also to define the satellites that orbit the planets (see Listing 5.1). Note in Listing 5.1 that the planets are first defined (those that orbit the sun). This is followed by each of the planets. Each planet that has satellites uses the orbits predicate to identify the satellites that orbit each of the planets (only a sample are shown in Listing 5.1). Finally, the gaseous_planet predicate is used to define the gaseous giants in the solar system.

LISTING 5.1: A knowledge base of facts about the Solar System.

```
orbits(sun, mercury).
orbits(sun, venus).
orbits(sun, earth).
orbits(sun, mars).
```

orbits(sun, jupiter).
orbits(sun, saturn).
orbits(sun, uranus).
orbits(sun, neptune).
orbits(earth, the_moon).
orbits(mars, phobos).
orbits(mars, deimos).
orbits(jupiter, metis).
orbits(jupiter, adrastea).

...

orbits(saturn, pan).
orbits(saturn, atlas).

...

orbits(uranus, cordelia).
orbits(uranus, ophelia).

...

orbits(neptune, naiad).
orbits(neptune, thalassa).

...

gaseous_planet(jupiter).
gaseous_planet(saturn).
gaseous_planet(uranus).
gaseous_planet(neptune).

With this set of facts, a set of rules can now be defined to embed additional knowledge into the database as well as support a small amount of reasoning. First, recall that a planet is defined as a major object that orbits the sun. This rule can use the orbits predicate with the sun to identify those items that are planets (and not satellites).

planet(P) :-
    orbits(sun, P).

As shown, any object (from our knowledge base) that orbits the sun is a planet. With this definition, we can easily define a rule for satellites. A satellite is simply an object that orbits a planet.

satellite(S) :-
    orbits(P, S), **planet**(P).

This predicate uses a conjunction which first uses the satellite object (S) to determine which objects (P) with the orbits predicate are satisfied. If this predicate produces a P object, and it's a planet (using the planet predicate), then the S is a satellite.

The next rule separates the gas giant planets (gaseous planets) from the terrestrial planets. Note that in the end of Listing 5.1, the gaseous planets are defined using the gaseous_planet predicate. This is used as shown below in the negated form (\+) in conjunction with the planet predicate, to determine if an object is a terrestrial planet.

terrestrial_planet(P) :-
>   **planet**(P) , \+ **gaseous_planet**(P).

Finally, with the satellite data that's provided, it's very simple to determine whether the object has no satellites. Given the planet object (which is validated with the planet predicate), this is used in conjunction with the orbits predicate to determine if no results are returned with the negation (\+).

no_moons(P) :-
>   **planet**(P) , \+ **orbits**(P, S).

Having a predicate that identifies that a planet has no satellites (no_moons), it's very simple to negate this to identify whether a planet has satellites (has_moons).

has_moons(P) :-
>   \+ **no_moons**(P).

This example illustrates an interesting property of knowledge representation and that of human accumulation of knowledge as well. Knowledge can be built on other knowledge. Given a set, and a distinction between a portion of that set, classifications can be further defined and refined from an initially small set of knowledge. For example, knowing that a planet orbits the sun, we know that all other objects that orbit an object other than the sun are satellites. A satellite is a moon of an object, so it's simple to determine those objects that have moons and those that don't. This property can also be a curse because as the relationships grow between the data, any error can have wide effects over the entire knowledge base.

Representing and Reasoning about an Environment.

In addition to simple reasoning with a database, Prolog can be used to represent an environment and to reason about it. Let's now explore a very simple map that identifies a set of locations and then look at a few functions that provide Prolog with the ability to traverse the map. Note in Figure 5.9 that our map is really nothing more than a simple graph. The connections in the map are bidirectional (so that you can get from Lyons to Longmont, and also from Longmont to Lyons).

Recall from Chapter 2 that in a graph, there exists a set of edges. An edge is a connection between two vertices on the graph. So the first item in our

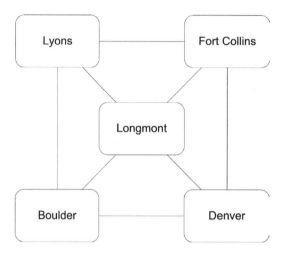

FIGURE 5.9: Map represented as a simple bidirectional graph.

knowledge base are the edges in the graph (which cities connect to which other cities). For this, we'll use a predicate called `edge`, which indicates an edge between the two objects (see Listing 5.2). Note here that only one direction is shown, as we'll let Prolog know about the bidirectional usage when we define the rules.

LISTING 5.2:   Defining the edges of our simple map for Prolog.

```
edge(lyons, fort_collins).
edge(lyons, longmont).
edge(lyons, boulder).
edge(boulder, longmont).
edge(boulder, denver).
edge(longmont, lyons).
edge(longmont, boulder).
edge(longmont, fort_collins).
edge(longmont, denver).
edge(fort_collins, denver).
```

With this set of facts defined, we can perform some queries with Prolog. For example, we can provide a city, and then query which cities are connected with the predicate:

```
| ?- edge(longmont, Y).
Y = lyons ? ;
```

```
Y = boulder ? ;
Y = fort_collins ? ;
Y = denver
yes
| ?-
```

We could also use the predicate in the form edge(X, longmont), but since we don't detail the bidirectional nature of our graph, this isn't as useful.

Next, a rule is defined to determine the *connectedness* of two cities. We'll call this rule connect, and it will return true if the cities are connected on the map by an edge, or false if they are not connected (see Listing 5.3). Note how this rule is constructed. We use the predicate edge to query whether an edge has been defined, but since we don't encode each direction in the facts, we can test both cases here to ensure that we catch a fact that indicates that the edge exists. Recall that the semicolon is a Boolean OR operation, so if one or the other is true, then we return true (that an edge, and connection exists).

LISTING 5.3: Defining a rule to test whether an edge exists.

```
connected( X, Y ) :-
        edge( X, Y ) ; edge( Y, X ).
```

Now let's explore a set of rules that can be used to determine one or more paths between cities in our simple map. We'll call the rule path, and it uses two other rules; traverse and reverse. Rule traverse is a recursive rule that searches for a path between a starting and ending city (labeled X and Y). It also maintains a Path variable, which is the query by which the rule is defined. Once traverse has found a path, the reverse rule is used to reverse the order of the path found to return it to the user (see Listing 5.4). Note the use of [X] in the traverse rule. The brackets indicate that a list is being built, and the contents of the list is defined as X, or the first city in the path.

LISTING 5.4: Rules to recursively determine paths.

```
path(X, Y, Path) :-
    traverse(X, Y, [X], Q),
    reverse(Q, Path).
```

Two high-level rules will be created to traverse the graph. The first (shown in Listing 5.5) is the special case of a path between just two cities. In this case, the connected predicate is used to determine this condition and no recursive calls are performed. Note that in the traverse call, the path is constructed with Y (end city) as the head and the path as the tail. This is done because the list is built in the order of the most recently visited city. The initial city is the last element in the list, and the most recently visited is the first item. When the reverse is used, the list will appear normally in output (first to last city).

LISTING 5.5:   First rule for traverse.

```
traverse(X, Y, P, [Y|P]) :-
    connected(X,Y).
```

The second more complex rule creates a recursive call after a number of tests (preconditions). First, the connected predicate is used to return the cities connected to the current city (X). This step determines the next possible steps in the path, for which there may be numerous. Each is returned as a list constructed separately (separate calls to traverse for separate paths). The next city to visit is called Z, and the next test is to ensure that the next city is not our destination (Z\==Y).

Finally, we use the member function to test whether the current city is part of the current path (since we won't visit a city more than once). If these tests pass, then we make a recursive call to traverse with Z as the current city (next to visit), and Y as the destination. The path is updated, adding Z to the city path. The calls then continue (for each path), until one or more of the tests fail, upon which the recursive calls stop and the call chain is unwound (returned to the main caller). (See Listing 5.6.)

LISTING 5.6:   Second recursive rule for traverse.

```
traverse(X, Y, V, Path) :-
    connected(X,Z), Z\==Y, \+member(Z,V),
    traverse(Z, Y, [Z|V], Path).
```

A query can now be performed to determine the available paths from a city to another city. An example of this process using Prolog is shown in Listing 5.7. Note that all permutations of the paths are returned.

LISTING 5.7:   A test query of the map knowledge base.

```
| ?- path(lyons, denver, P).
P = [lyons,fort_collins,denver] ? ;
P = [lyons,fort_collins,longmont,denver] ? ;
```

```
P = [lyons,fort_collins,longmont,boulder,denver] ? ;
P = [lyons,fort_collins,longmont,boulder,denver] ? ;
P = [lyons,longmont,denver] ? ;
P = [lyons,longmont,boulder,denver] ? ;
P = [lyons,longmont,fort_collins,denver] ? ;
P = [lyons,longmont,boulder,denver] ? ;
P = [lyons,boulder,denver] ? ;
P = [lyons,boulder,longmont,denver] ? ;
P = [lyons,boulder,longmont,fort_collins,denver] ? ;
P = [lyons,boulder,longmont,denver] ? ;
P = [lyons,boulder,longmont,fort_collins,denver] ? ;
P = [lyons,longmont,denver] ? ;
P = [lyons,longmont,boulder,denver] ? ;
P = [lyons,longmont,fort_collins,denver] ? ;
P = [lyons,longmont,boulder,denver] ? ;
(10 ms) no
| ?-
```

SEMANTIC WEB

The Semantic Web is the name behind an effort to change the way that the web is defined and interpreted. Today, the Internet is made up of hosts and content that is predominantly defined through the Hyper-Text Markup Language (or HTML). This language provides a way to add texture to web pages, so that instead of simply being text documents, other information can be included such as audio or graphical information. But HTML simply provides a way to *beautify* content so that it can be rendered in a device in an independent way.

A simple example of HTML is shown in Listing 5.8. This example defines a simple web page that includes a title (that is placed on the header of the browser) and a body that simply emits two paragraphs. Each paragraph in this example defines an author and a title that they've authored. Using the paragraph HTML tag (<p>), these lines are separated by a single line.

LISTING 5.8:   A simple example of HTML.

```
<html>
 <head>
```

```
  <title>Author List</title>
 </head>
 <body>
  <p>John Doe  Article A</p>
  <p>Jane Doe  Article B</p>
 </body>
</html>
```

So from Listing 5.8, we see that it's relatively easy to create a web page that can be viewed by any standard web browser. While this is useful, it's only useful from a human viewing perspective. The browser understands how to render the information given the markup, but it knows nothing of the content. If we're to build software agents that can read web pages and understand their content, something else is required. This is where RDF, or Resource Description Framework, can be applied.

RDF allows the definition of metadata within the markup, called *statements*. Each statement in RDF contains three structural parts, a subject, predicate, and object (see Listing 5.9). Also provided in this example is the namespace (coded `xmlns`), which provides a disambiguous space of names defined by a Uniform Resource Locator (or URL, a web address). The namespace provides a clarification of the terms used within the RDF.

LISTING 5.9:   A simple example of RDF.

```
<rdf:RDF
  xmlns:rdf="http://www.w3.org/2006/09/test-rdf-syntax-ns#"
  xmlns="http://schemas.mtjones.com/rdftest/">
 <rdf:Description="http://mtjones.com/rdf">
  <publications>
   <rdf:Description ID="mtjones.com">
    <article>
     <author>John Doe</author>
     <title>Article A</article>
    </article>
    <article>
     <author>Jane Doe</author>
     <title>Article B</article>
    </article>
   </rdf:Description>
  </publications>
```

```
</rdf:Description>
</rdf:RDF>
```

What's important from this example is that the data is provided in a format that makes it simple to parse and understand the elements of the data. This is because the data is marked with the meaning of the data (metadata). Note that article defines an author and title of an article (as defined by the author tag and the title tag). In this way, an RDF parser can embody an application (or software agent) with the ability to understand the data that's been provided.

COMPUTATIONAL KNOWLEDGE DISCOVERY

Computational Knowledge Discovery systems provide an interesting perspective on creativity and human knowledge creation. Many of these systems rely on the use of heuristics to constrain the search as well as the recursive application of a small set of discovery methods. They also commonly rely on the use of simple forms (of the initial knowledge) to aid in the discovery process. [Wagman 2000] Two of the most famous systems are BACON and the Automatic
Mathematician (AM).

The topic at hand differs from other machine learning techniques based on their methods for discovering knowledge. Machine-learning or data mining methods, produce knowledge in a variety of forms, such as decision trees. Knowledge (or Scientific) Discovery methods use formalisms such as equations producing other equations to represent the discovered knowledge. But each method looks at the initial data and the relationships of that data using a heuristic search to produce new knowledge.

One problem with computational knowledge discovery is that its use requires post-processing by a human to filter and interpret the resulting knowledge. From this perspective, computational knowledge discovery is better described as assisted knowledge discovery, as a human is commonly required to interpret and apply the results. But even with this drawback, computational knowledge discovery has produced new knowledge in many scientific fields (leading to publications in refereed literature).

The BACON System

BACON is actually a series of discovery systems developed over a number of years. One aspect of BACON is its ability to discover simple physical laws given the relationships between two variables. For example, using the simple general methods provided by BACON, two variables can be reviewed for their relationship. If one variable (X) increases and the other variable (Y) increases, then the INCREASING heuristic can be applied, causing BACON to analyze their ratio (X/Y). If one variable increases while the other decreases, then the DECREASING heurstic can be employed (causing BACON to analyze their product, XY). Finally, if the value X remains constant (or nearly constant), BACON can hypothesize that X maintains this value.

Note that while BACON is provided a series of data (of two variables), it has the capacity to create new data based on the predefined rules (providing ratios, products, and constants). BACON uses these new series as well in its attempt to analyze the data. While these rules are very simple, BACON used them to successfully rediscover Kepler's third law of planetary motion (see Eq 5.1, where d is the planet's distance from the Sun, p is its period, and k is a constant).

$$\frac{d^3}{p^2} = k \qquad \text{(Eq 5.1)}$$

Other variants of BACON employ even more advanced discovery procedures, but each follows a similar model of increasing complexity (more than two variables, numeric and symbolic variables, etc.).

The role of BACON is the construction of equations given a set of data using a variety of heuristics (fitting equations to data).

Automatic Mathematician (AM)

The Automatic Mathematician (or AM) is a mathematical discovery system with significant differences from BACON. AM was designed by Doug Lenat to discover new concepts in elementary mathematics and set theory. But rather than searching for a solution to a problem, or a predefined goal, AM simply follows "interesting" heuristics and generates new examples looking for regularities. When regularities are found, conjectures can be created.

When the AM is started, it's provided with a few facts about its domain (simple math concepts) using the *frame* knowledge representation technique. For example, AM could understand the concept of prime numbers. Given these concepts and rules of thumb, AM then applies these concepts based on their worth (the more interesting a rule, the more likely it is to be used).

AM uses a set of general methods to create new mathematical concepts (such as creating the inverse of an existing relation, or specializing by restricting the domain of a concept). The underlying model used by AM was small LISP programs, which represented a variety of mathematical concepts. New LISP programs, were generated and modified to represent new concepts (based on their interpretation with a LISP interpreter).

AM did not discover the concepts on its own, but relied on a human interpreter to review the data produced to understand what it found. AM did rediscover numerous mathematical concepts, such as prime numbers and Goldbach's conjecture but instead of identifying these characteristics, it instead has been criticized as providing the data to make the discovery with human review.

> **NOTE** *Doug Lenat followed the development of AM with another discovery system called EURISKO. This development, instead of searching for mathematical concepts, focused instead on the search for useful heuristics.*

ONTOLOGY

An Ontology is a core concept in modern knowledge representation, though the ideas behind it have been in existence since the beginning of KR. An ontology from the perspective of AI is a model that represents a set of concepts within a specific domain as well as the relationships between those concepts.

Recall the example of the semantic network in Figure 5.1. This is an ontology for the domain of places and capitals. The 'is-a' type of relationship defines a hierarchical taxonomy that defines how the objects relate to one another.

> **TIP** *Note that Figure 5.1 can also be defined as a set of Meronymy relations, as it defines how the objects combine to form composite objects (cities to states to countries to continents).*

An interesting use of an ontology is in the form of a language as a means to encode an ontology for the purposes of communicating knowledge between two entities (agents). This is explored in the next section.

COMMUNICATION OF KNOWLEDGE

Having a vast repository of knowledge is most useful if it can be shared and used from a variety of perspectives. Being able to share knowledge allows multiple disparate agents to cooperatively use the available knowledge, and modify the knowledge (such as is done in blackboard architectures).

 You can learn more about knowledge communication and sharing with agents in Chapter 14 "Agent Architectures." These are commonly called "Agent Communication Languages," or ACLs.

Examples of protocols that enable sharing of knowledge between agents include the Web Ontology Language (OWL) used in the Semantic Web, the Knowledge Query and Manipulation Language (KQML), and the Agent Communication Language (ACL).

COMMON SENSE

Computer systems that include some form of AI for a given problem domain can still rightly be considered unintelligent because they lack some of the most fundamental knowledge called common sense. For example:

- Objects fall toward Earth (due to gravity) and not up away from the Earth.
- If you get near a fire, you could be burned.
- It's dangerous to fly a kite in a lightning storm.

To enable reasoning at a common-sense level, a common-sense knowledge base is proposed that contains common-sense knowledge that most people possess. This knowledge base is constructed in a way that an application can use it to create inferences (to reason). Examples of the type of knowledge that is represented includes behavior of items, effects of actions (yelling at someone may make them angry), and preconditions of actions (one puts their socks on before their shoes). Many other topics could be covered such as the properties of objects (fire is hot), and descriptions of human behaviors (if someone is crying, then they may be sad).

An interesting example of a common-sense project is called Cyc. This project was created by Doug Lenat (who also created the Automatic Mathematician). The Cyc knowledge base includes over a million concepts and rules, which are defined in a language based on predicate calculus (similar to the LISP programming language). Examples of basic knowledge encoded in Cyc include:

(#$capitalCity #$Colorado #$Denver)

which encodes "Denver is the capital city of Colorado."

(#$genls #$Men #$Mortal)

which represents "All men are mortal." The Cyc knowledge base is partitioned into a number of collections of knowledge called *microtheories*. A microtheory is a contradiction-free of concepts and facts about a particular domain of knowledge (like an ontology). Microtheories can be related to one another and are organized into a hierarchy, supporting inheritance.

The development of Cyc and its inference engine continues, but the major work focus is primarily in knowledge engineering or hand-encoding knowledge and rules to represent basic common-sense knowledge.

CHAPTER SUMMARY

Knowledge representation focuses on the mechanisms by which information can be stored and processed in a way to make the information useful as knowledge. This chapter presented some of the more important mechanisms for knowledge representation, such as semantic networks and frames, and also methods that enable not only storage of knowledge, but also processing, such as propositional logic and first-order (or predicate) logic. Finally, applications of knowledge representation were explored including computational scientific discovery, and common-sense reasoning with the Cyc project.

REFERENCES

[Feigenbaum 1983] Feigenbaum, Edward A., McCorduck, Pamela "The Fifth Generation: Artificial Intelligence and Japan's Computer Challenge to the World." 1983.

[Wagman 2000] Wagman, Morton. "Scientific Discovery Processes in Humans and Computers: Theory and Research in Psychology and Artificial Intelligence," Praeger Publishers, 2000.

RESOURCES

Brachman, Ronald J., "What IS-A is and isn't. An Analysis of Taxonomic Links in Semantic Networks." *IEEE Computer*, 16: (10), October, 1983.

Langley, P. "BACON.1: A general discovery system." In Proceedings of the second biennial conference of the Canadian Society for Computational Studies of Intelligence," 173-180, 1978.

Lenat, D.B. "AM: An artificial intelligence approach to discovery in mathematics as heuristic search," Ph.D. Theses, AIM-286, STAN-CS-76-570, Stanford University, AI Lab, Stanford, 1976.

Lenat, D. B., and Brown, J.S. "Why AM and EURISKO appear to work." *Artificial Intelligence* 23(3):269-294, 1984.

Post, Emil "Introduction to a General Theory of Propositions," *American Journal of Mathematics* 43: 163-185.

Freud, Sigmund "The Interpretation of Dreams," Macmillan, 1913.

Object Management Group, "UML Specification," 2007.

Available online at: http://www.omg.org/technology/documents/modeling_spec_catalog.htm

Woods, W. "What's in a Link: Foundations for Semantic Nets," Representation and Understanding: Studies in Cognitive Science, Academic Press, 1975.

EXERCISES

1. Define knowledge representation in your own words. What are its most important characteristics?
2. Define two types of knowledge and their differences.
3. Consider a family tree, and represent this using a semantic network.
4. Frames include what is called a procedural attachment that can be used to trigger functions for various types of events. Describe these attachments and demonstrate how they can be used.
5. Define Modus Ponens and Modus Tollens and provide an example of each.
6. Define the universal and existential quantifier used in predicate logic.
7. Represent each of the following sentences in first-order logic:
   a. A whale is a mammal.
   b. Jane loves John.
   c. John knows Jane's father.
   d. If it's raining, then the ground is wet.
   e. If the switch is on and the light is off then the light-bulb is broken.
   f. All computers have a processor.
8. Describe the advantages of predicate logic over propositional logic.
9. Represent the sentence in 7.d in Prolog.
10. Describe the purpose behind the Semantic Web. What is its representation and how does it help?

6 MACHINE LEARNING

M achine learning, as the name implies, focuses on algorithms and methods that allow a computer to learn. Another way to think about this is from the perspective of learning by example. Given a set of data, machine learning can learn about the data and their relationships, producing information. In this chapter, machine learning will be investigated including a number of machine-learning algorithms. Algorithms to be explored include decision trees, Markov models, nearest neighbor learning, and others.

MACHINE-LEARNING ALGORITHMS

There exist numerous types of machine-learning algorithms. Some of the more popular approaches include supervised learning, unsupervised learning, and probabilistic learning.

Supervised learning algorithms imply that a teacher is present to identify when a result is right or wrong. The input data contains both a predictor (independent variable) and target (dependent variable) whose value is to be estimated. Through the process of supervised learning, the algorithm predicts the value of the target variable based on the predictor variables. Examples of supervised learning algorithms include perceptrons, backpropagation, and decision trees.

Unsupervised learning algorithms imply that learning occurs unsupervised, or without a teacher. In this case, there is no target variable, but instead relationships in the data that are exploited for classification (for example, patterns in the data). Examples of unsupervised learning include Hebbian Learning, Vector Quantization, and Adaptive Resonance Theory (ART).

Supervised and unsupervised learning alrogithms are explored in the neural network chapters (Chapters 8 and 9), in addition to the examples explored here.

Finally, probabilistic approaches to learning is a useful method in modern AI. This approach works on the principle that assigning probabilities to events can be done based on prior probabilities and observed data. This is useful because in theory this method can arrive at optimal decisions.

Supervised Learning

Supervised learning algorithms use training data that has been classified (has a target value for each training vector). The purpose of the supervised learning algorithm is to create a prediction function using the training data that will generalize for unseen training vectors to classify them correctly.

In this section, decision-tree learning is explored to construct a decision tree from observed behavior.

Learning with Decision Trees

One of the most intuitive and practical methods for supervised learning is the decision tree. A decision tree is the result of a classification process in which the source data is reduced into a predictor tree that represents a set of if/then/else rules. As an example, consider an observer that watched a FPS player and recorded their actions when confronted with an enemy. The result is shown in Table 6.1

Table 6.1:   Observed actions of a player in a first-person-shooter game.

Weapon	Ammo	Health	Behavior
Gun	Full	Low	Fight
Gun	Low	Full	Evade
Knife	Low	Full	Fight
Knife	Low	Low	Evade

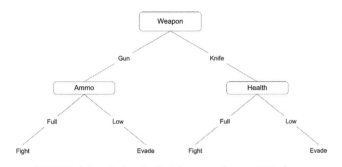

FIGURE 6.1:   **A simple decision tree for an FPS player.**

```
If ( (Weapon == Gun) && (Ammo == Full) ) then Fight
else if ( (Weapon == Knife) && (Health == Full) ) then Fight
else Evade
```

FIGURE 6.2:   **Conditional expression resulting from the simple decision tree.**

A simple example of a decision tree, created from the observed data in Table 6.1, is shown in Figure 6.1.

As shown in Figure 6.1 (and Table 6.1), this player has three predictor variables. These are Weapon (the weapon currently carried by the player), Ammo (the amount of ammunition carried by the player), and finally, Health (the level of health of the player). The interior nodes of the decision tree are the features, and the arcs out of the feature nodes are feature values. Each leaf in the tree is a category (or class). The breakdown of this decision tree results in a simple conditional expression shown in Figure 6.2.

This condition expression (representing the decision tree) defines that if the player has a gun with full ammo, it will fight. If the player has a knife and full health, it will fight. Otherwise, the player will evade. This is clearly shown in the simple conditional in Figure 6.2.

It's easy to see how the decision tree can be constructed from the data in Table 6.1, but with much larger data sets with many predictor variables, the task is considerably more difficult. The ID3 (Iterative Dichotomizer 3) algorithm automates this task through a form of top-down greedy search through the decision-tree space.

Decision-tree learning is a common technique used in data mining. Data mining is a larger field that studies the extraction of useful information from data sets. Data mining is a popular technique in financial analysis and also finds use in identifying fraud.

Using a decision tree is simply defined as starting at the root and taking the path through the tree whose feature values represent those of a given example. When the leaf of the tree is reached, the example has been classified.

Creating a Decision Tree

Creating a decision tree from a set of examples is a straightforward process. But the goal is to create a simple decision tree that is consistent with the training data. Simple can be ambiguous, but simpler decision trees tend to be more reliable and generalize better.

Creating a decision tree is a recursive process over the features of the data set, but it always begins with the determination of the root of the tree. To choose which feature to begin building the tree, the statistical property of information gain is used. The feature with the highest information gain is selected which specifies the feature most useful for classification.

Information gain is based on another idea from information theory called *entropy*, which measures the amount of information behind the feature. Entropy is defined in Eq 6.1.

$$E(S) = \sum -p(I)\log_2 p(I) \qquad \text{Eq 6.1}$$

Given a sample set (S), the sum is taken of the proportions of S that belong to class I. If all samples of S belong to the same class I, then entropy is 0. Entropy of 1.0 defines that the sample set (for class I) is completely random.

To calculate entropy for the Behavior listed in Table 6.1, we would apply Eq 6.1 as follows:

E(S) = -(2/5)Log2(2/5) + -(3/5)Log2(3/5)
E(S) = 0.528771 + 0.442179 = 0.970951

With the entropy calculated for the target (Behavior), the next step is to choose the feature with the highest information gain. To calculate the information gain for a feature, Eq 6.2 is used.

$$Gain(S,A) = E(S) - \sum_{v \in Values(A)} \frac{|S_v|}{S} E(S_v) \qquad \text{Eq 6.2}$$

Information gain identifies how much influence the given feature has over predicting the resulting category (in this case, Behavior). An example of calculating the information gain of feature Ammo is demonstrated as:

Gain(Sweapon) = E(S) - (2/4)*Entropy(Sgun) - (2/4)*Entropy(Sknife)

The entropy of a value of a given attribute is calculated based on the target feature. For example, the Weapon is value(Gun) in two of four examples. For the examples where Weapon has a value of Gun, the targets are split between Fight and Evade (1/2 for each). Therefore, the entropy for value of Gun is:

Entropy(Sgun) = -(1/2)Log2(1/2) - (1/2)Log2(1/2)
Entropy(Sgun) = 0.5 - 0.5 = 0.0

For examples where the Weapon has the value Knife, it's split as well (half have Knife, and when the example is Knife, the target Behavior is split between Fight and Evade, or 1/2).

Entropy(Sknife) = -(1/2)Log2(1/2) - (1/2)Log2(1/2)
Entropy(Sknife) = 0.5 - 0.5 = 0.0

So returning to the gain calculation for Weapon, the result is:

Gain(Sweapon) = 0.970951 - (2/4)*(0.0) - (2/4)*(0.0)
Gain(Sweapon) = 0.970951 - 0.0 - 0.0 = 0.970951

Next, the information gain for both Ammo and Health is calculated:

Gain(Sammo) = E(S) - (1/4)*Entropy(Sfull) - (3/4)Entropy(Slow)
Entropy(Sfull) = -(1/1)Log2(1/1) - (0/1)Log2(0/1)
Entropy(Sfull) = 0
Entropy(Slow) = -(1/3)Log2(1/3) - (2/3)Log2(2/3)
Entropy(Slow) = 0.528321 - 0.389975 = 0.138346
Gain(Sammo) = 0.970951 - (1/4)*0 - (3/4)*0.138346
Gain(Sammo) = 0.970951 - 0 - 0.103759 = 0.867192
Gain(SHealth) = E(S) - (2/4)*Entropy(Sfull) - (2/4)Entropy(Slow)
Entropy(Sfull) = -(1/2)Log2(1/2) - (1/2)Log2(1/2)
Entropy(Sfull) = 0.5 - 0.5 = 0.0
Entropy(Slow) = -(1/2)Log2(1/2) - (1/2)Log2(1/2)
Entropy(Slow) = 0.5 - 0.5 = 0.0
Gain(Shealth) = 0.970951 - (2/4)*0.0 - (2/4)*.0.
Gain(Shealth) = 0.970951 - 0.0 - 0.0 = 0.970951

The resulting gains are then:

Gain(Sweapon) = 0.970951 - 0.0 - 0.0 = 0.970951
Gain(Sammo) = 0.970951 - 0 - 0.103759 = 0.867192
Gain(Shealth) = 0.970951 - 0.0 - 0.0 = 0.970951

For a tie-breaker, we simply select the first largest information gain and use that as the largest. This yields Weapon as the feature to represent the

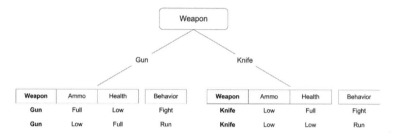

FIGURE 6.3: Bifurcation of the data set given a root feature decision.

root of the tree. The algorithm then continues, with the bifurcation of the data set into two sets, split by the selected feature and feature values, and the process continues to build the remainder of the tree (see Figure 6.3).

The process continues as above on the two legs of the tree. The entropy is calculated, and the information gain on each remaining feature to determine which to use to continue to develop the tree. One possible result was originally shown in Figure 6.1.

Characteristics of Decision-Tree Learning

As explored earlier, the ID3 algorithm uses a greedy form of search. This means that the algorithm picks the best attribute at each step, and does not return to re-evaluate earlier attribute choices. This can be problematic, as greedy doesn't necessarily mean optimal. The result can be a sub-optimal or unbalanced tree that does not yield the best segregation of features.

Decision treees that are large or are created from an small amount of training data tend to overfit (or over-generalize). In general, while larger decision trees are more consistent with the training data, smaller trees tend to generalize better. One way to manage this problem is to prune the training data to a smaller subset to avoid over-fitting.

The advantages of decision trees is that they are very fast (tend to classify in fewer decisions than the features of the data set) and are also easy to interpret. Most importantly, since a decision tree is inherently human-readable, it's very easy to understand how the classification works.

Unsupervised Learning

Recall that supervised learning learns from data that is preclassified (each training vector includes the target class). Unsupervised learning differs in that no target variable exists. All variables are treated as inputs, and therefore unsupervised learning is used to find patterns in the data. This allows the data to be reduced and segmented into its representative classes.

Markov Models

A useful example of a Markov model is the Markov chain, named after its creator, Andrey Markov. A Markov chain is a kind of probabilistic state machine that that can be easily trained given a set of training data. Each state can probabilistically lead to other states, but prior states have no relevance to subsequent state transitions (only the current state).

What makes Markov chains interesting is that they can be very easily created from observations. Take, for example, the idea of the smart home. The home monitors the actions of the occupant during the time that the occupant is home. Every evening, the occupant sets the alarm for 6 am (Sunday through Thursday). At 6 am, after the alarm sounds, the monitor notices that the bathroom light is turned on. Through observation, we capture the following over a week's training:

> Weekday, 6 am alarm, bathroom-light-on
> Weekend, no alarm, bathroom-light-off

With this data (five samples of weekday, two samples of weekend), it's visible that on weekdays, the alarm results in the observation that the bathroom light comes on with a probability of 1.0. With this data, the Smart Home could turn on the bathroom light when it sees the precursor event of the alarm going off.

This idea can be applied to a large variety of problems in the domain of prediction, clustering and classification. In the next section, the Markov chain is used to train character probability state machines to generate random words. These words are generated from a probabilistic state machine using regular words for training.

Word-Form Learning with Markov Chains

A simple Markov chain can be used to generate reasonable syntactically correct words using known words for training. To build random, but reasonable words the probability of letters following other letters is used. For example, if the word "the" were used as a training example four points of data can be collected. These are:

> the word begins with the letter 't'
> the letter 'h' follows the letter 't'
> the letter 'e' follows the letter 'h'
> the letter 'e' ends the word.

If we analyze a number of words this way, we can identify the frequency that letters start words, end words, and follow other letters. A table representation

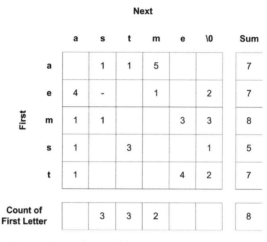

FIGURE 6.4: **The resulting letter transition matrix.**

is used to identify the beginning letter (rows) followed by the subsequent letter (columns). As an example, consider the word 'as' being analyzed. To start, the cell indicated by transition a->s is incremented (row 'a', column 's'). Then the transition s->'end' is incremented (shown as row 's', column '\0').

Consider the training sample consisting of the words:

mast, tame, same, teams,
team, meat, steam, and stem.

The product of analyzing these words is shown in Figure 6.4. For each word, the letter transitions are counted to arrive at the matrix representation. Note also that the sum of the rows is calculated (this is used later for word generation). The number of times a given letter occurred first is also counted (again, used in word generation).

Now that the matrix exists, how would a random word be created from this representation? For this, the counts are used as probabilities to determine which letter to use given a previously selected letter. To accomplish this, a random number is generated using the sum value as the bounds (the maximum random number that can be used). With this random value, roulette wheel selection is used to determine which letter from a row to use (depicted graphically in Figure 6.5 for row 'm').

Roulette wheel selection views the available options as a roulette wheel. Elements with zero probability of selection do not appear. Those with non-zero probability occupy a space on the wheel proportional to their frequency. For example, with a sum of 9, letter a is selected 2/9 of the time, or P(0.22).

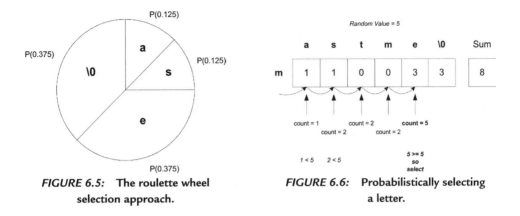

FIGURE 6.5:   **The roulette wheel**
selection approach.

FIGURE 6.6:   **Probabilistically selecting**
a letter.

For roulette wheel selection, a random value is selected which serves as the limit. A random starting point is selected (in this example, the first cell) and a count is incremented given the cell's contents (see Figure 6.6). If the count is greater than or equal to random value, then the letter is selected. Otherwise, the wheel continues and the next slot is accumulated. This process continues until the count value is the same or greater than the random value. When this test is satisfied, the letter is selected (in this case, 'e' is selected to follow the letter 'm'). The process would then continue for the letter 'e,' until the terminal character was selected ('\0') indicating that the word is complete. This follows the sample data, which indicates that the letter 'e' follows the letter 'm' 3/8's of the time or P(0.375)).

What's useful about this algorithm is that letters with higher frequencies (meaning higher numbers of occurrences in the training samples) are selected with a greater probability than letters with lower occurrences. This allows word generation (in this case) to probabilistically follow the training set.

Word Generation with Markov Chains

To generate a new random word, the first step is to define which letter to use first. For this, the vector (called 'count of first letter' in Figure 6.4) is used. A letter is selected randomly (per the earlier discussion using roulette wheel selection). With the first letter selected, we emit this letter, and then select the next letter using the current letter's row in the matrix (see Figure 6.4). Next letter selection was explored in Figure 6.6. When the letter selected is the NULL (or \0) character, the word is complete.

This can be demonstrated by hand using the representation matrix in Figure 6.4. In Table 6.2, the random value and resulting letter selected is shown.

Table 6.2: Sample iteration of word generation.

Random Value	Action
7	Iterate 'first letter vector,' select 'm'
1	Iterate matrix row 'm,' select 'a'
2	Iterate matrix row 'a,' select 't'
5	Iterate matrix row 't,' select 'e'
6	Iterate matrix row 'e,' select \0 (NULL)

The result is the generation of the random word 'mate' (not part of the training set). In the next section, the code to implement this capability is explored.

Markov Chain Implementation

The implementation of the Markov chain for random word construction requires two basic components. The first is the training element which reads the training file (called the corpus) and builds the matrix representation of the letter 'state machine.' The second element is the word generation element which uses the matrix representation to generate random words.

The complete implementation of the Markov-Chain demonstration can be found on the CD-ROM at ./software/ch6/markov.c.

The matrix is represented using a simple two-dimensional array as:

```
#define ROWS  28
#define COLS   28
unsigned int matrix[ROWS][COLS];
```

Indexes (row and column) 0 through 25 represent the letters 'a' through 'z.' Index 26 (row and column) represents the newline (end of word). Column 27 represents the sum of the particular row. Finally, row 27 represents the count of the given letter appearing as the first letter (see Figure 6.4).

Building the letter matrix (as illustrated in Figure 6.4) is a simple process that relies on a very simple state machine. The first state, called START_LTR_STATE, exists to identify that a single letter has been received and that another letter is required to increment a cell. In this state, when a character is received, the count of the first-letter-vector is incremented (which identifies how many times this character is the first in a word). After an initial character is received, the next state is entered called the NEXT_LTR_STATE. In this state, the transition counts are incremented (how often one character leads to another). When the next character received is

input	current state ⟶ next state		prev_char	Action
m	START_LTR_STATE	NEXT_LTR_STATE	–	Increment first letter cell for 'm'.
a	NEXT_LTR_STATE	NEXT_LTR_STATE	m	Increment matrix[m][a]
s	NEXT_LTR_STATE	NEXT_LTR_STATE	a	Increment matrix[a][s]
t	NEXT_LTR_STATE	NEXT_LTR_STATE	s	Increment matrix[s][t]
\0	NEXT_LTR_STATE	START_LTR_STATE	t	Increment matrix[t][\0]

FIGURE 6.7: **Recording a word's data with the parsing state machine.**

a terminal character (such as space, punctuation, etc.), this data is recorded (character at the end of a word), and then the state machine transitions back to the FIRST_LTR_STATE. This process is shown in Figure 6.7.

The state machine is implemented in function read_corpus shown in Listing 6.1. The function simply reads each line from the defined file, and uses the state machine to maintain letter transition counts in the matrix.

LISTING 6.1:   Creating the matrix representation from the training data.

```
int read_corpus( char *filename )
{
  FILE *fp;
  char line[MAX_LINE+1];
  int  i, state = START_LTR_STATE;
  char ch, prev_char;
  /* Open and test the corpus file */
  fp = fopen(filename, "r");
  if (fp == NULL) return -1;
  /* Loop through each line of the file */
  while (fgets(line, MAX_LINE, fp) != (char *)0) {
    /* Loop through the line */
    for (i = 0 ; ((i < MAX_LINE) && (line[i] != 0)) ; i++) {
      ch = tolower(line[i]);
      /* State machine for character handling */
      switch(state) {
        case START_LTR_STATE:
          /* We're on the initial letter, save it if non-terminal */
          if (!is_terminal(ch)) {
```

```
      prev_char = ch;
      matrix[FIRST_LETTER][to_idx(ch)]++;
      state = NEXT_LTR_STATE;
    }
    break;
  case NEXT_LTR_STATE:
    if (is_terminal(ch)) {
      /* If the next letter is a terminal, transition back */
      matrix[to_idx(prev_char)][26]++;
      state = START_LTR_STATE;
    } else {
      /* If the next letter is a non-terminal, increment the count */
      matrix[to_idx(prev_char)][to_idx(ch)]++;
      prev_char = ch;
    }
    break;
    }
   }
  }
  /* Fill in sum columns in the matrix */
  calculate_maximums();
  return 0;
}
```

When read_corpus has finished, the matrix is updated and represents the training data. The matrix can now be used to generate random words that mimic the structure of the words in the training data. Two functions are used for word generation, these are generate_word and select_letter.

Function generate_word (see Listing 6.2) is the higher-level function that selects letters to build a word. It begins by selecting a letter, but from the vector representing the frequency of letters appearing first (FIRST_ LETTER). Each new letter (row in the matrix) is requested using the current letter (representing the row from which to select). Once the terminal character is selected, the word is complete and the function returns.

LISTING 6.2:   Function generate_word to create a new random word.

```
void generate_word( void )
{
  int sel;
```

```
/* Select the first letter to use */
sel = select_letter(FIRST_LETTER);
/* Continue, selecting additional letters based upon
 * the last letter.
 */
while (sel != END_LETTER) {
  printf("%c", ('a'+sel));
  sel = select_letter(sel);
}
printf("\n");
return;
}
```

The core of the word creation algorithm is the select_letter function (see Function 6.3). This function implements the roulette wheel selection algorithm. The algorithm begins with the row, which represents the previous letter. This provides the row that is used to determine which letter will follow. A random value is created (max_val), which represents the limit (where the ball will stop in the roulette wheel). The row is then accumulated (starting at the first cell) until the max_val is reached or exceeded. At this point, the letter is returned. If the max_val is not reached, then the next cell is accumulated and the process continues.

Listing 6.3:   The select_letter function that probabilistically selects letters based on the current letter.

```
char select_letter( int row )
{
  int max_val;
  int i=0, sum = 0;
  /* Pick the maximum value (for roulette selection) */
  max_val = RANDMAX( matrix[row][MAX_COUNTS] )+1;
  /* Perform the roulette wheel */
  while (1) {
    /* Add in the current slot value */
    sum += matrix[row][i];
    /* If >= max_val, then select this letter */
    if (sum >= max_val) return i;
    /* Otherwise, skip to the next letter in the row */
    if (++i >= MAX_COUNTS) i = 0;
```

```
  }
  exit(0);
}
```

Generating random words from a program built from this source can result in interesting words, and also not so interesting words. For example, these words were generated from a sample corpus:

antinsubaized
sutosermed
eroconated
axpoged
porantide
arouded
anvilured
arketized

But more often than not, words like this can result:

rolacunficonged
phteroobund

From this perspective, extracting the more useful words from the nonsensical words can be done with human involvement. In other words, the application generates solution sets which are then reviewed by a human to identify those that have value (for example, if a new company or drug name were being searched). This is called human-assisted unsupervised learning and results in the best approach (software for search, human review for filtering).

Other Applications of Markov Chains

Markov chains and their variants can be found in a number of areas, including speech recognition, speech understanding, music composition, and a number of other areas. The simplicity of the algorithm makes it very efficient. The system has no idea of the events for which probabilities are being defined, all that's learned is probability between events within a system. But even without an understanding of the semantics behind the relationships, the system can still react to them (such as the alarm/bathroom-light example). The approach is also useful from the human-assisted learning perspective (with human operators considering the importance of the relationships found).

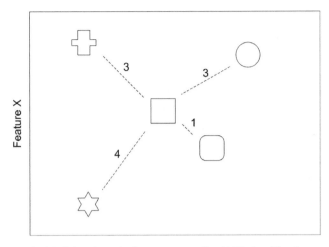

FIGURE 6.8: **Sample feature space for 1NN classification.**

Nearest Neighbor Classification

One of the earliest unsupervised learning algorithms that is also one of the simplest is called *nearest neighbor classification*. This algorithm classifies an unseen pattern or concept by finding the closest pattern in the known data set. This is what is meant by nearest neighbor. The class of the nearest neighbor in the multi-dimensional feature space is the class of the (unseen) test vector.

An example of this is shown in Figure 6.8. At the center of the feature space is a new sample that is yet to be classified. The distance between the new sample and other examples in the space is calculated. The closest example is used as the class to which this new sample should be clustered. In this example, the closest example is one unit away, and therefore the class of this example is used. Declaring the class based on the closest sample is called one nearest neighbor (1NN).

Calculating the distance between two feature vectors can be accomplished in a number of ways, but the most popular is the Euclidean measure. Another popular function uses the Manhattan distance. The Euclidean distance is calculated using Eq 6.3 for feature vectors p and q.

$$d = \sqrt{\sum_{i=1}^{n} (p_i - q_i)^2} \qquad \text{Eq 6.3}$$

Nearest neighbor (1NN) takes a simple but effective approach to classification. In the next section, a simple demonstration of 1NN is explored for animal classification.

1NN Example

The algorithm for 1NN is easily described and implemented. With 1NN, the sample (unclassified) feature vector is checked against all known examples. The class for the closest example is then used as the class for the sample feature vector.

For the example vectors, the table in Figure 6.9 is used. This contains a number of features that in certain combinations define a type of animal. Five types of animals are classified here using 14 example vectors and 10 attributes.

	Give Birth to Live Young	Lays Eggs	Feed Offspring with Own Milk	Covered with Hair	Warm-Blooded	Cold-Blooded	Covered with Feathers	Scaly Skin	Live in Water and Land	Breathe with Gills	Class
Squirrel	1		1	1	1						Mammal
Cat	1		1	1	1						Mammal
Frog		1				1			1		Amphibian
Duck		1			1		1		1		Bird
Bat	1		1	1							Mammal
Elephant	1		1	1	1						Mammal
Alligator		1				1		1			Reptile
Owl		1			1		1				Bird
Trout		1				1		1		1	Fish
Turtle		1				1		1			Reptile
Water Dragon		1				1			1		Amphibian
Elk	1		1	1	1						Mammal
Snake		1				1		1			Reptile
Salmon		1				1		1		1	Fish

FIGURE 6.9: Example feature vectors for animal classification.

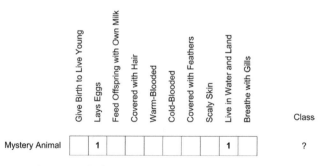

	Give Birth to Live Young	Lays Eggs	Feed Offspring with Own Milk	Covered with Hair	Warm-Blooded	Cold-Blooded	Covered with Feathers	Scaly Skin	Live in Water and Land	Breathe with Gills	Class
Mystery Animal	1								1		?

FIGURE 6.10: Distance calculation for the mystery animal to the known examples.

As an example, consider a newly discovered animal with the attributes shown by its feature vector (see Figure 6.10). What's observed is that the mystery animal lays eggs and lives in both the water and on land. The distance of the feature vector to each known example is calculated and the closest example used for the class (see Figure 6.11). In this case, the mystery animal is classified as an amphibian.

The implementation for 1NN is very simple and shown in Listing 6.4. As shown the calc_distance simply calculates the distance using each feature of the vector. The 1NN algorithm simply walks through each example vector and calculates the distance from the sample vector (see main). The closest vector is then used as the class.

The complete implementation of the 1NN demonstration can be found on the CD-ROM at ./software/ch6/one_nn.c.

LISTING 6.4: Sample implementation of the 1NN clustering algorithm.

```
#define MAX_FEATURES      10
#define MAMMAL            0
#define BIRD             1
#define FISH             2
#define AMPHIBIAN        3
#define REPTILE          4
typedef struct {
  int features[MAX_FEATURES];
  int class;
} sample_t;
#define MAX_SAMPLES       14
sample_t samples[MAX_SAMPLES] = {
/* LY LE FBM CWH WB CB HF SS LWL BWG */
{{  1, 0,  1,  1,  1, 0, 0, 0,  0,  0 }, MAMMAL },    /* Squirrel */
{{  1, 0,  1,  1,  1, 0, 0, 0,  0,  0 }, MAMMAL },    /* Cat */
{{  0, 1,  0,  0,  0, 1, 0, 0,  1,  0 }, AMPHIBIAN }, /* Frog */
{{  0, 1,  0,  0,  1, 0, 1, 0,  1,  0 }, BIRD },      /* Duck */
{{  1, 0,  1,  1,  0, 0, 0, 0,  0,  0 }, MAMMAL },    /* Bat */
{{  1, 0,  1,  1,  1, 0, 0, 0,  0,  0 }, MAMMAL },    /* Elephant */
{{  0, 1,  0,  0,  0, 1, 0, 1,  0,  0 }, REPTILE },   /* Alligator */
{{  0, 1,  0,  0,  1, 0, 1, 0,  0,  0 }, BIRD },      /* Owl */
{{  0, 1,  0,  0,  0, 1, 0, 1,  0,  1 }, FISH },      /* Trout */
{{  0, 1,  0,  0,  0, 1, 0, 1,  0,  0 }, REPTILE },   /* Turtle */
```

```
{{  0,  1,  0,  0, 0,  1, 0,  0,  1,  0 }, AMPHIBIAN }, /* Wtr Dragn */
{{  1,  0,  1,  1, 1,  0, 0,  0,  0,  0 }, MAMMAL },   /* Elk */
{{  0,  1,  0,  0, 0,  1, 0,  1,  0,  0 }, REPTILE },  /* Snake */
{{  0,  1,  0,  0, 0,  1, 0,  1,  0,  1 }, FISH }      /* Salmon */
};
char *names[5]={"Mammal", "Bird", "Fish", "Amphibian", "Reptile"};
double calc_distance( int *feature_vector, int example )
{
  double distance = 0.0;
  int i;
  /* Compute the distance for each feature of the vector */
  for (i = 0 ; i < MAX_FEATURES ; i++) {
    distance += sqr( (samples[example].features[i] - feature_vector[i]) );
  }
  return sqrt(distance);
}
int main( void )
{
  int i, class = 0;
  double distance, min = 100.0;
  int fv[MAX_FEATURES]={ 0, 1, 0, 0, 0, 0, 0, 0, 1, 0 };
  for (i = 0 ; i < MAX_SAMPLES ; i++) {
    /* Calculate distance between the sample and example_i vector */
    distance = calc_distance( fv, i );
    /* If this is the closest vector, save it */
    if (distance < min) {
      min = distance;
      class = samples[i].class;
    }
  }
  printf( "Class is %s\n", names[class] );
  return 0;
}
```

k-NN Example

A problem with 1NN classification is that it can be susceptible to noisy data. One solution to this problem is instead of simply classifying based on the closest neighbor, take the closest k neighbors and use the majority vote to determine the correct class (see Figure 6.11).

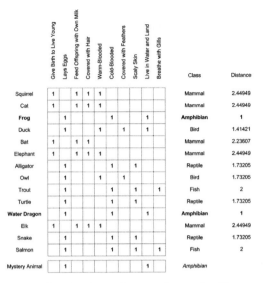

FIGURE 6.11: **Using the closest k examples to classify a new sample.**

The advantage of k-NN (where $k > 1$) is that the probability of misclassifying a sample is reduced because more examples can weigh in on the result. The k portion can be taken too far, and if the k value is too large, it can also result in misclassification. The value of k should therefore be small, but not too large. Unrelated examples influence the vote.

The implementation for k-NN is a variation of 1-NN in that k examples are used for classification instead of simply one.

The data representation for k-NN is identical to that one 1-NN, as shown in Listing 6.4. What differs is how the classification occurs once the Euclidean distances are calculated. Listing 6.5 provides the main function for k-NN classification. As shown, each distance is calculated for the feature vector fc (with calc_distance) and then saved in the distance array. Function count_votes is then invoked (with the k value) to find and count the voting examples.

The complete implementation of the k-NN demonstration can be found on the CD-ROM at ./software/ch6/k_nn.c.

LISTING 6.5:   Main function for the k-NN implementation.

```
int main( void )
{
  int i, class = 0;
  int fv[MAX_FEATURES]={ 0, 1, 0, 1, 0, 0, 0, 0, 1, 0 };
```

```
double distance[MAX_SAMPLES];
int k=3;
/* Walk through each example vector */
for (i = 0 ; i < MAX_SAMPLES ; i++) {
  distance[i] = calc_distance( fv, i );
}
/* Count, Sort and Return Winning Class */
class = count_votes( distance, k );
printf("Class is %s\n", names[class]);
return 0;
}
```

The calc_distance function is the same as shown in Listing 6.4. The next function, count_votes, is used to find the closest k examples to the sample vector and then to find the class represented by the majority of the examples. The function begins by moving the class members from the example vectors into a new list vector. The list is then sorted using the distance vector passed into the function. The class votes array is then zeroed and the top k members of the list (those closest to the unclassified sample) are counted. Finally, the class with the most votes is returned to the main function to emit the class to which the sample belongs (based on the majority vote of the closest k examples).

LISTING 6.6:   Function to find and count the closest k example vectors.

```
int count_votes( double *dist, int k )
{
  int i, list[MAX_SAMPLES];
  int votes[MAX_CLASSES];
  int sorted;
  int max, class;
  /* Move classes to the new temporary list array */
  for (i = 0 ; i < MAX_SAMPLES ; i++) list[i] = samples[i].class;
  /* Sort the list in ascending order of distance */
  sorted = 0;
  while (!sorted) {
    sorted = 1;
    for (i = 0 ; i < MAX_SAMPLES-1 ; i++) {
      if (dist[i] > dist[i+1]) {
        int temp = list[i];  list[i] = list[i+1]; list[i+1] = temp;
        double tdist = dist[i]; dist[i] = dist[i+1]; dist[i+1] = tdist;
```

```
    sorted = 0;
  }
 }
}
/* Count the votes */
for (i = 0 ; i < MAX_CLASSES ; i++) votes[i] = 0;
/* Add the vote to the particular class */
for (i = 0 ; i < k ; i++) {
  votes[list[i]]++;
}
/* Count the votes and return the largest class */
max = votes[0];
class = 0;
for (i = 1 ; i < MAX_CLASSES ; i++) {
  if (votes[i] > max) {
    max = votes[i];
    class = i;
  }
}
return class;
}
```

	Give Birth to Live Young	Lays Eggs	Feed Offspring with Own Milk	Covered with Hair	Warm-Blooded	Cold-Blooded	Covered with Feathers	Scaly Skin	Live in Water and Land	Breathe with Gills	Class	Distance
Squirrel	1		1	1	1						Mammal	2.23607
Cat	1		1	1	1						Mammal	2.23607
Frog		1				1			1		**Amphibian**	**1.41421**
Duck		1			1		1		1		**Bird**	**1.73205**
Bat	1		1	1							Mammal	2
Elephant	1		1	1	1						Mammal	2.23607
Alligator		1				1		1			Reptile	2
Owl		1			1		1				Bird	2
Trout		1				1		1		1	Fish	2.23607
Turtle		1				1		1			Reptile	2
Water Dragon		1				1			1		**Amphibian**	**1.41421**
Elk	1		1	1	1						Mammal	2.23607
Snake		1				1		1			Reptile	2
Salmon		1				1		1		1	Fish	2.23607
Mystery Animal		1		1					1		*Amphibian*	

2 votes Amphibian
1 vote Bird

FIGURE 6.12: **k-NN Example for Classification (k=3).**

The k-NN algorithm is much less susceptible to noise than the 1-NN and therefore can provide a much better classification than 1-NN. The value of k should be large enough to yield a representative set of voting examples, but small enough to avoid too small of a sample.

The process of k-NN is shown in Figure 6.12. The distance from each example to the sample vector (mystery animal) is performed and the top through chosen. In this case, the examples aren't sorted, but instead just selected from the list (shown in bold). In this example, two of the closest examples are from the amphibian class and one from the bird class.

The nearest neighbor algorithm k-NN is a great algorithm for classifying feature vectors using a set of known classified examples. Drawbacks can include the processing time required if the example set and feature vector are large. Its biggest advantage is its simplicity.

CHAPTER SUMMARY

While machine learning is one of the older techniques of AI, it remains useful and effective for general learning. In this chapter, the ideas behind supervised and unsupervised learning were explored and a collection of algorithms that demonstrate these approaches were given. Decision trees were introduced from the perspective of supervised learning, and also Markov chains and nearest neighbor algorithms from the unsupervised learning perspective. All are useful for learning and classification in a wide variety of problem domains.

RESOURCES

Anzai, Y. *Pattern Recognition and Machine Learning* New York, Academic Press, 1992.

Carbonell, J. (Ed.) *Machine Learning Paradigms and Methods* Boston, MA MIT Press, 1990.

Dasarthy, B. (Ed.). "Nearest Neighbor (NN) Norms: NN Pattern Classification Techniques," 1991.

Hastie, T. et al "The Elements of Statistical Learning," Springer, 2001.

Mitchell, T.M. "Machine Learning," McGraw-Hill, 1997.

EXERCISES

1. In your own words, define the core differences between supervised and unsupervised learning.

2. What is a common application of decision-tree learning?
3. Define entropy and its application to decision-tree learning. What can be inferred if entropy is zero or one?
4. What issues can result from creating decision trees from training sets that are too small or too large?
5. What other applications are useful for Markov chains?
6. In the Markov example presented in this book, only two letters are considered to build a probability matrix. Update the sample program to consider three letters in probability construction. How does this affect the production of random words?
7. Nearest neighbor classification uses a feature vector to represent known concepts. How could a first-person-shooter character (NPC) be defined such action-selection was performed with 1NN?
8. Describe the difference between 1NN and k-NN classification.
9. What is the primary issue with 1NN classification?
10. How does k-NN classification improve on the capabilities of 1NN classification?
11. What is the primary issue with k-NN classification?

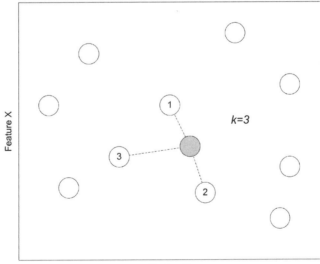

FIGURE 6.13: k-NN Example for Classification (k=3).

Chapter 7 EVOLUTIONARY COMPUTATION

Evolutionary Computation refers to a class of algorithms that utilize simulated evolution to some degree as a means to solve a variety of problems, from numerical optimization to symbolic logic. By simulated evolution, we mean that the algorithms have the ability to evolve a population of potential solutions such that weaker solutions are removed and replaced with incrementally stronger (better) solutions. In other words, the algorithms follow the principle of natural selection. Each of the algorithms has some amount of biological plausibility, and is based on evolution or the simulation of natural systems. In this chapter, we'll explore genetic algorithms, genetic programming, evolutionary strategies, differential evolution, and another biologically inspired algorithm: swarm intelligence.

SHORT HISTORY OF EVOLUTIONARY COMPUTATION

It's no surprise that evolution has been used as a metaphor for solving very difficult problems. Evolution in itself is a mechanism of incremental search, whereby more fit solutions to problems propagate to future generations, and less fit solutions gradually fade away. This process of natural selection provides a wonderful vehicle for finding solutions to difficult multivariate optimization problems.

While evolutionary algorithms have existed for quite some time, their use has increased as modern computing systems permit the evolution of larger populations of solutions to much more complex problems.

Evolutionary Strategies

One of the earliest uses of evolution occurred in the 1960s by Rechenberg. Rechenberg introduced evolution strategies as a means to optimize vectors of real-values to optimize physical systems such as airfoils. [Rechenberg 1965] In this early evolutionary strategy, the population size was restricted to two members, the parent and child. The child member was modified in a random way (a form of mutation), and whichever member was more fit (parent or child) was then allowed to propagate to the next generation as the parent. For example, as shown in Figure 7.1, the child member is more fit than the parent in the first generation, which results in it being the parent in the next generation.

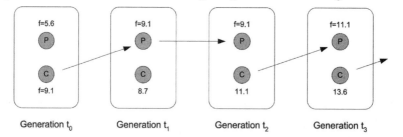

FIGURE 7.1: **Demonstrating the simple two member evolutionary strategy.**

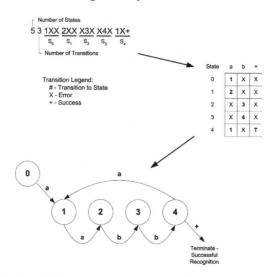

FIGURE 7.2: **Evolving finite state machines for a simple parsing task.**

Evolutionary Programming

Evolutionary Programming was also introduced and advanced in the 1960s by Fogel. With evolutionary programming, Fogel evolved populations of finite state machines (or automata) that solved various problems. [Fogel 1966] A finite-state machine is a graph with state transitions based on an input symbol and the current state (for example, many parsers are designed as finite-state machines). Fogel's method incrementally improved the population through random mutation of the state transitions.

The example shown in Figure 7.2 demonstrates one of the encodings that could be used for evolving finite-state machines. The goal is to evolve a finite-state machine that can recognize patterns such as aabb, aabbaabb, aabbaabbaabb, etc.

The upper left of Figure 7.2 is the finite-state machine raw encoding that can be mutated during evolution. This particular finite-state machine results in the state transition diagram shown in the middle right. This can be diagrammed as shown in the lower right of Figure 7.2, the state-machine diagram.

Genetic Algorithms

John Holland introduced the idea of genetic algorithms in the 1960s as a population-based algorithm with greater biological plausibility than previous approaches. Where evolutionary strategies and evolutionary programming used mutation as a way to search the solution space, Holland's genetic algorithm extended this with additional operators straight from biology. Potential solutions (or chromosomes) are represented as strings of bits instead of real values. In addition to mutation, Holland also used crossover and inversion to navigate the solution space (see Figure 7.3).

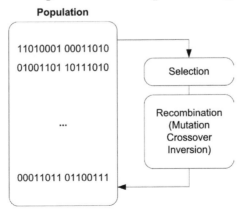

FIGURE 7.3:   **Holland's bit-string genetic algorithm.**

Holland also studied the mathematical foundation of his algorithms, looking more to understand them from a theoretical perspective than using them to solve problems.

NOTE ▸ *All living organisms consist of cells, where each cell contains a set of chromosomes (strings of DNA). Each chromosome is made up of genes, each of which can encode a trait (behavioral or physical). These chromosomes serve as the basis for genetic algorithms, where a potential solution is defined as a chromosome, and the individual elements of the solution are the genes.*

Genetic Programming

In 1990s, John Koza introduced the subfield called Genetic Programming. This is considered a subfield because it fundamentally relies on the core genetic algorithm created by Holland, and differs in the underlying representation of the solutions to be evolved. Instead of using bit-strings (as with genetic algorithms) or real-values (as is the case for evolutionary programming or evolutionary strategies), genetic programming relies on S-expressions (program trees) as the encoding scheme.

Consider the example shown in Figure 7.4. The population consists of two members, A and B. Using the crossover operator, a portion of A is grafted onto B, resulting in a new expression. Genetic programming also utilizes the mutation operator as a way of extending the population to the search space.

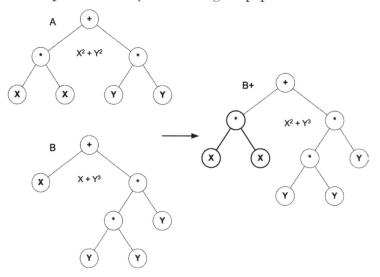

FIGURE 7.4:   **Using the crossover operator to create new S-expressions.**

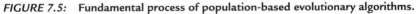

While Koza's representation focused on S-expressions, linear genetic programming has been introduced to evolve programs in standard machine (assembly) languages.

BIOLOGICAL MOTIVATION

The evolutionary algorithms covered in this chapter are all biologically plausible. In each case, the algorithms that we'll explore are population-based. Each of the algorithms operates on a population of entities, parallelizing the ability to solve a problem.

The first set of algorithms that we'll review (genetic algorithms, genetic programming, and evolutionary strategies) is truly evolutionary in nature. These algorithms involve natural selection across a population of potential solutions. Members of the population are born and eventually die, but pass on their genetic materials through the populations in search of a satisfactory solution. At the core of these algorithms is what's called *recombination*, or the combining and mutating of solutions that can change the material in the population. As the members of the pool change, only those that are fit can move onto the next population (potentially in more fit form). This process is illustrated in Figure 7.5.

FIGURE 7.5: Fundamental process of population-based evolutionary algorithms.

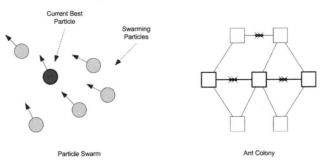

FIGURE 7.6: Optimization by natural system (particle swarm and Ant Colony Optimization).

The second set of algorithms that we'll explore is capable of solving a variety of problems using nature as a guide. The first algorithm, in the field of swarm intelligence, uses a population of particles that swarm with each other over a fitness landscape to solve various problems such as optimization. The best particle is used as the center of the swarm, with other particles swarming around it (looking for better solutions).

The second algorithm, Ant Colony Optimization, simulates a colony of ants and uses simulated pheromones to find solutions to various graph-related problems (as shown in Figure 7.6, where the pheromone trail identifies the shortest path through the graph).

GENETIC ALGORITHMS (GA)

Let's begin our discussion of evolutionary algorithms with the most popular and most flexible algorithm, the Genetic Algorithm. The genetic algorithm isn't really a single algorithm, but a collection of algorithms and techniques that can be used to solve a variety of problems in a number of different problem domains. For example, many consider genetic algorithms a technique for numerical optimization, but genetic algorithms can be used for much more (as we'll see later in the sample application).

The ability of the genetic algorithm to solve wide-ranging problems is derived from the method by which the solution is represented in the population. As we saw in the introduction, solutions can be represented as bit-strings (with an underlying representation), real-values, as well as more abstract entities such special encodings of LISP S-expressions. The genetic algorithm can be applied to many problems, and is limited primarily to the developer's ability to efficiently represent a solution. We'll see a number of possible solution encodings for Genetic Algorithms, Genetic Programming, and Evolutionary Strategies.

Genetic Algorithm Overview

The GA is a collection of algorithm recipes that can be used to evolve solutions to a range of different types of problems. We call it a recipe because there are a large number of variations of the GA that can be used. These variations are typically selected based on the type of problem to be solved.

Let's start with a discussion of the basic flow of the GA, and then we'll dig into the details and explore which variants are most useful. Note that the GA is called a population-based technique because instead of operating on a single potential solution, it uses a population of potential solutions.

The larger the population, the greater the diversity of the members of the population, and the larger the area searched by the population.

One attempt to understand why genetic algorithms work is called the Building-Block Hypothesis (BBH). This specifies, for binary GA, that the crossover operation (splitting two chromosomes and then swapping the tails) improves the solution by exploiting partial solutions (or building blocks) in the original chromosome. One can think of this as genetic repair, where fit building blocks are combined together to produce higher fitness solutions. Additionally, using fitness-proportionate selection (higher fit members are selected more often), less fit members and their corresponding building blocks, die out thus increasing the overall fitness of the population.

The overall genetic algorithm can be defined by the simple process shown in Figure 7.7. First, a pool of random potential solutions is created that serves as the first generation. For the best results, this pool should have adequate diversity (filled with members that differ more than they are similar). Next, the fitness of each member is computed. The fitness here is a measure of how well each potential solution solves the problem at hand. The higher the fitness, the better the solution in relation to others.

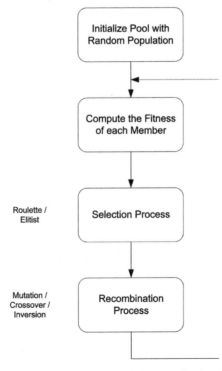

FIGURE 7.7: **Simple flow of the genetic algorithm.**

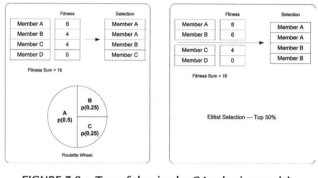

FIGURE 7.8: Two of the simpler GA selection models.

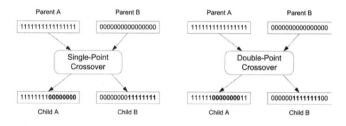

FIGURE 7.9: Illustrating the crossover operators in genetic recombination.

Next, members of the population are selected based on some algorithm. The two simplest approaches are roulette wheel selection, and elitist selection (see Figure 7.8). Roulette wheel selection is a probabilistic algorithm that selects members of the population proportionate with their fitness (the higher fit the member, the more likely it will be selected). In elitist selection, the higher fitness members of the population are selected, forcing the lesser fit members to die off.

Using roulette wheel selection (using the data from Figure 7.8), one likely selection result would be that two of Member A would be selected, and one each of Members C and D. Since Member A is of higher fitness that the other members, it has the privilege of propagating more chromosomes to the next population. Elitist selection in this model (shown in Figure 7.8) simply takes the upper 50% of the population's members (most fit), and then distributes these to the next generation.

Returning now to our GA flow, from the selection process, we have a number of members that have the right to propagate their genetic material to the next population. The next step is to recombine these members' material to form the members of the next generation. Commonly, parents are selected two at a time from the set of individuals that are permitted to propagate (from the selection process). Given two parents, two children

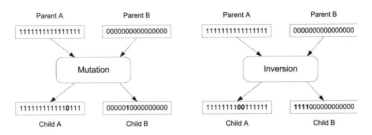

FIGURE 7.10: Illustrating the mutation and inversion genetic operators.

are created in the new generation with slight alternations courtesy of the recombination process (with a given probability that the genetic operator can occur). Figures 7.9 and 7.10 illustrate four of the genetic operators.

Figure 7.9 illustrates the crossover genetic operators. Using crossover, the parents are combined by picking a crossover point, and then swapping the tails of the two parents to produce the two children. Another variant of crossover creates two crossover points, swapping the genetic materials in two places.

Figure 7.10 covers the mutation operator and also the inversion operator. Each of these operators were the original genetic operators from Holland's original work. The mutation operator simply mutates (or flips) a bit. Note that in real-valued chromosomes, a slight change to the value can also be performed as mutation (small increment or decrement of the value). The inversion operator takes a piece of the chromosome, and inverts it. In this case, the range of bits are flipped.

Finally, we've discussed the process of the GA, but not how it terminates. There are a number of ways that we can terminate the process. The most obvious is to end when a solution is found, or one that meets the designer's criteria. But from the algorithm's perspective, we also need to account for the population, and its ability to find a solution.

Another termination criterion, potentially returning a suboptimal solution, is when the population lacks diversity, and therefore the inability to adequately search the solution space. When the members of the population become similar, there's a loss in the ability to search. To combat this, we terminate the algorithm early by detecting if the average fitness of the population is near the maximum fitness of any member of the population (for example, if the average fitness is greater than 0.99 times the maximum fitness). Once the population becomes too similar, the members have focused on similar areas of the search space, and are therefore incapable of branching out to new areas in search of more fit individuals.

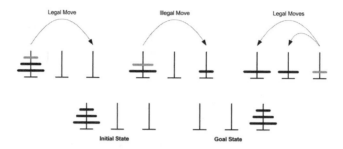

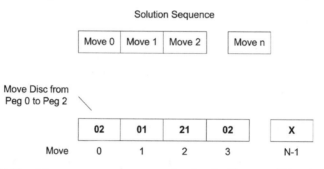

FIGURE 7.11: Legal moves for the Towers of Hanoi with initial and goal states.

FIGURE 7.12: Move sequence representation for the Towers of Hanoi problem.

> *The issue of lack of diversity in genetic algorithms results in premature convergence, as the members converge on a local maximum, not having found the global maximum. Early termination is one solution, but others include algorithm restart if this situation is detected.*

Genetic Algorithm Implementation

Let's now explore an implementation of a genetic algorithm to solve the Towers of Hanoi problem. This problem involves three pegs, with three unique-sized discs, and the goal of moving the discs from one peg to another. The constraint exists that a disc can be moved to a peg only if the peg is empty, or if the disc currently on the peg is larger than the peg to be moved (see Figure 7.11).

The first problem to solve is how to represent the sequence of moves to solve the problem in a form that can be evolved by the genetic algorithm. The first thing to consider is that there are only a handful of moves that are possible (though these may not always be legal, depending on the current configuration). If we number the pegs from zero to two, we can think about

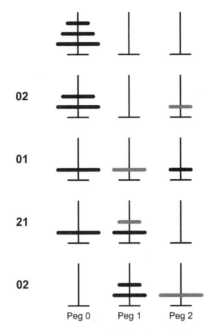

FIGURE 7.13: Illustrating the moves provided in the solution sequence in Figure 7.12.

the solution space as a sequence of moves whereby the move encodes the source peg and the destination peg.

From Figure 7.12, the first move '02' represents a move of the disc from peg 0 to peg 2. The next move '01' moves the disc from peg 0 to peg 1. The sequence of moves shown in Figure 7.12 can be shown visually as illustrated in Figure 7.13. The top configuration represents the initial configuration of the problem, and subsequent moves show how the configuration changes with each move (the grey disc is the last moved).

Let's now dig into the source that provides this representation (see Listing 7.1). The chromosome for the GA is sequence of moves, and each gene is a single move. We'll represent the moves very simply as integer numbers from 0 to 5. We'll decode the move number to the peg to/from command using the moves array. This allows us to avoid a direct representation, and provide a simpler format to the GA to evolve.

The Towers of Hanoi simulation is provided by the pegs array. This contains three structures representing the pegs, and up to three discs (with the number of discs currently on the peg defined by count). The solution is represented by the type solution_t. This contains the sequence of moves (plan), the number of active moves (op_count), and the current fitness evaluation.

Listing 7.1:   Representing the solution space for the Towers of Hanoi.

```
#define A_TO_B              0x01
#define A_TO_C              0x02
#define B_TO_A              0x10
#define B_TO_C              0x12
#define C_TO_A              0x20
#define C_TO_B              0x21
#define MAX_OPERATIONS    6
char moves[MAX_OPERATIONS]={
 A_TO_B, A_TO_C, B_TO_A, B_TO_C, C_TO_A, C_TO_B };
typedef struct {
  char peg[3];
  int  count;
} peg_t;
peg_t pegs[3];
#define NUM_OPERATIONS        12
typedef struct {
  int       op_count;
  unsigned char plan[NUM_OPERATIONS+1];
  double     fitness;
} solution_t;
```

The population of the GA is split into two parts. We'll keep an array of solutions as the current population, and another array as the next generation of solutions. The current and next generation cycle between each other as the algorithm is performed (next becomes current, etc.).

```
#define POPULATION_SIZE          200
solution_t solutions[2][POPULATION_SIZE];
```

Let's now look at the main loop for the GA, and then discuss the major functions that provide the process of evolution. We begin by randomly initializing the population of possible solutions with a call to initialize_population, and then calculate the fitness of each member (by testing each plan against a simulation of the Towers of Hanoi) using compute_population_fitness. We then enter the loop that invokes the core of the GA. The function perform_ga does a single cycle through the population, selecting the members to move on, and recombining them in the next generation. The fitness of each member is calculated again, and the fundamental statistics are emitted (minimum fitness, average fitness, and maximum fitness of the entire population).

This process continues while there's adequate diversity in the population (checking the average fitness against the maximum) and we haven't yet found a solution (a perfect solution being a fitness of 75.0).

Listing 7.2:   A snippet from the main loop for the genetic algorithm.

```
RANDINIT();
initialize_population( cur );
compute_population_fitness( cur );
while ((avg < (0.999 * max)) && (max < 75.0)) {
  cur = perform_ga( cur );
  compute_population_fitness( cur );
  if (((generation++) % 500) == 0) {
    printf("%6d: %g %g %g\n", generation, min, avg, max);
  }
}
```

The perform_ga function is shown in Listing 7.3, and is the core of the genetic algorithm implementation. It performs selection and recombination (using some support functions). The first step is identifying which index of the solutions array we'll use for the next generation (essentially the opposite of the current generation). We then walk through the current population, selecting two parents with the select_parent function. If crossover is to be performed (randomly, per the probability of crossover), then a crossover point is selected, and the tails swapped on the two parents (using the minimum of the op_counts to ensure the smallest possible sequence of moves).

Note also that as the genes (individual moves) are copied from the parent to the child, there's a possibility of mutation with the MUTATE macro. Each child receives the number of operations used by the parent (size of move plan).

Listing 7.3:   The core of the genetic algorithm.

```
int perform_ga( int cur_pop )
{
  int i, j, new_pop;
  int parent_1, parent_2;
  int crossover;
  new_pop = (cur_pop == 0) ? 1 : 0;
  for ( i = 0 ; i < POPULATION_SIZE ; i+=2 ) {
    /* i is child_1, i+1 is child_2 */
```

```
parent_1 = select_parent(cur_pop);
parent_2 = select_parent(cur_pop);
if (RANDOM() < CROSSOVER_PROB) {
  crossover = RANDMAX(
            MIN(solutions[cur_pop][parent_1].op_count,
                solutions[cur_pop][parent_2].op_count) );
} else {
  crossover = NUM_OPERATIONS;
}
for (j = 0 ; j < NUM_OPERATIONS ; j++) {
  if (j < crossover) {
    solutions[new_pop][i].plan[j] =
        MUTATE(solutions[cur_pop][parent_1].plan[j]);
    solutions[new_pop][i+1].plan[j] =
        MUTATE(solutions[cur_pop][parent_2].plan[j]);
  } else {
    solutions[new_pop][i].plan[j] =
        MUTATE(solutions[cur_pop][parent_2].plan[j]);
    solutions[new_pop][i+1].plan[j] =
        MUTATE(solutions[cur_pop][parent_1].plan[j]);
  }
}
solutions[new_pop][i].op_count = solutions[cur_pop][parent_1].op_
count;
solutions[new_pop][i+1].op_count = solutions[cur_pop][parent_2].op_
count;
}
return new_pop;
}
```

The select_parent function provides the roulette wheel selection algorithm (see Listing 7.4). This function walks through the current population, and tests each member with a probability function. If a random number is selected that is less than the fitness of the member over the sum of all members, then this member is selected as a parent and returned. The idea is that higher fitness members are selected more often, but occasionally, a less fit member is allowed to propagate. This is actually desirable because it increases the diversity of the overall population. If the entire population is checked, and no member is selected, then a random member of the population is returned.

Listing 7.4: Selecting a parent solution with roulette wheel selection.

```
int select_parent( int cur_pop )
{
  int i = RANDMAX(POPULATION_SIZE);
  int count = POPULATION_SIZE;
  double select=0.0;
  while (count--) {
    select = solutions[cur_pop][i].fitness;
    if (RANDOM() < (select / sum)) return i;
    if (++i >= POPULATION_SIZE) i = 0;
  }
  return( RANDMAX(POPULATION_SIZE) );
}
```

Finally, let's look at the fitness function (compute_fitness). This function is used by compute_population_fitness, which simply performs compute_fitness on the entire population, and collects the necessary statistics. The basic flow of this function is first to initialize the Towers of Hanoi simulation (pegs, peg contents, and disc counts). The member solution is then iterated executing each command, and performing the disc move that's specified. If the move is illegal (no disc on the source peg, or attempting to move a large disc over a smaller disc), then an illegal_moves counter is incremented, but the move is not performed to maintain a valid pegs configuration.

When all moves from the solution have been iterated, the fitness is calculated and returned. In this example, we calculate the fitness by giving a score of 25 for each disc that's on the correct peg. We then subtract from this the number of illegal moves that were attempted. The purpose of this is to evolve solutions that are optimal (no illegal moves attempted).

Listing 7.5: Calculating the fitness of a potential solution.

```
double compute_fitness( int cur_pop, int member, int trace )
{
  int i, from, to, disc=3;
  int illegal_moves = 0;
  int move;
  double fitness;
  /* Initialize the pegs */
  for (i = 0 ; i < 3 ; i++) {
```

```
  pegs[0].peg[i] = disc--;
  pegs[1].peg[i] = 0;
  pegs[2].peg[i] = 0;
}
pegs[0].count = 3;
pegs[1].count = 0;
pegs[2].count = 0;
for (i = 0 ; i < solutions[cur_pop][member].op_count ; i++) {
  /* Get the actual move from the moves array */
  move = moves[solutions[cur_pop][member].plan[i]];
  /* Find the source peg */
  from = (move >> 4) & 0xf;
  if (pegs[from].count == 0) {
    illegal_moves++;
  } else {
    /* Find the destination peg */
    to = move & 0xf;
    /* Ensure it's a legal move */
    if ((pegs[to].count == 0) ||
        (pegs[from].peg[pegs[from].count-1] <
         pegs[to].peg[pegs[to].count-1])) {
      /* Perform the move, update the pegs configuration */
      pegs[from].count--;
      pegs[to].peg[pegs[to].count] = pegs[from].peg[pegs[from].count];
      pegs[from].peg[pegs[from].count] = 0;
      pegs[to].count++;
    } else {
      illegal_moves++;
    }
  }
}
/* Calculate the fitness */
fitness = (double)(pegs[2].count*25) - (double)illegal_moves;
if (fitness < 0.0) fitness = 0.0;
return fitness;
}
```

Let's now look at the application in action. Listing 7.6 shows the output of the application (using a mutation probability of 0.01 and a crossover probability of 0.07).

The genetic algorithm implementation can be found on the CD-ROM at ./software/ch7/ga.c.

Listing 7.6: Sample output of the genetic algorithm of the Towers of Hanoi problem.

```
$ ./ga.exe
   1: 0 17.155 48
 501: 20 46.1 49
1001: 0 44.195 49
1501: 0 44.345 48
1578: 0 45.68 75
Trace : 02 01 21 02 10 12 02
```

The complete optimal solution to the Towers of Hanoi problem is shown in Figure 7.14. The least number of moves that solve this problem is seven. The visual execution of this plan is shown in Figure 7.14 (the optimal solution). In some cases, the algorithm will find a suboptimal plan. Commonly this occurs when a lack of diversity exists in the population. This is an expected problem with the GA, requiring either multiple runs, or an automatic restart when this situation is detected.

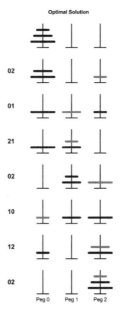

FIGURE 7.14: **The optimal solution to the Towers of Hanoi for three discs.**

GENETIC PROGRAMMING (GP)

As we discussed in the early part of this chapter, genetic programming is the biologically-inspired evolution of computer programs that solve a predefined task. For this reason, GP is nothing more than a genetic algorithm applied to the problem program evolution. Early GP systems utilized LISP S-expressions (as shown in Figure 7.4), but more recently, *linear genetic programming* systems have been used to evolve instruction sequences to solve user-defined programming tasks. [Banzhaf 1998]

Evolving complete programs with GP is computationally very expensive, and the results have been limited, but GP does have a place in the evolution of program fragments. For example, the evolution of individual functions that have very specific inputs and outputs and whose behavior can be easily defined for fitness evaluation by GP. To evolve a function, the desired output must be easily measurable in order to understand the fitness landscape of the function in order to incrementally evolve it.

> NOTE ▶
> *GP has also been applied to the evolution of physical hardware using programmable logic. This is an interesting area of research, but due to the inability to understand the complexity of the resulting design, met with limited success.*

Genetic Programming Algorithm

The genetic programming algorithm uses the same fundamental flow as the traditional genetic algorithm. The population of potential solutions is initialized randomly and then their fitness computed (through a simulation of executed instructions with the stack). Selection of members that can propagate into the next generation can then occur through fitness-proportionate selection. With this method, the higher fit the individual, the

Instruction	Description	Code
PUSH Pi	PUSH PI onto the stack	0
PUSH 2	PUSH 2 onto the stack	1
PUSH 3	PUSH 3 onto the stack	2
DUP	Duplicate the top element of the stack	3
SWAP	Swap the first two elements of the stack	4
MUL	Multiply the first two elements of the stack	5
DIV	Divide the first two elements of the stack	6
ADD	Add the first two elements on the stack	7

FIGURE 7.15: Sample instruction set encoding for the linear genetic programming example.

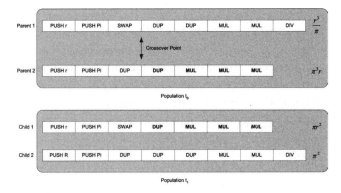

FIGURE 7.16: **Demonstrating the crossover genetic operator on two simple linear programs.**

higher the probability that they will be selected for recombination in the next generation.

The chromosome, or program to be evolved, is made up of genes, or individual instructions. The chromosome can also be of different lengths, assigned at creation, and then inherited during the evolution. We'll use a simple instruction set defined for the particular problem, as shown in Figure 7.15.

With this minimal number of instructions, we'll support computing a number of different types of functions (such as volume and area equations for two-and three-dimensional objects). Each of the instructions operates on the stack, either pushing a number to the stack, or manipulating the stack in some way.

Continuing with the GP algorithm, once two parents are selected, solutions are recombined with some small probability using the crossover and mutation operations. This process is shown below in Figure 7.16.

From Figure 7.16, we see how two unrelated programs can combine to produce a program to compute the area of a circle (child 1).

NOTE   *The architecture simulated here for GP is called a "zero-address" architecture. What makes this architecture unique is that it is a stack-focused architecture – there are no registers available. All arguments and processing occurs on the stack. This makes the instruction set very simple, which is ideal for evolving instruction sequences for complex operations.*

Let's look at one final example to fully understand the operation of these linear programs using a stack machine (see Figure 7.17). In this example, we have a simple four-instruction program (that computes the cube of the value at the top of the stack). The top of the figure represents the initial state before the program is executed. The instructions are shown at the right, with a pointer to the instruction last executed (with the instruction shown in bold). The stack is shown in the initial configuration with the value to be cubed (and a pointer to the next element that can be written).

The DUP instruction takes the top element of the stack and duplicates it (so that the first two elements of the stack will be the same). The MUL instruction multiples the first two elements of the stack, and then pushes the result back onto the stack (but consuming the initial two values). The result when all instructions have been executed is the cube of the initial value, stored at the top of the stack.

Remember that the representation is very important, and much care should be taken when designing it for the problem at hand. Since we'll be executing many of these programs during the evaluation phase of the algorithm (large population, many verification iterations), it must be simple and efficient. Let's now dig into the implementation to see how it works.

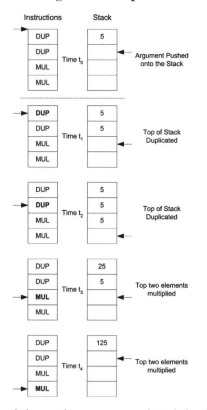

FIGURE 7.17: **Example instruction sequence and stack for the 'cube' program.**

Genetic Programming Implementation

Let's investigate an implementation of linear genetic programming to evolve the instruction sequence to solve a specific volume equation. Much of the implementation is shared with our existing genetic algorithm source, so we'll focus here on the core differences in the implementation (the chromosome representation, and the fitness calculation function).

The chromosome (potential program solution) is represented by the structure programs_t. This contains the number of instructions in the program (op_count) and the program itself (program). The fitness is the current fitness measure of the program (of op_count instructions). The two populations of program solutions is represented as the two-dimensional programs array. It's two dimensional because we need to represent the current and next generation (for the entire population size).

The full genetic programming implementation can be found on the CD-ROM at ./software/ch7/gp.c.

Finally, in Listing 7.7, is the list of legal instructions. Figure 7.15 shows the meanings of these instructions, and Figure 7.17 illustrates their use in a sample program.

Listing 7.7: **Program and population representation for the linear genetic programming example.**

```
#define NUM_INSTRUCTIONS 20
typedef struct {
  int       op_count;
  unsigned char program[NUM_INSTRUCTIONS];
  double    fitness;
} programs_t;
#define POPULATION_SIZE           2000
programs_t programs[2][POPULATION_SIZE];
#define PUSH_PI          0
#define PUSH_2           1
#define PUSH_3           2
#define DUP              3
#define SWAP             4
#define MUL              5
#define DIV              6
#define ADD              7
#define MAX_OPERATIONS   8
```

When defining an instruction set for genetic programming, design the instruction set around the problem, if possible. Specify the instructions that can contribute to the solution, rather than increasing the complexity with a large number of instructions that simply cloud the solution space.

Now let's look at the differences from our previous genetic algorithm example. The first difference is the method by which parent chromosomes are selected for recombination. In the previous example, we used roulette wheel selection, but in this example, we'll modify select_parent to provide a form of elitist selection (see Listing 7.8). We start at a random member and then work through the entire population looking for a member whose fitness is more than the average. When one is found, we simply return it (no probabilistic selection, other than beginning in a random location).

One advantage to this approach is that we can set the crossover and mutation probabilities high (to cover more of the search space) without much concern about losing existing good solutions.

Listing 7.8:   Choosing parents using an elitist selection algorithm.

```
int select_parent( int cur_pop )
{
  int i = RANDMAX(POPULATION_SIZE);
  int count = POPULATION_SIZE;
  double select=0.0;
  /* Step through each of the population's members */
  while (count--) {
    select = programs[cur_pop][i].fitness;
    /* Select this parent if its fitness is more than the average */
    if (select >= avg) return i;
    /* Check the next member of the population */
    if (++i >= POPULATION_SIZE) i = 0;
  }
  /* Nothing found greater than the average, return a random member */
  return( RANDMAX(POPULATION_SIZE) );
}
```

Finally, let's look at the fitness function. This function provides the simulation for the simple instruction set. Also within this function is the stack object from which the instructions will operate (see Figure 7.9). This function very simply operates as a virtual machine. It loops through the instructions, executing them given the data available on the stack. If the instruction is deemed illegal (overflows or underflows the stack), then the instruction is simply ignored, and we move on to the next instruction.

NOTE

Note that the loop iterates through the current program multiple times, to ensure it solves the equation for multiple sample values. We begin by pushing a random value onto the stack, and then executing each instruction serially. When the program is complete, we check the result and calculate a fitness value. This is based on there being one value left on the stack, and correctly calculating our sample equation (Eq 7.1).

Listing 7.9: Fitness function for the linear genetic programming example.

```
double compute_fitness( int cur_pop, int member )
{
  int i, instruction;
  int iteration = MAX_ITERATIONS;
  double fitness=0.0;
  double expected, d;
  stack_t stack;
  while (iteration--) {
    d = (double)RANDMAX(100)+RANDOM();
    expected = (PI * (d * d * d)) / 4.0;
    stack.index = 0;
    PUSH(stack, d);
    for (i = 0 ; i < programs[cur_pop][member].op_count ; i++) {
      /* Get the actual move from the moves array */
      instruction = programs[cur_pop][member].program[i];
      switch( instruction ) {
        case PUSH_PI:
          if (!IS_FULL(stack)) {
            PUSH(stack,PI);
          }
          break;
        case PUSH_2:
          if (!IS_FULL(stack)) {
            PUSH(stack,2.0);
          }
          break;
```

```
case PUSH_3:
 if (!IS_FULL(stack)) {
   PUSH(stack,3.0);
 }
 break;
case DUP:
 if (!IS_EMPTY(stack)) {
   double temp = POP(stack);
   PUSH(stack, temp);
   PUSH(stack, temp);
 }
 break;
case SWAP:
 if (stack.index >= 2) {
   double temp1 = POP(stack);
   double temp2 = POP(stack);
   PUSH(stack,temp1); PUSH(stack,temp2);
 }
 break;
case MUL:
 if (stack.index >= 2) {
   double temp1 = POP(stack);
   double temp2 = POP(stack);
   PUSH(stack, (temp1*temp2));
 }
 break;
case DIV:
 if (stack.index >= 2) {
   double temp1 = POP(stack);
   double temp2 = POP(stack);
   PUSH(stack, (temp1/temp2));
 }
 break;
case ADD:
 if (stack.index >= 2) {
   double temp1 = POP(stack);
   double temp2 = POP(stack);
   PUSH(stack, (temp1+temp2));
 }
 break;
```

```
      default:
        assert(0);
    }
  }
  /* Calculate the fitness */
  fitness += (1.0 / (double)stack.index);
  if (stack.stk[0] == expected) {
    fitness += 30.0;
    if (stack.index == 1) fitness += 10.0;
  }
}
fitness = fitness / (double)MAX_ITERATIONS;
return fitness;
}
```

The evaluation function that we're trying to solve in Listing 7.9 is the volume of a sphere (see Eq 7.1). There's a single variable for the equation, d, or the diameter of the sphere. This value is pushed onto the stack and the result should be a single value V (as defined by Eq 7.1).

$$V = \frac{\pi d^3}{6} \qquad \text{(Eq 7.1)}$$

Considering the equation, and some knowledge of the operation of the stack machine, one simple hand-crafted solution to the problem is:

PUSH 2, PUSH 3, MUL, SWAP, DUP, DUP, MUL, MUL, PUSH PI, MUL, DIV

which is a reasonable solution to the problem, but evolution doesn't know anything about the equation, and does a better job of finding solutions (squeezing one instruction away). Here are a number of other solutions that were evolved by the linear genetic programmer:

DUP, DUP, PUSH 2, PUSH 3, MUL, PUSH PI, DIV, MUL, MUL, MUL

DUP, SWAP, DUP, PUSH PI, MUL, MUL, PUSH 3, PUSH 2, MUL, DIV, SWAP, DIV

DUP, DUP, MUL, MUL, PUSH 2, DIV, PUSH 3, MUL, PUSH PI, DIV

DUP, DUP, PUSH 3, DUP, SWAP, ADD, DIV, DIV, PUSH PI, DIV, MUL

Note in the second example, that there's a superfluous instruction (SWAP, shown in italics). This instruction doesn't help in solving the equation, but it doesn't hurt either. The presence of this instruction has some biological plausibility, which should be mentioned. Molecular biologists have discovered what's called 'junk' DNA (or non-functional sequences of DNA) that are called introns. Researchers in genetic algorithms have actually found that the introduction of introns can actually improve the ability of genetic algorithms to solve complex problems. [Levenick 1991]

Genetic programming, in this case, linear genetic programming, is a useful metaphor for the evolution of instruction sequences for simple to moderately complex functions. It's not only useful to evolve highly optimized functions for specific problems, but can also be useful to study new and novel ways to solve problems.

EVOLUTIONARY STRATEGIES (ES)

Evolutionary Strategies (ES) are one of the oldest of the evolutionary algorithms, and remain quite useful. It's very similar to the genetic algorithm, but instead of focusing on binary strings (as did the original genetic algorithm), evolutionary strategies focus on the optimization of real-value parameters.

The evolutionary strategies algorithm was developed (in parallel to genetic algorithms) during the 1960s at the Technical University of Berlin (TUB), Germany by Rechenberg and Schwefel. Evolutionary strategies were initially designed to solve fluid dynamics problems through simulations. Their initial experiments utilized a population of one (parent + offspring, choosing the best to propagate further), since the optimization was done manually, without access to a computer to simulate the experiments. Even with this simple approach (which later evolved into a population-based technique) their results were successful.

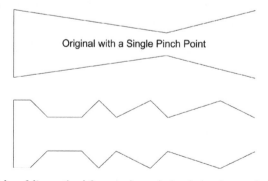

FIGURE 7.18: Schwefel's method for nozzle optimization using evolutionary strategies.

As the evolutionary strategy continued to be developed, it was successfully used by Schwefel to optimize the shape of a supersonic two-phase flashing nozzle. [EvoNews 1999] To optimize the shape of nozzles, Schwefel used an encoding that defined the diameter of the nozzle at various points across the tube (see Figure 7.18).

The original evolutionary strategy used a single parent, and produced a single child. This is called a $(1 + 1)$ strategy (one parent produces a single offspring). In general terms, these strategies are defined as $(\mu + \lambda)$, where μ parents are selected and λ offspring result. In this strategy, the population of $\mu + \lambda$ members all compete for survival. Another approach is referred to as (μ, λ), where μ parents are selected and λ offspring result. Only the λ offspring compete in the next generation, the μ parents are completely replaced in the next generation.

Evolutionary Strategies Algorithm

One of the unique aspects of the evolutionary strategies algorithm, and what makes the algorithm useful today, is that it's relatively simple to implement. Traditionally, the algorithm isn't as simple to understand as the genetic algorithm, but the approach that will be explored here will provide the basic concepts, and a couple of mutation simplifications proposed by Schwefel himself.

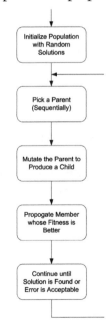

FIGURE 7.19:   **The fundamental evolutionary strategies algorithm.**

The flow of the evolutionary strategies algorithm is shown in Figure 7.19. We'll first walk through the high-level flow and then explore the details. The process begins with the initialization of the population. Each of the members of the population consists of a vector of real-values that represent the problem itself.

> NOTE
>
> *The evolutionary strategies algorithm is called a phenotypic algorithm, where the genetic algorithm is a genotypic algorithm. A phenotypic algorithm represents parameters of the system as the solution, where a genotypic algorithm represents an abstraction of the solution. Take for example, the modeling of the behavior of a system. In the phenotypic approach, the solutions would represent the parameter of the behavior itself, but in the genotypic approach, the solution would represent an intermediate representation of the behavior.*

The next step is producing the next generation by selecting parent solutions and generation offspring. We'll explore the simplest case of selection in ES where each parent has the potential to move into the next generation. Each parent is selected and an offspring generated given a mutation. The parent and child are then compared, and whichever has the better fitness is moved to the next generation. This process continues for each member of the current population. The algorithm can then terminate (if a solution is discovered), or continue for some number of generations.

Let's now explore what it means to mutate a parent to create an offspring. When we create random numbers (for example, with our RANDOM() function), the number is just as likely to be small as it is large (uniformly distributed). What we really want is primarily small random numbers, with an occasional larger random number. This allows the small random numbers to "tweak" the solution, with the larger random numbers for extending the solution in the fitness landscape. These types of random numbers are called normally distributed with an expectation rate of zero. To produce these random numbers, we first calculate two uniformly distributed random numbers (u1 and u2), and then use Eq 7.2 and 7.3 to produce the normally distributed random numbers.

$$z_1 = \sqrt{-2\ln(u_1)}\ \sin(2\pi u_2) \qquad \text{(Eq 7.2)}$$

$$z_2 = \sqrt{-2\ln(u_1)}\ \cos(2\pi u_2) \qquad \text{(Eq 7.3)}$$

One advantageous modification to our mutation scheme is to further limit the size of the changes that occur over time (similar to what occurs

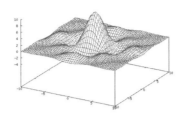

FIGURE 7.20: Plot of the sample function to be maximized by the evolutionary strategy.

in simulated annealing). To support this, we can use the current iteration ($iter_{cur}$) and max iteration ($iter_{max}$) to identify a multiplier, as shown in Equation 7.4).

$$m = \frac{(iter_{max} - iter_{cur})}{iter_{max}} \qquad \text{(Eq 7.4)}$$

Evolutionary Strategies Implementation

Let's now have a look at an implementation of evolutionary strategies for a function optimization problem. The goal of this problem is to find the parameters that maximize the function (result in the greatest value). We'll use the function shown in Eq 7.5, which is shown graphically in Figure 7.20.

$$z = (\sin(x)/x)*(\sin(y)/y)*\Phi \qquad \text{(Eq 7.5)}$$

Let's begin with a description of the fundamental structures that will be used by the evolutionary strategies algorithm. The two core elements of the evolutionary strategies is the size of the population, and the number of iterations that will occur (which is equivalent to the number of generations to be created). The solution_t typedef specifies the arguments (x and y) and the result (fitness). We'll create a two-dimensional array of these solution_t types, with the first dimension used to define the generation (which operates in a ping-pong fashion), and the second dimension used to define the members of the population.

Listing 7.10:   Fundamental structures for the evolutionary strategies algorithm.

```
#define MAX_POPULATION        50
#define MAX_ITERATIONS        20
```

```
typedef struct {
  double x;
  double y;
  double fitness;
} solution_t;
solution_t solutions[2][MAX_POPULATION];
```

The main loop for the evolutionary strategy is shown in Listing 7.11. We initialize the population with a random set of solutions using initialize_population, and then calculate the population's fitness with compute_population_fitness. We then iterate the maximum number iterations previously defined by MAX_ITERATIONS. A call to select_and_recombine creates the next generation of solutions, after which, we switch the current population (as defined by cur_pop) to the next. After evaluating the fitness of the entire population (via compute_population_fitness), we continue the process until the maximum number of iterations is reached.

Listing 7.11:   The main loop for the evolutionary strategy

```
int main( void )
{
  int cur_pop = 0;
  int i = 0;
  RANDINIT();
  initialize_population( cur_pop );
  compute_population_fitness( cur_pop );
  for (i = 0 ; i < MAX_ITERATIONS ; i++) {
    select_and_recombine( cur_pop, i );
    cur_pop = (cur_pop == 0) ? 1 : 0;
    compute_population_fitness( cur_pop );
    printf("%g %g %g\n", min, avg, max);
  }
  find_and_emit_best( cur_pop );
  return 0;
}
```

The core of the evolutionary strategy is in the selection and recombination of candidate solutions (see the function select_and_recombine, Listing 7.12). This function first determines which population index is the next generation (new_pop) and the current multiplier, which is used to scale any changes in the mutation (see Eq 7.4). We then walk through the entire current population (as passed in, pop).

For each member of the current population, we begin by generating our normally distributed random numbers (using Eqs 7.2 and 7.3). We then mutate the parent to create the offspring into the next generation (in an elitist fashion). If the offspring is not as fit as the parent, then the parent solution is copied to the next generation (overwriting the generated offspring). This process continues for each member of the existing generation.

Listing 7.12: Creating the next generation of the population.

```
void select_and_recombine( int pop, int iteration )
{
  int i, new_pop;
  double multiplier;
  double u1, u2, z1, z2, fitness;
  /* Figure out which population index is the next generation */
  new_pop = (pop == 0) ? 1 : 0;
  /* Equation 7.4 */
  multiplier = ((double)MAX_ITERATIONS - (double)iteration) /
                        (double)MAX_ITERATIONS;
  for (i = 0 ; i < MAX_POPULATION ; i++) {
    u1 = RANDOM(); u2 = RANDOM();
    /* Equation 7.2 */
    z1 = (sqrt(-2.0 * log(u1)) * sin( (2.0 * PI * u2))) * multiplier;
    /* Equation 7.3 */
    z2 = (sqrt(-2.0 * log(u1)) * cos( (2.0 * PI * u2))) * multiplier;
    /* Create the child as the mutated parent */
    solutions[new_pop][i].x = bound( solutions[pop][i].x + z1 );
    solutions[new_pop][i].y = bound( solutions[pop][i].y + z2 );
    fitness = compute_fitness( &solutions[new_pop][i] );
    /* If the child is less fit than parent, move the parent to child */
    if (fitness < solutions[pop][i].fitness) {
      solutions[new_pop][i].x = solutions[pop][i].x;
      solutions[new_pop][i].y = solutions[pop][i].y;
    }
  }
  return;
}
```

Note in Listing 7.12, the bound function is used to bound the values from -20 to 20 for both x and y.

Finally, we present the function to calculate the fitness of a given candidate solution. Using Eq 7.5, the function is evaluated, stored, and returned.

Listing 7.13:   Computing the fitness of a candidate solution.

```
double compute_fitness( solution_t *sol_p )
{
  double x,y;
  double fitness;
  /* Cache the arguments to simplify the equation */
  x = sol_p->x;
  y = sol_p->y;
  /* Equation 7.5 */
  fitness =
    sol_p->fitness =
        (sin(x)/x) * (sin(y)/y) * (double)10.0;
  return fitness;
}
```

The evolutionary strategies algorithm implementation can be found on the CD-ROM at ./software/ch7/es.c.

Let's now look at the algorithm in action. Note that the program will emit the fitness values (minimum, average, and maximum), for each generation. As can be seen in Listing 7.14, six generations are all that are required to get to within 90% of the maximum. The algorithm then tunes for 14 generations (to get within 99.9% of the maximum). Note that in the results, steps are taken in maximum fitness, where the maximum fitness appears dormant, and then a higher fit member is found. This has been observed in a number of evolutionary algorithms, and tied biologically to what's called *punctuated equilibrium*.

In the theory of punctuated equilibrium (from evolutionary biology), it has been found that reproducing species often show no evolutionary change through their lifetime. But when evolutionary change does occur, its effects are clearly seen in the ability of the new species to survive and adapt to its environment.

Listing 7.14:   Sample execution of the evolutionary strategies algorithm.

```
$ ./es
-1.86534 0.221798 3.15964
```

```
-1.57037 0.360016 3.15964
-0.194702 0.805424 8.64
-0.0959031 0.961668 8.64
-0.0959031 1.15622 8.7512
-0.0959031 1.24244 9.06489
-0.00876197 1.35238 9.69174
-0.00179016 1.3965 9.96464
-0.00179016 1.50873 9.96464
0.049577 1.54039 9.96464
0.049577 1.59179 9.96464
0.0596969 1.62029 9.96464
0.0596969 1.65329 9.98932
0.0596969 1.70359 9.98932
0.0596969 1.71321 9.98932
0.0596969 1.7309 9.98932
0.0596969 1.74583 9.98932
0.0596969 1.75184 9.98932
0.0596969 1.75429 9.98932
0.0596969 1.75759 9.99414
Best is [0.0561596, -0.0190792] = 9.99414
$
```

DIFFERENTIAL EVOLUTION (DE)

Differential Evolution (DE) is a more recent stochastic population-based evolutionary method (introduced by Storn and Price in 1996). It follows the standard evolutionary algorithm flow (mutation, recombine, select), but has some significant differences in how mutation and recombination is performed.

The fundamental idea behind DE is the use of vector differences (choosing two randomly selected vectors, and then taking their difference as a means to perturb the vector and probe the search space). The vector difference is then added to a third randomly selected vector, making the approach self-organizing.

DE also includes two tunable parameters, F (the weighting factor) and CR (the crossover probability). The weighting factor is applied to the difference vector. The crossover probability specifies the probability that multi-point crossover will occur for the initial vector and the resulting target vector.

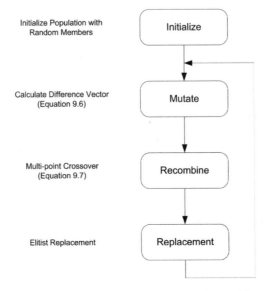

FIGURE 7.21: High-level flow of the differential evolution algorithm with noted differences for DE.

Differential Evolution Algorithm

The Differential Evolution algorithm is simple, but has some additional complexities in the number of activities that occur for recombination. Let's start with a big picture of the DE algorithm, and then explore the details of mutation and recombination.

The high-level flow for DE is shown in Figure 7.21. This is the fundamental evolutionary algorithm flow, but the details differ for mutation, recombination, and replacement.

There are a number of variations for DE, but we'll focus here on the nominal approach. After initialization, each of the members of the population undergoes mutation and recombination. Once recombination occurs, the new member is compared to the old member, and whichever fitness is better is moved to the next generation (replacement policy).

With our member in the current generation $(x_{i,G})$ we select three uniformly random members from the current generation that are unique $(x_{i,G} \mathrel{!=} x_{r1,G} \mathrel{!=} x_{r2,G} \mathrel{!=} x_{r3,G})$. Using these member vectors, we create what's known as a mutant vector, or donor vector, $(v_{i,G+1})$ in the next generation using the weighted difference of two of the vectors (r2 and r3) summed with the third vector (r1). This is shown in Eq 7.6.

$$(v_{i,G+1} = x_{r1,G} + F(x_{r2,G} - x_{r3,G}) \qquad \text{(Eq 7.6)}$$

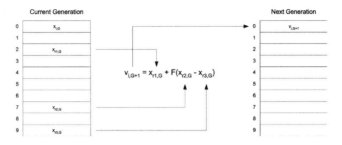

FIGURE 7.22:   **Mutation process in differential evolution.**

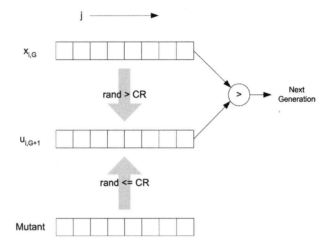

FIGURE 7.23:   **The DE crossover and replacement process.**

This new mutant vector has completed the mutation stage and is now ready for recombination. This process is shown graphically in Figure 7.22.

In this stage, we'll perform a multi-point crossover of the mutant vector $(v_{i,G+1})$ with our original vector from the current generation $(x_{i,G})$. This constitutes using elements from our mutant vector with the original member for fitness evaluation. This process is shown in Eq 7.7.

$$u_{j,i,G+1} = \begin{cases} f\,(rand \le CR) \; than \; (v_{j,i,G+1}) \\ f\,(rand > CR) \; than \; (v_{j,i,G}) \end{cases} \qquad \text{(Eq 7.7)}$$

The crossover process is performed on each element of the vector, with the resulting vector candidate being provided to the replacement process (see Figure 7.23). The current member and mutant are randomly permitted to contribute to the new vector. In the end, whichever vector has the greater fitness (new vector, or vector from the current generation) is permitted into the next generation.

Let's now explore a sample implementation of DE for function maximization. For comparative purposes, we'll use the function shown in Figure 7.20.

Differential Evolution Implementation

Let's begin with a discussion of how the DE objects will be represented in a program (see Listing 7.15). The fundamental vector type (vec_t) will be used to represent the vectors of real-values to be optimized. This is integrated into our member object (member_t), which also includes the fitness measure.

NOTE ▶ *Note that the population is two-dimensional in size. The first dimension represents the generation (two are used because we'll implement a ping-pong generation, where at any one time, the index represents the current generation, and the opposite index represents the next generation).*

We also maintain a best member_t that keeps the best member found so far (for housekeeping purposes).

We also define the tunable parameters here, F (the mutation factor) and CR (the crossover probability). These parameters can be tuned for the particular problem at hand, but are reasonable at their current levels for this optimization problem.

Listing 7.15:   DE types and symbolics.

```
#define MAX_ELEMENTS      2
typedef double vec_t[MAX_ELEMENTS];
#define MAX_POPULATION    10
#define MAX_ITERATIONS    100
typedef struct {
  vec_t args;
  double fitness;
} member_t;
member_t population[2][MAX_POPULATION];
member_t best = {{0.0,0.0},0.0};
#define F      ((double)0.5)
#define CR     ((double)0.8)
```

The main loop for DE is shown in Listing 7.16. This function implements the outer loop to the DE algorithm. It begins by initializing the current population (cur_pop), and then initializing the random number generator. The population is then initialized with a call to init_population, which not only initializes the vectors for each member, but also computes their initial fitness values (with a call to compute_fitness).

With initialization complete, we enter the DE algorithm. We'll provide no exit criteria, and instead simply execute the algorithm for some maximum number of iterations (MAX_ITERATIONS). Each iteration consists of performing the DE core algorithm (select_and_recombine) and then emitting the best member found so far (as stored in the best structure).

Listing 7.16:   The DE main loop.

```
int main()
{
  int i;
  int cur_pop = 0;
  RANDINIT();
  init_population( cur_pop );
  for (i = 0 ; i < MAX_ITERATIONS ; i++) {
    cur_pop = select_and_recombine( cur_pop );
    printf("Best fitness = %g\n", best.fitness);
  }
  return 0;
}
```

The core of the DE algorithm is implemented in the select_and_recombine function (see Listing 7.17). We begin by determining the index of the next generation (next_pop) and then initializing the best structure fitness to zero (in order to find the current best member in the population).

The next step is to iterate through each of the members of the population to create a new candidate solution. We cache the current index to the next generation member (mutant) to increase the readability of the code. Next, we create three random numbers (r1, r2, and r3) which are all unique, and differ from each other and the current member index (i).

The mutant vector is created next using Eq 7.6. Using the three members from the current population (as defined by our three random numbers), the mutant vector is created. With Eq 7.7, the crossover process is performed using the current member from the current generation, and the mutant vector. When complete, the fitness is computed with a call to compute_fitness.

At this point, we have a mutant vector with its fitness calculated. We compare the fitness of the mutant with the fitness of the current member, and whichever are greater moves into the next generation (the replacement process). We follow this with some housekeeping to keep track of the best vector found so far (emitted in the main function).

Listing 7.17:   The DE process of mutation, recombination, and replacement.

```
int select_and_recombine( int pop )
{
  int next_pop = (pop == 0) ? 1 : 0;
  int i, j;
  member_t *mutant;
  int r1, r2, r3;
  best.fitness = 0.0;
  for (i = 0 ; i < MAX_POPULATION ; i++) {
    /* Cache the target vector in the next generation */
    mutant = &population[next_pop][i];
    /* Calculate three random numbers (r1, r2, r3) which are all
     * unique.
     */
    do {
      r1 = RANDMAX(MAX_POPULATION);
    } while (r1 == i);
    do {
      r2 = RANDMAX(MAX_POPULATION);
      r3 = RANDMAX(MAX_POPULATION);
    } while ((r3 == r2) || (r3 == r1) || (r2 == r1) ||
        (r3 == i) || (r2 == i));
    /* Given the candidate member, and our random members, form a
     * 'mutant member' (Equation 7.6).
     */
    for (j = 0 ; j < MAX_ELEMENTS ; j++) {
      mutant->args[j] = population[pop][r1].args[j] +
              (F * (population[pop][r2].args[j] -
                  population[pop][r3].args[j]));
    }
    /* Perform crossover of 'mutant' vector with the current generation
     * member (Equation 7.7)
     */
```

```
   for (j = 0 ; j < MAX_ELEMENTS ; j++) {
     if (RANDOM() < CR) mutant->args[j] = population[pop][i].args[j];
   }
   mutant->fitness = compute_fitness( mutant );
   /* If the original member has a greater fitness than the mutant, copy
    * the original member over the mutant in the next generation.
    */
   if (population[pop][i].fitness > mutant->fitness) {
     for (j = 0 ; j < MAX_ELEMENTS ; j++) {
       mutant->args[j] = population[pop][i].args[j];
     }
     mutant->fitness = population[pop][i].fitness;
   }
   /* Housekeeping -- save the best member */
   if (mutant->fitness > best.fitness) {
     for (j = 0 ; j < MAX_ELEMENTS ; j++) {
       best.args[j] = mutant->args[j];
     }
     best.fitness = mutant->fitness;
   }
 }
 return next_pop;
}
```

Finally, the `compute_fitness` function is used to calculate the fitness of a member of the population. The pointer to the current member is passed in (of type `member_t`), and the coordinates are extracted to enhance readability. We bound the coordinates to the constraints of the function (the area that we intend to maximize) and then use Eq 7.5 to calculate and return the fitness.

Listing 7.18:   Calculating the fitness of a DE member.

```
double compute_fitness( member_t *member_p )
{
  double x,y;
  double fitness;
  /* Cache the coordinates to simply the function. */
  x = member_p->args[0];
  y = member_p->args[1];
```

```
/* Bound the location of the particle */
if ((x < -10.0) || (x > 10.0) ||
   (y < -10.0) || (y > 10.0)) fitness = 0.0;
else {
  /* Equation 7.5 */
  fitness =
     (sin(x)/x) * (sin(y)/y) * (double)10.0;
}
return fitness;
}
```

The differential evolution algorithm implementation can be found on the CD-ROM at ./software/ch7/de.c.

The algorithm does a very good job of quickly converging on a solution. Listing 7.19 shows a sample run of the DE implementation. In a very short time, the algorithm moves from poor solutions to an almost optimal solution (10.0).

Listing 7.19:   Sample run of the DE implementation.

```
$ ./de.exe
Best fitness = 0.662495
Best fitness = 0.662495
Best fitness = 0.963951
Best fitness = 3.66963
Best fitness = 4.8184
Best fitness = 4.8184
Best fitness = 5.54331
Best fitness = 5.54331
Best fitness = 7.48501
Best fitness = 7.48501
Best fitness = 9.78371
Best fitness = 9.78371
Best fitness = 9.97505
Best fitness = 9.97505
Best fitness = 9.97505
Best fitness = 9.99429
Best fitness = 9.99429
Best fitness = 9.99429
Best fitness = 9.99429
```

Best fitness = 9.99568
Best fitness = 9.99646
Best fitness = 9.99646
Best fitness = 9.9981
Best fitness = 9.9981
Best fitness = 9.9981
Best fitness = 9.99837
Best fitness = 9.99974
Best fitness = 9.99974
Best fitness = 9.99984
Best fitness = 9.99984
Best fitness = 9.99998
Best fitness = 9.99998
Best fitness = 9.99998
Best fitness = 9.99998
$

The prior run is shown plotted in Figure 7.24. As shown, the algorithm is quickly able to converge and then fine-tune the result to the near optimal solution.

While there's not yet a proof of convergence for the DE algorithm, it has been shown to be effective on a wide range of optimization problems. The original authors also found in a study that the DE algorithm was more efficient than both the genetic algorithm and simulated annealing.

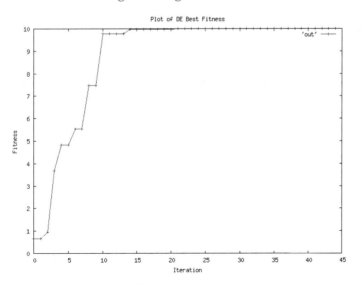

FIGURE 7.24: **Best fitness plot for the differential evolution implementation (population size 100).**

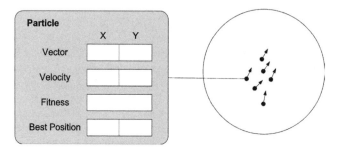

FIGURE 7.25: Anatomy of a particle in a larger storm.

PARTICLE SWARM OPTIMIZATION (PSO)

The last population-based algorithm that we'll explore in this chapter is called Particle Swarm Optimization (or PSO). PSO simulates a collection of particles that swarm with one another within an N-dimensional space (where N is the size of the solution vector). A very simple set of equations is used to implement a flocking behavior, which gives the particles some amount of freedom to search the N-dimensional search space, but also some constraints to exhibit flocking behavior by tracking the particle that has the current best performance.

A particle within the swarm exists as an object that contains a vector (with the same dimensionality as the solution space), a velocity (for each element of the dimensionality vector, resulting in the vector velocity), the fitness (for the current vector), and a vector representing the best position found so far (see Figure 7.25).

Particles in the swarm are influenced by two unique factors. The first is the best position (vector) of the particle itself, and the second is the global best position found by any particle in the swarm. Therefore, a particle is influenced by its best position, and also the best position of the swarm. The amount of influence of each is controllable, as we'll see in the discussion of the algorithm itself.

Let's now dig into the PSO algorithm, to understand how particles swarm, and the equations for swarm influence.

Particle Swarm Algorithm

The particle swarm optimization algorithm is very simple to understand, but is also quite effective for a variety of optimization problems. This section will explore the PSO algorithm in sufficient detail to implement a general function maximizer.

The use of particle swarms as an optimization technique is recent compared to the other evolutionary algorithms discussed thus far. The social behavior of birds flocking and fish schooling inspired Eberhart and Kennedy to create what they refer to as *swarm intelligence*.

The basic flow of the PSO is as follows. First, a population of random vectors and velocities are created as the swarm of particles. Initially, these particles are randomly placed, and each move in random directions, but as the algorithm is performed, swarming behavior emerges as the particles probe the multi-dimensional surface.

With our random set of particles, the fitness of each is evaluated and stored as the current fitness. We also keep track of a global best particle that has the best overall fitness. This particle, to some extent, is the center of the swarm. Note that we also keep track of the personal best vector for the particle, which is stored as the best position (see Figure 7.20). At this point, termination criteria could be applied. If a satisfactory solution is found, or some maximum number of iterations has been performed, the algorithm could exit, emitting the current global best solution found so far.

If the algorithm has not yet reached its termination criteria, the velocity of the particles is updated, and then each particle's position is updated (given its current position and current velocity). The process then continues by evaluating each particle's fitness, and checking our termination criteria.

Calculating the next position of an N-dimensional particle is shown in Eq 7.8. Each vector element (X_n) of particle (P) accumulates the velocity element (V_n) scaled by the time interval (t) over which the particle is to be moved.

$$P_{X_n} = P_{X_n} + P_{V_n} * \Delta t \qquad \text{(Eq 7.8)}$$

Recall that we also update the velocity after the particle is moved. As shown in Eq 7.9, there are two independent influences over the change in velocity, the current global best particle (defined as G_{X_n}), and the personal best for this particle (PB_{X_n}). For each term, there exists what's called an acceleration constant (c_1, c_2), which is used to determine how much influence the global or personal best solution has over the velocity equation.

To add some variability to the equation, we also include two uniform random numbers (R_1, R_2), which apply to the terms. How these uniform random numbers are generated provides some emphasis to one term over another (global vs personal best). The goal is to probe the solution space with greater variability.

$$P_{V_n} = P_{V_n} + (C_1 * R_1 * (G_{X_n} - P_{X_n})) + (c_2 * R_2 * (PB_{V_n} - P_{X_n})) \quad \text{(Eq 7.9)}$$

Using these very simple equations (Eq 7.8 for particle movement and Eq 7.9 for velocity adjustment), the PSO algorithm is able to minimize or maximize functions with an efficiency similar to genetic algorithms or evolutionary strategies.

Particle Swarm Implementation

As shown in the algorithm discussion, the implementation of particle swarm optimization is simple. Let's begin our discussion with a description of the representation of particles and the swarm in software.

In this implementation, we'll encode a solution as a two-dimensional object, with the fitness defined as the function of the vector arguments (two in this example, representing the x and y arguments). For the fitness function, we'll use the function shown in Figure 7.20 (as demonstrated by the evolutionary strategies algorithm).

Listing 7.20 provides the fundamental types and symbolics for the particle swarm optimization implementation. The most fundamental type is the vec_t, which defines our vector (in this example, it specifies an x and y coordinate). This vector type is used to represent the coordinate position (coord), the current velocity, and the personal best vector coordinates (best_coord). Structure particle_t collects these together as a single object to represent the entire particle. The particle swarm (of number **MAX_ PARTICLES**) is represented by the array particles. The particle_t type is also used to represent the current global best (gbest).

Listing 7.20:   Particle swarm types and symbolics.

```
typedef struct {
  double x;
  double y;
} vec_t;
typedef struct {
  vec_t coord;
  vec_t velocity;
  double fitness;
  vec_t best_coord;
  double fitness_best;
} particle_t;
#define MAX_PARTICLES        10
#define MAX_ITERATIONS       30
```

```
particle_t particles[MAX_PARTICLES];
particle_t gbest;
```

The flow of the particle swarm algorithm is implemented in the main function (see Listing 7.21). This initializes and seeds the random number generator (RANDINIT) and the initializes the particle population with random locations and velocities. The loop then iterates for the maximum number of iterations (MAX_ITERATIONS). For each iteration, each particle in the swarm is updated through a call to update_particle. After all particles in the swarm are updated, the current global best particle (gbest) is emitted so that the swarm's progress can be tracked.

Listing 7.21:   The particle swarm optimization main loop.

```c
int main( )
{
  int i, j;
  RANDINIT();
  init_population();
  for (i = 0 ; i < MAX_ITERATIONS ; i++) {
    for (j = 0 ; j < MAX_PARTICLES ; j++) {
      update_particle( &particles[j] );
    }
    printf("Current Best: %g/%g = %g\n",
        gbest.coord.x, gbest.coord.y, gbest.fitness);
  }
  return 0;
}
```

The core of the particle swarm optimization algorithm is provided in the update_particle function (see Listing 7.22). The function provides a number of capabilities, but begins with the update of the particle's position using Eq 7.6. With the particle's change in location, we calculate the new fitness of the particle with a call to compute_fitness. Next, using Eq 7.7, the velocity vector for the particle is updated (given the particle's personal best position and the position of the global best position).

Finally, the function performs some housekeeping to maintain the best positions. We first check to see if the fitness for the particle is better than the personal best fitness. If it is, we store this within the particle. If the particle's personal best has been updated, we check to see if it's better than the global best position. If so, we store this into the gbest particle.

Listing 7.22: Updating particle positions and velocities.

```
void update_particle( particle_t *particle_p )
{
  /* Update the particle's position (Equation 7.8) */
  particle_p->coord.x += (particle_p->velocity.x * dt);
  particle_p->coord.y += (particle_p->velocity.y * dt);
  /* Evaluate the particle's fitness */
  particle_p->fitness = compute_fitness( &particle_p->coord );
  /* Update the velocity vector (Equation 7.9) */
  particle_p->velocity.x +=
    ( (c1 * RANDOM() * (gbest.coord.x - particle_p->coord.x)) +
      (c2 * RANDOM() * (particle_p->best_coord.x - particle_p->coord.x))
  );
  particle_p->velocity.y +=
    ( (c1 * RANDOM() * (gbest.coord.y - particle_p->coord.y)) +
      (c2 * RANDOM() * (particle_p->best_coord.y - particle_p->coord.y))
  );
  /* If the fitness is better than the personal best, then save it. */
  if (particle_p->fitness > particle_p->fitness_best) {
    particle_p->fitness_best = particle_p->fitness;
    particle_p->best_coord.x = particle_p->coord.x;
    particle_p->best_coord.y = particle_p->coord.y;
    /* If the fitness is better than the global best, then save it. */
    if (particle_p->fitness_best > gbest.fitness) {
      gbest.fitness = particle_p->fitness_best;
      gbest.coord.x = particle_p->coord.x;
      gbest.coord.y = particle_p->coord.y;
    }
  }
  return;
}
```

The fitness function (compute_fitness) accepts a vector input, and extracts the elements of the vector for use in Eq 7.5 (see the previous discussion on the evolutionary strategies algorithm). Note that the bounds of the function are set to -10 to 10 for both axes. In the event the position falls outside of this box, a zero fitness is returned (see Listing 7.23).

Listing 7.23: Calculating the fitness of a particle.

```
double compute_fitness( vec_t *vec_p )
{
  double x,y;
  double fitness;
  /* Cache the coordinates to simply the function. */
  x = vec_p->x;
  y = vec_p->y;
  /* Bound the location of the particle */
  if ((x < -10.0) || (x > 10.0) ||
      (y < -10.0) || (y > 10.0)) fitness = 0.0;
  else {
    /* Equation 7.5 */
    fitness =
        (sin(x)/x) * (sin(y)/y) * (double)10.0;
  }
  return fitness;
}
```

The particle swarm optimization algorithm implementation can be found on the CD-ROM at ./software/ch7/ps.c.

Let's now look at the implementation in action. The implementation emits the current global best particle as it iterates (see Listing 7.24).

Listing 7.24: Sample output of the particle swarm implementation.

```
$ ./ps
Current Best: -9.13847 -1.40457 0.216992
Current Best: 0.9244 1.22842 6.62169
Current Best: 0.0934527 1.17927 7.82673
Current Best: 0.10666 1.17463 7.83906
Current Best: 0.119866 1.16999 7.85087
Current Best: 0.133073 1.16535 7.86217
Current Best: 0.14628 1.16071 7.87295
Current Best: 0.159487 1.15607 7.8832
Current Best: 0.172693 1.15143 7.89293
...
Current Best: -0.0890025 0.0432563 9.98369
Current Best: -0.0890025 0.0432563 9.98369
```

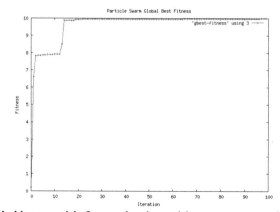

FIGURE 7.26:   Global best particle fitness showing quick convergence and then solution tuning with slowing velocities.

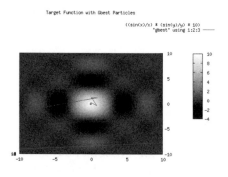

FIGURE 7.27:   Objective function with the global best particles overlaid.

Current Best: 0.016041 -0.0338574 9.99766
Current Best: 0.016041 -0.0338574 9.99766
Current Best: 0.0043322 -0.00436827 9.99994
$

As shown in Figure 7.26, the global best fitness converges very quickly to a solution (at around 70 iterations). The particle swarm is able to find a good solution rather quickly, but then tends to orbit this position due to its high velocity. But as the velocity equations slow down the particle swarm, the particles are able to fine-tune in order to find a better solution.

We can better visualize this process by looking at the objective function surface with the global best particles overlaid (see Figure 7.27). In this figure, we see the fitness of the function surface (the lighter the color, the better the fitness). The particle shows a very quick convergence onto a reasonable solution, and then fine-tunes at this peak to find the best solution. Note that what's shown here is the global best particle (found by the entire swarm of particles), and not the swarm of particles themselves.

The algorithm can be tuned by the two acceleration parameters (c_1 and c_2). These parameters determine how much influence the personal best vector and the global best vector have over the particle's trajectory. Recall that the velocity equation is used to change the velocity toward the particle's best position, or the global best position. This acceleration also includes a random element, to support probing the surface of the objective function in the hopes of escaping local minima.

Particle swarm optimization is another useful optimization method that is very biologically plausible. Like most other evolutionary methods, the PSO

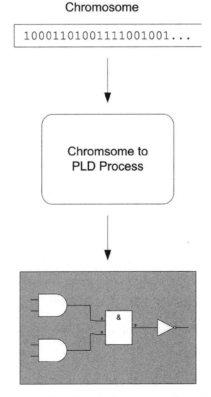

FIGURE 7.28: **Demonstration of evolution process from chromosome to PLD.**

relies on a population of candidate solutions to find the best solution. As can be seen from the sample implementation, PSO is simple, computationally inexpensive, and effective for function optimization.

EVOLVABLE HARDWARE

The use of evolutionary algorithms to generate hardware has been used in a similar way as GP is used to evolve software. Hardware evolution ranges from simple circuit design (such as for analog filters), or more complex products such as evolving the architecture for Programmable Logic Arrays (PLA, or Programmable Logic Device, PLD).

Evolving hardware solutions has been restricted to toy problems, but research in this area is promising. Nevertheless, hardware evolution does have its problems. For example, evolving circuits to problems tends to result in solutions that are difficult or impossible to understand. Evolution has no understanding of aesthetics or readability, and evolution commonly finds shortcuts that make their understanding difficult. The circuits found through evolution may not always be tolerant of noise or temperature, making their deployment difficult. In the end, using designs that are evolved commonly requires greater testing to ensure that all variability has been explored in the resulting design.

CHAPTER SUMMARY

While evolutionary algorithms are not new, you'll find continued research and even new algorithms being developed today (for example, differential evolution and swarm intelligence). Evolutionary algorithms borrow concepts from Darwinian natural selection as a means to evolve solutions to problems, choosing from more fit individuals to propagate to future generations. In this chapter we explored a number of evolutionary and biologically-inspired algorithms. After an introduction to evolutionary algorithms, we presented the genetic algorithm which is at the core of most evolutionary algorithms. Next, we explored genetic programming, an evolutionary means to generate code sequences. We then reviewed one of the original evolutionary methods, evolutionary strategies. Next, we reviewed the new method of differential evolution, and finished with a review of particle swarm optimization (a biologically plausible optimization method).

REFERENCES

[Banzhaf 1998] Banzhaf, W., Nordin, P., Keller, R.E., Francone, F.D., *Genetic Programming: An Introduction: On the Automatic Evolution of Computer Programs and Its Applications*, Morgan Kaufmann, 1998.

[EvoNews 1999] "Professor Hans-Paul Schwefel talks to EvoNews." 1999. Available online at: http://evonet.lri.fr/evoweb/news_events/news_features/article.php?id=5

[Fogel 1966] Fogel, L.J., Owens, A.J., Walsh, M.J. *Artificial Intelligence through Simulated Evolution*. Wiley, New York, 1966.

[Levenick 1991] Levenick, James R. "Inserting Introns Improves Genetic Algorithm Success Rate: Taking a Cue from Biology." Proceedings on the Fourth International Conference on Genetic Algorithms, 1991.

[Rechenberg 1965] Rechenberg, I. "Cybernetic solution path of an experimental problem." Technical Report Library translation No. 1122, Royal Aircraft Establishment, Farnborough, Hants., UK, 1965.

RESOURCES

Higuchi, Testuya; Liu, Yong; Yao, Xin (Eds.) *Evolvable Hardware, Genetic and Evolutionary Computation* Springer, 2006.

Iba, Hitoshi; Iwata, Masaya; Higuchi, Testuya "Machine Learning Approach to Gate-Level Evolvable Hardware," 1996.

Koza, J.R. (1990), *Genetic Programming: A Paradigm for Genetically Breeding Populations of Computer Programs to Solve Problems*, Stanford University Computer Science Department technical report STAN-CS-90-1314.

Particle Swarm Optimization website Available online at: http://www.swarmintelligence.org/

[Price, et al 1997] Price, K., and Storn, R. "Differential Evolution," Dr. Dobb's Journal, pp 18-24, 1997.

EXERCISES

1. Describe the first use of an evolutionary algorithm and how it worked.
2. Describe three of the evolutionary algorithms, and compare and contrast them.
3. Describe the fundamental flow of the genetic algorithm (each of the phases).

4. Describe the building-block hypothesis as defined for genetic algorithms.
5. Describe the differences between roulette wheel selection and elitist selection.
6. Describe the mutation and crossover operators for the genetic algorithm. What effect do they provide in the local search space?
7. Describe the inversion operator introduced by Holland.
8. What is a termination criteria?
9. Define premature convergence and then ways to combat it.
10. What other sequence-planning problems could be applied to the genetic algorithm? Describe one, and then discuss how you would implement this for evolution with the GA.
11. How was the genetic programming algorithm initially used (what kinds of programs were evolved)?
12. What are the fundamental problems with genetic programming?
13. The implementation of genetic programming in this book focused on a simple (zero address) instruction set. What value exists for simplifying the instruction set, and what problems could result with a larger more complex set?
14. Why does GP implementation perform the candidate program multiple times to record a fitness value?
15. The GP implementation found numerous solutions to the candidate problem (even with the simple instruction set). What does this say about the viability of this algorithm?
16. What is the basic difference between the evolutionary strategies algorithm and the genetic algorithm?
17. What problem was the early evolutionary strategies algorithm applied to with success?
18. Describe the basic differences between a *phenotypic* algorithm and a *genotypic* algorithm.
19. What is a uniformly distributed random number?
20. Describe the process of punctuated equilibrium.
21. Describe the basic process of the differential evolution algorithm. What are the processes of mutation, crossover, and replacement?
22. What effect do the F and CR tunable parameters have on the differential evolution algorithm?
23. In your own words, describe the basic process of the particle swarm optimization algorithm.
24. What is the definition of a particle in a particle swarm algorithm?
25. For a given particle in a swarm, define the two influences that specify how it should move in the solution space.

26. The velocity update equations for the particle swarm optimization algorithm included two random numbers. What affect do these random numbers have?

27. What affect do the two acceleration constants (c1 and c2) have on the particle swarm velocity equation?

28. What is evolvable hardware, and what are the primary issues that it faces?

Chapter 8 — NEURAL NETWORKS I

N eural networks are biologically motivated computing structures that are conceptually modeled after the brain. The neural network is made up of a highly connected network of individual computing elements (mimicking neurons) that collectively can be used to solve interesting and difficult problems. Once trained, neural networks can generalize to solve different problems that have similar characteristics. This chapter will introduce the basics of neural networks and introduce a number of supervised learning algorithms. In Chapter 11, we'll continue our exploration of neural networks and review some variants that can be used to solve different types of problems and in particular, those of unsupervised learning algorithms.

SHORT HISTORY OF NEURAL NETWORKS

The story of neural networks is interesting because, like AI itself, it's one of grand visions, eventual disappointment, and finally, silent adoption. In 1943, McCulloch and Pitts developed a neural network model based on their understanding of neurology, but the models were typically limited to formal logic simulations (simulating binary operations). In the early 1950s, researchers in neural networks worked toward neural network models with the support of neuroscientists.

But it wasn't until the late 1950s that promising models began to emerge. The Perceptron model, developed by Rosenblatt, was built for the purpose of understanding human memory and learning. The basic perceptron consisted of an input layer (for the stimulus) and an output layer (result) that was fully interconnected. Each connection was assigned a weight that was applied to the input stimulus (to which it was connected on the input layer). By adjusting the weights of the connections, a desired output could be formed for a given input. This allowed the perceptron to learn to recognize input patterns.

In the 1960s, another learning model emerged from Widrow and Hoff of Stanford University called ADALINE, or Adaptive Linear Element. This particular algorithm used least-mean-squares for adjusting the weights of the network, but this particular model could be implemented in the physical world using analog electronic components.

In 1969, the growing popularity of neural networks was brought to a halt. Marvin Minsky and Seymour Papert wrote a book entitled "Perceptrons" in which limitations of single-layer perceptrons were discussed, but then generalized to more powerful multi-layer models. The result was severe reductions in neural network research funding, and a corresponding reduction in the effort applied to the field. Luckily, several researchers continued to investigate neural network models, and successfully defined new models and methods for learning. In 1974, Paul Werbos developed the backpropagation algorithm, which permitted successful learning in multi-layer neural networks.

Since the 1970s, research and successful results in neural network design have attracted scientists back to the field. Many theoretical papers and practical treatments of neural networks have emerged, and neural networks can now be found outside of the lab and in real applications such as pattern recognition and classification. To support large neural networks, integrated circuits have been developed to speed the operation and training in production applications.

BIOLOGICAL MOTIVATION

In 1943, McCulloch and Pitts used their understanding of neurology to build a new information processing structure. The processing element of a neural network is modeled after a neuron, which is viewed as the fundamental processing element in our own brains.

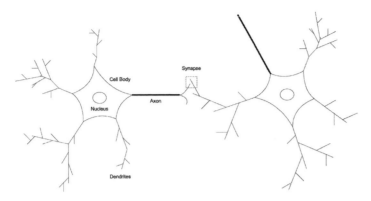

FIGURE 8.1: The neuron cell with inputs (dendrites) and outputs (axons).

The neuron is a simple processing device that has inputs (known as *dendrites*) and outputs (known as *axons*). The axon splits at its end into thousands of branches, each potentially influencing other neurons at a *synapse* (a small gap that separates axons and dendrites). When a neuron receives excitatory inputs that exceed its inhibitory inputs, a signal is transmitted down its axon to other neurons. This process continues in other neurons, creating a massively parallel network of neurons in an excited or inhibited state. Learning can then be defined as the altering of the synaptic junctions that change the manner in which one neuron is influenced by others.

> NOTE
> *While neural networks are modeled after our understanding of the way in which our brain works, surprisingly little is known about how our brains actually function. Through various types of inspection, we can see our brain in operation, but because of the massive number of neurons and interconnections between these neurons, how it works remains a mystery (though many theories exist).*

FUNDAMENTALS OF NEURAL NETWORKS

Let's begin with an exploration of neural networks applications, fundamental concepts behind neural networks, and then begin an investigation into a number of network models and learning algorithms.

You can find neural networks in a large variety of applications, from classification tasks (such as credit-risk assessment), data-processing tasks (adaptive signal processing), and approximation of arbitrary functions (time-series modeling and prediction). In this chapter, we'll explore neural networks for classification (character recognition and data classification).

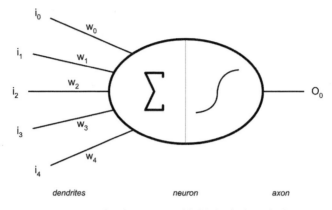

FIGURE 8.2: **Simple neuron with biological equivalents.**

A neural network is made up of one or more neurons, which is the basic processing element. A neuron has one or more inputs (dendrites), each of which are individualy weighted. A neuron has one or more outputs (axons) that are weighted when connecting to other neurons. The neuron itself includes a function that incorporates its inputs (via summation) and then normalizes its output via a transfer function (see Figure 8.2).

For each input of Figure 8.2, a weight is applied. These adjusted inputs are then summed and a transfer function is applied to determine the output. Eq 8.1 provides the equation for this simple neuron.

$$O_0 = f\left(\sum_{j=0}^{n} (i_j w_j)\right) \qquad \text{(Eq 8.1)}$$

Single Layer Perceptrons (SLPs)

Single Layer Perceptrons (or SLPs) can be used to emulate logic functions such as NOT, NOR, OR, AND, and NAND, but cannot be used to emulate the XOR function (two layers of neurons are required for this function). We'll explore this problem shortly.

Minsky and Papert documented the XOR limitation of single layer perceptrons, which ultimately resulted in vast reduction in neural network function during the 1970s.

A bias is also commonly applied to each neuron, which is added to the weighted sum of the inputs prior to passing through the transfer function. A weight is also commonly applied to the bias. The bias determines the level

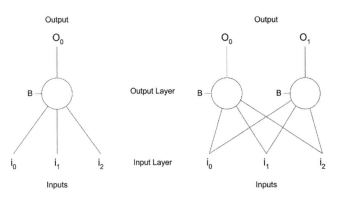

FIGURE 8.3:   **Examples of Single Layer Perceptrons (SLPs).**

of incoming activations (value of weighted inputs) that are required in order for the neuron to fire. The bias is commonly set to one, but a weight is also present for the bias which can be tuned by the learning algorithm.

An SLP should not be confused with a single neuron. Consider the network in Figure 8.3. This is also an SLP, because it consists of a single layer. For problems of higher dimensionality, we must use the MLPs, or Multi-Layer Perceptrons.

Representing SLPs is quite simple. As the inputs and weights have a one-to-one correspondence, it's easy to compute the output. Consider the simple code in Listing 8.1.

Listing 8.1:   Sample code illustrating SLP representation.

```
#define NUM_INPUTS  3
/* Note: +1 here to account for the bias input */
double weights[ NUM_INPUTS+1 ];
double inputs[ NUM_INPUTS+1 ];
int step_function( double input )
{
if (input > 0.0) return 1;
else return -1;
}
int calc_output( void )
{
int i;
double sum = 0.0;
/* Set the bias (could be done once at init) */
```

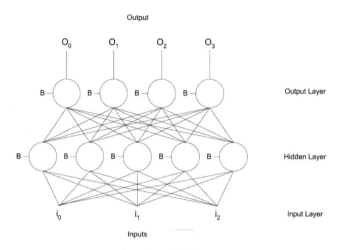

FIGURE 8.4:   **Example of a Multiple Layer Perceptron (MLP).**

```
inputs[NUM_INPUTS] = 1.0;
/* Compute the output (Equation 8.1) */
for (i = 0 ; i < NUM_INPUTS+1 ; i++) {
  sum += (weights[i] * inputs[i]);
}
/* Pass the output through the step (activation) function */
return step_function( sum );
}
```

Multi-Layer Perceptrons (MLPs)

As Minsky and Papert revealed in their book "Perceptrons," single layer perceptrons have the disadvantage that they can only be used to classify linearly separable data. But what was found a short time later is that by stacking the single layer perceptrons into multiple layer perceptrons (see Figure 8.4), the ability to solve any classification problem theoretically could be realized. The MLP can model practically any function of arbitrary complexity, where the number of inputs and number of hidden layers determine the function complexity.

The neurons in an MLP have the same basic attributes of the SLP (bias, etc.). But with multiple layers, the output from one layer becomes the input to the next. The implementation for the MLP is a bit more complicated, but remains straightforward (see Listing 8.2). Note here the use of an activation function for both the hidden and output nodes. The sigmoid function can be used to squash the output of the neuron to 0.0 to 1.0.

Listing 8.2:   Sample code illustrating MLP representation.

```
#define NUM_INPUTS                4
#define NUM_HIDDEN_NEURONS        4
#define NUM_OUTPUT_NEURONS        3
typedef mlp_s {
  /* Inputs to the MLP (+1 for bias) */
  double inputs[NUM_INPUTS+1];
  /* Weights from Hidden to Input Layer (+1 for bias) */
  double w_h_i[NUM_HIDDEN_NEURONS+1][NUM_INPUTS+1];
/* Hidden layer */
double hidden[NUM_HIDDEN+1];
  /* Weights from Output to Hidden Layer (+1 for bias) */
  double w_o_h[NUM_OUTPUT_NEURONS][NUM_HIDDEN_
NEURONS+1];
  /* Outputs of the MLP */
  double outputs[NUM_OUTPUT_NEURONS];
} mlp_t;
void feed_forward( mlp_t *mlp )
{
int i, h, out;
/* Feed the inputs to the hidden layer through the hidden
 * to input weights.
 */
for ( h = 0 ; h < NUM_HIDDEN_NEURONS ; h++ ) {
  mlp->hidden[h] = 0.0;
  for ( i = 0 ; i < NUM_INPUT_NEURONS+1 ; i++ ) {
    mlp->hidden[h] += ( mlp->inputs[i] * mlp->w_h_i[h][i] );
  }
  mlp->hidden[h] = sigmoid( mlp->hidden[h] );
}
/* Feed the hidden layer activations to the output layer
 * through the output to hidden weights.
 */
for( out = 0 ; out < NUM_OUTPUT_NEURONS ; out++ ) {
  mlp->output[out] = 0.0;
  for ( h = 0 ; h < NUM_HIDDEN_NEURONS ; h++ ) {
    mlp->outputs[out] += ( mlp->hidden[h] * mlp->w_o_h[out][h] );
  }
  mlp->outputs[out] = sigmoid( mlp->outputs[out] );
```

```
}
 return;
}
```

Listing 8.2 implements the MLP neural network shown in Figure 8.5. This MLP has four input cells, four hidden cells, and three output cells. Bias cells are implemented as input and hidden cells, but these have a constant value of 1.0 (though the weights can be adjusted to modify their effect).

Note the flow in Listing 8.2. First, we calculate the output of the hidden cells (using the input cells and the weights between the hidden and input cells), and then calculate the next layer up, which in this case is the output cells. This process is commonly referred to as feeding the data forward, or more simply, *feedfoward*.

NOTE ▶ *We can think of neural networks as parallel computing systems. Each neuron is a processing element that takes one or more inputs and generates an output. The inputs and outputs can be thought of as messages. In MLP architectures, the outputs can be sent to multiple other process elements for further processing. The parallel nature of neural networks comes into play with multiple neurons in a layer. Each of these neurons can process their inputs at the same time, making neural networks with large numbers of neurons in a layer faster in multi-processor architectures.*

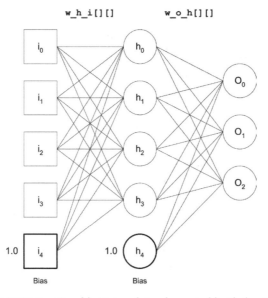

FIGURE 8.5:   Graphic Network Implemented in Listing 8.2

Supervised vs Unsupervised Learning Algorithms

There are two basic categories of learning algorithms for neural networks: supervised learning and unsupervised learning.

In the supervised learning paradigm, the neural network is trained with data that has known right and wrong answers. By calculating the output of the neural network and comparing this to the excepted output for the given test data, we can identify the error and adjust the weights accordingly. Examples of supervised learning algorithms include the Perceptron learning algorithm, Least-Mean-Squares learning, and Backpropagation (each of which will be explored in this chapter).

Unsupervised learning algorithms are those in which there's no answer given in the test data. What these algorithms do instead is analyze the data in order to understand their similarities and differences. In this way, relationships in the data can be found that may not have been apparent before. Examples of unsupervised learning algorithms include the k-Means clustering algorithm, Adaptive Resonance Theory (ART), and Kohonen Self-Organizing Maps (each of which, and more, will be discussed in Chapter 9).

Binary vs Continuous Inputs and Outputs

Neural networks can operate with a combination of input types. For example, we can use binary inputs (-1, 1) and binary outputs. We'll explore this in our first two examples of SLPs. For other uses, such as audio or video applications, we'll need continuous inputs (such as real-valued data). It's also possible to use combinations, such as continuous inputs and binary outputs (for classification problems).

Now that we have a basic understanding of neural network topologies and learning algorithms, let's start with an investigation of the perceptron and understand how it can be trained for simple pattern classification.

THE PERCEPTRON

A perceptron is a single neuron neural network that was first introduced by Frank Rosenblatt in the late 1950s. The perceptron is a simple model for neural networks that can be used for a certain class of simple problems called *linear separable* problems (otherwise called *linear discriminants*). These are often used to classify whether a pattern belongs to one of two classes (see Figure 8.6).

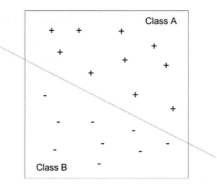

FIGURE 8.6: A linear discriminant can be used to classify input patterns into two classes.

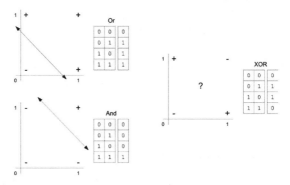

FIGURE 8.7: Viewing the linear discriminant for simple boolean functions.

So given a set of inputs describing an object (sometimes called a feature vector), a perceptron has the ability to classify the data into two classes if the data is linearly separable. Given the set of possible inputs, the task then is to identify the weights that correctly classify the data (linearly separate) into two classes.

> *Another name for the perceptron is the Threshold Logic Unit, or TLU. The TLU is a linear discriminator that given a threshold (whether the feature sum is greater than the threshold, or less than the threshold).*

The perceptron can accurately classify the standard boolean functions, such as AND, OR, NAND, and NOR. As shown in Figure 8.7, the AND and OR functions can be linearly separated by a line (in the case of two inputs, or a *hyperplane* for three inputs), but the XOR function is linearly inseparable. A bias component provides the offset of the line from the origin. If no bias existed, the line (or hyperplane) would be restricted to pass through the origin and the weights would only control the angle of the discriminant.

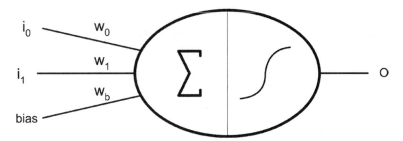

FIGURE 8.8: **Simple perceptron used for binary function classification.**

One result of Rosenblatt's work on perceptrons was the Mark I perceptron at Cornell Aeronautical Laboratory. The Mark I was an analog computer based on the perceptron that had a 20 by 20 retina and learned to recognize letters.

Perceptron Learning Algorithm

Perceptron learning is a supervised learning algorithm and is a simple procedure where the weights are adjusted to classify the training set. Each sample from the training set is applied to the perceptron, and the error (expected result minus the actual result) is used to adjust the weights. A learning rate is also applied (small number between 0 and 1) to minimize the changes that are applied at each step.

We'll use the perceptron shown in Figure 8.8 to illustrate the perceptron learning algorithm. The weights of the perceptron will initially be set to zero. There are two inputs with two corresponding weights and also a bias with a weight. The bias will be set to one, but the weight for the bias will be adjusted to alter its affect. Calculating the output of the perceptron can then be defined (Eq 8.2).

$$R = step\ (i_0 w_0 + i_1 w_1 + w_b) \qquad \text{(Eq 8.2)}$$

The step function simply pushes the result to 1.0 if it exceeds a threshold; otherwise, the result is -1.0.

Given a training set for our perceptron, we apply each of the elements of the training set to the perceptron and for each sample, adjust the weights based on the error. The error is defined as the expected result minus the actual result. Each is adjusted using Eq 8.3 (called the *Perceptron Rule*).

$$w_i = w_i + aTi_i \qquad \text{(Eq 8.3)}$$

In this equation, *(alpha)* is the learning rate (small number less than one), *T* is the target (or expected) result, and i_i is the input value for the current weight w_i. Eq 8.3 very simply adjusts the weight by incrementing or decrementing the weight based on the direction of the error and the corresponding input (which is identified by multiplying the expected result by the training input for this connection).

NOTE ▶ *The perceptron learning algorithm is an example of a supervised learning algorithm. We present a training set to our perceptron and penalize it when it arrives at the wrong answer (an incorrect classification).*

The application of the learning algorithm continues until no changes are made to the weights because all tests are properly classified.

Perceptron Implementation

The implementation of the perceptron learning algorithm is very simple (see Listing 8.3). In this implementation, the perceptron is trained with a training set (a boolean function), and after calculating the error (of desired vs actual result), the weights are adjusted per Eq 8.3. Calculating the output of the perceptron is shown in the compute function. This function implements the Eq 8.2. The training process continues for a maximum number of iterations, and when complete, the truth table is emitted for the boolean function.

Listing 8.3: Perceptron learning implementation.

```
#define MAX_TESTS    4
training_data_t training_set[MAX_TESTS]={
   {-1.0, -1.0, -1.0},
   {-1.0,  1.0,  1.0},
   { 1.0, -1.0,  1.0},
   { 1.0,  1.0,  1.0} };
double compute( int test )
{
  double result;
  /* Equation 8.2 */
  result = ((training_set[test].a * weights[0]) +
        (training_set[test].b * weights[1]) +
        (1.0            * weights[2]) );
  /* Clip the result */
  if (result > 0.0) result = 1.0;
  else result = -1.0;
```

```
    return result;
}
int main()
{
  int i, test;
  double output;
  int change;
  /* Initialize the weights for the perceptron */
  for ( i = 0 ; i < NUM_WEIGHTS ; i++ ) weights[i] = 0.0;
  /* Train the perceptron with the training set */
  change = 1;
  while (change) {
    change = 0;
    for ( test = 0 ; test < MAX_TESTS ; test++ ) {
      /* Test on the perceptron */
      output = compute( test );
      /* Perceptron Supervised Learning Algorithm */
      if ( (int)training_set[test].expected != (int)output ) {
        /* Use Equation 8.3 */
        weights[0] += ALPHA *
                  training_set[test].expected *
                  training_set[test].a;
        weights[1] += ALPHA *
                  training_set[test].expected *
                  training_set[test].b;
        weights[2] += ALPHA * training_set[test].expected;
        change = 1;
      }
    }
  }
  /* Check the status of the Perceptron */
  for (i = 0 ; i < MAX_TESTS ; i++) {
    printf(" %g OR %g = %g\n",
         training_set[i].a, training_set[i].b, compute(i) );
  }
  return 0;
}
```

 The perceptron learning implementation can be found on the CD-ROM at ./software/ch8/perceptron.c.

LEAST-MEAN-SQUARE (LMS) LEARNING

The LMS algorithm goes by a number of names, including the *Widrow-Hoff rule* and also the *Delta rule* (LMS was originally introduced by Widrow and Hoff in 1959). LMS is a fast algorithm that minimizes the Mean-Square Error (MSE). Recall from perceptron learning that the algorithm operates until it correctly classifies the entire training set. At this point, a solution has been found. But just how good is the solution? Is the data linearly separated by an optimal discriminator (as shown in Figure 8.6)?

Another approach is to train the perceptron using another termination criterion. So instead of training the perceptron until a solution is found, another criterion is to continue training while the MSE is greater than a certain value. This is the basis for the LMS algorithm.

NOTE ▶ *LMS learning is based on gradient descent, where the local minimum of the error is achieved by adjusting the weights proportional to the negative of the gradient. Additionally, the weights are adjusted with a learning rate (ρ) to allow it to settle into a solution and avoid oscillating around the MSE.*

First, let's explore the MSE. The MSE is simply the average of the weighted sum of the error for N training samples (see Eq 8.4).

$$MSE = \frac{\sum_{j=1}^{N}\left(R - C_j\right)^2}{N} \qquad (\text{Eq } 8.4)$$

In Eq 8.4, R is the output of the perceptron given the current set of weights multiplied by the current test inputs (C_j).

LMS Learning Algorithm

To train the perceptron using LMS, we iterate through the test set, taking a set of inputs, computing the output, and then using the error to adjust the weights. This process is done either randomly for the test set, or for each test of the set in succession.

The learning rule (see Eq 8.5) adjusts the weight based on the error (R-C, or expected minus actual output). Once the error is calculated, the weights are adjusted by a small amount (p) in the direction of the input (E). This has the effect of adjusting the weights to reduce the output error.

$$w_{t+1} = w + \rho(R - C)E \qquad \text{(Eq 8.5)}$$

One of the major differences between LMS and perceptron learning is that LMS can operate with real-values. Recall that perceptron learning operates solely with binary inputs.

 LMS is a standard tool for adaptive signal processing and can solve problems such as echo cancellation, noise cancellation, and equalization.

LMS Implementation

Like the perceptron algorithm, LMS is also very simple (see Listing 8.4). Initially, the weights vector is initialized with small random weights. The main loop then randomly selects a test, calculates the output of the neuron, and then calculates the error (expected result minus the actual result). Using the error, Eq 8.5 is applied to each weight in the vector (note that weight[2] is the bias, and its input is always 1.0). The loop then continues, where we check the MSE to see if it has reached an acceptable value, and if so, we exit and emit the computed truth table for the neuron.

Recall that single neuron models can only classify training data into two sets. In this case, the AND function is separable, so the neuron can be successfully trained. Nonseparable training sets will result in the algorithm never converging on a solution.

Listing 8.4:   LMS learning algorithm.

```
double weights[NUM_WEIGHTS];
#define MAX_TESTS    4
const training_data_t training_set[MAX_TESTS]={
 /* a    b   expected */
  {-1.0, -1.0, -1.0},
  {-1.0,  1.0, -1.0},
  { 1.0, -1.0, -1.0},
  { 1.0,  1.0,  1.0}
};
double compute_output( test )
{
  double result;
  result = ((training_set[test].a * weights[0]) +
        (training_set[test].b * weights[1]) +
```

```
          (1.0              * weights[2]) );
  return (result);
}
int classify( int test )
{
  double result;
  result = compute_output( test );
  if (result > 0.0) return 1;
  else return -1;
}
double MSE( void )
{
  int test;
  double sum = 0.0;
  /* Equation 8.4 */
  for (test = 0 ; test < MAX_TESTS ; test++) {
    sum += sqr( training_set[test].expected - compute_output(test) );
  }
  return ( sum / (double)MAX_TESTS );
}
int main()
{
  int i, test;
  double result, error;
  RANDINIT();
  /* Pick random weights for the perceptron */
  for ( i = 0 ; i < NUM_WEIGHTS ; i++ ) {
    weights[i] = RAND_WEIGHT;
  }
  /* Train the perceptron with the training set */
  while (MSE() > 0.26) {
    test = RANDMAX(MAX_TESTS);
    /* Compute the output (weighted sum) */
    result = compute_output(test);
    /* Calculate the error */
    error = training_set[test].expected - result;
    /* Delta Rule Learning Algorithm  (Equation 8.5) */
    weights[0] += (RHO * error * training_set[test].a);
    weights[1] += (RHO * error * training_set[test].b);
    weights[2] += (RHO * error);
```

```
    printf("mse = %g\n", MSE());
}
for (i = 0 ; i < MAX_TESTS ; i++) {
  printf(" %g AND %g = %d\n",
      training_set[i].a, training_set[i].b, classify(i) );
}
return 0;
}
```

The early ADALINE model (single layer perceptron) used the LMS algorithm for learning. ADALINE originally stood for "ADAptive LInear NEuron," but when neural network technology became unpopular, it was changed to "ADAptive LINear Element." [Gallant 1994]

The Least Mean Square algorithm implementation can be found on the CD-ROM at ./software/ch8/lms.c.

LEARNING WITH BACKPROPAGATION

Let's now investigate what can be considered the most popular of the MLP learning algorithms, backpropagation. The backpropagation algorithm can be succinctly defined as follows. For a test set, propagate one test through the MLP in order to calculate the output (or outputs). Compute the error,

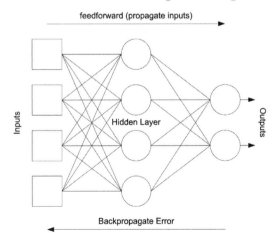

FIGURE 8.9: Simple network illustrating forward propagation and backward error propagation.

which will be the difference of the expected value and the actual value. Finally, backpropagate this error through the network by adjusting all of the weights; starting from the weights to the output layer and ending at the weights to the input layer (see Figure 8.9).

Like LMS learning, backpropagation adjusts the weights in an amount proportional to the error for the given unit (hidden or output) multiplied by the weight and its input. The training process continues until some termination criterion, such as a predefined mean-squared error, or a maximum number of iterations.

Backpropagation is one of the most popular learning algorithms, and is used to train neural networks for a variety of applications. We'll first look at the details of the algorithm, and then explore a neural network that can recognize numbers from a standard 5 by 7 character bitmap format.

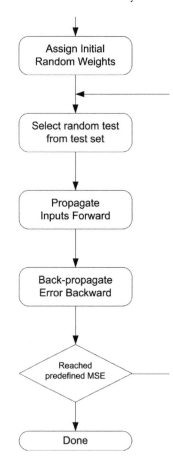

FIGURE 8.10: **A simplified flow of backpropagation.**

Backpropagation Algorithm

The backpropagation algorithm is a typical supervised learning algorithm, where inputs are provided and propagated forward to generate one or more outputs. Given the output, the error is calculated using the expected output. The error is then used to adjust the weights (see Figure 8.10). Propagating the inputs forward was previously explored in Listing 8.2.

It's important to note that there are two types of error functions for backpropagation. The first error function (Eq 8.6) is used for output cells, and the second is used only for hidden cells (Eq 8.7).

$$E_O = (Y_i - u_i)g'(u_i) \qquad \text{(Eq 8.6)}$$

$$E_h = (\sum_{i=1}^{i<n} (w_{h,i} E_O))g(u_h) \qquad \text{(Eq 8.7)}$$

Note that in both equations, u is the output of the given cell, otherwise known as its activation. Y is the expected or correct result. Finally, w represents all of the weights (from 1 to n) connecting the hidden cell to all inputs cells (in a fully connected network).

The activation, or transfer, function (g) to be used will be the standard sigmoid squashing function (see Figure 8.11). While g represents the sigmoid, g' represents the first derivative of the sigmoid, as shown in Eq 8.8.

$$g'(u) = u(1-u) \qquad \text{(Eq 8.8)}$$

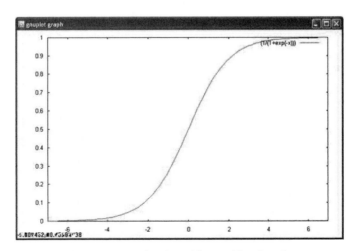

FIGURE 8.11:   **The sigmoid squashing function.**

At this point, given our test input and expected result, we have the error calculated for each output and hidden node. The next step is to use this error to adjust the corresponding weights for the node. We'll use Eq 8.9 for this purpose, which utilizes the error previously calculated for the node (whether hidden or output).

$$w_{i,j} = w_{i,j} + \rho E u_i \qquad \text{(Eq 8.9)}$$

For the given error (E) and activation (or cell output, u_i), we multiply by a learning rate (ρ) and add this to the current weight. The result is a minimization of the error at this cell, while moving the output cell activation closer to the expected output.

Backpropagation Implementation

Neural networks are a great tool for classifying a set of inputs to a set of outputs. Let's look at a very visual example of neural networks from the domain of pattern recognition. Consider the bitmap character images in Figure 8.12. We'll train a neural network to take the cells of this image as the input (35 independent cells) and activate one of ten output cells representing the recognized pattern. While any of the output cells could be activated, we'll take the largest activation as the cell to use in a style called *winner-takes-all*.

Since we could very simply implement a comparison classifier to recognize the pattern (by looking for the specific pattern at the input), we'll introduce noise to the pattern when we test the neural network. This will make the classification problem more difficult, and test the *generalization* features of the neural network.

Generalization is one of the greatest characteristics of neural networks. This means that after training a neural network with a set of training data, it can generalize its training to correctly classify data that it has not seen before. Generalization can be trained out of a neural network by training

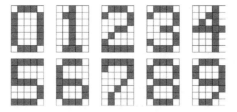

FIGURE 8.12: Sample bitmaps for training the number recognition neural network.

the network for too long with a data set. When this happens, the network overfits the data and is not able to generalize for new unseen data.

The neural network that we'll use is called a *winner-takes-all* network in which we have a number of output nodes, and we'll select the one that has the largest activation. The largest activation indicates the number that was recognized. Figure 8.13 shows the neural network that will be used for the pattern recognition problem. The input layer consists of 35 input cells (for each pixel in the image input), with 10 cells in the hidden layer. The output layer consists of 10 cells, one for each potential classification. The network is fully interconnected, with 350 connections between the input and hidden layer, and another 350 connections between the hidden layer and output layer (for a total of 700 weights).

For our implementation, let's first discuss the neural network representation (see Listing 8.5). We'll maintain three vectors containing the input values, current activations of the hidden layer and current activations of the output layer. Note that we'll also maintain an extra cell at the input and hidden layers which will represent the bias (set to a constant 1.0). The weights will be represented by two, two-dimensional arrays representing the hidden layer weights and the output layer weights.

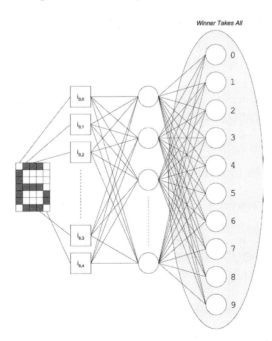

FIGURE 8.13: Neural network topology for the pattern recognition problem.

The full source implementation for backpropagation learning can be found on the CD-ROM at ./software/ch8/backprop.c. The following discussion provides only the relevant functions to illustrate backpropagation learning.

Listing 8.5:   Neural network representation (inputs, activations, and weights).

```
#define INPUT_NEURONS    35
#define HIDDEN_NEURONS   10
#define OUTPUT_NEURONS   10
double inputs[INPUT_NEURONS+1];
double hidden[HIDDEN_NEURONS+1];
double outputs[OUTPUT_NEURONS];
double w_h_i[HIDDEN_NEURONS][INPUT_NEURONS+1];
double w_o_h[OUTPUT_NEURONS][HIDDEN_NEURONS+1];
```

Computing the activations of the output cells is very straightforward (see Listing 8.6). Note the use of the sigmoid function to squash the activations into the range 0 to 1.

Listing 8.6:   Calculating the output activations with the `feed_forward` function.

```
void feed_forward( void )
{
  int i, j;
  /* Calculate outputs of the hidden layer */
  for (i = 0 ; i < HIDDEN_NEURONS ; i++) {
    hidden[i] = 0.0;
    for (j = 0 ; j < INPUT_NEURONS+1 ; j++) {
      hidden[i] += (w_h_i[i][j] * inputs[j]);
    }
    hidden[i] = sigmoid( hidden[i] );
  }
  /* Calculate outputs for the output layer */
  for (i = 0 ; i < OUTPUT_NEURONS ; i++) {
    outputs[i] = 0.0;
    for (j = 0 ; j < HIDDEN_NEURONS+1 ; j++) {
      outputs[i] += (w_o_h[i][j] * hidden[j] );
    }
    outputs[i] = sigmoid( outputs[i] );
```

```
}
}
```

The backpropagation algorithm (shown in Listing 8.7) is just slightly more complicated than feeding forward. Using Eq 8.6 and Eq 8.7, we calculate the error for the output and hidden nodes. Finally, the weights are updated given the hidden and output errors, input value, and a small learning rate.

Listing 8.7:   Updating the weights given the backpropagation algorithm.

```
void backpropagate_error( int test )
{
  int out, hid, inp;
  double err_out[OUTPUT_NEURONS];
  double err_hid[HIDDEN_NEURONS];
  /* Compute the error for the output nodes (Equation 8.6) */
  for (out = 0 ; out < OUTPUT_NEURONS ; out++) {
    err_out[out] = ((double)tests[test].output[out] - outputs[out]) *
              sigmoid_d(outputs[out]);
  }
  /* Compute the error for the hidden nodes (Equation 8.7) */
  for (hid = 0 ; hid < HIDDEN_NEURONS ; hid++) {
    err_hid[hid] = 0.0;
    /* Include error contribution for all output nodes */
    for (out = 0 ; out < OUTPUT_NEURONS ; out++) {
      err_hid[hid] += err_out[out] * w_o_h[out][hid];
    }
    err_hid[hid] *= sigmoid_d( hidden[hid] );
  }
  /* Adjust the weights from the hidden to output layer (Equation 8.9) */
  for (out = 0 ; out < OUTPUT_NEURONS ; out++) {
    for (hid = 0 ; hid < HIDDEN_NEURONS ; hid++) {
      w_o_h[out][hid] += RHO * err_out[out] * hidden[hid];
    }
  }
  /* Adjust the weights from the input to hidden layer (Equation 8.9) */
  for (hid = 0 ; hid < HIDDEN_NEURONS ; hid++) {
    for (inp = 0 ; inp < INPUT_NEURONS+1 ; inp++) {
      w_h_i[hid][inp] += RHO * err_hid[hid] * inputs[inp];
    }
```

```
    }
  return;
}
```

The main function (shown in Listing 8.8) performs the neural network training as well as the test of the trained network. The first step is initializing the network by setting each weight to a small random value (via a call to init_network). We then enter the training loop where a test is selected at random, the inputs loaded from the test into the inputs vector (set_network_inputs), and the output activation calculated (backpropagate_error). Finally, the MSE is calculated and tested against our termination criteria.

Listing 8.8:   The training and test loop (main function).

```
int main( void )
{
  double mse, noise_prob;
  int   test, i, j;
  RANDINIT();
  init_network();
  /* Training Loop */
  do {
    /* Pick a test at random */
    test = RANDMAX(MAX_TESTS);
    /* Grab input image (with no noise) */
    set_network_inputs( test, 0.0 );
    /* Feed this data set forward */
    feed_forward();
    /* Backpropagate the error */
    backpropagate_error( test );
    /* Calculate the current MSE */
    mse = calculate_mse( test );
  } while (mse > 0.001);
  /* Now, let's test the network with increasing amounts of noise */
  test = RANDMAX(MAX_TESTS);
  /* Start with 5% noise probability, end with 25% (per pixel) */
  noise_prob = 0.05;
  for (i = 0 ; i < 5 ; i++) {
    set_network_inputs( test, noise_prob );
    feed_forward();
```

```
for (j = 0 ; j < INPUT_NEURONS ; j++) {
  if ((j % 5) == 0) printf("\n");
  printf("%d ", (int)inputs[j]);
  }
printf( "\nclassified as %d\n\n", classifier() );
noise_prob += 0.05;
}
return 0;
}
```

The final step in the main function (Listing 8.8) is the neural network test. This test verifies the generalization capabilities of the neural network by inducing noise into the input image. We start by selecting one of the tests (a number to recognize) and then add increasing amounts of noise to the image. Once the noise is added (as part of the call to set_network_inputs), the output activations are computed (feed_forward) and then the classification emitted (through a call to classifier). This classifier function inspects each of the output activations, and chooses the largest one in the winner-takes-all fashion.

Figure 8.14 graphically illustrates the generalization capabilities of the network trained using error backpropagation. In both cases, once the error rate reaches 20%, the image is no longer recognizable.

What's shown in main is a common pattern for neural network training and use. Once a neural network has been trained, the weights can be saved off and used in the given application.

TIP

This approach for pattern recognition is considered brittle if you consider the rotation of the image by a small degree. A production character recognizer would instead use features of the image space, rather than requiring that pixels be roughly in the correct place.

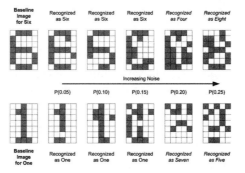

FIGURE 8.14: **The pattern recognition capabilities of the multi-Layer neural network.**

Tuning Backpropagation

Backpropagation is a great technique to train a neural network for a classification task. But there are a number of things that can be done to tune the algorithm either for better generalization, or for faster training. We'll explore some of these techniques here.

Training Variants

One of the problems that can be created in training is what's called "over-learning," or "over-fitting." The desire for the neural network is to provide a correct mapping of the test data, but maintain the ability to generalize for yet to be seen data. This is difficult to quantify, but the results of over-learning can be very apparent in the test stage.

There are a number of things that can be done to avoid over-learning. One of the simplest is called *early-stopping*. As the name suggests, we train for a limited amount of time. Practically, we can train until the training set is correctly classified, and ignore the MSE. In this way, we've not optimized the neural network to the data set, and its generalization capabilities should remain intact.

Another method to avoid over-learning is to incorporate noise into the training. Rather than simply provide the test set verbatim to the neural network, small amounts of noise can be induced to maintain some amount of flexibility in the network's generalization capability. The addition of noise keeps the network from being focused solely on the test data.

The network could also be trained with a subset of the available training data. In this way, the network is initially trained with the subset, and then tested with the remainder of the test data to ensure that it generalizes properly. The availability of lots of training data can also help in generalization and avoid overfitting.

Finally, one could maintain generalization capabilities by minimizing the changes made to the network as time progresses. Minimizing the changes can be achieved by reducing the learning rate. By reducing the changes over time, we reduce the possibility that the network will become focused on the training set.

Ultimately, there's no silver bullet. What can be done is to experiment with network topologies, number of hidden layers, number of hidden nodes per layer, learning rate, etc., to find the best combination that works for the problem at hand.

Weight Adjustment Variants

With backpropagation, there are a number of other weight adjustment strategies that can be applied that can speed learning or avoid becoming trapped in local minima. The first involves a momentum term where a portion of the last weight change is applied to the current weight adjustment round. Eq 8.1 shows an updated weight adjustment variant based on Eq 8.9. The difference is that a portion of the last weight change (identified as $\Delta w_{i,j}$) is accumulated using a small momentum multiplier (m), as shown in Eq 8.10. The last weight change is stored using Eq 8.11.

$$w_{i,j} = w_{i,j} + \rho E u_i + m \Delta w_{i,j} \qquad \text{(Eq 8.10)}$$

$$\Delta w_{i,j} = \rho E u_i \qquad \text{(Eq 8.11)}$$

Another useful weight adjustment technique is called *weight decay*. Weight decay can improve generalization in neural networks by suppressing irrelevant components of the weight vector by choosing the smallest vector that solves the particular problem. [Krogh 1995] Weight decay works by slowly decaying the weights of a neural network during training. Eq 8.12 is one method by which this can be done.

$$w_{i,j} = \lambda w_{i,j} \qquad \text{(Eq 8.12)}$$

In this equation, γ is a large number (such as 0.95) so that 5% of the weight is decayed for each iteration. In this way, large weights are penalized by larger amounts than small weights. This is a similar method to *weight elimination* (or *pruning*), whose goal is to remove connections between layers that do not contribute to the network's classification capabilities.

PROBABILISTIC NEURAL NETWORKS (PNN)

A useful neural network architecture with fundamental differences from backpropagation is called a Probabilistic Neural Network (or PNN). This architecture is similar to backpropagation in that it is feedforward in nature, but differs very much in the way that learning occurs. Both backpropagation and PNN are supervised learning algorithms, but PNN includes no weights in its hidden layer. Instead each hidden node represents an example vector, with the example acting as the weights to that hidden node. These are not adjusted at all. Figure 8.15 illustrates a sample PNN.

As shown in Figure 8.15, the PNN consists of an input layer, which represents the input pattern (or feature vector). The input layer is fully interconnected with the hidden layer, which consists of the example vectors

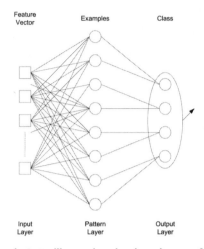

FIGURE 8.15: Sample PNN illustrating the three layers of the network model.

(the training set for the PNN). The actual example vector serves as the weights as applied to the input layer. Finally, an output layer represents each of the possible classes for which the input data can be classified. Note here that the hidden layer is not fully interconnected to the output layer. The example nodes for a given class connect only to that class's output node and none other. In the example PNN, our network has four classes for which there are two training examples each.

One other important element of the PNN is the output layer and the determination of the class for which the input layer fits. This is done through a winner-takes-all approach. The output class node with the largest activation represents the winning class. While the class nodes are connected only to the example hidden nodes for their class, the input feature vector connects to all examples, and therefore influences their activations. It's therefore the sum of the example vector activations that determines the class of the input feature vector.

PNN Algorithm

Calculating the class-node activations is therefore a simple process. For each class node, the example vector activations are summed, which are the sum of the products of the example vector and the input vector. The hidden node activation, shown in Eq 8.13, is simply the product of the two vectors (E is the example vector, and F is the input feature vector).

$$h_i = E_i F \qquad \text{(Eq. 8.13)}$$

The class output activations are then defined in Eq 8.14.,

$$c_j = \frac{\sum_{i=1}^{N} e^{\frac{(h_i-1)}{\gamma^2}}}{N} \qquad \text{(Eq. 8.14)}$$

where N is the total number of example vectors for this class, h_i is the hidden-node activation, and is a smoothing factor. The smoothing factor is chosen through experimentation. If the smoothing factor is too large, details can be lost, but if the smoothing factor is too small, the classifier may not generalize well.

What's interesting about the PNN is that there's no real training that occurs since the example vectors serve as the weights to the hidden layer of the network. Given an unknown input vector, the hidden node activations are computed and then summed at the output (class nodes) layer. The class node with the largest activation determines the class to which the input feature vector belongs.

As no training is required, classifying an input vector is fast, depending on the number of classes and example vectors that are present. It's also very easy to add new examples to the network. We simply add the new hidden node, and its output is used by the particular class node. This can be done dynamically as new classified examples are found. The PNN also generalizes very well, even in the context of noisy data.

Let's now look at the implementation of a PNN with a graphical example that will illustrate its classification capabilities.

Probabilistic neural networks are a form of normalized Radial-Basis Form (RBF) neural networks, where each hidden node is a "kernel" implementing a probability density function

PNN Implementation

Building a PNN is quite simple once the structures are in place to represent the training dataset (which fundamentally defines the weights between the hidden layer and the input layer). Let's begin with a short discussion of the dataset.

For this example, we'll implement a two-dimensional classifier so that we can visualize it graphically. The dataset represents points on a two-dimensional map that have been pre-classified into three classes. Each point is a feature vector that is represented by the example_t type.

```
#define DIMENSIONALITY        2
typedef structure example_s {
```

```
    int feature[DIMENSIONALITY];
} example_t;
```

A dataset is then defined as a collection of examples. We'll have a dataset per class, which is easily defined as:

```
#define EXAMPLES              10
typedef struct data_set_s {
example_t example[EXAMPLES];
} data_set_t;
#define CLASSES               3
data_set_t dataset[CLASSES] = {
/* Class 0 */
{ { {{13,  1}},
   {{11,  2}},
...
   {{13, 10}} } },
/* Class 1 */
{ { {{36,  4}},
   {{34,  5}},
...
   {{37, 11}} } },
/* Class 2 */
{ { {{24, 27}}.
   {{22, 29}},
...
   {{22, 38}} } }
};
```

We now have a collection of data points that are split into examples for our three classes. Let's now look at how these are used by the PNN algorithm to classify an unseen data point.

Listing 8.9 provides the `pnn_classifier` function. The sole purpose of this function is to take a feature vector (example), and identify the class to which it belongs. The function begins with an outer loop that iterates through each of the classes in the dataset. For each class, each of the examples is iterated, calculating the sum of the feature vector and example vector products.

Finally, the output array (class vector) is passed to a function called `winner_takes_all`, which returns the class with the largest activation. This is the class which the PNN classified as the example feature vector.

Listing 8.9: Implementation of the simple PNN classifier function.

```c
int pnn_classifier( void )
{
  int c, e, d;
  double product;
  double output[CLASSES];
  /* Calculate the class sum of the example multiplied by each of
   * the feature vectors of the class.
   */
  for ( c = 0 ; c < CLASSES ; c++ ) {
    output[c] = 0.0;
    for ( e = 0 ; e < EXAMPLES ; e++ ) {
      product = 0.0;
      /* Equation 8.13 */
      for ( d = 0 ; d < DIMENSIONALITY ; d++ ) {
        product +=
          (SCALE(example[d]) * SCALE(dataset[c].example[e].feature[d]));
      }
      /* Equation 8.14 -- part 1 */
      output[c] += exp( (product-1.0) / sqr(SIGMA) );
    }
    /* Equation 8.14 -- part 2 */
    output[c] = output[c] / (double)EXAMPLES;
  }
  return winner_takes_all( output );
}
```

The full source implementation for the probabilistic neural network classifier can be found on the CD-ROM at ./software/ch8/pnn.c. The previous source discussion provides only the PNN function to illustrate the classifier.

Let's now use the PNN classifier to classify the entire two-dimensional space in which our example feature vectors exist. In this example, the two-dimensional space is iterated to identify the class to which each point belongs. This classification is emitted, with space in place for the example feature vectors (see Listing 8.10).

Listing 8.10: Output of the PNN classifier over a two-dimensional space of three classes.

```
$ ./pnn
000000000000000000000000001111111111111111111111111
0000000000000 0000000000001111111111111111111111111
00000000000 0000000000000011111111111111111111111111
00000000000000 0000000000111111111111111111111111111
000000000 0000000000000011111111111 1111111111111
000000000000 00000000001111111111 111111111111111
00000000000 00 0000000011111111111 1 111111111111
000000000000000 0000001111111111111111111111111111
000000000000000000 0000001111111111 11 1111111111111
00000000000 0000000000011111111111 111111111111111
0000000000000 0000000011111111111111111111111111111
000000000000000000000001111111111 11 1 111111111111
000000000000000000000022111111111111111111111111111
000000000000000000000222222111111111111111111111111
000000000000000000022222222111111111111111111111111
000000000000000002222222222221111111111111111111111
000000000000000022222222222221111111111111111111111
000000000000022222222222222222221111111111111111111
000000000002222222222222222222222211111111111111111
000000000222222222222222222222222222211111111111111
000000002222222222222222222222222222222211111111111
000000222222222222222222222222222222222222211111111
000022222222222222222222222222222222222222221111111
002222222222222222222222222222222222222222222211111
022222222222222222222222222222222222222222222211111
22222222222222222222222222222222222222222222222111
22222222222222222222222222222222222222222222222221
222222222222222222222222 22222222222222222222222222
2222222222222222222222222222222222222222222222222222
222222222222222222222 222222222222222222222222222
222222222222222222222 222222222222222222222222222
222222222222222222222222 222222222222222222222222222
2222222222222222222222222222222222222222222222222222
22222222222222222222 2 222222222222222222222222222
222222222222222222222222 222222222222222222222222222
2222222222222222222222222222222222222222222222222222
222222222222222222222 222222222222222222222222222
222222222222222222222222 222222222222222222222222222
222222222222222222222222 222222222222222222222222222
2222222222222222222222222222222222222222222222222222
2222222222222222222222222222222222222222222222222222
2222222222222222222222222222222222222222222222222222
2222222222222222222222222222222222222222222222222222
2222222222222222222222222222222222222222222222222222
2222222222222222222222222222222222222222222222222222
2222222222222222222222222222222222222222222222222222
2222222222222222222222222222222222222222222222222222
2222222222222222222222222222222222222222222222222222
2222222222222222222222222222222222222222222222222222
2222222222222222222222222222222222222222222222222222
$
```

The example shown in Listing 8.10 illustrates the clustering capabilities of the PNN as applied to this simple problem. PNNs have been applied to complex problems such as speaker-independent speech recognition and many other applications.

OTHER NEURAL NETWORK ARCHITECTURES

In addition to single and multi-layer perceptrons, there are variations of neural network architectures that can support different types of problems. Let's look at two neural network architectures that support time-series (or signal) processing and feedback systems (or those with memory).

Time-Series Processing Architecture

Consider the time series shown in Figure 8.16. This signal could be a portion of speech, a fetal heartbeat, or the stock price of a company. The signal can be sampled at a given frequency and used as input to a neural network to predict a future value. The neural network could also be used to filter the input signal for noise cancellation.

In addition to sampling points from the time series, the neural network can operate over a window of the time series through the use of a sliding window. Using a sliding window allows the neural network to operate on multiple data points, making it a better predictor of future time-series behavior.

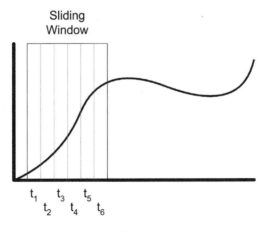

FIGURE 8.16:　Example of a time series with a sliding window.

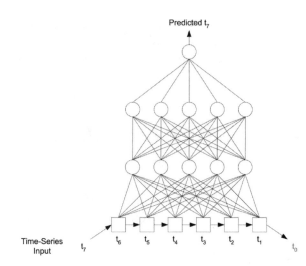

FIGURE 8.17: Example of a multi-mayer neural network for time-series prediction.

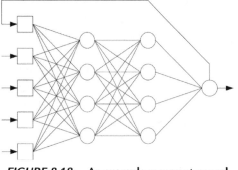

FIGURE 8.18:   An example recurrent neural
network (feedback).

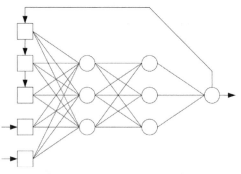

FIGURE 8.19:   A recurrent neural network
with longer term memory.

Figure 8.17 illustrates a four-layer, multi-layer perceptron for time-series processing. As input samples are acquired, the contents of the input nodes are shifted right (losing the right-most value) and then inserting the new value in the left-most node. The network is then fed-forward, resulting in an output activation (in this model, predicting the next value of the time series).

This particular network could be trained with backpropagation on a sample time series using the known value and predicted value to determine the error that is to be backpropagated for weight adjustment.

Neural networks, which operate over a window of time-series data, are often called tapped-delay-line networks, as there is an implicit delay between input samples as they shift down the line of inputs.

Recurrent Neural Network

A recurrent neural network is one that includes feedback connections, where higher layer nodes in the network feed lower layer nodes. Consider the recurrent neural network as shown in Figure 8.18. In this network model, the output feeds back as input to the next iteration.

Recurrent neural networks are very biologically plausible, as our own brains are recurrent. Neural networks with feedback are able to implement almost any arbitrary sequential behavior and are therefore useful in control systems, robotics, and many other applications.

Recurrent neural networks are also an interesting take on long-and-short term memory. The feedback loop provides the means for short-term memory (recalling the last output, in the example, and using it as an input). A tapped-delay-line could be used to keep the previous state longer (as in the tapped-delay-line model). The tapped-delay-line could also be modified to keep the last, 10th previous, and 100th previous output to give the network a longer history.

TIPS FOR BUILDING NEURAL NETWORKS

Neural networks can benefit from careful design of inputs, outputs, and internal structure. Let's explore a few techniques that can help in building efficient neural network architectures.

Defining the Inputs

How the inputs are defined to a neural network can help speed learning, or help to minimize the overall size of the neural network. Consider a set of inputs that describe the weather as one of four states {sunny, cloudy, raining, snowing}. A simple representation is to define an input node for each of the inputs, as shown in Figure 8.20.

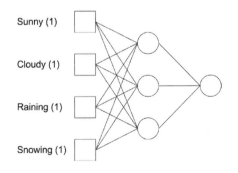

FIGURE 8.20: Using a single input per category.

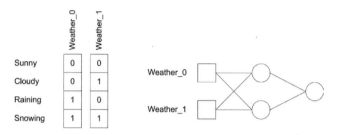

FIGURE 8.21: Using a binary encoding to reduce the number of inputs.

An alternative for a distinct set of inputs is to encode as a binary set of inputs (increasing the input information density, while reducing the number of input nodes that are necessary). Figure 8.21 illustrates this binary encoding.

Note that this works only for mutually exclusive inputs. Using real-valued inputs, we could set *sunny* and *cloudy* each to 0.5 (and raining and snowing to 0.0) to represent partly cloudy. Using real-valued inputs in this way provides a means of fuzziness to the input, and introduces the concept of probability or input confidence.

Defining the Outputs

The winner-takes-all model is great for determining a classification (mapping the inputs to a particular output node representing a class). Real-valued outputs are ideal for real-valued outputs representing signal values or time-series predictions.

Note that output values are not restricted to activations in the range 0 to 1.0 (as can be forced through the sigmoid activation function). Activations can take any real-value, including negative values, if the particular output activation function supports this.

It's also useful to use target output values of the range 0.1 to 0.9 (for a valid classification). This avoids saturating the weights in the network to force the activation toward the extremes.

Choice of Activation Functions

There are a number of activation functions that can be used, but it's important to note that the power of multi-layer neural networks is that they are non-linear. Therefore, using a linear activation function (for example) results in a linear activation.

For single-layer networks, linear activations and also step functions can be used. For multi-layer networks, the sigmoid, Gaussian, and hyperbolic tangent (tanh) can be used. The only requirement for backpropagation is that the activation function must be differentiable.

Number of Hidden Layers

A single hidden layer can model any continuous function, and is easily trained with backpropagation. With two hidden layers, any arbitrary function can be computed, with a complexity defined by the number of nodes. For this reason, neural networks with two hidden layers are universal computing devices. But neural networks with multiple hidden layers can be more difficult to train, and therefore, models with a single hidden layer should be used if the target problem supports this.

CHAPTER SUMMARY

Neural networks are an ideal solution to problems that can't be formulated easily to an algorithm, and for which lots of examples exist from which the network can be trained. Additionally, neural networks are highly parallel and distributed structures with the desirable property that they generalize well to unseen data. This chapter presented an introduction to neural networks using supervised learning algorithms, including perceptron learning, the delta-rule, backpropagation, and probabilistic neural networks.

REFERENCES

[Gallant 1994] Gallant, Stephen I. "Neural Network Learning and Expert Systems." MIT Press, Cambridge, Massachusetts., 1994.

[Krogh 1995] Krogh, Anders and Hertz, John A. "A Simple Weight Decay Can Improve Generalization." In Advances in Neural Information Processing Systems 4, Morgan Kauffmann Publishers, San Mateo CA, 1995, p. 950-957.

EXERCISES

1. Describe the difference between supervised and unsupervised learning.
2. What are the major components of a neural network?
3. Describe how learning occurs in neural networks.
4. What is the primary limitation of single-layer perceptrons?

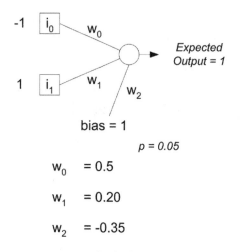

$p = 0.05$

$w_0 \quad = 0.5$

$w_1 \quad = 0.20$

$w_2 \quad = -0.35$

FIGURE 8.22: **Sample Single-Layer Network (SLP).**

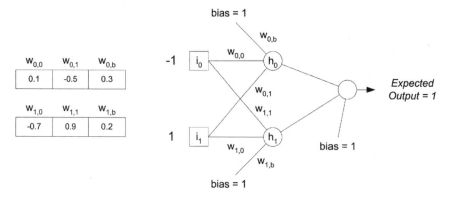

FIGURE 8.23: **Sample Multi-Layer Network (MLP).**

5. Multi-layer perceptrons include non-linear activation functions at the hidden and output layers - why is this important?
6. What is the purpose of the bias component?
7. Describe the fundamental process behind perceptron learning.
8. What is a principle advantage of the Delta rule over perceptron learning?
9. Describe the basic process behind learning with the Delta rule.
10. Consider the perceptron shown in Figure 8.22. Find the error and then calculate the new weights given the training example. After the new weights are available, recalculate the error for the given sample and verify that the error has been reduced given the prior weight adjustment.

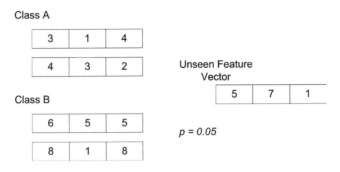

FIGURE 8.24: Sample class data for PNN calculation.

11. With the example neural network shown in Figure 8.23, calculate the weight adjustments using backpropagation learning. Recalculate the output to verify that the error has been reduced given the prior weight adjustment.

12. Describe the major architectural differences between MLP neural networks with backpropagation and probabilistic neural networks.

13. Using the test data shown in Figure 8.24, identify to which class the unseen feature belongs.

14. Describe a neural network architecture for time-series data prediction.

15. How can long-term memory be implemented in a neural network architecture?

9 NEURAL NETWORKS II

In Chapter 8, we explored a number of neural network architectures and learning algorithms that were able to train with a set of example data, and then generalize for unseen data. This is called *supervised learning*, as the network learns with the aid of a teacher (definition of output error). This chapter will present a different model for learning, called *unsupervised learning*. In this model, the network is given a set of raw data, for which it must analyze with no prior knowledge of its structure, and then classify it based on the inherent similarities.

UNSUPERVISED LEARNING

Unsupervised learning is a valuable method for data classification as it requires nothing more than raw data, and does not require an understanding of the underlying structure of the data. Unsupervised learning algorithms can in fact identify the underlying structure by segregating the data into distinct groups for later analysis. It does this by finding similarities in the raw data, and then grouping those pieces of data together. What unsupervised learning algorithms cannot do is name the clusters of data; it has no knowledge of why training data are grouped together, and what the grouping represents (see Figure 9.1). It simply identifies the similarities and clusters appropriately.

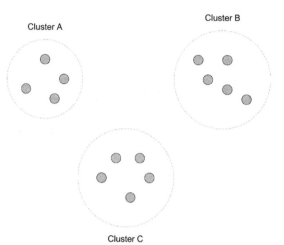

FIGURE 9.1: Unsupervised learning can cluster based on similarities, but has no knowledge of the meaning of the clusters.

NOTE ▼ *Reinforcement learning also uses a form of unsupervised learning.*

While conceptually simple, unsupervised learning is extremely valuable and can be used in a variety of problem domains. In addition to being used to identify the underlying structure of a set of raw data, it can also be used to compress or transform the data. We'll explore a number of unsupervised learning algorithms in this chapter, along with their relative strengths and weaknesses.

HEBBIAN LEARNING

The work of Donald Hebb represents the earliest development of a learning rule that is both biologically plausible and can be implemented as an algorithm.

This has been summarized concisely in what's called Hebb's postulate of learning:

"When an axon of cell A is near enough to excite a cell B and repeatedly or persistently takes part in firing it, some growth process or metabolic change takes place in one or both cells such that A's efficiency, as one of the cells firing B, is increased." [Hebb 1949]

In simpler terms, if two neuron cells are firing simultaneously, then any weight connecting between them should be increased. In this way, connected neurons reinforce each other to support learning. Note here that Hebb introduced the concept of increasing weights, but not decreasing weights. Nevertheless, Hebb's work served as the basis for further research in connectionist models, such as Frank Rosenblatt's work on the perceptron learning algorithm (see Chapter 8).

 In the period that Hebb introduced his work in neuron modeling, Norbert Weiner introduced the concept of Cybernetics, or the "control and communication in the animal and the machine." Cybernetics was a multi-disciplinary field that included such established fields as electrical engineering, mathematics, biology, neurophysiology, anthropology, and psychology.

Hebb's Rule

The basic idea behind Hebb's rule is that whenever there are two cells with similar activations, the weights that connect them should be strengthened. From a pattern recognition perspective, this provides the means to strengthen weights when inputs are similar, and to weaken them when they're dissimilar. This results in the very simple Eq 9.1, which implements the learning algorithm for Hebb's rule.

$$\Delta w_{ij} = \varepsilon x_j y_i \qquad \text{(Eq 9.1)}$$

where E is a learning rate ($0 < E <= 1$), x is the input, y is the output, and $w_{i,j}$ is the weight that connects them.

The neural network that uses the Hebb Rule is a very simple network that utilizes some number of input cells, and an identical set of output cells (see Figure 9.2). The network is fully interconnected, with weights connecting between each output cell and each input cell (so that every input has some influence over the output).

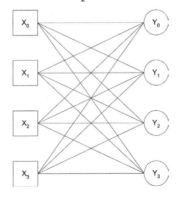

FIGURE 9.2: **Simple pattern recall network using Hebb's rule.**

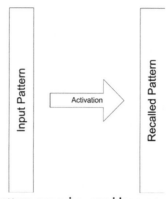

FIGURE 9.3:   **An abstract pattern recognizer provides a mapping between the input to the output.**

To train the network, we provide the network with the input pattern (and also duplicate the value of the input cells at the output, so that the Hebb rule builds the association). Once the weights have been trained using Hebb's learning rule, the network can recall output patterns from those presented to the input (the weights encode the memory of the patterns) as shown in Figure 9.3.

The major disadvantage with Hebb's Rule is that it can only create a map over orthogonal patterns of inputs. This is due to the lack of a hidden layer within the network.

Hebb Rule Implementation

Implementing the Hebb rule is quite simple, and can be done with a minimal amount of code. We'll represent our network as we have with other single-layer neural networks (see Chapter 10).

We'll show three functions from this implementation: locking in the input and expected output pattern, computing the activations, and the function implementing the Hebb rule.

The implementation of pattern recall using the Hebb rule can be found on the CD-ROM at ./software/ch9/hebb.c.

In the first function, we set the input pattern and also lock this same pattern into the output (define_pattern). This will be subsequently used by the Hebb rule to train the weights for the pattern (see Listing 9.1). The input and output vectors are also shown. Note that while the inputs are defined as integers, the outputs are double, since we used a real-valued learning rate. We'll use a linear threshold to clip the values, anything greater than 0 is a '1,' and anything equal to, or less than 0 is a '-1.'

Listing 9.1:   Setting the input and output patterns for Hebb learning.

```
int   inputs[MAX_CELLS];
double weights[MAX_CELLS][WEIGHTS_PER_ACTIVATION];
double outputs[MAX_CELLS];
void define_pattern( int *inp )
{
  int i;
  for (i = 0 ; i < MAX_CELLS ; i++) {
    inputs[i] = inp[i];
    outputs[i] = (double)inp[i];
  }
  return;
}
```

Computing the activations using Hebb's rule is shown in Listing 9.2 (compute_activations). For each output cell, we iterate through each input and accumulate it by multipling the associated weight by the input. Once the output activations have been computed, a step function is used to force the outputs to either a value of 1 or -1.

Listing 9.2:   Computing the output activations using Hebb's Rule.

```
void compute_activations( int adjust_weights )
{
  int out, weight;
  /* Compute the activations */
  for (out = 0 ; out < MAX_CELLS ; out++) {
    outputs[out] = 0.0;
    for (weight = 0 ; weight < WEIGHTS_PER_ACTIVATION ; weight++) {
      outputs[out] += (weights[out][weight] * (double)inputs[weight]);
    }
    /* Clip the outputs */
    if (outputs[out] > 0.0) outputs[out] = 1.0;
    else outputs[out] = -1.0;
  }
  return;
}
```

Finally, adjusting the weights with Hebb's rule is the simple process of accumulating weight changes using Eq 9.1. For each output cell, each weight connecting to the input is adjusted by multiplying the input by the output and a small learning rate (see Listing 9.3). This adjusts the weights in an effort to map the input vector to the output vector.

Listing 9.3: Weight adjustment with Hebb's rule.

```
void adjust_weights( void )
{
  int out, weight;
  /* Hebbian Learning Rule */
  for (out = 0 ; out < MAX_CELLS ; out++) {
    for (weight = 0 ; weight < WEIGHTS_PER_ACTIVATION ; weight++) {
    /* Equation 9.1 */
    weights[out][weight] += ETA * (outputs[out] *
(double)inputs[weight]);
    }
  }
  return;
}
```

To learn a new pattern, we simply specify a new image and load it with the define_pattern function. A call to `adjust_weights` can then be performed to create a mapping for the new pattern, for example:

```
{
  int pattern1[MAX_CELLS] = {-1,  1,  1, -1,
                  1, -1, -1,  1,
                  1, -1, -1,  1,
                  -1,  1,  1, -1 };
  define_pattern( pattern1 );
}
/* Train for Pattern 1 */
adjust_weights();
```

We can then test for this pattern by computing the output activations with a call to `compute_activiations`. Note that in this example, we've presented a partial input pattern in an attempt to test its recall capabilities:

```
/* Test for Pattern 1 */
{
```

```
    int patternA[MAX_CELLS] = {-1, -1, -1, -1,
                               -1,  1,  1, -1,
                                1,  1,  1,  1,
                                1,  1,  1,  1 };
  define_pattern( patternA );
  }
  show_activations();
```

Note that show_activations simply emits the input and output vector to illustrate the mapping.

Now let's look at the algorithm in action. We'll train our network for two distinct training patterns in a 4 by 4 matrix. Pattern one is a simple box, and pattern two is a representation of an 'X' pattern (see Figure 9.4).

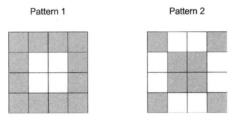

FIGURE 9.4: **Training patterns for the Hebb rule neural network.**

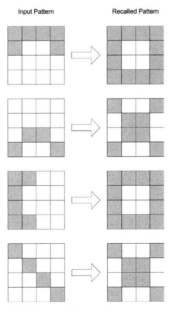

FIGURE 9.5: **Result of pattern recall using the Hebbian network.**

To test the recall capabilities of the network, we'll present the network with elements of the input pattern, but not the entire pattern (see Figure 9.5).

As is shown in Figure 9.5, Hebbian learning does a reasonable job of recalling patterns given pieces of the original patterns. The Hebb rule is very simple, and can be very effective when there's a strong correlation between the presented input pattern, and desired recall pattern.

SIMPLE COMPETITIVE LEARNING

In competitive learning, the output nodes of the network (which represent the distinct classes available for classification), compete with one another to fire and therefore represent the class of the feature vector at the input nodes.

> *Clustering is a very interesting technique with very practical applications. Clustering a raw data set allows a better understanding of the structure of the data. Using clustering, relationships in data can be found that could otherwise not be seen. One very useful example of clustering is in recommendation systems, where customer data is clustered. Customers in a given cluster are then unique classes of customers and their differences can be used to recommend purchases to those in the cluster who lack that purchase.*

The competitive learning network is made up of two layers. The first layer is the input layer and represents the feature vector, and the second layer is the output layer representing the class (see Figure 9.6).

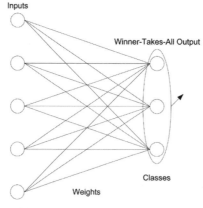

FIGURE 9.6: Sample competitive learning network.

The weights between the input and output layer encode the ability to classify a particular input feature vector to an output class node. In some competitive learning architectures, inhibitory connections between the output layer are included. These connections allow the output nodes to influence each other in a true competitive sense.

Vector Quantization

One example of competitive learning is called *vector quantization*. Vector quantization is a surprisingly simple network architecture and learning algorithm. The input layer has a number of nodes defined by the length of the feature vector, and the output layer has a number of nodes defined by the number of anticipated classes. Each output node connects to every input node by a trainable weight.

As each prototype vector (sample to classify) is applied to the network, a simple feedforward algorithm computes the activation of each output node, as defined by Eq 9.2. For each output node M, the sum of the products of the prototype vector (x) and weights determine the activation.

$$y_M = \sum w_{M,i} x_i \qquad \text{(Eq 9.2)}$$

A winner-takes-all approach then decides which particular output activation is chosen as the correct classification. But instead of choosing the largest activation (as we've seen with other approaches, such as Probabilistic Neural Networks), we choose the lowest activation, as it represents the class with the closest Euclidean distance to the input prototype vector. In this sense, the weights of the neural network define the centroid of all prototype vectors assigned to this class.

NOTE ▶ *Vector quantization effectively divides the prototype vector input space into a Voronoi tessellation. A Voronoi tessellation (named after Georgy Voronoi) is a decomposition of a space to a specific set of discrete objects in the space (such as centroids).*

After a prototype vector is found to be closest to a given class (output node), only the weights associated with this output node are updated. The weights associated with the winning output node (M) are updated for input x, and learning rate ρ, as shown in Eq 9.3.

$$w_{M,i} = w_{M,i} + \rho(x_i - w_{M,i}) \qquad \text{(Eq 9.3)}$$

The process of training continues until we reach some termination criteria. This could be after some number of runs, or when the network has reached equilibrium (no changes are made, such as prototype vectors changing classification).

Vector Quantization Implementation

Vector quantization, as illustrated by the introduction, is very easily implemented. We'll explore a few functions that make up the implementation, the remaining source can be found on the CD-ROM.

The implementation of object classification using vector quantization can be found on the CD-ROM at ./software/ch9/vq.c.

Let's begin with a discussion of the neural network representation for vector quantization (see Listing 9.4). In this approach, the prototype feature vectors are represented with the feature_vector_t type. This contains the current class to which the prototype belongs, and the feature vector itself (features).

The neural network is implemented very simply. Since there are no hidden layers, we need only maintain the value of the output nodes (the outputs array). The weights between the output layer and input layer are represented by a two-dimensional array (first dimension is the output node, second are the individual weights for the output node).

Listing 9.4:   Major types and variables.

```
#define MAX_FEATURE_VECTORS       40
#define MAX_FEATURES              3
typedef struct {
  int class;
  int features[MAX_FEATURES];
} feature_vector_t;
feature_vector_t fvec[MAX_FEATURE_VECTORS];
/*
 * Neural Network Representation for Vector Quantization
 */
#define OUTPUT_NODES      3                    /* Unique classes
 */
#define CLASSES               OUTPUT_NODES
double outputs[OUTPUT_NODES];
```

```
double weights[OUTPUT_NODES][MAX_FEATURES];
#define LEARNING_RATE          ((double)0.01)
```

Note that we'll normalize the feature vector so that the values scale to the range 0 to 1, but we'll not use the value zero and one (the extremes) to avoid saturating the weights of the network (see Figure 9.7).

Next, let's continue the implementation discussion with the main loop (see Listing 9.5). The main function provides a fundamental algorithm for vector quantization, including the termination criteria. We begin by first initializing the prototype feature vectors with a call to initialize_vectors. This function creates a random set of feature vectors given the feature length and available individual features (see the source on the CD-ROM for the details of this function). Next, we initialize the neural network with a call to initialize_network. This function simply takes the first N feature prototype vectors (N being the number of classes available for classification), and associates the output node with the feature vector. This is done through a call to updateNetwork, which initializes the weights for the output node given the prototype feature vector (we'll review this function shortly). Note that this can be problematic, especially if there are strong similarities between the first N feature prototype vectors, but it is simple, and works well given a good random distribution.

Next, we enter the main loop. This loop continues to operate while changes occur (and by change, we mean a feature prototype vector changing classes, based on the class feature centroids changing themselves). Each of the sample feature prototype vectors are applied in succession to the network, using the feed_forward function. This function returns the class to which the prototype was assigned. This information is then applied to the updateNetwork function, which updates the particular output node's (class's) weights given the current prototype feature vector. This process then continues for the next sample, until for each iteration through the sample set, no changes occur.

Feature Vector	Color	Texture	Shape	Value
	Red	Smooth	Box	*0.3*
	Blue	Rough	Sphere	*0.5*
	Black	Dimpled	Cylinder	*0.7*

FIGURE 9.7:   **Representing the prototype feature vector.**

Listing 9.5:   Vector quantization main loop (portion).

```
int main()
{
 int i, j;
 int sample = CLASSES;
 int class;
 changes = 0;
 /* Initialize the feature vectors */
 initialize_vectors();
 /* Initialize the neural network */
 initialize_network();
 /* Continue to run while feature vectors change classes */
 while (changes > 0) {
  if (sample >= MAX_FEATURE_VECTORS) {
   /* Reset the sample index */
   sample = 0;
   /* If no changes occurred in the last iteration, the exit,
    * otherwise, reset the changes counter to zero and continue.
    */
   if (changes == 0) break;
   else changes = 0;
  }
  /* Feed the sample prototype vector through the network. */
  class = feed_forward( sample );
  /* Update the weights for the winning output node (class). */
  updateNetwork( sample, class );
  /* Next sample */
  sample++;
 }
 ...
 return 0;
}
```

The feed_forward function implements the output node activations based on Eq 9.2 (see Listing 9.6). Given the input prototype feature vector index, we calculate the activations for each output node. This, using Eq 9.2, is the sum of the products of the weights for the particular class, and the values of the input feature vector. In a winner-takes-all fashion, we identify the output node with the lowest value, which represents the class to which the input feature vector belongs. Finally, we check to see if the feature vector has changed classes, and if so, we increment the changes variable to let the main loop that a class change occurred.

Listing 9.6:   Computing the output node activations with `feed_forward`.

```
int feed_forward( int feature_vector )
{
  int output, weight, best;
  double best_value;
  /* Compute each output node activation for the current
   * prototype vector.
   */
  for (output = 0 ; output < CLASSES ; output++) {
   outputs[output] = 0.0;
   /* Equation 9.2 */
   for (weight = 0 ; weight < MAX_FEATURES ; weight++) {
    outputs[output] +=
       weights[output][weight] *
         SCALE(fvec[feature_vector].features[weight]);
   }
  }
  /* Set the current best to class 0 */
  best = 0;
  best_value = outputs[0];
  /* Iterate through the remaining classes to identify which was best. */
  for (output = 1 ; output < CLASSES ; output++) {
   if (outputs[output] < best_value) {
    best = output;
    best_value = outputs[output];
   }
  }
  /* Keep track of when a prototype vector changes classes, for use as
   * a termination criteria.
   */
  if (best != fvec[feature_vector].class) {
   changes++;
   fvec[feature_vector].class = best;
  }
  return best;
}
```

Finally, during training, once we identify that a prototype feature vector belongs to a particular class, we update the weights for the class. This is done through a call to updateNetwork (see Listing 9.7). To the function, we provide the prototype vector index and the class to which it belongs. Each of the weights associated with the particular output node (class) is then updated per Eq 9.3. Note that we apply a learning rate to the weight update to provide a gradual change to the weights.

Listing 9.7:   Updating the weights for a particular class with updateNetwork.

```
void updateNetwork( int feature_vector, int class )
{
  int weight;
  for (weight = 0 ; weight < MAX_FEATURES ; weight++) {
    /* Equation 9.3 */
    weights[class][weight] += LEARNING_RATE *
        ( SCALE(fvec[feature_vector].features[weight]) -
        weights[class][weight] );
  }
  return;
}
```

Let's now see vector quantization in practice (Listing 9.8). Per the sample implementation, a set of random data is created that represents a variety of objects that differ in shape, size, and color. These are encoded into a feature vector (shape, texture, color) and applied to the network in order to train the weights. When training is complete (equilibrium is reached in the network), the classification is emitted.

For this set of randomized data, we see a very clear classification emerge from the data. From the feature vectors, we can see that class 0 contains all objects that have the box shape. Class 2 includes all objects that are smooth (except for boxes). Finally, Class 3 includes all objects not previously classified. This includes any object that isn't a box and isn't smooth. That's one possible classification, but given the number of box shapes that exist, it's not surprising that this particular categorization was found.

Listing 9.8:   Sample classification of random object data.

```
$ ./vq.exe
Class 0 contains:
```

```
 1 [BLACK ROUGH  BOX          ]
 2 [BLACK SMOOTH  BOX         ]
 3 [RED   SMOOTH  BOX         ]
 7 [BLACK SMOOTH  BOX         ]
 8 [BLACK SMOOTH  BOX         ]
13 [BLACK ROUGH   BOX         ]
16 [BLUE  SMOOTH BOX          ]
18 [BLACK DIMPLED BOX         ]
21 [RED   ROUGH  BOX          ]
23 [BLACK SMOOTH  BOX         ]
25 [BLACK SMOOTH  BOX         ]
27 [RED   ROUGH   BOX         ]
29 [RED   SMOOTH  BOX         ]
32 [RED   ROUGH   BOX         ]
39 [RED   DIMPLED BOX         ]
```

Class 1 contains:

```
 0 [BLACK SMOOTH  SPHERE      ]
12 [BLACK SMOOTH  SPHERE      ]
14 [RED   SMOOTH  SPHERE      ]
15 [BLUE  SMOOTH  SPHERE      ]
17 [RED   SMOOTH  SPHERE      ]
24 [RED   SMOOTH  CYLINDER    ]
26 [RED   SMOOTH  CYLINDER    ]
33 [BLUE  SMOOTH  CYLINDER    ]
34 [RED   SMOOTH  CYLINDER    ]
37 [RED   SMOOTH  CYLINDER    ]
```

Class 2 contains:

```
 4 [BLUE  DIMPLED CYLINDER    ]
 5 [BLACK DIMPLED SPHERE      ]
 6 [BLACK ROUGH   SPHERE      ]
 9 [BLACK ROUGH   SPHERE      ]
10 [BLACK DIMPLED CYLINDER    ]
11 [BLACK ROUGH   SPHERE      ]
19 [BLACK ROUGH   SPHERE      ]
20 [BLUE  ROUGH   SPHERE      ]
22 [BLACK ROUGH   SPHERE      ]
28 [BLUE  DIMPLED CYLINDER    ]
30 [RED   ROUGH   CYLINDER    ]
```

```
31 [BLACK ROUGH   CYLINDER      ]
35 [RED   DIMPLED CYLINDER      ]
36 [BLACK ROUGH   SPHERE        ]
38 [BLACK DIMPLED SPHERE        ]
$
```

Note that this method was unsupervised. The algorithm had no knowledge of the data, but did a reasonable job of segregating the data based on characteristics of the data. In one cluster, the data is segmented based on the shape, but in another, it's segmented based on a texture.

The simplicity of this algorithm makes it a great choice for clustering. One primary disadvantage of the algorithm is that the number of output classes must be defined up front. This is a significant disadvantage because it assumes that we have some general knowledge of the data and how it should be classified.

In addition to its clustering capabilities, you'll find vector quantization in other applications such as image and audio compression, and even speaker recognition. Identifying a speaker is an interesting problem and fundamentally comes down to a classification problem. The incoming voice audio is reduced to a feature vector, which is applied to a vector quantizer to identify the class (or speaker) that fits best.

K-MEANS CLUSTERING

A very popular algorithm for unsupervised clustering of feature vector data is called *k-Means* (where there are k clusters, and the average of the cluster contents determine the cluster centroid). This algorithm is popular primarily because it works relatively well and is extremely simple both to understand and to implement (see Figure 9.8).

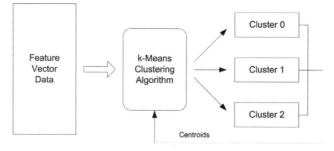

FIGURE 9.8:   Basic flow of the *k*-Means clustering algorithm.

FIGURE 9.9:   Demonstrating a centroid change with the loss of a data item.

The fundamental approach to k-Means clustering is based on centroids representing the average of the current set of feature vectors contained within the cluster. The centroid is the average of all feature vectors, and is recalculated whenever an object moves into or out of a cluster. Choosing a cluster for a given feature vector is based on the Euclidean distance of the feature vector and the available cluster centroids (see Figure 9.9). The closer the Euclidean distance, the higher the probability the feature vector belongs to the cluster.

Note that each time a cluster changes, its centroid also changes (as it's recalculated after every change). This means that over the duration of the algorithm, as the cluster's membership changes, the centroids change, which can mean that additional feature vectors can change cluster membership. For this reason, a typical termination criteria is an iteration through all feature vectors with none changing cluster membership.

k-Means Algorithm

The k-Means algorithm is one of many clustering algorithms, but remains popular due to its simplicity. It's also relatively efficient, but does have some disadvantages (such as inefficient methods for defining the clusters at initialization time). Let's first explore the details of the k-Means algorithm, and then we'll discuss the advantages and disadvantages of this method.

NOTE   *As with vector quantization, we'll use a very simple feature vector to discuss and explore k-Means in an implementation. Feature vectors will describe objects in terms of a number of dimensions (color, texture, and shape).*

We begin with a set of prototype feature vectors that are to be clustered based on their similarities and differences (see the flow shown in Figure 9.10). The number of clusters (k) must also be defined *a priori*. Each cluster has an associated centroid feature vector which represents the average of the prototype feature vectors contained within that cluster.

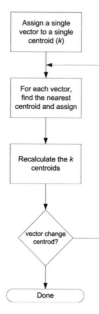

FIGURE 9.10: Basic flow of the _k_-Means clustering algorithm.

A centroid is defined as the center of the mass. In this context, the centroid is the center of a set of multi-dimensional prototype feature vectors.

We then take k of the prototype feature vectors and assign one each to the available clusters. These k prototype feature vectors can be picked at random, but ideally, we would choose vectors that are dissimilar. The simplest approach is to choose the first k feature vectors and assign them to the clusters. With the clusters now containing one prototype feature vector, we initialize the centroid. Since the cluster contains only one prototype feature vector, the centroid is equal to the prototype feature vector.

Next, we iterate through each of the available prototype feature vectors, and compute the Euclidean distance of the centroid to the prototype feature vector (see Eq 9.4, i is the feature index, x is the input feature vector, and c is the centroid). We pick the nearest centroid (defined as the smallest Euclidean distance) and assign the prototype vector to that centroid. We then recalculate the centroids to take into consideration their new members. Note that this can be done after each evaluation or in a batch mode where the feature vectors are assigned, and then the centroids updated at the end.

$$d = \sqrt{\sum_i^{i<n}(x_i c_i)^2} \qquad \text{(Eq 9.4)}$$

If at the end of evaluating all prototype feature vectors, none have changed clusters, we can assume that we've reached equilibrium and the clustering is complete. If a centroid did change (because of gaining and/or losing a prototype feature vector), we re-evaluate each prototype vector again. Recalculating the centroid simply involves summing the prototype feature vectors and dividing the resulting vector by the total number of prototype vectors in the cluster.

The primary disadvantage of k-Means is that the number of clusters must be defined *a priori*. This can require some experimentation for the problem at hand, to identify how many clusters should be present to properly classify the data. As defined in the introduction, initialization of the clusters can also be problematic. Therefore, multiple runs of the algorithm may be required to find a proper classification.

That's the basic algorithm for k-Means clustering. Let's now explore a sample implementation that clusters objects (based on Figure 9.7).

k-Means Implementation

To demonstrate the k-Means algorithm, we'll reuse the data infrastructure from the vector quantization example (object classification based on shape, color, and texture). The prototype vectors contain both a feature vector and the current class to which the prototype vector belongs. The centroids are represented as a floating-point vector (see Listing 9.9). The centroids differ from the prototype feature vectors because the centroids will represent the average of the member prototype vectors, and therefore require floating-point precision.

Listing 9.9:   k-Means types and symbolic constants.

```
#define MAX_FEATURE_VECTORS     40
#define MAX_FEATURES            3
typedef struct {
  int class;
  int features[MAX_FEATURES];
} feature_vector_t;
/* Prototype Feature Vectors */
feature_vector_t fvec[MAX_FEATURE_VECTORS];
/* Number of clusters */
#define K               3
/* Cluster Centroids */
double centroids[K][MAX_FEATURES];
```

We'll present a few of the functions that implement the k-Means algorithm: the entire implementation can be found on the CD-ROM. For the purposes of explanation, we'll explore the k-Means main loop, identifying the nearest centroid, computing the geometric distance, and finally recalculating a centroid given the current prototype feature vectors.

The implementation of object classification using k-Means clustering can be found on the CD-ROM at ./software/ch9/kmeans.c.

The k-Means main loop implements the high-level algorithm for *k*-Means clustering (see Listing 9.10). It begins by initializing the random set of prototype feature vectors, and then assigning some number of them (**K**) to clusters. Once we have a set of initialized clusters (with one random item each), we calculate the centroid values for the clusters for later use by the algorithm.

The main loop for k-Means then begins, with the termination criteria that all clusters are satisfactorily classified (no prototype vectors moved in the last iteration). Note that we iterate through the prototype vectors backwards because the first K has been assigned to the clusters as part of the initialize_membership function. As part of the iteration, we first call the partition_feature_vector to identify to which cluster the prototype feature vector belongs. If the vector changes classes, we recalculate the centroid for the cluster that lost the vector as well as the cluster that gained it.

Listing 9.10:   The k-Means algorithm main loop.

```
void k_means_clustering( void )
{
  int done = 0, i;
  int old, new;
  int proto_vector;
  /* Create the random set of prototype feature vectors */
  initialize_prototype_vectors();
  /* Set K vectors to clusters (to initialize the centroids) */
  initialize_membership();
  /* Compute the centroids for each cluster */
  for (i = 0 ; i < K ; i++) {
    compute_centroids( i );
  }
  while (!done) {
    done = 1;
```

```
/* Iterate through the available prototype feature vectors */
for (proto_vector = MAX_FEATURE_VECTORS-1 ; proto_vector >= 0 ;
    proto_vector--) {
  /* Find the cluster to which this prototype vector belongs */
  new = partition_feature_vector( proto_vector );
  /* Did the prototype feature vector change classes */
  if (new != fvec[proto_vector].class) {
    old = fvec[proto_vector].class;
    fvec[proto_vector].class = new;
    /* Recompute the affected centroids (-1 = not yet clustered) */
    if (old != -1) {
      compute_centroids( old );
    }
    compute_centroids( new );
    done = 0;
  }
 }
 }
}
```

The function partition_feature_vector is used to identify the cluster with the centroid nearest the prototype feature vector under review. The algorithm iterates through each of the available clusters, and calculates the Euclidean distance from the prototype feature vector to the cluster's centroid with a call to geometricDistance. As each distance is calculated, the cluster representing the lowest distance is saved and returned as the cluster to which this prototype vector should be moved.

Listing 9.11:   Finding the nearest cluster.

```
int partition_feature_vector( int proto_vector )
{
  int cluster, best = 0;
  double gdCur, gdBest = 999.99;
  /* Find the centroid that best matches the prototype feature vector */
  for (cluster = 0 ; cluster < K ; cluster++) {
    gdCur = geometricDistance( proto_vector, cluster );
    /* Keep track of the closest cluster centroid */
    if (gdCur < gdBest) {
      best = cluster;
```

```
   gdBest = gdCur;
  }
 }
 return best;
}
```

Calculating the Euclidean distance between the prototype feature vector and the cluster centroid is done with a call to geometricDistance. Using Eq 9.4, we step through each element of the vector, summing the squares of the difference. After each element of the vector has been iterated, the square root of the result is returned.

Listing 9.12:   Computing the geometric distance between the feature vector and the centroid.

```
double geometricDistance( int proto_vector, int centroid )
{
  int feature;
  double gd = 0.0;
  /* Equation 9.4 */
  for (feature = 0 ; feature < MAX_FEATURES ; feature++) {
   gd += ( ((double)fvec[proto_vector].features[feature] -
             centroids[centroid][feature]) *
         ((double)fvec[proto_vector].features[feature] -
             centroids[centroid][feature]) );
  }
  return( sqrt(gd) );
}
```

Finally, the `compute_centroids` function is used to recalculate the centroid for the defined cluster. This function very simply sums the fields of the prototype feature vectors that are contained within the current cluster, and then divides each field by the total number. The resulting centroid represents the multi-dimensional center of the cluster's prototype feature vectors.

Listing 9.13:   Recalculating the cluster centroids.

```
void compute_centroids( int cluster )
{
  int proto_vector, feature;
```

```
int total = 0;
/* Clear the centroid vector */
for (feature = 0 ; feature < MAX_FEATURES ; feature++) {
  centroids[cluster][feature] = 0.0;
}
/* Calculate the centroid vector for the current cluster */
for (proto_vector = 0 ; proto_vector < MAX_FEATURE_VECTORS ;
     proto_vector++) {
  if (fvec[proto_vector].class == cluster) {
    for (feature = 0 ; feature < MAX_FEATURES ; feature++) {
      centroids[cluster][feature] +=
          (double)fvec[proto_vector].features[feature];
    }
    total++;
  }
}
/* Compute the average for the centroid */
for (feature = 0 ; feature < MAX_FEATURES ; feature++) {
  centroids[cluster][feature] /= (double)total;
}
return;
}
```

Let's now look at a sample result of the k-Means algorithm (see Listing 9.14). Class 0 is clearly a cluster of smooth objects, and Class 2 contains red objects that are not smooth. Class 1 then becomes all objects that are neither red, nor smooth.

Listing 9.14:   Sample k-Means classification of random object data.

```
$ ./kmeans.exe
Class 0 contains:
        5 [RED   SMOOTH  BOX      ]
        6 [RED   SMOOTH  BOX      ]
        7 [RED   SMOOTH  BOX      ]
        8 [RED   SMOOTH  SPHERE   ]
       11 [BLACK SMOOTH  SPHERE   ]
       12 [BLACK SMOOTH  BOX      ]
       14 [BLUE  SMOOTH  CYLINDER ]
       16 [BLACK SMOOTH  BOX      ]
```

```
17 [BLACK SMOOTH  CYLINDER ]
19 [BLUE  SMOOTH  BOX      ]
24 [RED   SMOOTH  CYLINDER ]
25 [RED   SMOOTH  SPHERE   ]
30 [RED   SMOOTH  BOX      ]
31 [BLACK SMOOTH  CYLINDER ]
32 [BLUE  SMOOTH  SPHERE   ]
33 [BLUE  SMOOTH  CYLINDER ]
35 [BLACK SMOOTH  CYLINDER ]
36 [BLACK SMOOTH  BOX      ]
39 [RED   SMOOTH  SPHERE   ]
```

Class 1 contains:

```
 0 [BLUE  DIMPLED CYLINDER ]
 1 [BLACK DIMPLED CYLINDER ]
 4 [BLUE  DIMPLED BOX      ]
 9 [BLACK ROUGH   SPHERE   ]
10 [BLUE  DIMPLED SPHERE   ]
15 [BLACK ROUGH   SPHERE   ]
18 [BLUE  DIMPLED CYLINDER ]
20 [BLUE  DIMPLED BOX      ]
22 [BLACK DIMPLED SPHERE   ]
23 [BLUE  DIMPLED SPHERE   ]
26 [BLUE  DIMPLED CYLINDER ]
27 [BLUE  ROUGH   SPHERE   ]
29 [BLACK DIMPLED BOX      ]
34 [BLUE  DIMPLED CYLINDER ]
```

Class 2 contains:

```
 2 [RED   DIMPLED CYLINDER ]
 3 [RED   ROUGH   SPHERE   ]
13 [RED   DIMPLED SPHERE   ]
21 [RED   DIMPLED CYLINDER ]
28 [RED   DIMPLED CYLINDER ]
37 [RED   ROUGH   SPHERE   ]
38 [RED   ROUGH   CYLINDER ]
```

$

Recall that from initialization, the first k prototype feature vectors are assigned to their same numbered cluster (vector 0 to cluster 0, vector 1 to cluster 1, etc.). Note in this example that while prototype vector 2 remained in cluster 2, prototype vector 0 moved to cluster 1 (since cluster 0 was used to classify smooth objects).

The k-Means algorithm is a useful algorithm because it's simple and works well. It's not without its issues (such as *a priori* definition of k, and sensitivity to initialization), but these can be combated through multiple runs of the algorithm on the data set.

> *It's good to note that there's no theoretical solution for understanding the optimal number of classes for any dataset. An experimental solution is to execute the k-Means algorithm on the dataset multiple times and review the results. Fewer clusters mean better generalization in the results, where more clusters tends to end in clusters with very specific attributes and a risk of over-fitting.*

For k-Means and vector quantization, the primary disadvantage is that the number of clusters must be predefined. Let's now explore an algorithm that can dynamically create new clusters when the dataset warrants them.

ADAPTIVE RESONANCE THEORY (ART)

Adaptive Resonance Theory is a collection of models for unsupervised learning. In this section, we'll focus solely on ART-1, which is applicable to binary input vectors. For continuous variables, the ART-2 algorithm can be used.

ART-1 in particular was designed to resolve the stability-plasticity dillema. This refers to a conflict in the ability to maintain old learned information while still being adaptive to learn new information. An algorithm is defined as plastic if it can adapt to new information. Additionally, an algorithm is stable if it can retain previously learned knowledge. The goal then is to create an algorithm that can retain previously learned knowledge while at the same time integrating newly discovered knowledge. In this way, the algorithm is both stable and plastic. Many clustering algorithms are one or the other, but not necessarily both.

As we discussed in k-Means clustering, an interesting advantage to ART-1 is in its ability to create a new cluster if the underlying data warrants. It accomplishes this with a vigilance parameter that helps to determine when to cluster a feature vector to a "close" cluster, or when to simply create a new cluster into which this feature vector is inserted.

ART-1 Algorithm

The ART-1 algorithm is simple, not quite as simple as the k-Means algorithm, but straightforward, nonetheless. Let's begin with a quick overview of ART-1 and then we'll dig deeper into the algorithm to understand how it works.

We begin the algorithm with a set of unclustered feature vectors and some number of clusters. We take each feature vector, in turn, and attempt to find the cluster to which it's closest. If no clusters are found that are near the feature vector, we create a new cluster and assign the feature vector to it. Otherwise, with a cluster that's near the feature vector, we test how close the feature vector is to the cluster. If the feature vector is near the cluster, then we assign the feature vector to the cluster, and update the cluster. Otherwise, we continue to test the feature vector to all available clusters. If all available clusters have been exhausted, then we simply assign the feature vector to a new cluster.

We then start the process again with a new feature vector. If we work through all available feature vectors, and none change their cluster, all samples have been satisfactorily clustered and the process is complete. That's ART-1 in a nutshell. Now let's explore a little further to understand how the algorithm maintains both stability and plasticity.

First, each feature vector is a binary string of a given width (n). Each cluster is represented by a vector that is the boolean AND operator of all feature vectors contained within the cluster (see Figure 9.11).

Note from Figure 9.11 that the width of the feature vector (and the cluster, which must be the same) is defined as n (or 8). We'll use the symbol p to represent the current cluster (typically indexed, as in p_i). The symbol I represents the current feature vector. Finally, symbols β and ρ are constant values, and we'll discuss these shortly.

Given a feature vector, and a list of available clusters (initially, all will be empty), the first step is to test the similarity of a feature vector to the cluster's vector. This is done using Eq 9.5.

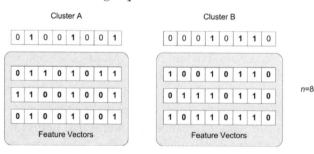

FIGURE 9.11: **Boolean AND relationship of feature vectors to the cluster vector for ART-1.**

$$\frac{||p_i \cap I||}{\beta + ||p_i||} > \frac{||I||}{\beta + n} \qquad \text{(Eq 9.5)}$$

Note that in Eq 9.5, the double vertical bars simply represent the number of 1s that are set in the particular vector. For example, the vector representing cluster A in Figure 9.11 would be 3. The inverted 'U' represents the boolean AND operation between the cluster vector and the current feature vector.

The similarity test in Eq 9.5 calculates how near the feature vector is to the cluster vector. The higher the value, the closer the vector is to the cluster. Therefore, if Eq 9.5 is satisfied, then the feature vector can be defined as sufficiently close to the cluster. If this equation fails for all cluster vectors, then we simply create a new cluster for this feature vector and continue to the next feature vector. Otherwise, if it is sufficiently close, we test for vigilance acceptability. The β parameter is used as a "tie-breaker" to give deference to clusters with more 1s in the case that the feature vector and cluster are similar. This parameter is typically a small number (greater than zero and less than n).

The vigilance test is the final determiner for whether the feature vector should be added to the particular cluster (see Eq 9.6).

$$\frac{||p_i \cap I||}{||I||} \geq \rho \qquad \text{(Eq 9.6)}$$

This equation simply identifies if the feature vector is sufficiently close to the cluster (as a ratio of the matching 1s between the feature vector and the cluster). This means that if vigilance (ρ) is high (such as 0.9) more clusters will tend to be created, and if vigilance is low, then fewer clusters are created. If ρ is set to 1.0, then the feature vector must match the cluster exactly in order to join it.

If the feature vector fails the vigilance test, and there are no further clusters to test, then a new cluster is created for this feature vector (as there are no similar clusters available).

Note that while clusters are created, feature vectors may drop out of a cluster and into another based on new feature vectors being added, and adjusting the cluster vector. When no cluster changes are made for an entire iteration through the available feature vectors, the algorithm is complete.

When a feature vector joins a cluster, the cluster's vector must be updated to incorporate the features of the new addition. If the feature vector

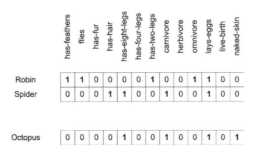

	has-feathers	flies	has-fur	has-hair	has-eight-legs	has-four-legs	has-two-legs	carnivore	herbivore	omnivore	lays-eggs	live-birth	naked-skin
Robin	1	1	0	0	0	0	1	0	0	1	1	0	0
Spider	0	0	0	1	1	0	0	1	0	0	1	0	0
Octopus	0	0	0	0	1	0	0	1	0	0	1	0	1

FIGURE 9.12: Representing an animal's characteristics for the ART-1 algorithm.

added is the only member of the cluster, then the cluster vector is identical to the feature vector. Otherwise, each of the cluster's feature vectors (I_i) is assimilated using Eq 9.7.

$$p = p \cap I_i \qquad \text{(Eq 9.7)}$$

ART-1 is stable (retains knowledge), but is also plastic in that it can indefinitely incorporate new knowledge given a sufficient number of clusters. Let's now explore the implementation of ART-1 for an object classification task.

ART-Implementation

Let's start with a discussion of the clustering problem at hand and then review the representation for the feature vector and cluster vector. To demonstrate the ART-1 algorithm, we'll use a feature vector representing attributes of a number of animals (see Figure 9.12). These characteristics include whether the animal gives live birth, or lays eggs, or whether the animal has fur, hair, or naked-skin, etc.

The implementation of animal clustering using ART-1 can be found on the CD-ROM at ./software/ch9/art1.c. The major functions that make up ART-1 are explored here, but the entire implementation is provided on the CD-ROM.

Both feature vectors and clusters are represented with the vector_t type. This contains not only the binary feature vector, but a union which represents the current class (in the case of a feature vector, for fvec) or the member count (in the case of a cluster, pvec). The feature vectors are statically initialized, while the clusters (pvec) are initialized with a call to initialize_prototype_vectors.

Listing 9.15:   Feature vector and cluster representation for ART-1.

```
/* Number of clusters */
#define MAX_CLUSTERS            5

/* Number of prototype feature vectors */
#define MAX_FEATURE_VECTORS     19

/* Size (width) of feature vector */
#define MAX_FEATURES            13

typedef struct {
  union {
    int class;              /* For Feature Vectors */
    int count;              /* For Clusters       */
  } u;
  int features[MAX_FEATURES];
} vector_t;

/* Prototype Feature Vectors */
vector_t fvec[MAX_FEATURE_VECTORS]={

/* Robin    */ { {-1}, { 1, 1, 0, 0, 0, 0, 1, 0, 0, 1, 1, 0, 0 } },
/* Spider   */ { {-1}, { 0, 0, 0, 1, 1, 0, 0, 1, 0, 0, 1, 0, 0 } },
/* Cat      */ { {-1}, { 0, 0, 1, 0, 0, 1, 0, 0, 0, 1, 0, 1, 0 } },
/* Salmon   */ { {-1}, { 0, 0, 0, 0, 0, 0, 0, 0, 0, 1, 1, 0, 1 } },
/* Mouse    */ { {-1}, { 0, 0, 1, 0, 0, 1, 0, 0, 0, 1, 0, 1, 0 } },
/* Moose    */ { {-1}, { 0, 0, 0, 1, 0, 1, 0, 0, 1, 0, 0, 1, 0 } },
/* Bat      */ { {-1}, { 0, 1, 1, 0, 0, 0, 1, 0, 0, 1, 0, 1, 0 } },
/* Dog      */ { {-1}, { 0, 0, 1, 0, 0, 1, 0, 0, 0, 1, 0, 1, 0 } },
/* Snake    */ { {-1}, { 0, 0, 0, 0, 0, 0, 0, 1, 0, 0, 1, 0, 1 } },
/* Lion     */ { {-1}, { 0, 0, 1, 0, 0, 1, 0, 1, 0, 0, 0, 1, 0 } },
/* Iguana   */ { {-1}, { 0, 0, 0, 0, 0, 1, 0, 0, 0, 1, 1, 0, 1 } },
/* Dolphin  */ { {-1}, { 0, 0, 0, 0, 0, 0, 0, 1, 0, 0, 0, 1, 1 } },
/* Zebra    */ { {-1}, { 0, 0, 1, 0, 0, 1, 0, 0, 1, 0, 0, 1, 0 } },
/* Horse    */ { {-1}, { 0, 0, 1, 0, 0, 1, 0, 0, 1, 0, 0, 1, 0 } },
/* Ostrich  */ { {-1}, { 1, 0, 0, 0, 0, 0, 1, 0, 1, 0, 1, 0, 0 } },
/* Penguin  */ { {-1}, { 1, 0, 0, 0, 0, 0, 1, 0, 0, 0, 1, 0, 0 } },
/* Tiger    */ { {-1}, { 0, 0, 1, 0, 0, 1, 0, 1, 0, 0, 0, 1, 0 } },
/* Platypus */ { {-1}, { 0, 0, 1, 0, 0, 1, 0, 1, 0, 0, 1, 0, 0 } },
/* Octopus  */ { {-1}, { 0, 0, 0, 0, 1, 0, 0, 1, 0, 0, 1, 0, 1 } }
};
```

```
/* Clusters */
vector_t pvec[MAX_CLUSTERS];

/* Algorithm constants */
#define BETA                    ((double)8.0)
#define VIGILANCE               ((double)0.2)
```

Let's now have a look at the support functions for ART-1, which include creating a new cluster, adding a feature vector to a cluster, and recomputing the vector for a cluster.

Creating a new cluster involves finding a cluster that's empty, and then adding the defined feature vector to it. The feature vector's class is then adjusted for the cluster and the cluster's count set (see Listing 9.16). The routine begins by searching for a cluster that has no members. If one is not found, the feature vector remains unclustered (class set to -1) and the function returns. Otherwise, the cluster vector is copied from the feature vector, and the feature vector class and cluster count are initialized.

Listing 9.16:   Creating a new cluster with `create_new_cluster`.

```
void create_new_cluster( int vector )
{
  int cluster, i;
  /* Find an empty cluster */
  for (cluster = 0 ; cluster < MAX_CLUSTERS ; cluster++) {
    if (pvec[cluster].u.count == 0) break;
  }
  /* No cluster available -- unclassified */
  if (cluster == MAX_CLUSTERS) {
    fvec[vector].u.class = -1;
    return;
  }
  /* Set the feature vector's class to this new cluster */
  fvec[vector].u.class = cluster;
  /* Copy the feature vector to the cluster */
  for (i = 0 ; i < MAX_FEATURES ; i++) {
    pvec[cluster].features[i] = fvec[vector].features[i];
  }
  pvec[cluster].u.count = 1;
  return;
}
```

Adding a feature vector to an existing cluster (one with existing members) is achieved with the function add_to_cluster. The first thing this function must do is determine if the feature vector is being removed from another cluster (if the class is not -1). If another cluster is losing this feature vector, then we must reset the class for the feature vector and then make a call to recompute_cluster to redefine the cluster's vector. Then, we add the feature vector to the intended cluster and recompute its vector (with another call to recompute_cluster).

Listing 9.17:   Adding a feature vector to a cluster with add_to_cluster.

```
void add_to_cluster( int cluster, int vector )
{
  int old_cluster;
  /* If feature vector had previously been clustered */
  if (fvec[vector].u.class != -1) {
    old_cluster = fvec[vector].u.class;
    fvec[vector].u.class = -1;
    pvec[old_cluster].u.count--;
    recompute_cluster( old_cluster );
  }
  /* Add the feature vector to the new cluster */
  fvec[vector].u.class = cluster;
  recompute_cluster( cluster );
  pvec[cluster].u.count++;
  return;
}
```

Now let's bring it all together with the ART-1 main loop. This function, art1, implements the fundamental ART-1 algorithm, using the previously discussed vector support functions. We iterate through each of the feature vectors, looking for the nearest cluster. This begins with the similarity test (per Eq 9.5), which is followed by the vigilance test (Eq 9.6). If the feature vector is near the cluster and passes the vigilance test, then the feature vector is added to the cluster (through a call to add_to_cluster). If the feature vector is not clustered after checking all of the available clusters, then a new cluster is created for it using create_new_cluster. This process continues until no changes to clusters are made.

Listing 9.18:   The ART-1 main loop (art1).

```
void art1()
{
  int done = 0, cluster, i, clustered;
  vector_t result;
  double max, sim, res_magnitude, fvec_magnitude, pvec_magnitude;
  while (!done) {
    done = 1;
    /* Iterate through each of the prototype feature vectors */
    for (i = 0 ; i < MAX_FEATURE_VECTORS ; i++) {
      clustered = 0;
      /* Iterate through each of the active clusters */
      for (cluster = 0 ; cluster < MAX_CLUSTERS ; cluster++) {
        /* Skip empty clusters */
        if (pvec[cluster].u.count == 0) continue;
        /* Mask the feature vector with the cluster vector */
        vectorAnd( &result, &fvec[i], &pvec[cluster] );
        res_magnitude = (double)vectorMagnitude( &result );
        fvec_magnitude = (double)vectorMagnitude( &fvec[i] );
        pvec_magnitude = (double)vectorMagnitude( &pvec[cluster] );
        max = res_magnitude / ( BETA + fvec_magnitude );
        sim = pvec_magnitude / ( BETA + (double)MAX_FEATURE_VECTORS
);
        /* Test similarity of feature vector to cluster */
        /* Equation 9.5 */
        if (max > sim) {
          /* Feature vector is sufficiently similar to cluster.  Next, test
           * for vigilance acceptability (Equation 9.6).
           */
          if ( (res_magnitude / pvec_magnitude) >= VIGILANCE ) {
            if (fvec[i].u.class != cluster) {
              add_to_cluster( cluster, i );
              done = 0;
            }
            clustered = 1;
            break;
          }
        }
      }
    } /* clusters loop */
```

```
    if (!clustered) {
      /* Add to an empty cluster */
      create_new_cluster( i );
      done = 0;
    }
  } /* vectors loop */
  }
  return;
}
```

Let's now have a look at ART-1 in action. Listing 9.19 shows the result of clustering the animal feature vector data shown in Listing 9.15 (with the feature columns shown in Figure 9.12). What's shown is a reasonable clustering of the data into five classes. Class 0 represents animals that fly while Class 1 contains all animals that are carnivores. Class 2 includes all four-legged animals and Class 3 has a single member (salmon), representing fish. Finally, Class 4 represents non-flying birds, but have clustered based on their having feathers and laying eggs.

Listing 9.19:   Sample output of ART-1 clustering.

```
$ ./art1.exe
Class 0 contains:
     0 [1 1 0 0 0 0 1 0 0 1 1 0 0 ] Robin
     6 [0 1 1 0 0 0 1 0 0 1 0 1 0 ] Bat
Class 1 contains:
     1 [0 0 0 1 1 0 0 1 0 0 1 0 0 ] Spider
     8 [0 0 0 0 0 0 0 1 0 0 1 0 1 ] Snake
     9 [0 0 1 0 0 1 0 1 0 0 0 1 0 ] Lion
    11 [0 0 0 0 0 0 0 1 0 0 0 1 1 ] Dolphin
    16 [0 0 1 0 0 1 0 1 0 0 0 1 0 ] Tiger
    17 [0 0 1 0 0 1 0 1 0 0 1 0 0 ] Platypus
    18 [0 0 0 0 1 0 0 1 0 0 1 0 1 ] Octopus
Class 2 contains:
     2 [0 0 1 0 0 1 0 0 0 1 0 1 0 ] Cat
     4 [0 0 1 0 0 1 0 0 0 1 0 1 0 ] Mouse
     5 [0 0 0 1 0 1 0 0 1 0 0 1 0 ] Moose
     7 [0 0 1 0 0 1 0 0 0 1 0 1 0 ] Dog
    10 [0 0 0 0 0 1 0 0 0 1 1 0 1 ] Iguana
    12 [0 0 1 0 0 1 0 0 1 0 0 1 0 ] Zebra
```

13 [0 0 1 0 0 1 0 0 1 0 0 1 0] Horse
Class 3 contains:
3 [0 0 0 0 0 0 0 0 0 1 1 0 1] Salmon
Class 4 contains:
14 [1 0 0 0 0 0 1 0 1 0 1 0 0] Ostrich
15 [1 0 0 0 0 0 1 0 0 0 1 0 0] Penguin

Note that these clusters were based on a β of 8.0 and a ρ of 0.2. By decreasing the vigilance parameter, we could classify the feature data into fewer clusters.

The ART-1 algorithm is a useful clustering algorithm with the obvious advantage over k-Means in that new clusters can be created if the feature data requires it. ART-1 can also be tuned using the B ("tie-breaker") and p (vigilance) parameters. Regardless of these settings, ART-1 is stable in that once the clusters have formed, performing additional iterations of the algorithm on the same data will not change the clusters.

HOPFIELD AUTO-ASSOCIATIVE MODEL

As our final example of unsupervised learning, let's explore the Hopfield auto-associative model for pattern recall. Recall the discussion of a simple auto-associator early in this chapter for Hebbian learning.

An auto-associative network has the ability to store the set of training examples so that they can be recalled later. Additionally, if incomplete or noisy input patters are provided, the auto-associative model can recall the original pattern (or memory), making them operate as a Content-Addressable Memory (or CAM).

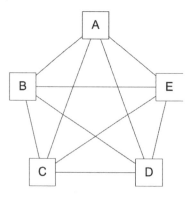

FIGURE 9.13:   The Hopfield auto-associative network uses a recurrent weight structure.

We'll focus on the Hopfield model here, which is a recurrent neural network with discrete inputs and activations (in the domain {-1, 1}). Every input connects to every other input, but self-connections are not permitted. Additionally, the inputs and outputs are the same cells (see Figure 9.13).

Early learning algorithms for auto-associators were commonly called one-shot learning algorithms. Using this algorithm, the training examples are used once to generate the weights for the network, rather than tuning the weights by iterating through the examples multiple times. One-shot learning is both simple, and also very fast.

Hopfield Auto-Associator Algorithm

Building a simple Hopfield auto-associator is quite simple, and the algorithm is very straightforward. The first step is the creation of the weights for the recurrent neural network. This is done by summing the outer products of each training example that is to be "memorized" by the network (see Eq 9.8).

$$W = \sum E_i E_i \qquad \text{(Eq 9.8)}$$

In our example implementation, we'll use a one-dimensional vector to represent the examples. The result will be a two-dimensional matrix of weights (but the diagonal will be zero, as self-connections are not permitted). The weight matrix is summed over the examples that are to be trained.

We now have a weight matrix that can be used for recall of training examples. To validate the recall features of the weight matrix, we can apply the weight matrix to the example vector to produce the activation. It's important to note that depending on the size of the vector, and number of training examples, not all examples will be stored in their entirety. Therefore, some examples may not be fully recalled. It is shown that for N cells in the Hopfield network (for the discrete case), 0.15N training examples can be memorized. [Gallant 1994]

NOTE *When considering recall, there are two fundamental modes by which this can operate. In the synchronous mode, all cells are updated at the same time, and therefore, each cell is able to use its inputs statically (as none of the other cells are changing while the cell is updated). In the asynchronous mode, the cells of the network fire independently and asynchronously of one another. This means that the recall is dependent on the firing order, and therefore multiple cycles may be required in order reach a state of equilibrium.*

During recall, each cell of the recall vector is a sum of the products of the current input and associated weights (see Eq 9.9). Further, the output is bound to the discrete range of {-1, 1} using the sign function (1 if $S_i>=0$, -1 if $S_i<0$).

$$S_i(t) = \sum_j w_{i,j} u_j(t) \qquad \text{(Eq 9.9)}$$

The pattern recall Y can therefore be defined as a simple matrix product of the test (example) vector E, and the weight matrix W (see Eq 9.10).

$$Y = E \cdot W \qquad \text{(Eq 9.10)}$$

Let's now explore a sample implementation of the discrete Hopfield algorithm that demonstrates pattern recall, even in the presence of noise.

Hopfield Implementation

Let's begin with a discussion of the network representation and the essential types that are used to implement the Hopfield algorithm (see Listing 9.20). We'll use a 9 by 9 matrix for patterns in the Hopfield implementation, but represent them as a one-dimensional vector of size N. As we're implementing the discrete model of Hopfield, a two-dimensional int array is used to represent the weights. The weights array can be viewed as the first dimension representing the source vector index, and the second dimension representing the weight index to the alternate cells.

The type example_t is used to represent the examples, inputs vector, and outputs vector. Recall that we're implementing symmetric updates, so we'll maintain separate input and output vectors. A single example is shown in Listing 9.20, which demonstrates the representation of the training vector.

Listing 9.20:   Fundamental types and symbolics for Hopfield implementation.

```
#define M                    9
#define N                    (M*M)
#define MAX_EXAMPLES         4
typedef int example_t[N];
int weights[N][N];
example_t inputs;
example_t outputs;
#define SGN(x)          ((x) >= 0 ? 1 : -1)
example_t examples[MAX_EXAMPLES]={
 /*Plus */ {  1,  1,  1,  1, -1,  1,  1,  1,  1,
```

```
     1,  1,  1,  1, -1,  1,  1,  1,  1,
     1,  1,  1,  1, -1,  1,  1,  1,  1,
     1,  1,  1,  1, -1,  1,  1,  1,  1,
    -1, -1, -1, -1, -1, -1, -1, -1, -1,
     1,  1,  1,  1, -1,  1,  1,  1,  1,
     1,  1,  1,  1, -1,  1,  1,  1,  1,
     1,  1,  1,  1, -1,  1,  1,  1,  1,
     1,  1,  1,  1, -1,  1,  1,  1,  1},
     ...
};
```

The first step in the Hopfield algorithm is the training of the weights using the example training data (Listing 9.21). We iterate through each of the training examples, summing their outer products to produce a new matrix of connection weights. Note that self connections are not permitted, so a zero diagonal will be present in the weight matrix.

Listing 9.21:   Generating the weights array using the example vectors.

```
void generate_weights_from_examples( void )
{
  int e, r, c;
  /* First, clear the weights */
  for (r = 0 ; r < N ; r++) {
    for (c = 0 ; c < N ; c++) {
      weights[r][c] = 0;
    }
  }
  /* Equation 9.8 */
  for (e = 0 ; e < MAX_EXAMPLES ; e++) {
    for (r = 0 ; r < N ; r++) {
      for (c = 0 ; c < N ; c++) {
        /* Don't permit self-connections */
        if (r == c) continue;
        weights[r][c] += examples[e][r] * examples[e][c];
      }
    }
  }
  return;
}
```

Listing 9.22 shows the function for computing the network activations. This very simply is a matrix multiplication of the input matrix (1 by 81) by the connection weight matrix (81 by 81) resulting in the output matrix (81 by 1). We then scale the activations (output matrix) using the SGN function to bound it to the discrete output values (-1 and 1).

Listing 9.22   Computing the output activations for a given input vector.

```
void compute_activations( void )
{
  int r,c;
  int temp[N][N];
  bzero( (void *)temp, sizeof(temp) );
  for (r = 0 ; r < N ; r++) {
    for (c = 0 ; c < N ; c++) {
      if (r == c) continue;
      temp[r][c] += inputs[r] * weights[r][c];
    }
  }
  for (c = 0 ; c < N ; c++) {
    outputs[c] = 0;
    for (r = 0 ; r < N ; r++) {
      outputs[c] += temp[r][c];
    }
    outputs[c] = SGN(outputs[c]);
  }
  return;
}
```

Using the Hopfield network model for training and recall (using the functions discussed here) is then a simple linear process (see Listing 9.23). It begins with the generation of the connection weight matrix (generate_weights_from_examples). Next, we take a training example and copy it to the inputs matrix, with some amount of noise (using set_inputs_to_example). Finally, we compute the output activations using compute_activations and then emit the resulting output matrix with emit_result.

Listing 9.23   Using the Hopfield network model.

```
generate_weights_from_examples();
set_inputs_to_example( e, noise );
```

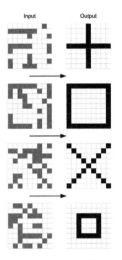

FIGURE 9.14: Sample activations for the Hopfield model implementation.

compute_activations( );
emit_result(outputs);

Let's now look at the Hopfield network model in action. We'll use a 9x9 matrix to represent the input and output matrices. The implementation supports four different input patterns with increasing amounts of noise to test the recall capabilities of the network. Figure 9.14 demonstrates one instance of pattern recall for each of the four patterns. On the left side are the inputs patterns (sample pattern with up to 20% noise) and on the right is the activation of the Hopfield network (the original input pattern).

Note the similarities between Hopfield's model and the Hebbian learning model. Weight connections are strengthened when the example cells are similar in sign, and are weakened when the signs of the cells are different.

CHAPTER SUMMARY

This chapter explored a variety of unsupervised neural network architectures and learning algorithms. Unsupervised learning algorithms are useful to discover the underlying structure of a data set. We began with a biologically plausible learning method for patterns called Hebbian Learning and demonstrated its pattern storage and recall capabilities. Next, we explored a number of clustering algorithms that were capable of segregating data based on their similarities and differences. Algorithms explored included vector quantization, k-Means clustering, and Adaptive Resonance Theory (ART-1). Finally, we ended the chapter with a return to pattern storage and recall with a discussion of the Hopfield auto-associator (another biologically plausible model).

REFERENCES

[Gallant 1994] Gallant, Stephen I. *Neural Network Learning and Expert Systems*. The MIT Press, Cambridge, Massachusetts, 1994.

[Hebb 1949] Hebb, D.O., *The Organization of Behavior: A Neuropsychological Theory*. Wiley, New York, 1949.

EXERCISES

1. Explain some of the uses of unsupervised learning algorithms.
2. Define the fundamental idea behind Hebbian learning.
3. Using the Hebb rule implementation on the CD-ROM, experiment with two different datasets. In the first, use patterns that are similar, and in the second use patterns that are very different. How does recall differ in the presence of noise or incomplete input patterns?
4. In a typical winner-takes-all network, the largest activation is used as the proper classification. What is the relevance of using the smallest activation in vector quantization?
5. Define the type of neural network used for vector quantization, and explain the learning algorithm.
6. What is a primary disadvantage of vector quantization?
7. Describe the fundamental ideas behind k-Means clustering and the use of centroids for cluster representation.
8. Define the primary advantage and disadvantage of the k-Means clustering algorithm.
9. What are the issues for k-Means cluster initialization, and in what ways could it be improved?
10. What is meant by the terms plastic and stable for a clustering algorithm?
11. Describe the basic process of the ART-1 algorithm.
12. What is the purpose of the vigilance test in the ART-1 algorithm?
13. Describe the purpose of the Beta and Rho parameters for ART-1.
14. The Hopfield auto-associative model is useful for biologically plausible memory storage and recall. Describe its architecture and learning algorithm.
15. What is one-shot learning and what are its advantages?
16. Both Hebbian learning and Hopfield can be used for pattern storage and recall. Describe the fundamental differences between these two approaches.

Chapter 10 ROBOTICS AND AI

From the early days of AI, robots have existed as the physical embodiment of AI algorithms and methods. Outside of the realm of simulations, robots allowed AI algorithms to interact and explore the real world. Robotics also fit the mold of early Strong AI, where the desire was to create an intelligent machine (ideally in our image). In this chapter, we'll explore the fundamentals of robotics and its application of AI.

INTRODUCTION TO ROBOTICS

While AI and robotics can be considered two independent disciplines, they are inexorably tied given the benefits they provide one another. AI provides the means to embed intelligence into a physical robot, where a robot provides the means to visualize the behavior that is provided by an AI algorithm. Therefore, the two disciplines complement one another.

This chapter will begin with an introduction to robotics, its history, and then a short discussion of a taxonomy of robotics. The chapter will then explore robotics in greater detail, reviewing the various interfaces and architectures.

What is a Robot?

ISO (International Standard) 8373 defines a robot this way:

An automatically controlled, reprogrammable, multipurpose, manipulator programmable in three or more axes, which may be either fixed in place or mobile for use in industrial automation applications.

But this older definition can unfairly constrain the definition of a robot. Joseph Engelberger, a pioneer in early industrial robotics, defines a robot as follows:

I can't define a robot, but I know one when I see one.

Like art, this definition fits robotics the best as modern-day robots exist as a wide spectrum of designs to fit a given need. Early robots were viewed as fantastical entities, built of tin and represented by evil intentions. The realistic view is less hysterical. The first robot was a tele-operated boat that was demonstrated at an 1898 exhibition by Nikola Tesla (with the end goal being a wireless torpedo). [WikiRobot] The term Robot would not be coined for another 20 years, when it was used in Karel Capek's science fiction play, "Rossum's Universal Robots."

Another way to define a robot is through its decomposition. A robot is an entity that satisfies some goal and is made up of a platform (consisting of some form of mechanicals), a source of power (stored, or gathered in real-time), a set of sensors to perceive the environment, a set of actuators to move and/or manipulate the environment, and finally, a source of intelligence for rational decision making (see Figure 10.1).

Using a model of decomposition to define a robot permits the breakdown of the components to identify how and where they are applied. As we'll see, every robot is different based on its application. The mechanicals, sensors, and actuators can be very different from a satellite (a form of an autonomous robot) when compared to an autonomous underwater robot. What can be very similar is the AI algorithms applied to the problem.

In the following sections, we'll explore these components in greater detail to understand how the *intelligence* block interacts with the various other components.

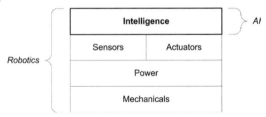

FIGURE 10.1:   A robot from the perspective of decomposition.

A Sampling from the Spectrum of Robotics

A concise history of robotics is beyond the scope of this book, but a summary of some of the more important epochs in robotic history will be presented.

The first mobile robot that incorporated artificial intelligence algorithms was called Shakey and was built from 1966 through 1972 at SRI (the Stanford Research Institute). Shakey was a mobile robot that included a TV camera, range finder, and bump sensors to sense its environment. The Shakey platform was connected to a PDP-10 and PDP-15 computer via a radio link. Shakey's AI was built on three levels of action. At the bottom were the basic action routines (for moving, turning, and basic route planning). At the intermediate layer was control that linked lower-level activities together to create more complex tasks. At the highest level was the planner that could execute plans to achieve goals. Later, in the 1970s at Stanford, Hans Moravec built a mobile robot cart that included a very robust vision system. This provided the robot with greater autonomy and resulted in some of the first 3D environment mapping experiments.

Robots in the early days weren't restricted to the ground. Some objects representing robots took flight to the Moon, Venus, Mars, and beyond. While Sputnik was the first artificial Earth satellite, it had a couple of sensors but no actuators (except for a transmitter that generated "beeps" for those listening via radio on the ground). Using our model shown in Figure 10.1, Sputnik lacked only in intelligence.

Other important robotic spacecraft included Luna 2, a Soviet Lunar impacter (1959), and Venera 7. Venera 7 was a Soviet spacecraft that succeeded in the first soft landing on another planet (Venus) in 1970. The U.S. followed six years later with the Viking-1 Mars lander (and while not mobile, it did include a robotic arm for soil sampling).

NOTE *Some examples of robots that are operated remotely are called tele-robots. These types of robots are useful where the robot can survive (at least for a time) where a human would not. A prime example is on the surface of Mars, such as Viking 1.*

Another type of robot constructed at MIT was called Kismet (developed by Cynthia Breazeal). Kismet is another non-traditional robot in that it's simply a head, but includes a variety of input devices (audio, video and proprioception) as well as effectors to enable facial expressions (such as moving its ears, eyebrows, eyelids, lips, and head). The goal of Kismet was to study human social interaction. Kismet could simulate human behaviors, demonstrating (simulated) human emotion and appearance through facial expressions and vocalizations. An interesting side effect of this research was that these characteristics gave the robot a personality.

NOTE ▼ *New research focuses on emotions and their influence over intelligence and learning. It's understandable that emotions would be helpful in building machines that can more easily interact with humans. Emotions can be problematic (imagine a paranoid AI auto-pilot), but not all emotions are irrational and emotions can result in a more rational robot.*

In more recent history, Honda demonstrated a very advanced humanoid robot in Yokohama, Japan called Asimo. Asimo is a humanoid robot, meaning that it resembles a human with legs and arms. Asimo was designed for real-life environments, and can grasp objects and walk around an environment (including the use of stairs). This robot incorporates a variety of human-like sensors including vision and hearing, and is able to recognize objects, gestures from humans, and even recognize faces and sounds. For example, Asimo can understand pointing gestures for attention or movement.

Finally, the DARPA grand challenge, a competition to build autonomous ground vehicles that race between two locations in difficult terrain, continues to push the envelope for autonomous robotics. The first challenge, in 2004, saw many organized teams, but not a single robot finished the course. By 2005, five vehicles had completed the difficult course (led by Stanford and Carnegie Mellon).

NOTE ▼ *Combining AI and vehicles is not new; in fact, Carnegie Mellon introduced ALVINN (or Autonomous Land Vehicle In a Neural Network) in the 1990s. A 30 by 32 two-dimensional retina (using input from a video camera) fed a five-layer neural network (trained via backpropagation). The output of the neural network determined the direction that the vehicle should travel. Using this method, the vehicle controlled by ALVINN could autonomously drive and stay on a road.*

Taxonomy of Robotics

While modern robotics still fails to live up to the expectations set by science fiction, robotics has grown from the early mobile carts and robotic appendages. Today, robots not only navigate on land, but also in the air and in the water. In this section, a short taxonomy of robotics will be presented, listing some of the various types of robots that have been developed or are under active research.

Fixed

Many of the industrial robots in use today are of the fixed variety. Robotic arms perform assembly and welding to very precise specifications, repeatedly without mistakes. These robotic arms include a manipulator or tool at their extremity and one or more joints to give the arm the ability to move around in its space.

Legged

The legged variety of robot can also be called the *walking* or *hopping* style of robot. Robots with one leg (called monopods, such as the one built at the MIT Leg Laboratory) hop in a style similar to a pogo stick. Bipedal robots (those with two legs) mimic human locomotion (such as Asimo). But more legs are also interesting, such as quadrupeds (four legs), hexapods (six legs), and octapods (eight legs).

Wheeled

A popular variety of robot given its simplicity is the mobile, or wheeled robot. Hobbyist robotic platforms are commonly of this design due not just to its simplicity, but the minimal cost. The control of the mobile platform is relatively simple when compared to a legged variety of robot. For example, a mobile robot is stable without control, where a legged robot must dynamically balance to be stable.

Underwater

Underwater robots are very useful, but require different forms of locomotion. Many tele-robots of this variety are called ROVs, or Remotely Operated Vehicles. These can take a number of forms, mimicking what nature has taught us about navigating in water. Not only have underwater robots been demonstrated that mimic fish, but also crab and lobster structures. Robotic worms have also been used to provide locomotion.

Aerial

Robots of the aerial variety, like underwater robots, have a number of different mechanisms for movement. For example, traditional aerial robots can use common aircraft models (such as a plane or heliocopter). Even a passenger airliner can be considered a flying robot, as humans typically attend to the operation of the plane but the auto-pilot (a form of AI). [WikiRobot] Satellites are another example of an aerial robot, though they have an entirely different set of sensors and actuators (sun sensors, gyroscopes for sensing, momentum wheels, and thrusters for effectors).

Other Types of Robots

Finally, there are a number of other types of robots which don't fit cleanly within the previously defined categories. This is because they could apply equally to the other robot types.

Polymorphic, or shape-changing, robots have the ability to self-reconfigure based on the particular task at hand. These robots are multi-functional and can tackle a variety of tasks by reconfiguring themselves. The robot's design indicates how polymorphic it is. The SuperBot, designed at the USC Polymorphic Robotics Lab, is an early example of a reconfigurable robot. This robot can reconfigure itself to walk, crawl, roll, or climb.

Distributed robots, or robot swarms, are another interesting aspect of robotics. In this model, multiple robots swarm together to perform a task. This can be viewed serially (such as ants cooperating to move food from a location back to the nest) or at the same time (such as working together to move an object that an individual robot could not move). Robot swarms are an interesting area of research today, including topics such as task distribution and communication. How do individual robots communicate with one another, and how are assignments made in the absence of a centralized planner?

Hard vs Soft Robotics

While most robots are hard in nature (made physically in the real world), there is another category of robots that don't exist physically. These are called *soft* robots and exist within the confines of computer systems. But instead of robot simulations, these soft robots include a *soft* set of sensors and effectors that allow them to interact and navigate their environments. For example, a soft robot (called a web spider) can navigate the Internet using the HTTP protocol to communicate with services on a given machine. Using advanced mobility protocols, agents can move around a network, transporting themselves from one machine to another bringing their state with them. An example of this is the Aglets framework from IBM that provides a Java framework for agent mobility using the Agent Transport Protocol (or ATP).

BRAITENBURG VEHICLES

A discussion of robotics would not be complete without at least mentioning what are now known as Braitenberg vehicles. Valentino Braitenberg was a cybernetician, someone who studied the processes of biological and mechanical (and electronic) systems, particularly in the context of comparing them to natural or biological systems. Braitenberg's book "Vehicles" remains a worthwhile read.

Braitenberg vehicles can be thought of as a set of thought experiments for robotic systems with simple but effective control systems. As an example, take the simple robot shown in Figure 10.2. This two-wheeled robotic platform (with a front castor wheel) includes two light sensors (the left sensor and right sensor) at the front that directly attach to the motors on the wheels (the left motor and right motor). When light shines in a sensor, it proportionally drives the motor to which it attaches. When the light shines in the left sensor, it drives the right motor moving it toward the light sensor. If the light shines to the right sensor, the left motor is driven, causing the left motor to turn (thus causing the robot to travel right toward the light). This simple control system demonstrates an attractive behavior (the robot is attracted toward the light).

An alternative robotic architecture is shown in Figure 10.3. In this example the sensors attach to the same side wheel motors. This has the opposite effect, in that light shining in (for example) the left sensor drives the left motor causing the robot to turn away from the light source. This similar behavior occurs for the right sensors and right motor. This is an example of repulsive behavior, the robot moves away from the light source.

Light shining in both motors has a proportional effect, but still leaning toward a strong effect to the sensor to which a stronger light signal is received. From these simple examples, you can see how a very simple architecture can yield very interesting behaviors.

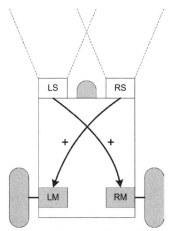

FIGURE 10.2: A simple Braitenberg vehicle demonstrating attractive behavior.

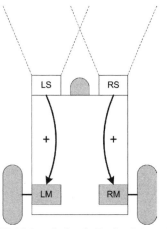

FIGURE 10.3: A simple Braitenberg vehicle demonstrating repulsive behavior.

NATURAL SENSING AND CONTROL

Before we talk about the various robotic sensors, actuators, and control systems, it's important to explore the senses, effectors, and control mechanisms that we as humans use.

From the human perspective, there are five classical senses (see Table 10.1). These are the sense of sight (vision), hearing (audition), taste (gustation), smell (olfaction), and touch (tactition). These basic senses give us the ability to perceive the world around us. There are also other senses at work. For example, humans have the ability of proprioception, or kinethetic sense.

This sense allows us to be aware of ourselves and our bodies. Humans also have the ability of balance, or equilibrioception, and the ability to sense heat or cold through thermoception.

Table 10.1:   Five classical human senses.

Sense	Sensor	Description
Vision	Eyes	The Sense of Sight (Electromagnetic Waves)
Auditon	Ears	The Sense of Hearing (Pressure Waves)
Gustation	Tounge	The Sense of Taste (Chemicals)
Olfaction	Nose	The Sense of Smell (Chemicals)
Tactition	Skin	The Sense of Touch (Pressure)

But there are also senses that are not available to humans, but exist in other organisms (see Table 10.2). For example, some animals have the ability to sense infrared light. Bats, for example, use echolocation to determine the position of objects. The detection of electric fields (electroception) and fluctuations in magnetic fields (magnetoception) is also available to certain animals (such as fish, bees, and birds).

Table 10.2:   Examples of non-human senses.

Sense	Description
Echolocation	Detection of Objects through echo
Electroception	Detection of Electric Fields
Magnetoception	Detection of Fluctuation of Magnetic Fields

While many robots include senses modeled after humans, it's not necessarily advantageous. The complexity of some human senses (such as vision) can be supported by other simpler mechanisms such as touch sensors and ultrasonic detectors (for object location).

Humans also include a variety of effectors that are used to manipulate the environment. In addition to the obvious mechanisms such as our arms and hands to manipulate objects, or legs which provide us with mobility, humans have the ability to speak to communicate with others in our environments. There are also effectors which are hidden, such those embodied in non-verbal communication. These mechanisms permit communication which is indirect (and many times, unintentional).

PERCEPTION WITH SENSORS

The sensors available to robotic systems are open to the imagination and the needs of the robotic application. Artificial sensors can mimic those of human sensors, but extend them in ways that are useful. For example, robotic eyes can see outside of the human visual range and see heat. Robotic ears can amplify or hear beyond the human frequency range. See Table 10.3 for a list of sensors and their human counterparts.

Table 10.3:   Robotic sensors and the human counterparts.

Human Sense	Robotic Sensors
Vision	Camera, Infrared Camera, Radiation Sensors, Ranging Sensors
Audition	Microphone
Gustation	Chemical Sensors
Olfaction	Chemical Sensors
Tactition	Contact (bump) Sensors, Force Sensors
Proprioception	Wheel Encoders
Equilibrioception	Tilt Sensor, Accelerometer, Gyroscope
Thermoception	Thermocouple

Robots can include vision capabilities using simple CCD (Charge-Couple-Device) cameras, or video cameras. Sonar is also possible, which provides a lesser form of vision (identifying when objects are near). Cameras can also include infrared for heat detection, or sensors that detect radiation ("seeing" in other spectrum). A metal detector can also be viewed as a form of vision (though obviously different than our own). Audition can be performed using microphones, but not only in the human audible spectrum. Higher or lower frequencies can also be measured.

The sense of gustation and olfaction can be provided through an array of chemical sensors. These sensors can be used to detect biological, chemicals or radiation. Tactition is one of the more common sensors available on robots, such as contact sensors.

Other robotic sensors can be used for the other senses, such as wheel encoders (to measure the rate at which the wheels are turning) for proprioception. The sense of equilibrioception can be provided by tilt-sensors, acceleratometers, or a gyroscope. Finally, a thermocouple can be used to detect heat to provide thermoception.

ACTUATION WITH EFFECTORS

The effectors (or actuators) available to a robot are varied, and depend on the goal of the robot itself. Some of the more common include motors that can be used to drive wheels or end-effectors, which consist of a device at the end of a robotic arm (such as a gripper, a paint sprayer, or other tool). Like sensors, actuators are driven based on the task at hand and are open to the imagination.

ROBOTIC CONTROL SYSTEMS

As defined earlier in this chapter, a robot is made up of a number of things, but three key elements are the sensors, effectors, and the control system. The sensors allow the robot to perceive its environment, the effectors the ability to manipulate its environment, and the control system provides a way to map sensors (the perception of the environment) to the effectors (to rationally interact with the environment). This is shown in Figure 10.4, and is an important aspect of robotic control systems.

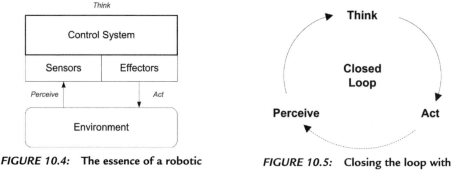

FIGURE 10.4: The essence of a robotic system.

FIGURE 10.5: Closing the loop with feedback for effective control.

Another way to think about this is shown in Figure 10.5. The loop aspect is important because the act of control should be viewed as a cycle, starting with perception, leading to decision-making, and ending in control. This implies feedback, which is the basis for control. If the robot were to try to control the environment with sensors, this would be called an open loop (as there's no feedback, there's no way to guarantee proper action). By closing the loop (sense-control-act) feedback is incorporated, resulting in an effective control system.

A common feedback mechanism in robotics is the *shaft encoder*. A shaft encoder measures the rotation rate of a shaft. This is commonly done with a photoreflector which reflects light back to a phototransistor (the sensor). The transitions between reflective spots and non-relective surfaces result in a pulse train that can be counted (see Figure 10.6). The counter coupled with a real-time clock can then be used to determine the rate at which the shaft (and wheel) is turning.

Using the shaft encoder, the speed of the wheel (and corresponding object propelled by the wheel) can be measured. This allows the robot to roughly determine its relative position. By enabling the motor, the control system could count off eight pulse transitions to measure a complete turn of the wheel. While fundamental, this shaft encoder example illustrates the concept of feedback in a control system. Without a shaft encoder, there could be no practical way to understand how far the robot traveled. This is an example of an open-loop system (no feedback).

SIMPLE CONTROL ARCHITECTURES

Robotic platforms can use a large number of control architectures to achieve their desired goals. In the following sections, a few of the more popular architectures are explored. While these architectures are useful, they're also conceptually simple and easy to implement.

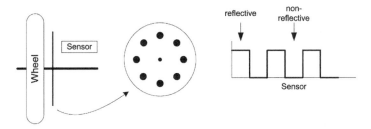

FIGURE 10.6: **Using a shaft encoder to determine wheel speed.**

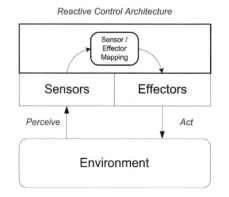

Reactive Control Architecture

FIGURE 10.7:   The reactive control system architecture.

The key to control architectures is that no single architecture is best. Each are applicable to different scenarios, and the architecture should match the problem at hand.

Reactive Control

The reactive control architecture is one where there's no real intelligence. Instead, the control system reacts to its sensors and drives its actuators (simple stimulus-response). This architecture is shown in Figure 10.7. Note here that the sensors map to the effectors in a direct mapping.

In this architecture, the sensors are read and directly mapped to the effectors. This differs from a deliberative architecture where some consideration is made about the sensors and internal state. The deliberative architecture is the more classical intelligent approach, as consideration is made about the state of the environment (sensors) and the state of the robot (internal state).

An advantage to this architecture is that it's very simple and very fast. Since no deliberation is made about which action should be performed based on sensors inputs, the direct mapping provides for a fast response time. This architecture is also very useful in dynamic environments. Since the robot simply responds to the immediate environment, it can react equally well to static or dynamic environments. The disadvantage to this architecture is that it's fundamentally unintelligent and has no capacity to learn.

Subsumption

Rodney Brook's subsumption architecture grew from the belief that human-level intelligence could not be built from the ground up, but instead must be built from simple behaviors that collectively could exhibit emergent higher-level behavior.

Building a robot that used simple behaviors was not new, but the problem that existed was how to coordinate those simple behaviors such that the right behavior could be in control at the right time. Using insects as a model, Brooks moved forward with an architecture that had no real central control mechanism, but instead a shared control architecture where behaviors were active in parallel, but only one in control at a time.

The subsumption architecture exhibits a number of properties that model aspects of insects very well. There exist prewired behaviors (as explored in the reactive architecture), but layers of behaviors with the ability to subsume control of lower behaviors when appropriate.

Conside the control system shown in Figure 10.8. The sensors are provided to the behaviors, and the effectors are driven by the behaviors. Note the parallel nature of this processing. Each behavior module has access to the sensor inputs and effector outputs. But only one behavior is permitted control at a time (by inhibiting execution of other behaviors). For example, if no objects are in the area of movement, then the upper-level module may subsume control. In this case, the explore behavior will have control. But if the robot is low on power, then the *seek power* behavior can subsume the explore behavior. While the robot is seeking power, the *object avoidance* behavior can take control if needed (if an object is in the area of movement).

The subsumption architecture is advantageous over the reactive architecture because it can incorporate more complex goal-oriented behaviors. Each level in the subsumption architecture can be thought of as

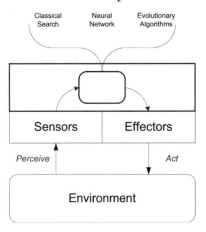

FIGURE 10.8: The subsumption control system architecture.

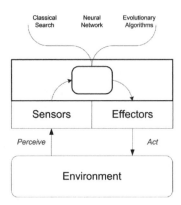

FIGURE 10.9:   Applying other AI algorithms to robot control systems.

a level of competence. From low-level reactive behaviors, to higher-level deliberative behaviors, each are competent but in different ways. But the subsumption architecture is not without its problems. The development of real robots using subsumption found that a large number of behaviors resulted in highly complex systems that were difficult to debug. Even with these complexities, subsumption remains a useful architecture.

Other Control Systems

Throughout this book, there are a number of algorithms and methods that would apply as a control architecture for a robot. These include neural networks, classical search algorithms, or evolutionary algorithms.

MOVEMENT PLANNING

Planning is an integral part of intelligent robot behavior. Planning is one of the key differentiators between intelligent human behavior, and seemingly random insect behavior. In this section, two interesting approaches to movement planning will be explored.

Complexities of Motion Planning

One of the major complexities of motion planning is in environments that are dynamic. Consider movement planning in an environment that does not change. Then consider how planning differs in an environment that is constantly changing. Dynamic environments offer considerable challenges to motion planning.

One approach to planning in dynamic environments is what is called *anytime planning*. Traditional planning algorithms will create a complete plan from start to finish. The problem that this creates is that the plan becomes brittle if the underlying assumptions change (such as in dynamic environments). Anytime planning is an algorithm that can be interrupted during the planning process, but still result in a workable plan. The more time that is given to the planning algorithm, the better the resulting plan. This is useful in dynamic environments because a plan can be created, and while that plan is executed (and the environment changes), the planner can continue to refine the plan dynamically given new information.

Cell Decomposition

Planning a robot's movement through an environment can be accomplished through a number of methods, and a conceptually simply method is called Cell Decomposition. The idea behind cell decomposition is to decompose the free space of the robot's environment into smaller regions called cells. Once the cells are defined, a graph can be created using the adjacency information from the cells. With the graph, a traditional search algorithm can be used to determine a path from the start cell to the end cell.

An example of cell decomposition begins with Figure 10.10. In this figure, a sample environment is shown with free space (clear) and obstacles

FIGURE 10.10: Sample robot environment with free space and obstacles.

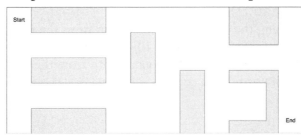

FIGURE 10.11: Environment decomposed into cells.

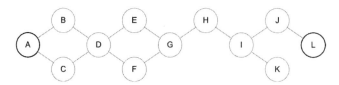

FIGURE 10.12:   **A graph represenation of Figure 10.11.**

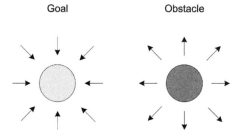

FIGURE 10.13:   **Potential field example of a goal and obstacle.**

(shown in gray). At the upper left-hand corner is the start position, and at the bottom right is the end goal.

Next, the free space in the environment is decomposed into cells. This is done in this example by drawing parallel line segments at the boundary of each obstacle. The bounded free space is then labeled to uniquely identify it (see Figure 10.11).

Then, using the adjacency information from the cell decomposition, a graph is constructed (see Figure 10.12). From this representation, simple graph algorithms can be used to plan a path from the start position (in cell A) to the goal position (in cell L).

Potential Fields

Potential fields is a very efficient method to provide robot movement in both static and dynamic environments. With the potential field method, the robot is considered a particle moving through a field containing a set of influences. The influences are potential fields that define how the particle should behave when in proximity to them.

Consider the potential fields shown in Figure 10.13. The goal has a potential field that attracts the robot, while the obstacle has a repulsive field that opposes the robot.

A robot then navigating an enviroment with other objects appears as shown in Figure 10.14. In this diagram, the robot avoids the obstacle (as it is repulsed by it) but then migrates toward the goal (as it is attracted to it).

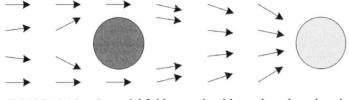

FIGURE 10.14: Potential field example with an obstacle and goal.

What makes potential fields so efficient is that at any instance in the environment, the motion of the robot is determined by the potential field at the robot's current location. If a new obstacle is added to the environment, the potential field is adjusted given the new influence (additive), so the approach can also work in dynamic environments.

An issue with potential fields is the possibility of local minimums, which can result in the robot being stuck in a position. This problem can be overcome by including mechanisms to escape the local minimum when it is detected.

TIP

Many other techniques exist for navigating environments. Landmark-based navigation uses easily recognizable landmarks to determine position. This technique has been applied to spacecraft using star fields as the recognizable landmarks. Using four well-known stars (based on their brightness), a spacecraft can determine its orientation. Other methods such as visibility graphs and Voronoi diagrams are also useful.

GROUP OR DISTRIBUTED ROBOTICS

Group or distributed robotics is an interesting area of research today. In this area, a group of robots accomplish a task that alone they could not accomplish. Swarms of identical robots can also be used to complete tasks much faster than a single robot acting on its own. Applications include agriculture and construction.

An important element in group robotics is their ability to communicate with one another to relay information about the task at hand. Examples from nature include stigmergy, in which insects communicate through their environment. Ants, for example, communicate with one another through pheromone trails that are deposited in the environment. Similar behaviors are seen in termites who also use pheromones, but in their case they are used to construct nests.

ROBOT PROGRAMMING LANGUAGES

To simplify the task of programming robot systems, and also for educational purposes, a number of robot programming languages have been developed. Examples include LAMA from MIT and the RAPT language from the University of Edinburgh.

From an educational perspective, a useful language developed by Richard Pattis of Stanford University is Karel (named after the Czech writer who coined the term robot). Karel is a language with a simple syntax that is also reminiscent of LOGO (another educational programming language). Karel has been updated to include object-oriented semantics, which goes by the name Karel++.

ROBOT SIMULATORS

Robot simulations offer another way to test and validate robotic algorithms without physical development. These algorithms also provide a way to verify algorithms prior to embedding them into physical embodiments.

Some of the more interesting include the Open Dynamics Engine, which is a physics library for simulating rigid body dynamics. Simbad is a 3D robot simulator that allows immediate visualization of programmed behaviors. Finally, TeamBots is a portable multi-agent robotic simulator that includes visualization for teams of soccer-playing robots.

CHAPTER SUMMARY

The field of robotics and AI are inexorably tied because robotics permit the visualization of AI algorithms in the physical world. Robotics exhibit the true systems level of AI, as there are distinct inputs (sensors), outputs (effectors), and the AI algorithms that provide rational decision-making. Robotics is an interesting area of study because they encompass many elements of AI. The algorithms demonstrated throughout this book are applicable to AI systems, from search for use in planning, to neural networks and evolutionary systems for learning. Robotics are the extension of AI algorithms into the real world.

REFERENCES

[WikiRobot] "Robot," Wikipedia free encyclopedia. Available online at: http://en.wikipedia.org/wiki/Robot

RESOURCES

[Braitenberg] Braitenberg, Valentine *Vehicles, Experiments in Synthetic Psychology.* MIT Press, 1986.

[Shakey] "Shakey the Robot," SRI International. Available online at:
Available online at http://www.sri.com/about/timeline/shakey.html

Breazeal, Cynthia "Sociable Machines: Expressive Social Exchange Between Humans and Robots." Sc.D. dissertation, Department of Electrical Engineering and Computer Science, MIT, 2000.

Hawes, Nick "Anytime Planning for Agent Behavior," School of Computer Science, The University of Birmingham, 1997.

Jones, M. Tim, "Open Source Robotics Toolkits," IBM Developerworks, 2006.
Available online at: http://www-128.ibm.com/developerworks/linux/library/l-robotools/

Krough, B. H. "A Generalized Potential Field Approach to Obstacle Avoidance Control," Proc. of International Robotics Research Conference, Bethlehem, Pennsylvania, August, 1984.

MIT Leg Laboratory. Available online at: http://www.ai.mit.edu/projects/leglab

Pattis, Richard E. Karel *The Robot: A Gentle Introduction to the Art of Programming.* John Wiley & Sons, 1981.

Whal, F. M., Thomas, U. "Robot Programming - From Simple Moves to Complex Robot Tasks," Institute for Robotics and Process Control, Technical University of Braunschweig, 2002.

EXERCISES

1. What are the major elements of a robot from the perspective of decomposition?

2. Compare the early development of robotics to those being developed today. How have advancements in the field of electronics affected robotics research today?

3. What was one of the earliest implementations of a self-driving vehicle, and which AI method was used?

4. What applications can you envision for shape-changing robots in the future?

5. What advantages exist for robotic simulations over the development of real physical robot embodiments? What issues to simulations present?

6. Using the example Braitenberg vehicles shown in this chapter, what other Braitenberg-like architectures can you see? How do alternate connections between sensors and motors (such as inhibition) affect the robot's behavior?

7. What is meant by open and closed loops in control systems?

8. Compare the two motion planning methods discussed in this chapter (cell decomposition and potential fields). What are the advantages and disadvantages of each?

9. Distributed robotics pertains to the distribution of a problem to a group of robots. What problems exist in this domain and what advantages?

Chapter 11

INTELLIGENT AGENTS

In this chapter, we'll explore the topic of Intelligent Agents. The definition of an intelligent agent can be difficult to succinctly provide, as the term has been used in a variety of settings. A common definition of an intelligent agent from the perspective of artificial intelligence is an autonomous entity that exists in an environment and acts in a rational way. What is rational is dependent on the environment. For example, is the agent attempting to solve a problem, or protect itself against other entities? In this chapter, we'll discuss the various types of agents, their applications, architectures, and languages.

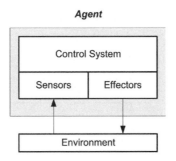

FIGURE 11.1:   The fundamental anatomy of an agent.

ANATOMY OF AN AGENT

An agent is commonly made up of a number of elements. These include one or more sensors that are used to perceive the environment, one or more effectors that manipulate the environment, and a control system. The control system provides a mapping from sensors to effectors, and provides intelligent (or rational) behavior (see Figure 11.1).

This anatomy can be applied to humans, as a first example. The human body has a rich set of sensors that cover a wide variety of domains. This includes vision (eyes), smell (nose), hearing (ears), taste (tongue), touch (various including skin), balance (vestibular sense), nociception (pain), and others. The human body also has a number of effector systems, including our fingers, limbs (arms and legs), and other various motor control systems. The control system includes our brain and central nervous system.

This can also be applied to other types of agents, both virtual and physical. A web spider, for example, is a virtual agent that gathers and filters information for another party. A web spider uses a primary sensor of the HyperText Transport Protocol, or HTTP, as a means to gather data from web pages. Its control system is an application, which can be written in almost any language, that drives the behavior of the web spider. This behavior includes web-data parsing and filtering. The web spider can identify new links to follow to collect additional information, and use the HTTP protocol to navigate the web environment. Finally, the web spider can communicate with a managing user through email using the Simple Mail Transport Protocol, or SMTP. The user can configure the web spider for collection, navigation, or filtering, and also receive emails indicating its current status (see Figure 11.2).

A web spider is one example of an agent, but we've not yet described the properties that separate an agent from a program.

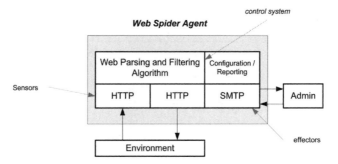

FIGURE 11.2: Web spider as an agent.

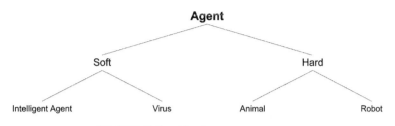

FIGURE 11.3: **Simple agent taxonomy.**

NOTE *Another useful perspective of agents is that of an agency. An agent is an intermediary between two or more parties. For example, the previous web spider agent example illustrates this property of an agency. The web spider is an intermediary agent for web-data gathering and filtering for a user. The web spider acts on the user's behalf for data gathering, given a set of constraints from the user. We'll look at an example of this application later.*

A robot can also be considered an agent. A robot includes a variety of sensors including vision (cameras, ultrasonic transducers, infrared detectors), hearing (microphones), touch (bump sensors), as well as other types of sensors for pressure, temperature, and movement detection (accelerometers). Effectors include motors (to drive wheels, tracks, or limbs), and a speaker for sound vocalization. A robot can also include a number of other effectors that can manipulate the environment, such as a vacuum, a water pump, or even a weapon.

While a complete taxonomy of agents is not feasible, we can reduce agents to a small tree, as shown in Figure 11.3. This division splits agents into hard and soft agents. Animals (including humans) and robots fall into the hard agents category, while software, or intelligent, agents (and viruses) fall into the soft category. Franklin and Graesser first identified viruses as agents in their 1996 taxonomy. [Franklin/Graesser 1996]

AGENT PROPERTIES AND AI

We can think of agents as a super-set of artificial intelligence. What makes a program an *agent* is that it utilizes one or more properties that exhibit some type of intelligence (or at least exhibit properties that appear intelligent). We'll now explore some of the properties that form the basis of intelligent software agents (see Table 11.1).

Table 11.1: Agent properties.

Property	Description
Rationale	Able to act in a rational (or intelligent) way
Autonomous	Able to act independently, not subject to external control
Persistent	Able to run continuously
Communicative	Able to provide information, or command other agents
Cooperative	Able to work with other agents to achieve goals
Mobile	Able to move (typically related to network mobility)
Adaptive	Able to learn and adapt

Rationale

The property of rationality simply means that the agent does the right thing at the right time, given a known outcome. This depends on the actions that are available to the agent (can it achieve the best outcome), and also how the agent's performance is measured.

Autonomous

Autonomy simply means that the agent is able to navigate its environment without guidance from an external entity (such as a human operator). The autonomous agent can therefore seek out goals in its environment, whether to sustain itself or solve problems. An example of an autonomous agent is the remote agent that rode along in NASA's Deep Space 1 spacecraft.

Persistent

Persistence implies that the agent exists over time and continuously exists in its environment. This property can also imply that the agent is stateful in conditions where the agent must be serialized and moved to a new location (as would be the case for mobile agents).

Communicative

An agent having the ability to communicate provides obvious advantages to agent systems. Agents can communicate with other agents to provide them with information, or communicate with users (for whom the agent represents). An example of agent communication was shown in Figure 11.2.

Cooperative

Related to the property of communication is the property of cooperation. This property implies that an agent can work with other agents to collectively solve problems in an environment. In order to cooperate, agents must have the ability to communicate (in some form or another). A related property is that of deception. Instead of communicating to cooperatively solve a problem, an agent can communicate disinformation to deceive another agent to maxmize its own reward.

Mobile

Mobility in agent systems is commonly defined as the agent's ability to migrate between systems over a network. This can be done autonomously, using a framework that supports this functionality (such as the Aglets mobile agent framework). Mobility also applies to viruses, which use either email (SMTP) or the web (HTTP) to move among systems and users.

NOTE ▶ *It's difficult to classify agents in one dimension when they're actually multi-dimensional. For example, an agent that is both mobile and cooperative (implying communication) can also be called Distributed Artificial Intelligence (DAI) or Distributed Problem Solving (DPS).*

Adaptive

The last, but likely most important, is the ability for an agent to learn and adapt to the environment. From the perspective of the agent, learning means creating a mapping of sensors to effectors that demonstrate intelligent behavior, or behavior that satisfies a set of defined constraints. To adapt means that these mappings are flexible, and can be modified due to changes in the environment.

AGENT ENVIRONMENTS

Whether an agent's environment is the Internet, virtual landscape of a game, or the unique space of a problem environment, all environments share a common set of characteristics. These characteristics are shown in Table 11.2.

Table 11.2:   Agent environment properties. [Russell/Norvig 2003]

Property	Description
Observability	Are all elements visible to the agent?

Change	Does the environment change (dynamic) or does it stay the same (static) and change only when the agent performs an action to initiate change?
Deterministic	Does the state of the environment change as the agent expects after an action (deterministic), or is there some randomness to the environment change from agent actions (stochastic)?
Episodic	Does the agent need prior understanding of the environment (prior experience) to take an action (sequential), or can the agent perceive the environment and take an action (episodic)?
Continuous	Does the environment consist of a finite or infinite number of potential states (during action selection by the agent)? If the number of possible states is large, then the task envirionment is continuous, otherwise it is discrete.
Multi-Agent	Does the environment contain a single agent, or possibly multiple agents acting in a cooperative or competitive fashion.

Given this taxonomy of agent properties, how would sample agents be classified such as a Non-Player Character (NPC) from a game environment, or a Chess program (or Chess Agent)?

A Chess-playing agent would be classified as shown in Table 11.3.

Table 11.3:   Properties of a Chess agent.

Property	Description
Fully Observable	The Chess board is fully observable to the Chess agent, nothing is hidden.
Static	The environment changes based on actions of the Chess agent and those of the opponent. But during the period when the Chess agent is making a decision for a move, the environment (Chess board) does not change.
Determistic	The Chess board changes based on the move selected by the agent, and therefore the environment is deterministic.

Episodic	The Chess agent operates in episodes, alternating between agent moves and opponent moves.
Multi-Agent	The Chess board environment can be classified as single agent (if the opponent is not considered) or as multi-agent, considering that an opponent operates on the environment in a competitive fashion.

Now let's look at the classification of a very different environment, that of a first-person-shooter (FPS) game environment. In this case, the environment is a virtual environment that is occupied by numerous NPCs and typically one or more human players. The classification for this environment is provided in Table 11.4.

Table 11.4:   Properties of a non-player character agent.

Property	Description
Partial Observability	First-person shooter genre games commonly use the real-world aspect of concealment and the ability to hide as a core part of the game experience. This means that another character in the game may not be visible to the player, making the environment only partially observable.
Dynamic	By definition, FPS games are dynamic. Players and NPCs compete or cooperate in the environment in real-time, and therefore the environment dynamically changes without any action taken by the observing agent.
Stochastic	The enviroinment of an FPS is stochastic (not deterministic). An action taken by an agent at one time may not result in the same response when taken again (such as shooting at another player). The agent may miss, or score a non-lethal hit to the opposing agent. Therefore, determinism is not a common characteristic to interesting FPS game environments.
Continuous	The FPS environment is continuous, as compared to an episodic environment such as a turn-based strategy game. For this reason, the continuous style

	environment for an FPS can be considered a real-time strategy.
Multi-Agent	An FPS environment is interesting by the fact that it's multi-agent. Typically, these are competitive environments, though some also include cooperative elements through support NPC agents.

Even though the Chess-game environment appears to be quite a bit simpler than that of an NPC agent in an FPS, the task at hand for a Chess agent is considerably more difficult. While the environment in an FPS game is much more dynamic and random, the agents are typically built with state-machine behaviors and minimal amounts of AI. The Chess-board environment is deterministic, but action selection is the key. Therefore, the Chess-playing agent includes much greater complexity (as illustrated in Chapter 4, AI and Games).

AGENT TAXONOMIES

Now that we've provided an introduction to agent properties and the characteristics of agent environments, let's explore some of the major agent types that exist in preparation for discussing agent applications.

Interface Agents

One of the earliest applications of intelligent agents was in the design of intelligent user interfaces. To minimize information overload on a user, intelligent user agents were built to reduce the amount of information presented to a user as a way to help the user focus on what is most important at any given time.

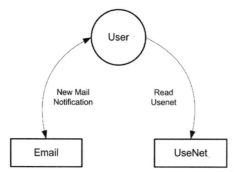

FIGURE 11.4: **A user scenario for email and UseNet.**

For example, consider a user that uses email and the UseNet. When new email arrives, typically an icon appears or a sound is played to indicate that new email is available. The user can then bring up their mail client to identify the sender of the email to decide whether to read it now, or wait until later. This user may also occasionaly review UseNet newsgroups for new information about a given topic (see Figure 11.4).

To combat the information overload and help the user focus on what's most important, an intelligent agent interface was proposed to assist the user in filtering what information should be presented when. To assist, the agent would need to learn about the user's needs. This was typically done in a learning phase, where the agent would monitor what the user did under which circumstances. For example, if the user always read emails from a given sender, the agent could emit the email notification only when email was received by that person. Also, if the user read UseNet posts about a given topic, the agent could autonomously monitor the UseNet for these posts, and then notify the user at some later time.

The goal of the intelligent interface agent is to minimize the information overhead on the user by learning under what circumstances certain actions are taken. This minimizes interruptions on the user, allowing them to focus more on what's important (see Figure 11.5).

Early development of intelligent interface agents focused on web interfaces, but others exist as well (which we'll explore in the section on agent applications).

Virtual Character Agents

A useful agent application that takes on a number of forms is called *virtual character agents*, or *synthetic agents*. These agents can take on a number of

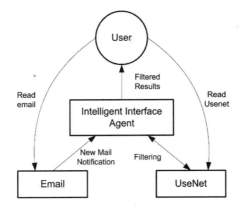

FIGURE 11.5: **An intelligent interface agent to minimize distractions.**

forms, focused on their particular application. These range from synthetic agents, and game agents (non-player characters), and conversational agents (otherwise known as chatbots).

Entertainment Agents

Synthetic agents are a special type of agent used in virtual reality environments. These types of agents can be used as characters in computer-generated (CG) movies or for training purposes in military simulations. Various movie studios have adopted CG and produced a variety of feature-length films using CG synthetic characters. Rather than each character being animated by an animator, a character is created complete with articulated joints and then trained to move. The animator can then simply request the character to move or perform an action, rather than specify it on a frame-by-frame basis.

An interesting variation on the entertainment agent is the "talking head" created at Ananova. Ananova is the first virtual newscaster that reads news from real-time news information using text-to-speech technology and computer animation to create a lifelike newscaster that lip syncs with the text being spoken.

Game Agents

One of the most common uses of agents, and a test bed for the development of AI is in the genre of video games (see also Chapter 4, AI and Games). Called Non-Player Characters in games (NPCs), these agents bring life to a variety of games by introducing characters that are autonomous and add to the realism of video games. NPCs can be cooperative in games; in other words, characters that work with the play in the game. NPCs can also be neutral characters in the game that provide guidance or help to the player during the game (or simply add to the ambient background of open-world games). But NPCs are more often competitive, working against the player from satisfying the desired goals of the game (for example, enemy NPCs in war or fantasy games).

To enable the development of NPCs, many games include scripting capabilities with APIs focused on the integration of realistic NPC behaviors. One of the more prominent examples of this capability is called UnrealScript, which was developed for the UnrealEngine of the popular Unreal Tournament first-person-shooter. UnrealScript is an object-oriented scripting language of the Java flavor.

The simplest implementation of an NPC is the reactive (or reflexive) agent. This agent includes no state, and instead directly maps an action from the current set of inputs.

A simple (though incomplete) example of an NPC in UnrealScript is shown in Listing 11.1. The function SpawnSimpleActor is used to create a new NPC. This function picks a random location and spawns the new character at that location. The state code implements the behaviors of the agent.

Listing 11.1:   Extending the actor class for a simple NPC.

```
class SimpleActor extends Actor;
var int Health;
// Spawn a new SimpleActor
function SpawnSimpleActor()
{
  local SimpleActor SA;
  local vector NewLocation;
  // Pick a new location
  NewLocation = Location + VRand();
  NewLocation.Z = Location.Z;
  // Spawn SimpleActor there
  SA = Spawn(class'SimpleActor',,,NewLocation);
}
// State Code
auto state Waiting
{
  function Touch( actor Other )
  {
    GotoState( 'Moving' );
  }
Begin:
  sleep( 5 );
  goto 'Begin';
}
auto state Moving
{
  Begin:
    // Move around
    GotoState( 'Waiting' );
}
DefaultProperties
{
```

```
// Specify Defaults
Health=100
}
```

 Many game environments implement NPC characters using the scripted Finite-State Machine (FSM) model. This model is conceptually simple and makes it easy to build characters with complex behaviors.

ChatterBots

Chatterbots, or conversational agents, have a long history in AI. As discussed in Chapter 1, Alan Turing proposed what is now known as the "Turing Test" as a means to judge the intelligence of a computing system. The test was based on the machine's ability (to make a judge operator) believe that it was speaking to another human, instead of a machine. If a judge couldn't tell the difference between a human and a machine, then it could be inferred that the machine possessed the characteristics of intelligence. This was really nothing more than a test of a machine's linguistic aspects, and not entirely intelligence.

There currently exists no academic focus on competing in the Turing test, but a less stringent form has resulted in a number of competitive solutions. The Loebner Prize awards prizes to the conversational agent that demonstrates the most human-like conversation.

Eliza and Parry

One of the earliest examples of a conversational agent is Joseph Weizenbaum's Eliza (written in the LISP language). Eliza was written in 1966 and in general, simply rephrased the input back to the human, typically in the form of a question. Listing 11.2 provides a sample conversation with Eliza.

Listing 11.2:   A conversation with Eliza.

```
Patient:  I'd like to talk about my mother.
Eliza:    What else comes to mind when you think of your mother?
Patient:  She wants to control me and run my life.
Eliza:    Your life?
Patient:  Yes, there are times that I have one.
Eliza:    You are sure.
Patient:  Why don't you think I have a life?
Eliza:    Do you believe I don't think you have life?
```

Eliza simply looked for patterns, and then rephrased, or picked a random comment. You can see how this is done in Chapter 15, which offers an introduction to the POP-11 language.

Another interesting and early example of a conversational agent was Parry. This agent differed from Eliza, in that instead of pretending to be a therapist, Parry simulated a patient with paranoid schizophrenia. Listing 11.3 provides a sample conversation between Parry and Eliza from RFC 439 (January 1973). [RFC 439]

Listing 11.3:   A conversation between Parry and Eliza.

Eliza:	Please go on.
Parry:	Do you know anything about bookies?
Eliza:	What makes you think I know anything about bookies?
Parry:	A bookie didn't pay me off once.
Eliza:	What does that suggest to you?
Parry:	I beat up the bookie who did not pay off, and I thought he might use his friends in the underworld to get even with me.
Eliza:	What else would you like to discuss?
Parry:	What do you know about racketeers?
Eliza:	Why do you ask?
Parry:	What experience have you had gambling?
Eliza:	Why does that question interest you?
Parry:	I like horseraces.
Eliza:	What else do you like?
Parry:	I know the mob controls the big rackets.
Eliza:	Who are you really talking about?

Parry, like Eliza, used patterns to formulate a response to a prior question or comment. It was written in meta-LISP on the DEC PDP-10 in the early 1970s.

Artificial Intelligence Markup Language (AIML)

AIML, or Artificial Intelligence Markup Language, is an interpeter that can be used to build conversational agents. As its name implies, AIML is a dialect of the Extensible Markup Language, or XML, which is a meta-language that allows definition of data, as well as its meaning and structure. Take the following example of a simple AIML template. In AIML, the fundamental unit of knowledge is called a *category*. A category contains a pattern (the input pattern) and the template (the response).

```
<category>
 <pattern>WHO ARE YOU</pattern>
 <template>Who I am is not important.</template>
</category>
```

AIML also supports variables, so that you can store information learned from the user. This can then be introduced later in the conversation.

AIML is a useful tool for building conversational agents, and has won the Loebner Prize for most human computer three times, in addition to other awards.

Mobile Agents

Mobile agents are those agents that possess the characteristics of mobility. This means that the agents have the ability to migrate from one host computer to another. This may seem like a trivial characteristic, but the advantages to mobility are both subtle and important.

Consider the agent example in Figure 11.6. In this example, the agent is stationary at a host node and collecting data from another node. The physical constraint in this example is that the network be available for communication. If the network becomes unavailable, the ability for the agents to communicate is severed resulting in a brittle system.

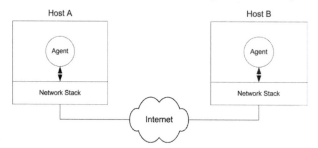

FIGURE 11.6:   **The brittleness of non-mobile software.**

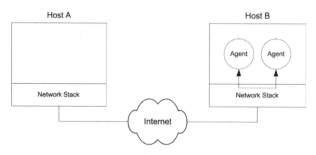

FIGURE 11.7:   **Increasing system reliability with mobile software.**

An alternative is to bring the data collection software to the source. As shown in Figure 11.7, a mobile agent migrates from Host A to Host B where the data is sourced. This agent could be a control system (in the simplest case, a thermostat), that reads the source data and then interacts with the system to make adjustments. In this model, the mobile agent interacts with the data collection agent at the source. Further, the agent could collect and filter data, and then return to the original host. This type of agent could be useful in situations where full-time connections are not always practically possible (such as satellites in low-earth orbit).

Mobile agents, which can also be viewed as a form of a virus, have potential in many areas of computing. Outside of data collection, mobile agents are an interesting method for software deployment. For example, customer purchasing software could accept a mobile agent that packages the software, or is the software itself. The agent could maintain licensing with a server, and also keep in touch with a remote server to ensure that patches are up-to-date.

With mobile agents, a communication theme emerges. Agents, particularly those that are mobile, require the means to communicate either locally or remotely. Later in this chapter, we'll explore some of the protocols that are used for agent communication (some designed specifically for this purpose).

Mobile agents have been used in a variety of applications including process control and network monitoring. Network monitoring is an ideal application for mobile agents. An agent is provided details of data collection, and then disbursed into a network. The agent collects data, and either communicates the data back to a central server, or migrates back to itself with its data.

Process control is another interesting application. Instead of purely collecting data from remote servers, the agents must also monitor and control the devices to which they're attached. Prior to migrating, the agents can be configured for their particular destination. From this perspective, mobile agents are an interesting deployment method for distributed systems.

IBM's aglets framework for Java is an interesting example of a mobility API. Aglets use what's called a ticket to identify where the agent is to be migrated. The agent use itself creates a ticket, and then calls the dispatch method with this ticket to serialize the Java program and migrate to the destination (see Listing 11.4). Once dispatched is called, the agent and its data are packaged and restarted at the defined destination.

Listing 11.4:   Java aglets as a mobility API.

```
public class MyAgent extends Aglet {
  public void run()
```

```
{
  ....
  QoC qoc = new QoC( QoC.NORMALINTEGRITY, QoC.
NOCONFIDENTIALITY );
  Ticket ticket = new Ticket( "atp://192.168.1.100/", qoc );
  try {
    // Serialize and migrate to the host defined by the ticket
    dispatch( ticket );
  } catch(Exception excp ) {
    excp.printStackTrace();
  }
  ...
}
}
```

In this example, a URL is defined for ticket. The URL specifies "atp" which represents the Agent Transfer Protocol. This protocol implements the ability to migrate aglets between hosts (where each support the ATP).

To enable the mobility with agents, frameworks are commonly built to provide this capability. Examples include IBM's Aglets framework, and also ANTS, or Active Node Transfer System. Another useful adaptation of mobile agents is what's called Active Networking, where packets transferred through a network contain data interpreted as code. These active packets (sometimes called capsules) can be used for various applications, including router configuration.

User Assistance Agent

One of the earliest applications for intelligent agents was for the purpose of simplifying our experiences when dealing with computers. Let's explore some of these applications from the perspective of the modern-day Internet.

Email Filtering

A simple example is that of email. When a new email arrives, our computers typically notify us of this fact using either a visual que (a mailbox flag) and possibly a tone indicating that our focus should change from whatever we happen to be doing to that of reading and responding to email. In some cases, this is what we'll naturally do (in the case of important email). But in other cases, such as spam or lower priority emails, we'd rather ignore this to avoid the interruption and continue with our work.

The email example is a perfect one for *agentification*. The agent first enters a state in which it monitors the actions of the user from the perspective of input stimulus (such as new email). This is the learning phase. When an email arrives, the user opens the mail client and scans the newly received email. Some of the emails are read, some are simply deleted, and others remain unread for some time. Over time, the agent can build probabilities that model the user's behavior. When the agent is able to model the user to a sufficient threshold (for example, 95% stimulus A results in response B), then it can mediate for the user in the domain of email. If an email arrives for which the user normally reads immediately (above the 95% threshold), the agent could present a window to the user that identifies that the email was received, and asks the user if they would like to read it. Otherwise, if the email falls below the threshold, the agent could withhold the email notification, so that the user is not disturbed by the new information.

An example agent that implements intelligent email handling is Maxims. This agent was developed in Common LISP for the Macintosh platform and learned to intelligently prioritize email for a user, as well as sorting and archiving. The Maxims agent also used caricatures to convey the state of the agent to the user. In this way, the user could know if the agent was working, suggesting, or unsure of what to do (as well as other emotive states). [Lashkari 1994]

Many new mail clients provide the ability to classify the route email according to user-defined rules. These features provide a mechanism for this capability, though it can be difficult to classify them as agents.

Information Gathering and Filtering

Information gathering and filtering is another useful example of using agents for user assistance. Keeping up on the latest information in our fields is important, but can be very time-consuming. But rather than do this work on our own, Internet search agents can do this work for us, providing the results when something new is available.

An interesting example of information gathering and filtering is the Google Alerts service. Google Alerts allow a user to create search 'alerts' which are search keywords. When Google runs across an item that matches your search criteria, it collects these links together and then emails you on a periodic basis. The emails are in the form of text plus a URL link, making it simple to review the new information and then present it in an easy-to-use format.

Other User-Assistance Applications

Many other applications have been developed in the category of user assistance. These include applications that require communication between agents. One example is a calendar agent which is used to schedule a person's time. The calendar agent representing a user negotiates meetings with other calendar agents to optimize all participants' time. Other examples include auction agents, which communicate with other auction agents to bid on goods per a user's request.

Hybrid Agents

In most cases, agents can't be classified succinctly by a single label as most are hybrid in nature. Instead of a single characteristic, such as mobile, agents implement multiple characteristics, such as mobile and communicative.

Consider an interface agent that securely relays information between consoles in an operations center. The agent consolidates the information to be relayed and then migrates to the destination console. Once there, it opens a window to the console's user (first authenticating the user to ensure it's the right person) and then provides the data in its needed form. This agent demonstrates a number of characteristics such as mobility, autonomy, and the ability to communicate (with a user in this context) through a defined interface.

> NOTE ▶ *The ability for agents to communicate for purposes of relaying information or directions is most often noted as the characteristic of communication. This characteristic has also been defined as a social ability where agents interact with one another for both collaboration and coordination.*

AGENT ARCHITECTURES

Let's now explore some of the agent architectures that have been created to support the development of agent systems. We'll first discuss the meaning of architecture, and then review some of the more important types of agent architectures that have been created. We'll then finish this discussion with a review of some of the agent architectures that have been developed and review some of the applications for which they can be used.

What is Architecture?

When we refer to architecture, we're referring to a framework from which applications can be built. Architectures are commonly defined to support a specific type of problem, such as dependable, or real-time. Architectures are commonly defined from a perspective or a viewpoint. This perspective could be from a functional view, code view, or user view (to name a few from the Recommended Practice for Architecture Description of Software-Intensive Systems).

Agent architectures, like software architectures, are formally a description of the elements from which a system is built and the manner in which they communicate. Further, these elements can be defined from patterns with specific constraints. [Shaw/Garlin 1996]

A number of common architectures exist that go by the names *pipe-and-filter* or *layered* architecture. Note that these define the interconnections between components. Pipe-and-Filter defines a model where data is moved through a set of one or more objects that perform a transformation. Layered simply means that the system is comprised of a set of layers that provide a specific set of logical functionality and that connectivity is commonly restricted to the layers contiguous to one another.

From the perspective of agent architectures, patterns can exist that support the development and operation of agents. For example, components can exist to provide communication between agents. Other components can support perception (viewing the agent's environment) and also actions (manipulating the environment). These types of components simplify the development task for agent designers, allowing them to concentrate on their particular task at hand instead of common environmental concerns.

It should be noted that architecture can be applied at multiple levels to agent systems. An agent itself can have architecture. Consider patterns that define how particular agents are developed. There are also lower-level architectures that provide the agent environment (as would be the case for mobile agent architectures).

In this section, we'll introduce a variety of architecture types as a precursor to explore specific frameworks that have been created for agent development.

Types of Architectures

Based on the goals of the agent application, a variety of agent architectures exist to help. This section will introduce some of the major architecture types and applications for which they can be used.

Reactive Architectures

A reactive architecture is the simplest architecture for agents. In this architecture, agent behaviors are simply a mapping between stimulus and response. The agent has no decision-making skills, only reactions to the environment in which it exists. Figure 11.8 illustrates this architecture.

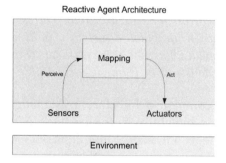

FIGURE 11.8:   Reactive architecture defines a simple agent.

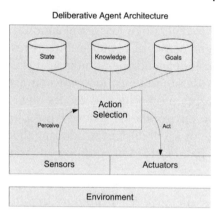

FIGURE 11.9:   A deliberative agent architecture considers its actions.

As shown in Figure 11.8, the agent simply reads the environment and then maps the state of the environment to one or more actions. Given the environment, more than one action may be appropriate, and therefore the agent must choose.

The advantage of reactive architectures is that they are extremely fast. This kind of architecture can be implemented easily in hardware, or fast in software lookup. The disadvantage of reactive architectures is that they apply only to simple environments. Sequences of actions require the presence of state, which is not encoded into the mapping function.

Deliberative Architectures

A deliberative architecture, as the name implies, is one that includes some deliberation over the action to perform given the current set of inputs. Instead of mapping the sensors directly to the actuators, the deliberative architecture considers the sensors, state, prior results of given actions, and other information in order to select the best action to perform. The deliberative architecture is shown in Figure 11.9.

The mechanism for action selection as shown in Figure 11.9 is undefined. This is because it could be a variety of mechanisms including a production system, neural network, or any other intelligent algorithm.

The advantage of the deliberative architecture is that it can be used to solve much more complex problems than the reactive architecture. It can perform planning, and perform sequences of actions to achieve a goal. The disadvantage is that it is slower than the reactive architecture due to the deliberation for the action to select.

Blackboard Architectures

The blackboard architecture is a very common architecture that is also very interesting. The first blackboard architecture was HEARSAY-II, which was a speech understanding system. This architecture operates around a global work area call the *blackboard*. The blackboard is a common work area for a number of agents that work cooperatively to solve a given problem. The blackboard therefore contains information about the environment, but also intermediate work results by the cooperative agents (see Figure 11.10).

The example shown in Figure 11.10 illustrates how a blackboard architecture could be applied to an agent system. In this example, two separate agents are used to sample the environment through the available sensors (the sensor agent) and also through the available actuators (action agent). The blackboard contains the current state of the environment that is constantly updated by the sensor agent, and when an action can be performed (as specified in the blackboard), the action agent translates this action into

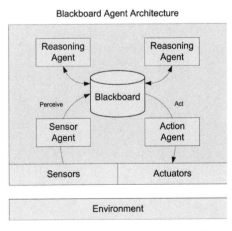

FIGURE 11.10: **The blackboard architecture supports multi-agent problem solving.**

control of the actuators. The control of the agent system is provided by one or more reasoning agents. These agents work together to achieve the goals, which would also be contained in the blackboard. In this example, the first reasoning agent could implement the goal definition behaviors, where the second reasoning agent could implement the planning portion (to translate goals into sequences of actions).

Since the blackboard is a common work area, coordination must be provided such that agents don't step over one another. For this reason, agents are scheduled based on their need. For example, agents can monitor the blackboard, and as information is added, they can request the ability to operate. The scheduler can then identify which agents desire to operate on the blackboard, and then invoke them accordingly.

The blackboard architecture, with its globally available work area, is easily implemented with a multi-threading system. Each agent becomes one or more system threads. From this perspective, the blackboard architecture is very common for agent and non-agent systems.

Belief-Desire-Intention (BDI) Architecture

BDI, which stands for Belief-Desire-Intention, is an architecture that follows the theory of human reasoning as defined by Michael Bratman. Belief represents the view of the world by the agent (what it believes to be the state of the environment in which it exists). Desires are the goals that define the motivation of the agent (what it wants to achieve). The agent may have numerous desires, which must be consistent. Finally, Intentions specify that the agent uses the Beliefs and Desires in order to choose one or more actions in order to meet the desires (see Figure 11.11).

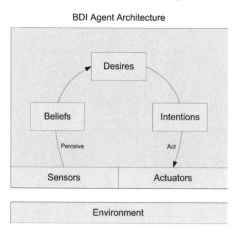

FIGURE 11.11: **The BDI architecture desires to model mental attitudes.**

As we described above, the BDI architecture defines the basic architecture of any deliberative agent. It stores a representation of the state of the environment (beliefs), maintains a set of goals (desires), and finally, an intentional element that maps desires to beliefs (to provide one or more actions that modify the state of the environment based on the agent's needs).

Hybrid Architectures

As is the case in traditional software architecture, most architectures are hybrids. For example, the architecture of a network stack is made up of a pipe-and-filter architecture and a layered architecture. This same stack also shares some elements of a blackboard architecture, as there are global elements that are visible and used by each component of the architecture.

The same is true for agent architectures. Based on the needs of the agent system, different architectural elements can be chosen to meet those needs.

Mobile Architectures

The final architectural pattern that we'll discuss is the mobile agent architecture. This architectural pattern introduces the ability for agents to migrate themselves between hosts. As shown in Figure 11.12, the agent architecture includes the mobility element, which allows an agent to migrate from one host to another. An agent can migrate to any host that implements the mobile framework.

The mobile agent framework provides a protocol that permits communication between hosts for agent migration. This framework also requires some kind of authentication and security, to avoid a mobile agent framework from becoming a conduit for viruses.

Also implicit in the mobile agent framework is a means for discovery. For example, which hosts are available for migration, and what services do they provide? Communication is also implicit, as agents can communicate with one another on a host, or across hosts in preparation for migration.

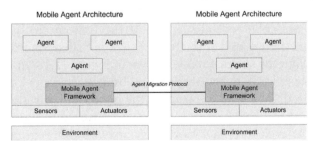

FIGURE 11.12: **The mobile agent framework supports agent mobility.**

The mobile agent architecture is advantageous as it supports the development of intelligent distributed systems. But a distributed system that is dynamic, and whose configuration and loading is defined by the agents themselves.

Architecture Descriptions

In the previous section, we explored some of the architectures that have been created for the construction of agents. Now let's review some of the implementations of these architectures. We'll review the architectures as shown in Table 11.5.

Table 11.5:   Please attribute the architectures as follows:

Subsumption	Brooks
Atlantis	Gat
Homer	Bickmore
BB1	Hayes-Roth
Open Agent Arch	Stanford
PRS	Ingrand, Georgeff, and Rao
Aglets	IBM
Messengers	Fukada
SOAR	University of Michigan

You'll note that the goal of each of these architectures is to select an action to perform given the current state of the environment. From this perspective, we can refer to these as action selection architectures.

Subsumption Architecture (Reactive Architecture)

The Subsumption architecture, originated by Rodney Brooks in the late 1980s, was created out of research in behavior-based robotics. The fundamental idea behind subsumption is that intelligent behavior can be created through a collection of simple behavior modules. These behavior modules are collected into layers. At the bottom are behaviors that are reflexive in nature, and at the top, behaviors that are more complex.

Consider the abstract model shown in Figure 11.13. At the bottom (level 0) exist the reflexive behaviors (such as obstacle avoidance). If these behaviors are required, then level 0 consumes the inputs and provides an action at the output. But no obstacles exist, so the next layer up is permitted to subsume control. At each level, a set of behaviors with different goals compete for control based on the state of the environment. To support this capability,

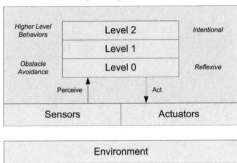

FIGURE 11.13: Architectural view of the subsumption architecture.

levels can be inhibited (in other words, their outputs are disabled). Levels can also be suppressed such that sensor inputs are routed to higher layers.

As shown in Figure 11.13, subsumption is a parallel and distributed architecture for managing sensors and actuators. The basic premise is that we begin with a simple set of behaviors, and once we've succeeded there, we extend with additional levels and higher-level behaviors. For example, we begin with obstacle avoidance and then extend for object seeking. From this perspective, the architecture takes a more evolutionary design approach.

Subsumption does have its problems. It is simple, but it turns out not to be extremely extensible. As new layers are added, the layers tend to interfere with one another, and then the problem becomes how to layer the behaviors such that each has the opportunity to control when the time is right. Subsumption is also reactive in nature, meaning that in the end, the architecture still simply maps inputs to behaviors (no planning occurs, for example). What subsumption does provide is a means to choose which behavior for a given environment.

Behavior Networks (Reactive Architecture)

Behavior networks, created by Pattie Maes in the late 1980s, is another reactive architecture that is distributed in nature. Behavior networks attempt to answer the question, which action is best suited for a given situation. As the name implies, behavior networks are networks of behaviors that include activation links and inhibition links.

An example behavior network for a game agent is shown in Figure 11.14. As shown in the legend, behaviors are rectangles and define the actions that the agent may take (attack, explore, reload, etc.). The ovals specify

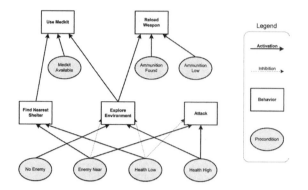

FIGURE 11.14: Behavior network for a simple game agent.

the preconditions for actions to be selected, which are inputs from the environment. Preconditions connect to behaviors through activation links (they promote the behavior to be performed) or inhibition links (that inhibit the behavior from being performed).

The network in Figure 11.14 illustrates a typical NPC in an FPS game environment. The environment is sampled, and then the behavior for the agent is selected based on the current state of the environment. The first thing to note is the activation and inhibition links. For example, when the agent's health is low, attack and exploration are inhibited, leaving the agent to find the nearest shelter. Also, while exploring, the agent may come across medkits or ammunition. If a medkit or ammunition is found, it's used.

Maes' algorithm referred to competence modules, which included preconditions (that must be fulfilled before the module can activate), actions to be performed, as well as a level of activation. The activation level is a threshold that is used to determine when a competence module may activate. The algorithm also includes decay, such that activiations dissipate over time.

Like the subsumption architecture, behavior networks are instances of Behavior-Based Systems (BBS). The primitive actions produced by these systems are all behaviors, based on the state of the environment.

Behavior networks are not without problems. Being reactive, the architecture does not support planning or higher-level behaviors. The architecture can also suffer when behaviors are highly inter-dependent. With many competing goals, the behavior modules can grow dramatically in order to realize the intended behaviors. But for simpler architecture, such as the FPS game agent in Figure 11.14, this algorithm is ideal.

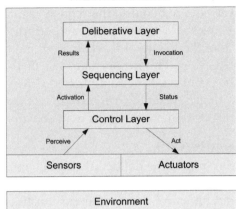

FIGURE 11.15: **The three-layer architecture of ATLANTIS.**

ATLANTIS (Deliberative Architecture)

The goal of ATLANTIS (A Three-Layer Architecture for Navigating Through Intricate Situations), was to create a robot that could navigate through dynamic and imperfect environments in pursuit of explicitly stated high-level goals. ATLANTIS was to prove that a goal-oriented robot could be built from a hybrid architecture of lower-level reactive behaviors and higher-level deliberative behaviors.

Where the subsumption architecture allows layers to subsume control, ATLANTIS operates on the assumption that these behaviors are not exclusive of one another. The lowest layer can operate in a reactive fashion to the immediate needs of the environment, while the uppermost layer can support planning and more goal-oriented behaviors. The fundamental architecture of ATLANTIS is provided in Figure 11.15.

In ATLANTIS, control is performed from the bottom-up. At the lowest level (the control layer) are the reactive behaviors. These primitive-level actions are capable of being executed first, based on the state of the environment. At the next layer is the sequencing layer. This layer is responsible for executing plans created by the deliberative layer. The deliberative layer maintains an internal model of the environment and creates plans to satisfy goals. The sequencing layer may or may not complete the plan, based on the state of the environment.

This leaves the deliberation layer to perform the computationally expensive tasks. This is another place that the architecture is a hybrid. The lower-level behavior-based methods (in the controller layer) are integrated with higher-level classical AI mechanisms (in the deliberative layer). Interestingly, the deliberative layer does not control the sequencing layer, but instead simply advises on sequences of actions that it can perform. The advantage of this architecture is that the low-level reactive layer and higher-level intentional layers are asynchronous. This means that while deliberative plans are under construction, the agent is not susceptible to the dynamic environment. This is because even though planning can take time at the deliberative layer, the controller can deal with random events in the environment.

Homer (Deliberative Arch)

Homer is another interesting deliberative architecture that is both modular and integrated. Homer was created by Vere and Bickmore in 1990 as a deliberative architecture with some very distinct differences to other architectures. Some of the notable differences include a temporal planner and a natural language processor.

At the core of the Homer architecture is a memory that is divided into two parts. The first part contains general knowledge (such as knowledge about the environment). The second part is called *episodic knowledge*, which is used to record experiences in the environment (perceptions and actions taken). The natural language processor accepts human input via a keyboard, and parses and responds using a sentence generator. The temporal planner creates dynamic plans to satisfy predefined goals, and is capable of replanning if the environment requires. By temporal, we mean that the planner can plan actions to take place within a given time, which can be replanned if this does not occur. The architecture also includes a plan executor (or interpreter), which is used to execute the plan at the actuators. The architecture also included a variety of monitor processes.

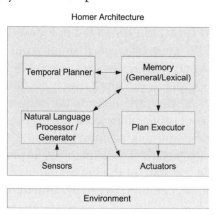

FIGURE 11.16: **The architecture of Homer integrates separate fields of AI.**

The basic idea behind Homer was an architecture for general intelligence. The keyboard would allow regular English language input, and a terminal would display generated English language sentences. The user could therefore communicate with Homer to specify goals and receive feedback via the terminal. Homer could log perceptions of the world, with timestamps, to allow dialogue with the user and rational answers to questions. Reflective (monitor) processes allow Homer to add or remove knowledge from the episodic memory.

Homer is an interesting architecture implementing a number of interesting ideas, from natural language processing to planning and reasoning. One issue found in Homer is that when the episodic memory grows large, it tends to slow down the overall operation of the agent.

BB1 (Blackboard)

BB1 is a domain-independent blackboard architecture for AI systems created by Barbara Hayes-Roth. The architecture supports control over problem solving as well as explaining its actions. The architecture is also able to learn new domain knowledge.

BB1 includes two blackboards; a domain blackboard which acts as the global database and a control blackboard, which is used for generating a solution to the given control problem. The key behind BB1 is its ability to incrementally plan. Instead of defining a complete plan for a given goal, and then executing that plan, BB1 dynamically develops the plan and adapts to the changes in the environment. This is key for dynamic environments, where unanticipated changes can lead to brittle plans that eventually fail.

As a blackboard architecture, knowledge sources introduce new knowledge to the blackboard for one or more users. The change of knowledge in a blackboard serves as a trigger for operation by users. In BB1, control solutions are dynamically generated using knowledge from the domain blackboard from control knowledge in the control blackboard. A scheduler manages which blackboard users should get the ability to execute.

Open Agent Architecture (Blackboard)

The Open Agent Architecture (or OAA) is a blackboard architecture in which all agents communicate through the blackboard (via a server process). The server process acts in a number of roles. It coordinates activities between the client agents (deciding which can act on knowledge on the blackboard) as well as providing communication between client agents. When knowledge is applied to the blackboard (through the server), the server decides which agent should be notified and then schedules them accordingly. An architectural view of the

OAA is provided in Figure 11.16A.

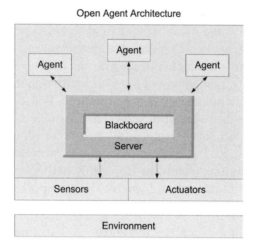

FIGURE 11.16A: **The OAA uses a blackboard and a server for coordination.**

The language used to communicate between agents in OAA is an extension of Prolog. A new agent registers itself with the server, and can install triggers that monitor incoming data into the blackboard. The trigger serves as a request such that when knowledge arrives, the server can route the data to the agent for further processing. Agents may also communicate with other agents through the server. This can be done for the purpose of requesting activities of other agents. The server (and blackboard) also provide the means for broadcast communications to globally coordinate between the agents.

The OAA is a useful generic architecture for multi-agent programming with a common communication structure. The agent communication language, using Prolog, makes it useful to communicate not only generic requests and responses, but also knowledge and semantic queries.

Procedural Reasoning System (BDI)

The Procedural Reasoning System (PRS) is a general-purpose architecture that's ideal for reasoning environments where actions can be defined by predetermined procedures (action sequences). PRS is also a BDI architecture, mimicking the theory on human reasoning.

PRS integrates both reactive and goal-directed deliberative processing in a distributed architecture. As shown in Figure 11.17, the architecture is able to build a world-model of the environment (beliefs) through interacting with environment sensors. Actions can also be taken through an intentions module. At the core is an interpreter (or reasoner) which selects a goal to meet (given the current set of beliefs) and then retrieves a plan to execute

Procedural Reasoning System Architecture

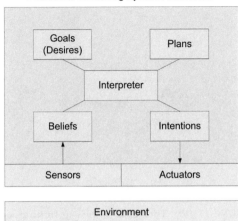

FIGURE 11.17:   **PRS is a BDI architecture for plan execution.**

to achieve that goal. PRS iteratively tests the assumptions of the plan during its execution. This means that it can operate in dynamic environments where classical planners are doomed to fail.

Plans in PRS (also called knowledge areas) are predefined for the actions that are possible in the environment. This simplifies the architecture because it isn't required to generate plans, only select them based on the environment and the goals that must be met. While planning is more about selection than search or generation, the interpreter ensures that changes to the environment do not result in inconsistencies in the plan. Instead, a new plan is selected to achieve the specific goals.

PRS is a useful architecture when all necessary operations can be predefined. It's also very efficient due to lack of plan generation. This makes PRS an ideal agent architecture for building agents such as those to control mobile robots.

Aglets (Mobile)

Aglets is a mobile agent framework designed by IBM Tokyo in the 1990s. Aglets is based on the Java programming language, as it is well suited for a mobile agents framework. First, the applications are portable to any system (both homogeneous and heterogeneous) that is capable of running a Java Virtual Machine (JVM). Second, a JVM is an ideal platform for migration services. Java supports serialization, which is the aggregation of a Java application's program and data into a single object that is restartable. In this case, the Java application is restarted on a new JVM. Java also provides

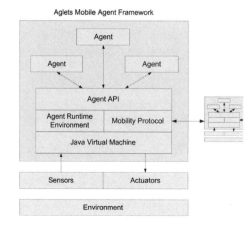

FIGURE 11.18:   **The aglets mobile agent framework.**

a secure environment (sandbox) to ensure that a mobile agent framework doesn't become a virus distribution system.

The Aglets framework is shown in Figure 11.18. At the bottom of the framework is the JVM (the virtual machine that interprets the Java bytecodes). The agent runtime environment and mobility protocol are next. The mobility protocol, called Aglet Transport Protocol (or ATP), provides the means to serialize agents and then transport them to a host previously defined by the agent. The agent API is at the top of the stack, which in usual Java fashion, provides a number of API classes that focus on agent operation. Finally, there are the various agents that operate on the framework.

The agent API and runtime environment provide a number of services that are central to a mobile agent framework. Some of the more important functions are agent management, communication, and security. Agents must be able to register themselves on a given host to enable communication from outside agents. In order to support communication, security features must be implemented to ensure that the agent has the authority to execute on the framework.

Aglets provides a number of necessary characteristics for a mobile agent framework, including mobility, communication, security, and confidentiality. Aglets provide weak migration, in that the agents can only migrate at arbitrary points within the code (such as with the dispatch method).

Messengers (Mobile)

Messengers is a runtime environment that provides a form of process migration (mobile agency). One distinct strength of the messengers environment is that it supports strong migration, or the ability to migrate at arbitrary points within the mobile application.

The messengers environment provides the hop statement which defines when and where to migrate to a new destination. After migration is complete, the messengers agent restarts in the application at the point after the previous hop statement. The end result is that the application moves to the data, rather than using a messaging protocol to move the data to the agent. There are obvious advantages to this when the data set is large and the migration links are slow.

The messengers model provides what the authors call Navigational Programming, and also Distributed Sequential Computing (DSC). What makes these concepts interesting is that they support the common model of programming that is identical to the traditional flow of sequential programs. This makes them easier to develop and understand.

Let's now look at an example of DSC using the messengers environment. Listing 11.5 provides a simple program. Consider an application where on a series of hosts, we manipulate large matrices which are held in their memory. This can be simply demonstrated on Listing 11.4.

Listing 11.5: Example of distributed sequential computing.

```
// Begin on host A
r1 = value(A)
// Hop to host B
hop(B)
r2 = f1(r1, B)
// Hop and end at host C
hop(C)
r3 = f2(r2, C)
```

What's interesting about this simple program, and a strength of the messengers approach, is that the resulting program has the same structure and flow as the original sequential variant. The only difference between this program, and a single processor non-distributed variant is that hop statements are inserted to initiate transfer of the program to the new host.

Another useful application of DSC is in the domain of sensor networks. Rather than moving sensor data among hosts for processing, messenger applications migrate to the sensor nodes (such as multi-megapixel imagers), process them (calculate their centroids), and migrate their results on to subsequent processing nodes.

Soar (Hybrid)

Soar, which originally was an acronym for State-Operator-And-Result, is a symbolic cognitive architecture. Soar provides a model of cognition along with an implementation of that model for building general-purpose AI systems. The idea behind Soar is from Newell's unified theories of cognition. Soar is one of the most widely used architectures, from research into aspects of human behavior to the design of game agents for first-person-shooter games.

The goal of the Soar architecture is to build systems that embody general intelligence. While Soar includes many elements that support this goal (for example, representing knowledge using procedural, episodic, and declarative forms), but Soar lacks some important aspects. These include episodic memories and also a model for emotion.

Soar's underlying problem-solving mechanism is based on a production system (expert system). Behavior is encoded in rules similar to the if-then form. Solving problems in Soar can be most simply described as problem-space search (to a goal node). If this model of problem solving fails, other methods are used, such as hill climbing. When a solution is found, Soar uses a method called *chunking* to learn a new rule based on this discovery. If the agent encounters the problem again, it can use the rule to select the action to take instead of performing problem solving again.

AGENT LANGUAGES

Agents can be built in any language, though a number of agent-focused languages (and language extensions) are available to simplify their development. In this section, we'll explore some of the languages and language extensions that can be used for agent development.

Telescript

Telescript is both a language and environment for the development of agents and agent societies. It's also one of the oldest languages that focus solely on agent development (including those with mobile attributes). Telescript was an object-oriented language that was interpreted by the environment. Telescript could also integrate with C applications for building large systems.

The two primary elements of Telescript are the agent and place (each represented as base classes). Using these classes, mobile and communicating agents can be developed along with locations for them to migrate and interact. Telescript includes the necessary security controls for places to authenticate one another (through the platform interconnect protocol) to support the secure transport of mobile agents.

A very simple example of Telescript migration is provided in Listing 11.6. In this example, a Telescript function is provided encapsulate the movement method (go). As with the aglets framework, a ticket is used to represent the request to travel to a remote host. The go method is used to initiate the transfer. Note below that the '*' symbols represent the object being manipulated, in this case, the current object.

Listing 11.6:   A simple method in telescript.

```
changeLocation: op (locName: Telename; locAddress: Teleaddress) =
{
 // Clear events
 *.disableEvents( );
 *.clearEvents( );
 // Move to new location
 *.go( Ticket(locName, locAddress) );
};
```

Telescript was an interesting language, following the heritage of Smalltalk (the original object-oriented language). Unfortunately, Telescript was a proprietary language and environment and lacked the developer and research community to survive.

Aglets

As described in the agent architectures section, Aglets is a Java-based framework for agent construction. In particular, the Java extensions provide the means for migration of agents (including their data) between hosts that support the Aglets framework. The Aglet framework was developed at IBM's Tokyo research laboratory.

As with Telescript, Aglets supports the development of mobile agents (using the Aglet class), and also places (implemented as Aglet contexts). Given their mobility, Aglets communicate using messages which are supported by the framework. The Aglets framework also support a global namespace, such that each Aglet is given a unique identifier.

The Aglets API supports the creation of Aglets, cloning of Aglets (duplication), disposal (removal of the Aglet), and other behaviors. This API is interesting because it extends a currently popular language with agent characteristics. This means that developers need not learn a new language in order to deploy agents (and potentially complex semantics), but instead simply the new classes for an existing language.

An example of Aglet's mobility mechanism is provided in Listing 11.4.

Obliq

Obliq was an interpreted language developed by the Digital Equipment Corporation (DEC). The goal was to create a language in which networking and migration was a part of the core kernel. The language supports the migration of procedures across a network as a closure. This provides a secure form of migration which minimizes the agent's access to remote host resources (only those provided by the remote side).

Obliq uses the concept of the hop instruction to migrate to a new host. The agent is migrated, along with its suitcase, which represents the data that it may carry with it to the new host. When the agent arrives at the new host, it receives a briefing, which represents the data made available to it by the host (a containment mechanism). The briefing can contain more than just data, and may also describe functions available to the agent and the new host as well as other agents that are available.

Agent TCL

Agent TCL, as the name implies, is a set of extensions for agent programming using TCL (Tool Command Language developed at the University of California at Berkeley). Agent TCL transforms the standard TCL language and interpreter into a transportable agent system.

One of the features provided by agent TCL is migration. This is provided by a new command called `agent_jump`. When the `agent_jump` command completes, the agent restarts at the new host at the command following the previously executed `agent_jump` command.

In addition to migration using the `agent_jump` command, Agent TCL supports those features common in agent frameworks. For example, communication using message passing, agent creation, cloning, and destruction commands, and the required features of security.

A portion of a simple example is shown in Listing 11.7.

Listing 11.7:   Simple example of agent TCL migration.

```
# Catch any exceptions that occur for the agent_jump command
if {[catch {agent_jump $machine} result]} {
  # Unable to migrate to $machine
```

```
    puts "Couldn't migrate..."
} else {
  # Migrated to $machine
  # Notify parent agent of migration
  agent_send $agent(root) 0 "I'm here.\n"
}
```

Agent TCL is another interesting example of an existing popular language that's been extended for agent development.

Traditional Languages

Agent systems have been developed in a wide range of languages, from the specialized languages designed for AI (domain-specific languages) and also the more traditional languages in wide use today (C, C++, and others). While the development of certain types of agent systems may require specialized capabilities (such as those demonstrated by mobile agent systems, or natural language systems), an intelligent application can be developed in any language, from LISP to object-oriented scripting languages such as Ruby.

AGENT COMMUNICATION

In the domain of multi-agent systems, communication is an important characteristic to support both coordination and the transfer of information. Agents also require the ability to communicate actions or plans. But how the communication takes place is a function of its purpose. In this section, we'll explore some of the popular mechanisms for communication and their semantics.

KQML (Knowledge Query and Manipulation Language)

The KQML is an interesting example of communication from a number of facets. For example, communication requires the ability to locate and engage a peer in a conversation (communication layer). A method for packaging the messages is then necessary (messaging layer), and finally an internal format that represents the messages and is sufficiently expressive to convey not only information but requests, responses, and plans (content layer).

In a network of KQML-speaking agents, there exists programs to support communication. These consist of facilitators that can serve as name servers to KQML components, and help find other agents that can satisfy a given agent's request. A KQML router supports the routing of messages and is a front-end to a specific KQML agent.

As KQML was originally written in Common LISP, it's message representation follows the LISP example (balanced parentheses). A KQML message can be transferred to any particular transport (such as sockets) and has a format that consists of a performative and a set of arguments for that performative. The performative defines the speech act which defines the purpose of the message (assertion, command, request, etc.). For example, the following describes the KQML message structure (see Listing 11.8). The performative-name defines the particular message type to be communicated (evaluate, ask-if, stream-about, reply, tell, deny, standby, advertise, etc.). The sender and receiver define the unique names of the agents in the dialogue. The content is information specific to the performative being performed. This content is defined in a language (how to represent the content), and an ontology that describes the vocabulary (and meaning) of the content. Finally, the agent can attach a context which the response will contain (in-reply-to) in order to correlate the request with the response.

Listing 11.8:   The structure of a KQML message.

```
(performative-name
  : sender X
  : receiver Y
  : content Z
  : language L
  : ontology Y
  : reply-with R
  : in-reply-to Q
)
```

Let's now look at an example conversation between two KQML agents. In this example, an agent requests the current value of a temperature sensor in a system. The request is for the temperature of TEMP_SENSOR_1A that's sampled at the `temperature-server` agent. The content is the request, defined in the prolog language. Our agent making the request is called `thermal-control-appl`.

```
(ask-one
  :sender thermal-control-appl
  :receiver temperature-server
```

```
    :language prolog
    :ontology CELSIUS-DEGREES
    :content "temperature(TEMP_SENSOR_1A ?temperature)"
    :reply-with request-102
)
```

Our agent would then receive a response from the temperature-server, defining the temperature of the sensor of interest.

```
(reply
  :sender temperature-server
  :receiver thermal-control-appl
  :language prolog
  :ontology CELSIUS-DEGREES
  :content "temperature(TEMP_SENSOR_1A 45.2)"
  :in-reply-to request-102
)
```

KQML is very rich in its ability to communicate information as well higher-level requests that address the communication layer. Table 11.6 provides a short list of some of the other KQML performatives.

Table 11.6: KQML performatives.

Performative	Description
evaluate	Evaluate the content of the message
ask-one	Request for the answer to a question
reply	Communicate a reply to a question
stream-about	Provide multiple responses to a question
sorry	Return an error (can't respond)
tell	Inform an agent of a sentence
achieve	A request of something to achieve by the receiver
advertise	Advertise the ability to process a performative
subscribe	Subscribe to changes of information
forward	Route a message

KQML is a useful language to communicate not only data, but the meaning of the data (in terms of a language and ontology). KQML provides a rich set of capabilities that cover basic speech acts, and more complex acts including data streaming and control of information transfer.

ACL (FIPA Agent Communication Language)

Where KQML is a language defined in the context of a university, the FIPA ACL is a consortium-based language for agent communication. ACL simply means Agent Communication Language and it was standardized through the Foundation for Intelligent Physical Agents consortium. As with KQML, ACL is a speech-act language defined by a set of performatives.

NOTE ▸ *The FIPA, or Foundation for Intelligent Physical Agents, is a non-profit organization that promotes the development of agent-based systems. It develops specifications to maximize the portability of agent systems (including their ability to communicate using the ACL).*

The FIPA ACL is very similar to the KQML, even adopting the inner and outer content layering for message construction (meaning and content). The ACL also clarifies certain speech-acts, or performatives. For example, communication primitives are called *communicative acts*, which are separate from the performative acts. The FIPA ACL also uses the Semantic Language, or SL, as the formal language to define ACL semantics. This provides the means to support BDI themes (beliefs, desires, intentions). In other words, SL allows the representation of persistent goals (intentions), as well as propositions and objects.

Each agent language has its use, and while both have their differences, they can also be viewed as complementary.

XML

XML is the eXtensible Markup Language and is an encoding that represents data and meta-data (meaning of the data). It does this with a representation that includes tags that encapsulate the data. The tags explicitly define what the data represents. For example, consider the ask-one request from KQML. This can be represented as XML as shown below:

```
<msg>
<performative>ask-one</performative>
<sender>thermal-control-appl</sender>
<receiver>temperature-server</receiver>
<sensor-request>TEMP_SENSOR_1A</sensor-request>
<reply-with>request-102</reply-with>
</msg>
```

There are some obvious similarities to XML and KQML. In KQML, the tags exist, but use different syntax than is defined for XML. One significant difference is that KQML permits the layering of tags. Note here that the <msg> tag is the outer layer of the performative and its arguments. XML is very flexible in its format and permits very complex arrangements of both data and meta-data.

XML is used in a number of protocols, including XML-RPC (Remote Procedure Call) and also SOAP (Simple Object Access Protocol). Each of these use the Hyper Text Transport Protocol (HTTP) as its transport.

CHAPTER SUMMARY

Intelligent agents are an interesting exploration in artificial intelligence as they are key users of AI methods and techniques. While agents can be viewed as an end application of AI, their study introduces concepts of intelligent systems and fundamental architectures for their implementation. This chapter provided an introduction to agent systems, characteristics, and architectures. You'll find agent systems in games, web applications (such as user assistance) as well as internally in complex and distributed applications.

RESOURCES

[ANTS 2003] "Active Networks at the University of Washington," 2003. Available online at: http://www.cs.washington.edu/research/networking/ants/.

[Aglets 2002] "Aglets Software Development Kit," 2002, IBM. Available online at: http://www.trl.ibm.bom/aglets/.

[Bratman 1987] "Intention, Plans, and Practical Reason," CSLI Publications, 1987.

[Brooks 1986] "A Robust Layered Control System For a Mobile Robot," *IEEE Journal of Robotics and Automation*, April 1986.

[Google Alerts] Google Alerts, 2006. Available online at: http://www.google.com/alerts

[Gat 1991] Gat, E. "Integrating planning and reacting in heterogeneous asynchronous architecture for mobile robots," SIGART Bulletin 2, 1991.

[Hayes-Roth 1984] Hayes-Roth, Barbara, "BB1: An architecture for blackboard systems that control, explain, and learn about their own behavior," Stanford University, 1984.

[IEEE-1471] "Recommended Practice for Architecture Description of Software-Intensive Systems." Also known as ISO/IEC DIS 25961.

Kotz, et al, "Agent Tcl: Targeting the Needs of Mobile Computers," *IEEE Internet Computing*, July/August 1997.

Labrou, et al. "Agent Communication Languages: The Current Landscape," University of Maryland, Baltimore County, IEEE Intelligent Systems, March/April 1999.

Labrou, et al. "A Proposal for a new KQML Specification," TR CS-97-03, 1997.

Available online at: http://www.cs.umbc.edu/kqml/papers/kqml97.pdf

Laird, John, Newll, Allen, and Rosenbloom, Paul. "Soar: An Architecture for General Intelligence," *Artificial Intelligence*, 33:1989.

Mabry, Susan L., Bic, Lubomir, F. "Bridging Semantic Gaps with Migrating Agents," International Conference on Parallel and Distributed Computing Systems (PDCS), 1999.

Muscettola, et al. "Remote Agent: To Boldly Go Where No AI System Has Gone Before," *Artificial Intelligence*, 1998.

Newell, Allen *Unified Theories of Cognition* Harvard University Press, 1990.

Nicolescu, Monica, and Mataric, Maja. "A hierarchical architecture for behavior-based robots," Proceedings, First International Joint Conference on Autonomous Agents and Multi-Agent Systems, pages 227-233, Bolgna Italy, July 2002.

"Soar (cognitive architecture)," Wikipedia. Available online at:

http://en.wikipedia.org/wiki/Soar_(cognitive_architecture)

REFERENCES

Franklin, S., and Graesser, A. "Is It an Agent or Just a Program? A Taxonomy for Autonomous Agents" from the Proceedings of the Third International Workshop on Agent Theories, Architectures, and Languages, 1996.

Lashkari, Y.; Metral, M.; and Maes, P. 1994. "Collaborative Interface Agents." In the proceedings of the Twelfth National Conference on Artificial Intelligence, 444-450. Menlo Park, CA.

Shaw, M., and Garlin, D. *Software Architecture: Perspectives on an Emerging Discipline* Prentice-Hall, 1996.

Stuart Russell, Peter Norvig. *Artificial Intelligence: A Modern Approach* Second Edition, Addison-Wesley, 2003.

Ananova, Virtual Newscaster. Available online at:

http://www.ananova.com/video

[RFC 439], Cerf, V. "Parry Encounters the Doctor," January 21, 1973.

EXERCISES

1. In your own words, define how an agent and a program differ.
2. Define the major agent properties and how they affect an agent.
3. Given the agent environment properties in Table 11.2, provide two environment examples and the properties they support.
4. What other types of interface agents could be used in an Internet environment?
5. Explore a game environment that supports NPC scripting. How rich is the script and what kinds of behaviors could be implemented?
6. Describe how Eliza carried out a seemingly intelligent conversation with a user.
7. Define an advantage of mobile agents over typical systems that rely on remote communication.
8. If you were to create a new mobile agent framework, describe the manner in which serialization and migration would occur. How would your approach differ from the mobile agent frameworks discussed in this text?
9. Compare and contrast the reactive and deliberative agent architectures.
10. Explain how communication and coordination work in a blackboard architecture.
11. While subsumption and behavior networks are both reactive architectures, they are architecturally very different. Define the two architectures and how they compare and differ.
12. Homer is a deliberative agent architecture. What is unique about Homer, and for which applications would it be used?
13. Explain the planning mechanism used by the Procedural Reasoning System.
14. Telescript and aglets are both mobile agent runtime environments. Define how each specifies migration.

12 BIOLOGICALLY INSPIRED AND HYBRID MODELS

F rom the perspective of biologically intelligent systems, we find a hybrid of methods at play. Humans are adept at numerical computation and symbolic computation. We support associative memories, and can recall images and concepts based on incomplete facts. We are highly parallel and connectionist in nature. In short, we are a hybrid of independent methods that integrate together and result in the highest form of intelligence on the planet. In this chapter, we'll explore some of the hybrid methods that result from integrating different AI techniques together.

CELLULAR AUTOMATA (CA)

Cellular Automata, or CA, is an interesting example of systems with very simple rules that exhibit very complex behavior. CAs are discrete systems that have been used in a variety of contexts, from theoretical biology to computability theory. A CA is what's known as *Turing complete* as it can be used to compute any computable function, albeit in an unusual fashion.

The first cellular automaton was developed by John Von Neumann and was based on a conversation with Stanislaw Ulam. The purpose of this first CA was as a vehicle to understand the conceptual requirements for self-replicating machines.

CAs can be simply described as a finite-state machine. The states of a system are then a function of some collection of other states in the system. At a discrete time step, each state of the system is updated given the other current states of the system, producing a globally changing system. These changes can exhibit computation, classification, and even self-replication.

Let's now look at some cellular automata classes to better understand their capabilities.

One-Dimensional CAs

The simplest form of CA is the one-dimensional CA. This consists of a row of cells, where each cell follows a globally defined set of rules. Each cell has a given state, which is altered at each discrete time step using the global rules. The cell states can be binary, or take on multiple values.

Additionally, the rules can be simple (such as using the cell states to the current cell and its two neighbors) up to many neighbors indicating a large number of rules.

Note that in the case of a rule set that incorporates the state of the current cell and that of its two neighbors, there are eight rules possible. A

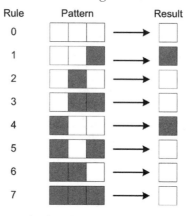

FIGURE 12.1: **Simple rule set for our one-dimensional CA.**

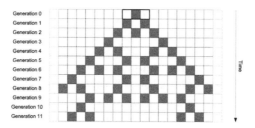

FIGURE 12.2: **Generational behavior of the simple one dimensional CA.**

sample rule set is shown in Figure 12.1. These rules simply define that a cell is born when a cell in the previous generation appears to its left or right (but only one) of the current neighborhood.

The result of this rule set (from Figure 12.1) is shown in Figure 12.2, given the initial generation 0. Note the neighborhood shown in Generation 0 as the bold line in the center (which will use rule 2). We can think of the cells as living (dark cell) and empty (white cell). The rules then define the birth criteria for a new cell given the state of its neighbors.

Given such simple rules, the CA is capable of generating very complex and interesting patterns. But while interesting, one-dimensional CAs are quite limited. Let's now take a more detailed look at the CA that extends another dimension.

Two-Dimensional CAs

The most famous two-dimensional CA was introduced in the 1970s by John Conway (and popularized through Scientific American). This was called the *Game of Life*. First, the universe for this CA is a two-dimensional grid. Each cell has eight neighbors (for a given cell in the grid, each cell that surrounds the cell is a neighbor). Like the one-dimensional CA, life occurs in generations. At each generational step, a new universe is created from the old. This means that if a cell dies, survives, or gives birth, it occurs in the next generation (where each cell is manipulated in parallel and births in the new generation do not contribute to neighbors in the old generation).

The rules of Conway's Game of Life are very simple (see the Conway neighborhood shown in Figure 12.3). If a cell is currently alive and has less than two neighbors, then it dies in the next generation. If a cell is currently alive and has two or three neighbors, then it survives into the next generation.

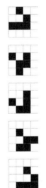

FIGURE 12.3: Illustration of the Conway
neighborhood for a specific cell.

FIGURE 12.4: Translation of the glider
object using Conway's rules.

But if a cell is alive, and has more than three neighbors, then it dies from overcrowding. Finally, if a cell is vacant but has three neighbors, then it becomes alive in the next generation. From this very simple set of rules, very complex behaviors are possible, even to the extent of being Turing complete.

Note that for Conway's rule, only the number of neighbors is relevant. This means that there can be a maximum of 18 rules (nine rules for each of the cell on or off state). Other rule systems could instead use specific cell configurations (for a maximum of 512 rules).

A simple example that shows the changes to a universe over time is shown in Figure 12.4. This example illustrates what is called a *glider*. This object moves (translates) diagonally one cell every four generations.

Conway Application

Implementing Conway's game of life is very simple. A portion of this is provided below to demonstrate Conway's rule. Two complete universes must be maintained which alternately represent the present and past. The contents of the present universe are generated from the past using Conway's rules. Once we determine which universe is the past and which is the present, we simply apply the rules to the past to identify which cells are set (or reset) in the future.

The complete source for the Conway's life application can be found on the CD-ROM at ./software/ch12/life.c. This application uses ncurses, which is available in GNU/Linux, or in Cygwin for Windows. Also on the CD-ROM are sample CA pattern files that can be used to demonstrate interesting CA objects.

Listing 12.1:   Conway's Life Rule Implementation in C.

```
void generateUniverse( int gen )
{
int y, x, neighbors, past, newcell;
 /* Which is the previous universe to test from? */
 past = (gen == 0) ? 1 : 0;
 /* Evaluate each cell from the past to determine what the future cell
  * should be.
  */
 for (y = 0 ; y < MAX_Y_GRID ; y++) {
```

```
for (x = 0 ; x < MAX_X_GRID ; x++) {
  /* Compute neighbors cells around the current */
  neighbors = cell(past,y-1,x-1) + cell(past,y-1,x) +
          cell(past,y-1,x+1) + cell(past,y,x-1) +
          cell(past,y,x+1)   + cell(past,y+1,x-1) +
          cell(past,y+1,x)   + cell(past,y+1,x+1);
  /* Conway rule
   *
   * Death    (cell on, less than 2 neighbors)
   * Survival (cell on, 2 or 3 neighbors)
   * Birth    (cell off, 3 neighbors)
   * Otherwise, new cell is off
   *
   */
  newcell = 0;
  if (cell(past,y,x) && (neighbors < 2)) newcell = 0;
  if (cell(past,y,x) && ((neighbors == 2) || (neighbors == 3)))
    newcell = 1;
  if ((!cell(past,y,x)) && (neighbors == 3)) newcell = 1;
  /* Birth, survival, or death */
  cell(gen,y,x) = newcell;
  }
 }
 return;
}
```

While Conway's rule uses eight neighbors to determine the cell state, we could increase the size of the neighborhood for different interactions. Also, what's described here is a homogeneous where each cell implements the same rule, but cells could operate with different rules, based on their location or based on a global system state (heterogeneous CA).

FIGURE 12.5: **Cellular automata glider gun (P30).**

The output of the sample application is shown in Figure 12.5. This shows a P30 glider gun emitting gliders (to the lower right).

Turing Completeness

The Turing completeness of CA (ability to emulate another computational model with CA) was proven in Stephen Wolfram's "A New Kind of Science." This book showed that rule 110 of a one-dimensional two-state CA exhibited the ability to create structures that would support universal computation. This was exciting because it opened up the possibility of natural physical systems supporting universal computation.

Emergence and Organization

Cellular Automata, and Conway's Life, is interesting because even with simple rule sets such as Conway's, characteristics such as emergent complexity appear. Emergence is a property of complex systems and can be very simply described as the appearance of complex system behaviors from the interactions of the lower-level elements of the system. The term self-organization has also been used to describe CA, where the internal organization of a system increases in complexity without any external guidance or pressure.

ARTIFICIAL IMMUNE SYSTEMS

Autonomic computing systems are those systems that have the ability to manage themselves for self-configuration, self-optimization, self-protection, and self-healing. Such systems perform these tasks in a way that mimics human biology. Our autonomic nervous system, for example, maintains our heart rate and

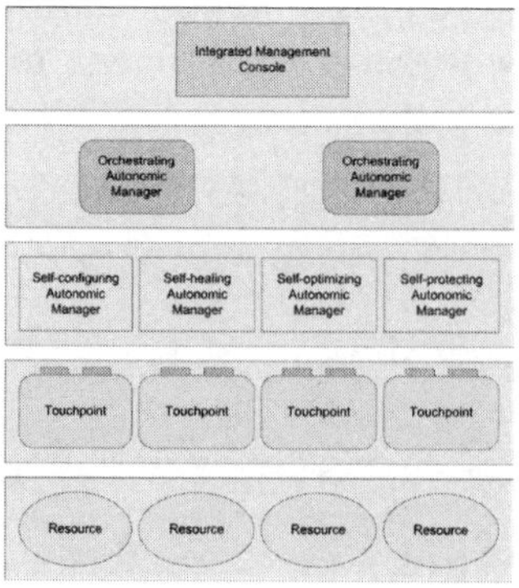

FIGURE 12.6: The layered architecture of an autonomic computing system.

stabilizes our body temperature without our conscious involvement. In the same way, an autonomic computing system allows system administrators to focus on higher-level business goals instead of the details of system management.

An autonomic computing system is made up of several components that work in concert to implement self-management capabilities. These components are implemented in a layered architecture, as shown in Figure 12.6.

At the bottom of the architecture are *managed resources*, which make up the elements that the system will monitor and control. These elements can be high-level information technology (IT) systems (such as servers) or applications within a single system. The interface to the managed resource is called a *touchpoint*. The touchpoint provides a set of Get and Set operations for monitoring and managing the resource.

At the next level are *touchpoint autonomic managers*. These autonomic managers work with the touchpoint to gather data about one or more resources. An autonomic manager commonly implements an intelligent algorithm to provide self-management, and when a change is required, you use the touchpoint again to alter the environment. Each autonomic manager implements a policy of self-management for self-configuration, self-healing, self-optimization, or self-protection.

Another set of autonomic managers is called the *orchestrating autonomic managers*. These managers provide coordination capabilities over several lower-level autonomic managers. Finally, at the top of the architecture is the *management console*, which you use to monitor the activities of the autonomic computing system and also define the policies to be used in self-management.

Self-Management capabilities

Control can exist at multiple layers within the autonomic computing system architecture but is most often implemented in the autonomic

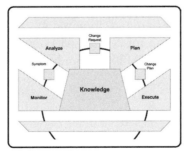

FIGURE 12.7: Control loop for an autonomic computing element.

managers. The embedded control loop follows a specific flow, though not all elements may be implemented. Figure 12.7 illustrates the elements of the control loop.

The *monitor* element collects and filters incoming data, which results in a *symptom*. The symptom is fed to the *analyze* element, which analyzes the symptom, potentially performs modeling and analysis of the symptom, identifies the course of action to take (if any), and generates a *change request*. From the change request, the *plan* element creates a *change plan* to achieve the goal. Finally, the *execute* element executes the plan to achieve the intended change. The *knowledge* element encapsulates the shared data that the monitor, analyze, plan, and execute elements use.

This collection of control loops at the various layers in the autonomic computing structure implements the attributes of self-management. These attributes include:

- Self-configuring
- Self-healing
- Self-optimizing
- Self-protecting

Autonomic managers can implement a single self-management attribute and operate within that domain. Orchestrating autonomic managers can work with the lower-level autonomic managers within attributes (such as self-configuring) or across attributes to achieve higher-level goals.

Touchpoints

A *touchpoint* is an interface to an underlying managed resource. The touchpoint implements sensor and effector behaviors that higher-level autonomic managers can use to manage the resource. The sensors gather information about a resource, and the effectors change the state or behavior of the underlying resource. A touchpoint may simply present a sensor/effector interface in the form of an API, or it may implement some level of internal intelligence to offload from higher-level managers (such as data filtering or data aggregation).

Touchpoint Autonomic Managers

The touchpoint autonomic managers provide intelligence for managing resources through their touchpoints. These managers may implement the control loop (or pieces of it) depending on the goal of the manager.

A touchpoint autonomic manager implements a policy that you define (from a management console) to provide for self-configuration, self-healing, self-optimization, or self-protection. It may do this using a single touchpoint, or it may work with multiple touchpoints of different types to achieve its goal.

These touchpoints may also provide an interface for orchestrating autonomic managers. An orchestrating autonomic manager may manage across self-management disciplines and therefore provide control over two or more touchpoint autonomic managers.

Orchestrating Autonomic Managers

A touchpoint autonomic manager manages a single resource through the touchpoint for that managed resource. Orchestrating autonomic managers coordinate across touchpoint autonomic managers to provide system-wide autonomic behavior.

Orchestrating autonomic managers may operate in one of two configurations. In the first configuration, the managers coordinate touchpoint autonomic managers of the same type (such as self-configuration autonomic managers). In the second configuration, the managers coordinate across disciplines (such as working with a self-protecting touchpoint autonomic manager and a self-healing touchpoint autonomic manager). In either case, the orchestrating autonomic managers have greater visibility into the system to be managed and can better contribute to overall system management.

Further, autonomic managers at all layers can work against each other to achieve their goals. An orchestrating autonomic manager that views the underlying system from a greater perspective (having greater visibility into the overall system than a focused autonomic manager) can more optimally manage the system from one or more self-management disciplines. For example, consider two self-optimizing autonomic managers that attempt to manipulate a common parameter for independent goals. It's possible that in their competing goals, they de-tune each another, resulting in no optimization. An orchestrating autonomic manager could help arbitrate situations such as these.

Integrated Management Console

At the top of the layered autonomic computing architecture is the Integrated Management Console (see Figure 12.8). This console is the user interface (UI) for the autonomic system. It allows you to manage the system and define the policies for self-management. It also allows you to monitor the activities of the autonomic system. Depending on the behavior of the system, you can change policies to better manage the system and achieve your goals.

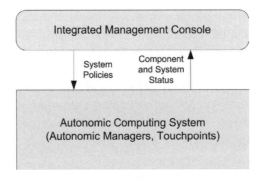

FIGURE 12.8: Integrated Management Console.

The integrated management console provides a single platform that can monitor and manage all elements of the autonomic computing system. This management includes not only initial configuration but also run-time monitoring and tuning. In the next tutorial, you'll see an example of an integrated management console built on the HTTP web protocol.

Autonomic Summary

Autonomic systems is an interesting architectural pattern for the development of intelligent systems. It's built around a layered architecture with very distinct responsibilities at each of the layers. The autonomic systems pattern can be used to develop a wide range of systems, from those that protect and manager servers (such as IBM's goal for autonomic systems) to the development of intelligent agent systems.

ARTIFICIAL LIFE

Artificial Life (or alife) is the study of life through simulation. It's also more commonly associated with the evolution of simple life forms that exhibit some desired behavior. For example, early alife simulations focused on the ability to breed creatures with varying control systems that could survive in their environments. Other simulations focused on economic behaviors and trading, and others on the synthesizing of life, albiet in a form different than our own.

   Note that the earlier discussion of Cellular Automata was a form of artifical life (prior to the term being coined). CAs are low-level implementations of artificial life (at the cell level) where the rules and state of the environment determine behaviors.

In this section, we'll explore some of the examples of artificial life and then look at a simple simulation that demonstrates the basic properties of artificial life and simulated evolution.

Echo

John Holland, a pioneer in the field of complex adaptive systems, created one of the earliest artificial life simulations called Echo. Holland's Echo provides an environment where agents interact in activities such as combat, mating, and trade. Along the way, agents develop strategies to survive and compete in environments that are resource constrained. The environments and agents include the necessary "knobs" to tweak the simulation's parameters to provide the ability to play "what-if" experiments.

Holland's Echo remains an important artificial-life simulation and is unique in its economic modeling.

Tierra

Tierra is another interesting simulator for the evolution of artificial life (from Tom Ray). In particular, the life in this simulator consists of evolved programs. The environment consists of a simulated computer where the evolved life execute. The programs vie for CPU time (energy) to execute and then reproduce in the environment (the RAM-space).

With Tierra, very complex behaviors have been evolved, including complex interactions between agents. For example, evolutionary arms races have been observed including host/parasite relationships of agents. Tom Ray's Tierra is another useful simulator for the study of evolution and ecology of novel agents in a unique environment.

Simulated Evolution

Let's now look at a simulation that provides the basic elements necessary to support evolution through natural selection. We'll start with a review of the environment, and then review the bug (agent in the environment), its sensors, and available actions. Finally, we'll look at a portion of the simulation to better understand how it works.

Environment

The environment for our simulation is a simple N x N grid. The environment contains cells that can be empty, or occupied by a bug or food. The environment typically contains a number of cells with food, and a lesser number of bugs.

The goal is to evolve a bug such that it can survive in the environment. With each step that the bug takes, it loses energy. If the bug's energy falls to zero, then it dies and is replaced by a mutated version. But if the bug is the oldest in the simulation, then it is allowed to be reborn without mutation. This allows the simulation to breed in an elitist fashion. The best bug is reborn without modification, but lesser bugs are mutated in the hopes that the mutation produces a better bug. If it does, one could postulate that evolution is occurring.

If a bug moves into a cell that contains food, then the food is consumed by the bug and a new food item placed somewhere else in the environment (into an empty cell). Each time food is consumed, energy is increased for the bug. But each time a move is made, energy is consumed. The goal, therefore, is to create a bug that is constantly in search of food to minimize energy use and maximize energy consumption.

The Bug (or Agent)

The bugs that populate the environment are provided with a reactive control system that reads the current state of the surrounding environment, and then chooses an option based on the sensor inputs. Let's begin with a discussion of the input sensor.

Figure 12.9 provides a diagram of the bug's field of perception. The bug is at the center (and if food had been present, it would have been consumed). There are eight separate fields in the bug's view. At the top left (field 0) are four cells. If a food item is present in any one of these, then the sensor input 0 is set. Similarly, sensor 1 contains two cells, and if either of them contain a food item, the sensor input is set.

0	0	1	2	2
0	0	1	2	2
3	3	B	4	4
5	5	6	7	7
5	5	6	7	7

FIGURE 12.9:   **Bug's field-of-view in the environment.**

Bug Sensor

0	1	2	3	4	5	6	7
1	0	1	1	0	0	0	1

FIGURE 12.10:   **Sample environment with sensor classification.**

Let's the look at the application of the sensor for a bug in an environment (see Figure 12.10). This example shows a 9 by 9 fragment of the environment. The cells marked with 'F' are food, while the center marked 'B' is the location of the bug in question. The bold lines differentiate the sensor inputs as defined before in Figure 12.9. At the bottom of Figure 12.10 is the sensor input that results from the environment. Note that the number of elements isn't as important as the existence of a food item in that sensor region.

The bug is provided with a minimal set of actions, essentially the ability to move North, South, East, or West as a single move. The reactive control system for the agent is then simply a sensor mapping for direction given a classification of the inputs. The classification that matches closest is the one permitted to execute. Note that in the case of a tie, we'll take the first action that was encountered. A sample classifier is shown in Figure 12.11. The classifier can be difficult to read, as it's a function of the environment, but one thing that does stand out is that the agent has a motivation to move to the East (as it matches all sensor inputs excepot for North). This particular classifier was evolved by the simulator and could survive for tens of thousands of moves.

Let's now look at the moves that will be made by our bug given the evolved control system shown in Figure 12.11. In Figure 12.12 is our original environment from Figure 12.10. We'll apply the classifer and count the number of matches (number of times a sensor is non-zero, and the classifier element is non-zero). The sum of these determines the applicability of the classifier to the current environment. The one with the highest (or the first if there is more than one) is chosen as the action to take.

For the initial position of the bug (as shown in Figure 12.12), the classifier counts are North (2), South (3), West (2), and East (4). Using the largest match (4), the bug makes a move to the East. The remaining moves can be determined by the reader, but considering the agent's initial energy

	0	1	2	3	4	5	6	7
N	1	1	1	0	0	0	0	0
S	1	0	1	0	0	1	1	1
W	1	0	1	0	0	1	1	0
E	1	0	1	1	1	1	1	1

FIGURE 12.11: Sample classifier evolved in the simulation.

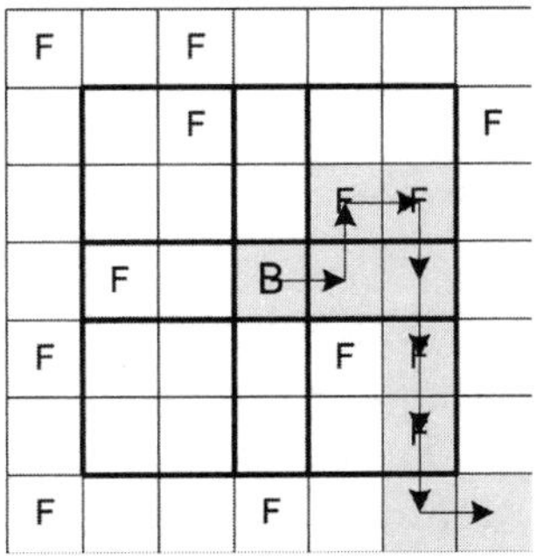

FIGURE 12.12: Moves selected by the bug given the classifer in Figure 12.11.

of 10, a food value of 5, and the cost of a move 1, the agent's ending energy is 20. The control system evolved for this bug is obviously beneficial and allows it to find and consume food in its environment.

In Listing 12.2 is the core of the simulation which is used to determine the next move to make for the current bug. Any number of bugs can be competing in the environment at the same time, so this focuses on one. After adjusting the bug's age, the current sensors are evaluated given the bug's position and the environment. The sensors are then matched to the classifiers and the one that matches best is chosen. The bug is moved, and if food is at the new location, it is consumed and the bug's energy is increased.

The full source for the artificial life simulation can be found on the CD-ROM at ./software/ch12/simevol.c.

Listing 12.2: Core of the bug simulation - the action selection routine.

```c
void makeMove( bug_t *bug )
{
  unsigned char sensors[MAX_SENSORS];
  unsigned char c_sum[MAX_CLASSIFIERS];
  int x, y, c, s;
  /* Age the bug so we know how long it lived */
  bug->age++;
  /* Keep track of the oldest bug */
  if (bug->age > maxAge) maxAge = bug->age;
  /*
   * Sensors:
   *  00122
   *  00122
   *  33.44
   *  55677
   *  55677
   *
   */
  y = bug->loc.y;
  x = bug->loc.x;
  /* Function env returns the contents of the cell */
  sensors[0] = env(y-2,x-2) + env(y-2,x-1) + env(y-1,x-2) + env(y-1,x-1);
  sensors[1] = env(y-2,x)   + env(y-1,x);
  sensors[2] = env(y-2,x+2) + env(y-2,x+1) + env(y-1,x+2) + env(y-1,x+1);
```

```
sensors[3] = env(y,x-2)  + env(y,x-1);
sensors[4] = env(y,x+2)  + env(y,x+1);
sensors[5] = env(y+2,x-2) + env(y+2,x-1) + env(y+1,x-2) + env(y+1,x-1);
sensors[6] = env(y+2,x)  + env(y+1,x);
sensors[7] = env(y+2,x+2) + env(y+2,x+1) + env(y+1,x+2) + env(y+1,x+1);
/* Match the classifiers to the sensors */
for (c = 0 ; c < MAX_CLASSIFIERS ; c++) {
  c_sum[c] = 0;
  for (s = 0 ; s < MAX_SENSORS ; s++) {
    if ( bug->classifier[c][s] && sensors[s] ) c_sum[c]++;
  }
}
/* Now pick the classifier (action) with the closest match */
s = 0;
for (c = 1 ; c < MAX_CLASSIFIERS ; c++) {
  if (c_sum[c] > c_sum[s]) s = c;
}
/* Remove the bug from the current location */
setLocation( bug->loc.y, bug->loc.x, " " );
/* Change location */
bug->loc.y = upd(bug->loc.y+actions[s].y);
bug->loc.x = upd(bug->loc.x+actions[s].x);
/* Is there food at this new location? */
if (environment[bug->loc.y][bug->loc.x]) {
  /* Consume food and increase energy */
  bug->life += FOOD_VALUE;
  environment[bug->loc.y][bug->loc.x] = 0;
  /* Add another food to the environment */
  findEmptySpot( &y, &x );
  environment[y][x] = 1;
  setLocation( y, x, "*" );
}
/* Reduce energy for move */
bug->life--;
/* Bug has died, mutate */
if (!bug->life) mutateBug(bug);
/* Place the bug back into the environment */
setLocation( bug->loc.y, bug->loc.x, "B" );
return;
}
```

If the bug dies because it runs out of energy, a function called mutateBug is invoked. This function checks to see if the current bug is the longest lived of the current set, and if so, it's allowed to be reborn without mutation. Otherwise, the classifiers of the bug are mutated at a given rate. The bug's age is then set to zero (a newborn) and the simulation continues. This is the natural selection portion of the simulation. If the bug is the best, it is the fittest and is permitted to continue without modification. Otherwise, the bug is mutated at some rate and the new bug is evaluated in the environment. This allows the simulation to maintain the best bug, but then mutate the others that don't measure up with the intent that these will evolve into better bugs.

When that happens, the older elitist bug will be mutated, causing the process of competition to continue.

Variations of Artificial Life

In addition to artificial life used in the form of natural selection and synthetic evolution, the concepts have also been applied in such fields as artificial chemistry. This was started in the artificial-life community as a way to simulate the processes of chemical reactions.

Lindenmayer Systems

Lindenmayer Systems (otherwise known as L-systems) are a model of biological development that's based on mathematical formalisms. An interesting characteristic of biological forms is that they are branched in their growth. The two most prevalent uses of L-systems are in the generation of fractals and in the realistic modeling of plants. But L-systems have found there way into other applications such as generation of neural network structures (nodes and their connections). This section will provide an introduction to L-systems and the basics of grammar rewriting systems.

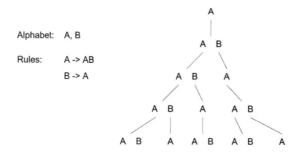

FIGURE 12.13:   **Simple L-system illustrating a basic transformation.**

At the core of an L-system is a rewriting system. Given an alphabet, and a set of rules for alphabet transformation, the ability to transform an element from the alphabet, or a sequence of elements from the alphabet is provided. This is sometimes referred to as a substitution system.

Let's now look at a couple of simple examples. The first is shown in Figure 12.13 and demonstrates an L-system of a two-letter alphabet and two rules. At each step, the current string is rewritten to the string below. Each letter undergoes a transformation, as indicated by the connecting lines.

Another example is provided in Figure 12.14. In this example, our alphabet consists of the numbers 0 and 1. Note the symmetry produced by this substitution system. At every other generation, the initial string is reproduced but at twice the size.

Each of these examples are a class of L-systems called deterministic and context-free. From the branching behaviors seen in the previous two examples, we can see how they could be applied to neural network architectures. Now let's look at how L-systems are used to generate graphical structures, which could also be used for neural network structures.

Consider the example shown in Figure 12.15. With a single rule, we're able to generate a branching tree structure. But note at the rightmost portion of the figure is the representation as a two-layer neural network.

		01
		110
		0011
Alphabet:	0, 1	111100
		00001111
Rules:	1 -> 0	111111110000
	0 -> 11	0000000011111111
		1111111111111111100000000
		00000000000000001111111111111111

FIGURE 12.14: Simple L-system illustrating symmetry of string generation.

Alphabet: A, B

Rules: A -> BAA

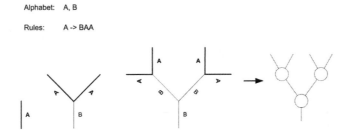

FIGURE 12.15: Simple L-system resulting in a neural network topology.

FIGURE 12.16: A plant structure created by simple L-system rules.

L-systems (of the bracketed form) can develop very life-like plant structures (as shown in Figure 12.16). The bracketed L-system includes operators for pushing and popping branches. This allows a trunk to be branched, to operate on that branch, and then revert back to the trunk.

FUZZY SYSTEMS

Fuzzy logic is an ideal way to take analog concepts from the real world and make them manageable in the discrete world of computer systems. Instead of dealing with crisp values and their semantics, we deal instead with membership in sets that represent the semantics of the value system. In this way, we can operate in the domain of conditional expressions using degrees of membership in fuzzy membership functions.

Fuzzy logic was created by Lotfi Zadeh at the University of California at Berkeley in 1965. The method was controversial, but adopted with success in Japan in a variety of successful applications. Adoption in the U.S. was much slower, but applications have grown with this method. This is because fuzzy logic can be easily implemented in low cost and low-end microprocessors.

Introduction to Fuzzy Logic

From a control perspective, fuzzy logic solves a real problem when considering the semantics of values. In human language, we talk about discrete states, but this creates problems for continuous ranges of values. For example, we can refer to temperature as *hot* or *cold*, but what do they really mean? Further, if we try to build logic based on a discrete factor such as *cold*, we quickly run into problems. The continuous nature of things like temperature are not well suited for the binary nature of logic. For example,

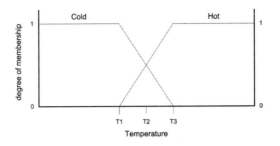

FIGURE 12.17: Fuzzy logic membership for temperature.

if we have just two temperatures, then there's a temperature by which we transition from *cold* to *hot*, and the real world doesn't work that way.

The answer is to use a mechanism that takes real-world ranges and translates them into discrete states, but in a fuzzy way. For example, instead of our temperature being hot or cold, our temperature is instead a member of the states. Let's look at an example to illustrate this further.

Figure 12.17 provides graph indicating the membership functions for our temperature states. A membership function is one that defines the degree of membership for a value to a given state (instead of simple true or false, as would be the case for traditional logic). For example, if our temperature is T1 or below, then we can say that the temperature is 1.0 cold and 0.0 hot. But since the membership for hot is 0, we can omit it. On the other side, temperature T3 is 1.0 hot and 0.0 cold (or simply, Hot).

Between T1 and T2 is where fuzzy logic begins to make sense. For example, at temperature T2, the fuzzy temperature is 0.5 cold and 0.5 hot. So it's neither hot, nor cold. This allows us to refer to temperatures in human terms, while allowing a computer to deal with them in a numeric sense (in terms of membership in a temperature category).

> NOTE *Note in Figure 12.17 that there's not a distinct jump from the cold state to the hot state. Instead there's a gradual transition from cold (1.0 / 0.0) to warm (0.5 / 0.5) to hot (0.0 / 1.0) with many intermediate states between. This is the power behind fuzzy logic. Rather than distinct steps, there's a gradual transition between the two.*

Fuzzy Logic Mapping

Let's now explore how we would represent the fuzzy membership in a simple application. Let's return to our temperature example, but in this case, we'll note values for each in order to develop the membership functions.

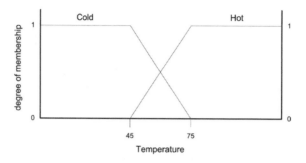

FIGURE 12.18: **Temperature membership functions.**

Figure 12.18 provides a graph of the membership functions for the cold and hot temperatures. As shown, if the temperature is 45 degrees F or below, then it's cold. If it's 75 degrees F or above, the temperature is hot. At a temperature of 60 degrees F, it's both cold (0.5) and hot (0.5).

We can represent this very easily as is shown in Listing 12.3. The two membership functions m_cold and m_hot test for the extreme, and then the slope to determine the membership degree. The slope calculation returns the y value between two x coordinates.

Listing 12.3:   **Encoding fuzzy logic membership functions for temperature.**

```
/* Calculate y value of slope between two x coordinates */
#define downslope(x, left, right) ((right-x) / (right-left))
#define upslope(x, left, right) ((x-left) / (right-left))
float m_t_cold(float x)
{
  float left = 45.0;
  float right = 75.0;
  if    (x <= left) return 1.0;
  else if (x >= right) return 0.0;
  else return downslope(x, left, right);
}
float m_t_hot(float x)
{
  float left = 45.0;
  float right = 75.0;
  if    (x <= left) return 0.0;
  else if (x >= right) return 1.0;
  else return upslope(x, left, right);
```

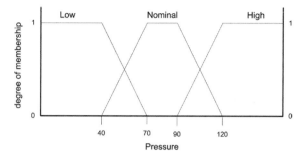

FIGURE 12.19: **Pressure membership functions.**

```
}
int main( )
{
  float x;
  x = 45.0;
  printf("%fF is Cold(%f) and Hot(%f)\n", x, m_t_cold(x), m_t_hot(x));
  x = 60.0;
  printf("%fF is Cold(%f) and Hot(%f)\n", x, m_t_cold(x), m_t_hot(x));
  x = 75.0;
  printf("%fF is Cold(%f) and Hot(%f)\n", x, m_t_cold(x), m_t_hot(x));
  return 0;
}
```

To build a fuzzy logic application, let's introduce one more set of fuzzy membership functions. These will represent pressures, but these will be a little different than those for temperature. For our pressure measurement, we'll provide three fuzzy membership functions; low, nominal, and high. But in this case, we'll introduce a trapezoid membership function for nominal that extends to both the low-and high-pressure fuzzy values (see Figure 12.19).

These new pressure membership functions are implemented as shown in Listing 12.4. The low and high pressure is implemented similarly to the temperature functions. The nominal pressure function includes support for two slope functions and also a plateau.

Listing 12.4: Encoding fuzzy logic membership functions for pressure.

```
float m_p_low( float x )
{
  float left = 40.0;
```

```
    float right = 70.0;
    if    (x <= left)  return 1.0;
    else if (x >= right) return 0.0;
    else return downslope(x, left, right);
}
float m_p_nominal( float x )
{
  float left_b = 40.0;
  float left_t = 70.0;
  float right_t = 90.0;
  float right_b = 120.0;
  if    (x <= left_b) return 0.0;
  else if ((x > left_b) && (x < left_t))
    return upslope(x, left_b, left_t);
  else if (x >= right_b) return 0.0;
  else if ((x > right_t) && (x < right_b))
    return downslope(x, right_t, right_b);
  else if (x >= right_b) return 0.0;
  else return 1.0; /* For Plateau */
}
float m_p_high( float x )
{
  float left = 90.0;
  float right = 120.0;
  if    (x <= left)  return 0.0;
  else if (x >= right) return 1.0;
  else return upslope(x, left, right);
}
```

Fuzzy Logic Operators

The term fuzzy logic implies that there are logical operations that can be performed. Fuzzy logic is applied as a set of if/then rules using the fuzzy membership functions. The fuzzy logic operators mimic those provided in traditional logic, but differ in their details. The three fuzzy logical operators are NOT, AND, and OR. These are defined as:

```
NOT x = ( 1.0 - x )
x AND y = minimum( x, y )
x OR y = maximum( x, y )
```

The resulting values are normalized to arrive at a binary logic value. If the result is 0.5 or greater, then the normalized value is 1.0. Otherwise, the normalized value is 0.0. Listing 12.5 explores the implementation of these operators.

Listing 12.5: Fuzzy operators implmentation.

```
#define EXTEND(x)     (((x) < 0.5) ? 0.0 : 1.0)
float f_and( float x, float y )
{
  if (x < y) return x;
  else return y;
}
float f_or( float x, float y )
{
  if (x < y) return y;
  else return x;
}
```

Fuzzy Control

Let's use our previously defined temperature and pressure membership functions to demonstrate the fuzzy operators in a fuzzy control system. In the previous listings, we provided membership functions for a device from which we can read temperatures and pressures. Our device has a control mechanism that can be throttled high, medium, or low, depending on the state of the sensors. Let's now define a couple of rules to control the throttle (see Listing 12.6).

Listing 12.6: Natural language rules for managing the throttle.

```
if (temperature is hot) AND (pressure is high) then
        throttle = low
endif
if ((temperature is cold) AND
    (pressure is low) OR (pressure is nominal)) then
        throttle = high
endif
```

The rules shown in Listing 12.5 are very easily translated into an application using fuzzy logic as shown in Listing 12.6 (note that the

EXTEND function simply extends the fuzzy value to a binary value). These functions provide the fuzzy rules for throttle management given temperature and pressure values.

Listing 12.6:   Fuzzy rules for throttle management.

```
if ( EXTEND( f_and( m_t_hot(t), m_p_high(p) ))) {
 /* Set throttle to high */
}
if ( EXTEND( f_and( m_t_cold(t), f_or( m_p_low(p), m_p_nominal(p)))))
{
 /* Set throttle to low */
}
```

This simple example illustrates the power behind fuzzy logic. Given a set of natural language rules, real-world analog values can be transformed into fuzzy values which can then be manipulated through a set of fuzzy operators. This makes it easier to understand and debug.

Fuzzy logic brings the fuzzy nature of the real world to the binary nature of computer systems. You'll find fuzzy logic in image processing, machine vision, robot navigation, medicine, and in telecommunications.

EVOLUTIONARY NEURAL NETWORKS

An interesting combined biological metaphor of AI is the evolution of neural networks. As we explored in Chapter 8, neural networks can be trained and constructed in a number of ways, but evolution of neural networks offers some signficant advantages to other methods. For example, by evolving neural networks, we can not only evolve the weights of a network, but also its topology (the connectivity of the neurons). This allows us to construct networks with very specific constraints, such as size, or minimal connectivity but still solve the problem at hand.

In this section, we'll explore two methods for neural network evolution and then return to our artificial-life example to evolve networks to control bugs in synthetic environments.

Genetically Evolved Neural Networks

One of the most common and simplest methods for evolving neural networks is simple weight evolution. This implies that the architecture of the network

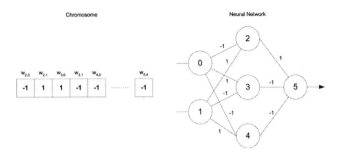

FIGURE 12.20: Combining neural networks with genetic algorithms.

is already formed, and what's missing is the weights that connect the cells of the network.

The evolution of the weights is provided by the genetic algorithm. For this reason, this type of solution is typically called GANN (or Genetic Algorithms/Neural Networks). The weights of the neural network are defined in a chromosome which has a direct mapping to the weights of the network. Figure 12.20 shows an example of this representation. On the left is the chromosome that represents the weights of the network; each weight is represented as its own gene in the chromosome.

Once a random population of chromosomes is created, their fitness is based on how well they solve the given problem when the weights in the chromosome are applied to the neural network. The better they solve the problem, the more likely they are to be selected for recombination and to survive to future generations. Recall the discussion of Genetic Algorithms in Chapter 7.

The basic disadvantage to this method is that an assumption is made on the architecture that it will solve the problem at hand. This assumption may not be correct, but the network architecture can be altered and new weights evolved. This property can sometimes be advantageous if we're attempting to understand the limits of a given network architecture. Given a small network, how well does it solve a given problem? Or given a particular network topology, can it solve a given problem? In this way, we can choose a network that classifies perhaps 95% of the inputs, but 5% are left unclassified, which may be suitable for the problem at hand.

Another method for the evolution of neural networks involves creating both the network architecture and the weights. This means that the weights and the architecture of the network must be encoded into the chromosome. A very common way to achieve this is by creating a chromosome that unfolds into a connectivity matrix. The connectivity

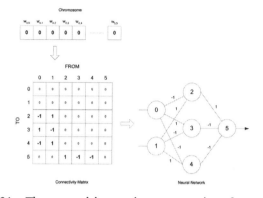

FIGURE 12.21: The connectivity matrix representation of a neural network.

matrix defines the weights between the cells of the network. For example, in Figure 12.21, we see the entire flow from chromosome to connectivity matrix to neural network. The chromosome is a simple one-dimensional string that is folded to become a two-dimensional matrix. Each cell in the matrix represents a single weight. Wherever a zero appears in the matrix, no connection exists.

Using this method, we can evolve neural networks of various sizes and connectivity. The example shown in Figure 12.21 is a simple multilayer feed forward network, but this method also supports recurrent connections (where neurons feed back to neurons in lower layers). Connections that bridge unconnected layers are also possible (for example, input layer neurons feeding directly to the output layer).

Evolving the weights and topology has some interesting advantages over simple weight evolution. Many times the correct network architecture is not intuitive. There are also times that the problem is simpler than we originally thought, and therefore a simpler solution can be found. The fitness parameters for the genetic algorithm can be tuned to not only find the solution to the problem, but also the one that requires the fewest number of neurons, or fewest connections between neurons. For this reason, evolving the network topology is preferred.

Another approach to neural network evolution (related to the genetic algorithm) is through what can be called *synthetic evolution* (or situated evolution). In this method, the neural networks compete with one another in a form of survival of the fittest. In genetic algorithms, this can be called *elitist* selection, as only the fittest is permitted to remain in the population. All other members must be mutated in some way to extend the search for an optimal network.

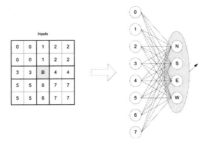

FIGURE 12.22: **Agent field-of-view to neural network inputs.**

Simulated Evolution Example

Let's return to our bug example for artificial life, and apply the concepts of neural network evolution. Recall that the environment is made up of a grid that contains cells of food, other bugs, or nothing. Bugs survive by occupying the same cell food (which is consumed), thereby increasing their health. For each move that a bug makes, it's health is reduced. Therefore, the bug must find food, otherwise it will die. Therefore, the neural network controlling the bug must be in constant search of food.

Recall from Figure 12.9 that the field of perception for the bug is the 24 surrounding cells. These cells are grouped into eight regions that serve as the input to the neural network (see Figure 12.22).

The agent implements a simple two-layer neural network. Each cell in the input layer connects to each cell of the output layer. The output layer contains four cells, which represent the actions that are possible by the bug (North, South, East, West). The neural network implements the winner-takes-all strategy, which simply means that the output node with the largest value is the cell that fires (the action to be taken).

The power that guides the evolution of the bugs is simply survival of the fittest. If a bug is the most fit (longest living), then it is permitted to be reborn without mutation. Any bug that dies (and is not the most fit) is mutated and then reborn. In this way, lesser fit bugs are modified and have the potential to be reborn with a better strategy, thereby taking the most fit role and forcing the previously fit bug to be mutated. This process continues for some number of iterations, and in the end, the best bug is emitted with its neural network. The action selection routine for the neural network version of the simulated bugs is shown in Listing 12.7.

The complete source for evolved neural network application can be found on the CD-ROM at ./software/ch12/nnevol.c. This application uses ncurses, which is available in GNU/Linux, or in Cygwin for Windows.

Listing 12.7:   Neural network action selection function.

```
void makeMove( bug_t *bug )
{
  short sensors[MAX_SENSORS];
  short outputs[MAX_ACTIONS];
  int x, y, a, s, best;
  /* Age the bug so we know how long it lived */
  bug->age++;
  /* Keep track of the oldest bug */
  if (bug->age > maxAge) maxAge = bug->age;
  /*
   * Sensors:
   *   00122
   *   00122
   *   33.44
   *   55677
   *   55677
   *
   */
  y = bug->loc.y;
  x = bug->loc.x;
  /* Function env returns the contents of the cell */
  sensors[0] = (env(y-2,x-2)+env(y-2,x-1)+env(y-1,x-2)+env(y-1,x-1)) ? 1 : 0;
  sensors[1] = (env(y-2,x)  +env(y-1,x)) ? 1 : 0;
  sensors[2] = (env(y-2,x+2)+env(y-2,x+1)+env(y-1,x+2)+env(y-1,x+1)) ? 1 : 0;
  sensors[3] = (env(y,x-2)  +env(y,x-1)) ? 1 : 0;
  sensors[4] = (env(y,x+2)  +env(y,x+1)) ? 1 : 0;
  sensors[5] = (env(y+2,x-2)+env(y+2,x-1)+env(y+1,x-2)+env(y+1,x-1)) ? 1 : 0;
  sensors[6] = (env(y+2,x)  +env(y+1,x)) ? 1 : 0;
  sensors[7] = (env(y+2,x+2)+env(y+2,x+1)+env(y+1,x+2)+env(y+1,x+1)) ?
1 : 0;
  /* Feedforward the input sensors through the neural network */
  for (a = 0 ; a < MAX_ACTIONS ; a++) {
    outputs[a] = 0.0;
    for (s = 0 ; s < MAX_SENSORS ; s++) {
      outputs[a] += bug->network[a][s] * sensors[s];
    }
  }
  best = 0;
```

```
/* Winner-takes-all output node selection */
for (a = 1 ; a < MAX_ACTIONS ; a++) {
  if (outputs[a] > outputs[best]) best = a;
}
/* Remove the bug from the current location */
setLocation( bug->loc.y, bug->loc.x, " " );
/* Change location */
bug->loc.y = upd(bug->loc.y+actions[best].y);
bug->loc.x = upd(bug->loc.x+actions[best].x);
/* Is there food at this new location? */
if (environment[bug->loc.y][bug->loc.x]) {
  /* Consume food and increase energy */
  bug->life += FOOD_VALUE;
  environment[bug->loc.y][bug->loc.x] = 0;
  /* Add another food to the environment */
  findEmptySpot( &y, &x );
  environment[y][x] = 1;
  setLocation( y, x, "*" );
}
/* Account for move */
bug->life--;
/* Bug has died */
if (!bug->life) mutateBug(bug);
setLocation( bug->loc.y, bug->loc.x, "B" );
return;
}
```

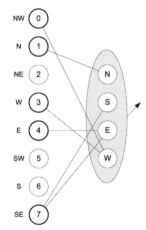

FIGURE 12.23: **Sample evolved agent neural network.**

A sample bug that was able to survive for many thousands of iterations is shown in Figure 12.23. This neural network contains only six connections, but remains a stable strategy for finding food in the environment. Each of the four actions are covered by inputs, but based on action selection, some actions are favored over others. For example, the winner-takes-all will select the largest output cell, but if there's a tie, it will choose the largest that was found first. In this way, if there's a tie between all actions, the North action will be chosen.

NOTE ► *The neural network shown in Figure 12.23 shows only activitory links (inputs contribute positively toward actions). The network could have also included inhibitory links leading to more complex strategies.*

The strategy is fairly straightforward from looking at the network. If food lies to the North, then the North action is taken. If food is to the Southeast, then the South action is taken. But if food lies to both the Southeast and to the East, then the East action is taken (East is also selected if food lies to the East). Finally, if food lies to the West or NorthWest, then the West action is taken. This strategy is shown visually in Figure 12.24. In this example, we can see the agent's preference to move North and East when food lies in those directions.

The use of evolved neural networks is interesting in this application because in effect the evolution provides a form of training with competetion. The best bug is permitted to remain in the environment without being mutated, but once a new bug appears that is more fit, then it takes over the most fit role and the previous bug's neural network is mutated. In this way, the bugs compete against one another to not be mutated. Mutation isn't necessarily a bad thing, as ultimately a mutated bug will take the most fit spot.

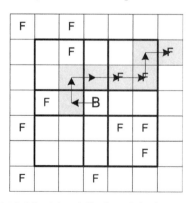

FIGURE 12.24: **Visual display of the bug's strategy.**

ANT COLONY OPTIMIZATION (ACO)

Ant Colony Optimization, or ACO, is a biologically inspired optimization method that is very useful for solving problems in physical space. As the name implies, ACO is an optimization algorithm using simulated ants. Recall that ants have the ability to build invisible trails made up of pheromones. These trails can be used to lead ants to and from food, thus optimizing their roundtrip times to the food and back to the nest.

In the same way that ants place down pheromone trails to collectively optimize the food forraging strategy (in a process known as stigmergy), this same concept can be used in a variety of problem domains, from network routing to pathfinding, and more.

The basic idea behind ACO can be visualized with a graph. Consider the nodes of a graph as locations, and edges as the path between those locations. A collection of ants are distributed around the graph and then probabilistically choose their path based on the strength of the pheromone on the edges open for them to take. The higher the pheromone level on an edge, the more likely they are to take that edge. After the ants complete a tour of the graph, their tour is measured (using whatever scheme is meaningful for the problem), and a new pheromone is placed on the tour representative with its fitness. Over time, the correct path becomes clear, and each ant begins to take the path found by others. From this simple description, one can see how this models the strategy used by ants using the process of stigmergy.

Traveling Salesman Problem (TSP)

Let's now have a look at the ACO algorithm as applied to the traveling salesman problem (finding the shortest or cheapest path through a graph of

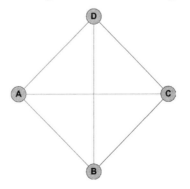

FIGURE 12.25: **Simple graph to demonstrate TSP tours.**

locations, visiting each location only once). The Traveling Salesman Problem (or TSP) was first explored in the 1800s.

Consider the simple graph shown in Figure 12.25. This simple graph consists of four cities (labeled A-D). Each city is connected to each other, so that the salesman can take any path. This means that a tour through all cities could be A->C->D->B->A (for a complete tour, the salesman must end back at the originating city), or A->B->D->C->A. Each of these tours is suboptimal, with one of the two optimal tours being A->B->C->D->A.

The TSP is an NP-hard problem, but various algorithms and heuristics have been devised to solve it (such as branch-and-bound algorithms or progressive improvement algorithms). ACO may not find the optimal path, but it will find a good one.

An interesting advantage to the ACO algorithm to TSP is dynamic changes to the cities. For example, if cities are added or removed, the ACO can run continuously and adapt to the changes dynamically, yielding a good solution.

ACO Algorithm

The elements that make up the ACO are the graph (set of cities, assuming fully interconnected and bidirectional), and a population of ants. Each ant maintains a set of information about its movement, what cities it has visited, and which remain for the tour. The length of the tour is also calculated along the way, which is used by the ant algorithm.

The ant algorithm then relies on a number of simple steps that are repeated for some number of iterations. These are:

- Distributing Ants to the Graph
- Performing a Tour with Each Ant
- Calculating the Tour Cost
- Distributing Pheromone
- Evaporating Pheromone

Ant Distribution to the Graph

Initialization of the algorithm begins with the distribution of the ants to the graph. The ants are as evenly distributed to the cities in the graph as is possible. The entry point of each ant becomes the first city in its tour.

 For best results, the number of ants should be equal to the number of cities (number of nodes in the graph).

Once ants are distributed, the next step is for each to visit each of the cities to make up a tour. This next step involves path selection.

Path Selection

The mechanism by which an ant selects the next city to visit is based on a relatively simple probability equation. This equation (Eq 12.1) determines the probability that a city should be visited. Note that when the ant is sitting on its first location for the initial tour, each path to the next city has equal probability of being selected.

$$P = \frac{\tau(r,u)^\alpha * \eta(r,u)^\beta}{\sum_k \tau(r,u)^\alpha * \eta(r,u)^\beta} \qquad \text{(Eq 12.1)}$$

The level of pheromone on a edge of the graph (between two locations) is represented by $\tau(r,u)$ and the distance between the distance between the current location and candidate location is represented by $\eta(r,u)$. Each of these parameters is adjusted for the effect by which they will have over the path selection. The α parameter, with a value between 0 and 1, represents how much influence the pheromone plays in the path selection. The β parameter, with a value between 0 and 1, represents how much influence the distance measure plays. As shown by Eq 12.1, the cities left to be visited are calculated and summed (with k representing the cities left to visit). The ratio of the current candidate city calculation to the sum of this calculation is then the probability that the path should be selected. We'll see how this is calculated and used shortly.

This process continues until each ant makes a complete tour of the graph (visits each city). When the tour is complete, pheromones are managed in the graph as defined by the following two steps.

Pheromone Intensification

Now that each of the ants has completed a tour of the graph (visited each of the nodes), the pheromone is distributed to the edges in an amount that commensurates with the length of the tour. The shorter the tour, the higher the pheromone that is distributed to the particular edges that make up the tour. The amount of pheromone distributed is based on Eq 12.2.

$$\Delta \tau_{ij}^k(t) = \frac{Q}{L^k(t)} \qquad \text{(Eq 12.2)}$$

In this equation, $\Delta \tau_{ij}^k(t)$ represents the amount of pheromone to intensify on the path, Q is a constant value, and $L^k(t)$ is the length of the tour (over k

cities). Note that this equation is applied on each edge individually, where i and j represent the edge between the cities. Eq 12.3 is then used to apply the pheromone to the particular edge. Note also here that ρ is used to control the amount of pheromone to apply. This will be a value between 0 and 1.

$$\tau_{ij}(t) = \tau_j(t) + (\Delta\tau_{ij}^k(t) * \rho) \qquad \text{(Eq 12.3)}$$

Pheromone Evaporation

Initial tours of the ants may use many of the edges that are available, but over time, better tours through the locations are found (as defined by the length of the tour), and more pheromone is placed on these paths. Pheromone evaporation reduces the intensity of pheromones on all paths and helps make clear where the best paths are (to be used by the path selection equation in Eq 12.1).

Eq 12.4 is the evaporation algorithm, which is applied to all edges once the ant tour is complete. Note here that ρ is repeated again, but in the inverse to the pheromone intensification (Eq 12.3).

$$\tau_{ij}(t) = \tau_{ij}(t) * (1-\rho) \qquad \text{(Eq 12.4)}$$

New Tour

Once all ants make a complete tour of all locations, the pheromone is intensified on the paths taken by the ants, and pheromone evaporated, the next step is to allow the ants to take another tour. Note that since pheromone is on the paths in an intensity based on the tour length, ants will probabilistically follow the best paths while randomly selecting other ones. In this way, given the α and β parameters, pheromone is intensified on the best path while allowing the ants to explore randomly. The ants will take some number of tours, either based on a user-defined maximum, or after some duration of a new best tour not being found.

Sample Use

Using the ACO for the traveling salesman problem is quite simple to implement and yields very good solutions. In this section, we'll look at some of the implementation details of the ACO. The focus will be the functions devoted to path selection, and pheromone intensification and evaporation.

The complete source for the ACO TSP program can be found on the CD-ROM at ./software/ch12/ants.c.

Choosing the path an ant takes through all possible edges (to unvisited cities) is accomplished with the function choose_next_city (see Listing 12.8). The first task is to compute the denominator for Eq 12.1. This is performed by searching through the tabu list (for the cities that have not been visited), and then computing the denominator. This denominator is then used to complete Eq 12.1 and results in a probability value. This value is used with a random number to determine which city should be visited next (searching through the tabu list to identify the cities that have not yet been visited).

For efficiency reasons, the distances between cities is precalculated and then used here (precomputed_distance). This allows a very fast lookup, rather than the math instructions involved in calculating it on the fly. This requires a bit more memory to store, but yields benefits in faster execution.

Once a new city is selected, the ant's data structures are updated (`tabu, tour_length`, etc.). If the tour is complete, we complete the ant's tour to the initial city to complete the path.

Listing 12.8:   Selecting the next city in the ant's tour.

```
void choose_next_city( ANT_T *ant )
{
  int from, to;
  double d=0.0, p;
  from = ant->current_city;
  /* If city not yet visited */
  for (to = 0 ; to < NUM_CITIES ; to++) {
    if (ant->tabu[to] == 0) {
      /* Equation 12.1 */
      d += pow(pheromone[from][to], alpha) *
          pow( (1.0 / precomputed_distance[from][to]), beta);
    }
  }
  /* Probabilistically select the next city */
  to = 0;
  while (1) {
    /* If city not yet visited */
    if (ant->tabu[to] == 0) {
      /* Equation 12.1 */
      p = (pow(pheromone[from][to], alpha) *
          pow( (1.0 / precomputed_distance[from][to]), beta)) / d;
```

```
    if (RANDOM() < p) break;
  }
  to = ((to+1) % NUM_CITIES);
}
/* We have our new destination, update for the new city */
ant->next_city = to;
ant->tabu[ant->next_city] = 1;
ant->tour[ant->tour_index++] = ant->next_city;
ant->tour_length +=
      precomputed_distance[ant->current_city][ant->next_city];
if (ant->tour_index == NUM_CITIES) {
  ant->tour_length +=
        precomputed_distance[ant->tour[NUM_CITIES-1]][ant-
>tour[0]];
}
ant->current_city = ant->next_city;
return;
}
```

Once all tours are complete, the pheromone is intensified on those edges that were used by the ants. Each ant is iterated, and then each edge of the tour for each ant is used to calculate the pheromone level to add (see Listing 12.9).

Listing 12.9:   Intensifying pheromone levels on the paths that the ants used.

```
void intensify_pheromone_trails( void )
{
  int from, to, i, city;
  for (i = 0 ; i < NUM_ANTS ; i++) {
    for (city = 0 ; city < NUM_CITIES ; city++) {
      from = ants[i].tour[city];
      to  = ants[i].tour[((city+1)%NUM_CITIES)];
      /* Equation 12.2 / 12.3 */
      pheromone[from][to] += ((qval / ants[i].tour_length) * rho);
      pheromone[to][from] = pheromone[from][to];
    }
  }
  return;
}
```

The next step is to evaporate pheromone from the ant trails (see Listing 12.10). Just like intensifying pheromone on the trails, evaporating applies to all edges and simply removes a small amount of pheromone (depending up the value of ρ). Pheromone evaporation is the inverse of intensification. For example, if ρ was 0.9, then during pheromone intensification, only 90% of the pheromone level would be added. During evaporation, only 10% of the pheromone would be removed.

Listing 12.10:   Evaporating pheromone from the ant trails.

```
void evaporate_pheromone_trails( void )
{
  int from, to;
  for (from = 0 ; from < NUM_CITIES ; from++) {
   for (to = 0 ; to < NUM_CITIES ; to++) {
    /* Equation 12.4 */
    pheromone[from][to] *= (1.0 - rho);
    if (pheromone[from][to] < 0.0) pheromone[from][to] = BASE_
PHEROMONE;
   }
  }
  return;
}
```

A sample result of the algorithm is shown in Figure 12.25. This illustrates a 20-city TSP and a reasonable (though sub-optimal) solution.

The ACO has more practical applications than the TSP. It has been applied to other problems (including NP-Hard problems). Examples include

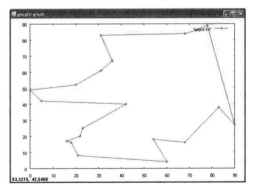

FIGURE 12.25:   **A sample solution of a 20-city TSP using the ant algorithm.**

dynamic and adaptive network routing, vehicle routing for logistics, and even for discovery of classification rules.

ACO Parameters

A number of parameters exist that allow a developer to control the way in which the algorithm works. The four parameters are shown in Table 12.1. The number of ants to be used is also a useful variable; typically it's the number of cities in the problem space. Finally, the number of iterations can also be useful, especially if the ants are allowed to explore (and favor pheromone and distance equally).

Table 12.1: ACO parameters for tuning

α	Favor Pheromone Level over Distance
β	Favor Distance over Pheromone Level
ρ	Intensification/Evaporation value
Q	Constant Value for Pheromone Distribution

AFFECTIVE COMPUTING

Affective computing is all about emotion, but from two different perspectives. First, it's about the detection and classification of emotions of a user. Second, it's about the synthesis of emotions from a computer to a user. Let's explore what this means and why it's important.

Emotions are a critical aspect of human communication (a side-band, if you will, of information). Consider the emotion of confusion. If a computer could detect this emotion from a user, it could alter the way in which it's presenting information. In order to present a computer as a believable entity, emotion must be part of its communication (either through speech, or acts of speech).

Emotions may also be more fundamental in nature than intelligence. For example, animals are capable of understanding emotion in humans (consider a dog's response to a human's gestures or speech), and while they're intelligent, it's certainly at a different level.

Characterizing Human Emotion

Characterizing human emotion can occur in numerous ways, but provide different types of information. For this reason, a hybrid approach is necessary for a complete and unambiguous view of the emotion of a human. Speech is a multi-channel interface, and in addition to the information being conveyed, information is also available in the patterns and pitch of the speaker. For example, the pitch of the speech, the speed of the speech, and the inflections in the speech that can be tuned by emotion, are all detectable through a microphone and software for analysis.

Gestures are also an important channel of communication for emotion. Some of this information is context-dependent. For example, inattention is an important gesture to understand for learning, but is even more important when used to understand a driver's awareness. Hand gestures are also important, as are posture and facial expressions.

Other important indicators of emotion include physiological parameters, most of which can require more than just visually monitoring a subject. Gauging a person's temperature can be done through infrared, but heart rate or blood pressure requires more invasive monitoring.

Giving a computer the ability to characterize and understand a human's emotive state is very important in future human-computer interfaces. With this we can build systems that not only communicate with a user (from the perspective of Strong AI), but can use subtle queues to build more efficient interfaces.

Synthesizing Emotion

Synthesizing human emotion in machines is an important aspect of Strong AI, particularly for the development of believable characters (computer agents) or in robotic systems. But human emotions are very complex and multi-dimensional. For example, happiness and sadness can be considered polar opposites, but a human can be both happy and sad at the same time, so they're not opposite ends of a spectrum. Considering the variety and depth of human emotion, synthesizing an agent with believable emotions will be difficult indeed.

Research exists to pursue the simulation of emotions given its importance to a number of applications, from Strong AI to computer game agents. The emotions to be synthesized are based on what's available to the simulated agent. Computer agents (those in computer games or other applications) typically have a full range of channels, as characters are typically fully modeled with synthesized speech. But visualization of emotions is the simpler aspect of this problem.

The more difficult problem of synthesizing emotion is generating emotion from a variety of internal agent states. How do these internal states map to the dimensionality of emotion? First steps would involve minimizing the emotive states to a more manageable set, and then evolving this set with experience.

Emotions may also play an important role in the internal function of simulated agents. Consider the survival response of animals. Animals can intellectually understand a situation and determine a response, but emotions and other physiological factors certainly apply in determining a rationale response to a situation.

RESOURCES

Dittrich, Peter, et al. "Artificial Chemistries - A Review," University of Dortmund, 2001.

Dorigo, M. and Blum, C. "Ant Colony Optimization Theory: A Survey," *Theoretical Computer Science*, 344(2-3):243-278, 2005.

Dorigo, M., Stutzle, Thomas. "Ant Colony Optimization," MIT Press, 2004.

Gambardella, et al. "Ant Colony Optimization for Vehicle Routing in Advanced Logistics Systems," Multi-Agent-Systems, 2003.
Available online at: http://www.idsia.ch/~luca/MAS2003_18.pdf

Holland, John. "Echo Artificial Life Simulator"
Available online at: http://www.santafe.edu/~pth/echo/

J. von Neumann. *The Theory of Self Reproducing Automata* University of Illinois Press, Urbana Illinois, 1966.

Lindenmayer, A. "Mathematical models for cellular interaction in development I.Filaments with one-sided inputs," *Journal of Theoretical Biology*, 1968.

Liu, Bo, Abbas, H.A, McKay B. "Classification rule discovery with ant colony optimization," Intelligent Agent Technology, IAT 2003, 2003.

Prusinkiewicz P., Lindenmayer A. "The Algorithmic Beauty of Plants," Springer-Verlag, New York, 1990.

Wolfram, Stephen. *A New Kind of Science* Wolfram Media, Inc., 2002.

Zadeh, Lotfi. "The birth and evolution of fuzzy logic," International Journal of General Systems 17, 1990.

Chapter **13** # THE LANGUAGES OF AI

W hile AI algorithms and techniques can be implemented in a wide spectrum of languages, there are a number of languages that are better suited to AI problems. For numerical AI problems such as neural networks or genetic algorithms, languages such as C are effective. For relational problems that depend on predicate logic, Prolog is ideal. Historically, LISP has been the foundational AI language as it emerged during the early days of AI (referred to as a functional language). In the end, any language can be used to build AI applications, but some are better suited to certain problems than to others. This chapter will introduce the major language taxonomies, and then explore the major languages used in AI to identify the applications for which they're best suited.

LANGUAGE TAXONOMY

Programming languages are a very interesting area of study, as they each fundamentally do the same thing; they allow a programmer to solve problems using a computer. But how they solve those problems can vary in a wide spectrum. For example, where loops are a common programming construct in C or Ada, recursion is commonly used to emulate loops in a language like Haskell, or LISP. Each language provides fundamentally the same functionality, but each does so in very different ways.

Another example is the comparison of imperative languages to object-oriented languages. In an imperative language, a system is built up from a set of functions in a hierarchy. Files typically act as containers for functions that logically belong together (such as functions that implement a queue). In an object-oriented system, containers for like functions and data are encapsulated into objects. The object embodies a data structure and the functions that operate on the data. A system is then built from a collection of objects.

Table 13.1 lists six of the major language types, from functional languages to concurrent languages.

Table 13.1:   Major language types.

Type	Focus
Functional	Builds programs as functions over types.
Imperative	Builds programs as commands over data.
Object-Oriented	Builds programs from cooperative collections of objects.
Logic	Draws conclusions from facts and relationships.
Concurrent	Uses multiple processes with communication.

NOTE▶ *Most programming languages, particularly the ones that we'll explore here, are what is known as Turing Complete. This means that the language has the computational power equivalent to the abstract computing model called the Turing Machine. Simply, this means that using the language we are able to perform any computational task (regardless of efficiency of simplicity of the solution).*

In the early days of AI, the focus of AI systems development was symbolic languages like LISP (1950s) and logic languages such as PROLOG (1970s). But as we've seen in this book, a variety of languages can be used for AI development. Let's look at the popular programming language paradigms, and how they apply to AI systems development.

Functional Programming

Functional programming is a paradigm deeply rooted in the theoretical framework called the *Lambda calculus*. Functional programming is based on a number of characteristics including higher-order functions, first-class functions, recursion, a lack of side effects, continuations, and closures to name just a few.

Table 13.1:   Sample functional languages.

Language	Year Introduced	Focus
LISP	1958	The original functional progamming language.
Scheme	1975	Elegant and simplified dialect of LISP.
ML	1980	A pure and strict functional language.
Haskell	1987	General purpose pure but lazy functional language.

Functional programming is best understood my comparing it to the imperative programming paradigm. Rather than relying on the sequential execution of commands that alter memory and state, functional programming relies on the application of functions over data. Let's now look at the major characteristics of functional programming.

Higher-order functions are a primary attribute to functional programming. A higher-order function is one simply that either is able to take a function as input, or return a function as output. This concept is common in mathematics; for example, the derivative in the calculus maps one function to another.

The classification of languages has become more difficult, as languages strive to support multiple programming paradigms. For example, Ruby and Python are object-oriented scripting languages, but each support the ability for programming using functional characteristics.

Many languages provide support for higher-level functions, including modern languages such as Python. The map function is used to apply a function to a list, as shown in Listing 13.1.

Listing 13.1:   Using the Python map function.

```
>>> def square(x): return x*x
...
>>> map(square, [1, 2, 3])
[1, 4, 9]
>>>
```

First-class functions are otherwise known as first-class objects, and lack the restrictions typically associated with other elements of a language. For example, in a language that supports first-class functions, we could create functions dynamically (see Listing 13.2), treat them as data (or vice-versa), pass functions to other functions, or return them from functions. First-class functions are values, just like any other data, and can be stored within data structures. While languages like C can store functions (or references to functions) in data structures, pass them to other functions, or return them from functions, C does not provide support for dynamic function creation.

Listing 13.2:   First-class functions in the Ruby language.

```
irb> def mult_by( factor )
irb> return Proc.new( |n| n*factor )
irb> end
=> nil
irb> mult_by_5 = mult_by(5)
irb> mult_by_2 = mult_by(2)
irb> mult_by_5.call(10)
=> 50
irb> mult_by_2.call(8)
=> 16
irb>
```

Recursive functions are functions that call themselves. This is typically how iteration is performed within function languages. Since recursion can imply maintaining a stack of return addresses, many languages that rely on recursion implement what is known as tail recursion. This obviates the need for a stack, which is efficient for both memory and processing.

Listing 13.3:   Using recursion in LISP to compute the factorial.

```
(defun fact (n)
(if (= n 1)
              1
             ( * n (fact (- n 1)))))
```

Closures are an interesting characteristic to functional programming, and are related to first-class functions. A closure is a dynamic function (sometimes anonymous) that is passed into a different lexical context for use. For example, closures can be used to create dynamic special purpose functions, such as filters.

Imperative Programming

The defining characteristic of imperative programming (otherwise known as procedural programming) is that computation is the sequential execution of statements that change program state.

The earliest imperative language was FORTRAN, developed in 1954. FORTRAN was developed by one of the pioneers of early computing, John Backus (while employed at, IBM). FORTRAN is at the root of a very large language tree that includes BASIC, Pascal, Modula, C, Ada, and a huge number of domain-specific languages such as Python and Ruby.

Table 13.2: Sample imperative languages

Language	Year Introduced	Focus
FORTRAN	1957	First general-purpose programming language.
ALGOL	1958	Second imperative programming language.
C	1972	Pervasive procedural programming language.
POP-11	1975	Multi-paradigm programming language.
Ada	1983	Multi-paradigm concurrent programming language.

We can also think of machine languages (or assembly languages) as imperative languages. The instructions of a given computer architecture are also an example of an imperative language. The instructions of a machine language not only alter memory, but also the machine state (status flags, for example).

Listing 13.4 illustrates the organization of a simple imperative program in BASIC. Note how this example can be described as a recipe. For example, request the user's name through the terminal, get the user's name, and finally emit the user's name through the terminal.

Listing 13.4: Illustrating the sequential commands of an imperative language (BASIC).

```
print "Please type in your name :"
read name
print "Hello, " + name
end
```

While recursion is permitted in imperative languages, these languages lack tail-recursion and therefore they are less efficient than functional implementations. Commonly, loops provide the iteration capabilities (as shown in the factorial implementation in Listing 13.5). As shown here, the while reserved word in C implements the looping behavior while the expression '(n > 0)' remains true.

Listing 13.5:   Computing the factorial in an imperative language (C).

```c
unsigned long factorial( int n )
{
unsigned long fact = 1;
while( n > 0 ) {
   fact = fact * n;
   n--;
}
return fact;
}
```

Object-Oriented Programming (OOP)

Object-Oriented Programming (or OOP) is a paradigm in which programs are constructed from a set of objects that connect to one another. Objects are able to message other objects through their public interfaces, while objects also maintain a set of private interfaces (and data) that are used internally by the objects themselves. Objects typically encapsulate some logical functionality of a system A sample of object-oriented languages through four decades is provided in Table 13.3.

Table 13.3:   Sample of object-oriented languages.

Language	Year Introduced	Focus
Simula 67	1967	First object-oriented programming system.
C++	1970	C language with object-oriented extensions.
Smalltalk	1970	Dynamic and reflective programming.
Ruby	1993	Pure interpreted object-oriented language.

A few of the fundamental characteristics are classes and objects, inheritance, encapsulation, and polymorphism.

A *class* is an abstract entity that defines behaviors (the actions that it can perform) and attributes (the characteristics for the class). *Objects* are instantiated from a class, going from an abstract entity to a physical instance of the class. Take, for example, a class that represents an NPC (non-player character) in a game. The attributes could specify the NPC's damage and the weapon that it's carrying (which itself could be represented by another object). The class behaviors could include the actions that the NPC may perform (attack, move, defend, etc.).

An example class is shown in Listing 13.6. In this simple example, our class exports two behaviors, set_value and area. The behavior set_value (which is also called a method) allows the initialization of an internal value. The second behavior, area, returns the square of the internal value. A sample main function is also presented that creates two instances of the Csquare class and demonstrates their methods.

Listing 13.6:   Illustrating a class and two objects with C++.

```
#include <iostream.h>
using namespace std;
class Csquare {
  int h;
  public:
    void set_value( int );
    int  area( void );
};
void Csquare::set_value( int in_h )
{
  h = in_h;
  return;
}
int Csquare::area( void )
{
  return h*h;
}
int main()
{
  Csquare s, t;
  s.set_value( 5 );
  t.set_value( 5 );
  cout << "s area = " << s.area() << endl;
```

```
cout << "t area = " << t.area() << endl;
return 0;
}
```

Inheritance is the ability for classes to inherit the characteristics of other classes. In this way, we can build base classes that define default behavior, and then create subclasses that amend these behaviors. For example, in designing a game, we might specify a class for an NPC. This class provides the base set of features that all NPCs share. Then, we can create subclasses that specialize the base class for more specific characters in the game.

As shown in Listing 13.7, we create an NPC_Base class that provides our base set of behaviors. From this, we create a Barbarian subclass, and a Villager subclass, that refine the behaviors for the character type. At the end of the listing, we create two objects of the two subclasses to demonstrate the specialization.

Listing 13.7:   Illustrating inheritance with Ruby.

```
> class NPC_Base
>   def move
>     puts "Move the NPC"
>   end
>
>   def behavior
>     puts "Just stand there"
>   end
> end
>
> class Villager<NPC_Base
>   def behavior
>     puts "Loiter"
>   end
> end
>
> class Barbarian<NPC_Base
>   def behavior
>     puts "Attack!"
>   end
> end
>
```

```
> fred = Villager.new
> hans = Barbarian.new
> fred.behavior
Loiter
> hans.behavior
Attack!
>
```

Note here that the behavior method has been replaced from the base class in the subclasses. This is an example of *polymorphism*, where the same method achieves different results based on the particular subclass for which an object is an instance.

Finally, the concept of *encapsulation* (otherwise known as information hiding) allows a class to hide the details of its internal operations. A class exports what is necessary as far as methods and instance data goes for proper operation, but hides what the external world is not necessary to know.

Logic Programming

Logic programming, first introduced by John McCarthy in 1958, is based on pattern-directed execution of rules to arrive at a goal. While logic programming is based on mathematical logic, logic programming is much more constricted than the capabilities of mathematical logic. Specifically, logic programming implements what is known as *horn clauses*. A horn clause (specifically a definite clause) can be shown as:

$$X_0 \text{ if } X_1 \text{ and } X_2, \text{ and } \ldots X_n$$

which means that if all X_1 through X_n is true, then X_0 is true. A special case of the horn clause is a simple fact, which is simply specified as:

$$X_0.$$

The horn clause can then be thought of as a fact being true if all prerequisites of the fact are true. For example:

mortal(X) if man(X)

which means that if the atom identified by X is a man, then X is also mortal. This can be demonstrated in Prolog as follows, with first the definition of a fact, and then a query, testing a given query:

```
?- man(Socrates).
?- mortal(X) :- man(X).
?- mortal(Socrates)?
Yes
?-
```

In this example, we specify a new fact (Socrates is a man). We then define that all men are mortal with a rule. Finally, we check to see if Socrates is a mortal, which evaluates to 'Yes.'

Later in this chapter, we'll review logic programming in more depth, from the perspective of a couple of different languages. Recently, non-functional languages have begun to integrate logic capabilities (such as Mercury, shown in Table 13.4).

Table 13.4:   Sample logic languages.

Language	Year Introduced	Focus
PROLOG	1972	Logic programming using Horn clauses.
Gödel	1991	General purpose, logic programming.
Oz	1995	Multi-paradigm concurrent constraint programming.
Mercury	1995	Multi-paradigm language for logic programming.

LANGUAGES OF AI

Considering the spectrum of applications of artificial-intelligence applications, a single language would not provide all of the capabilities necessary. For example, C is ideal for numerical applications such as those illustrated by neural networks or genetic algorithms. But the specialized needs of expert systems make Prolog an ideal choice. Further, for applications that require dynamicity (such as creating new functions on the fly), LISP provides the necessary functionality. Some language-to-application mappings are provided in Table 13.5.

Table 13.5:   Artificial intelligence applications and their languages.

Application	Language
Expert System	POP-11, Prolog, LISP

Dynamic Applications	LISP, Scheme, Dylan
Computer Vision	C
Natural Language Systems	Prolog, Oz
Evolutionary Systems	C, DSLs

In the remainder of this chapter, we'll dig further into a number of languages commonly used to build AI applications. This includes LISP, Scheme, Prolog, Erlang, POP-11, Smalltalk, and a look at some domain-specific languages that provide functionality useful for AI applications.

The LISP Language

The LISP language is one of the oldest languages still in use today. LISP shares this distinction with other ancient languages like FORTRAN and COBOL (COmmon Business Oriented Language). But these other languages, like LISP, have evolved over the years, and look very different than their initial offerings. Having said that, the fundamental attributes of these languages remain. For example, the FORTRAN continues to use the imperative approach, and LISP is still based on the functional approach.

LISP is one of the most unique languages (within the AI domain and outside). LISP stands for LISt Processing, as both data and LISP programs are represented as lists. Further, data and programs can be (and usually are) represented as lists of lists. With programs and data represented in identical ways (which makes LISP a homoiconic language), it's easy to understand how LISP functions can generate data to be used as another LISP function.

Let's now dig further into the LISP language, learn about its origin, and then explore a few example programs.

The History of LISP

John McCarthy (now at Stanford University) introduced the ideas behind LISP while at MIT in 1958. In 1960, he published a paper which served as the design for LISP, and implementations began to appear shortly thereafter. McCarthy's notation used what was called bracketed M-expressions, but this notation was abandoned in early implementations for S-expressions, which are still in use today.

While many consider LISP to be an archaic language, LISP is worthwhile to learn because of the fundamental ideas upon which it's based.

LISP quickly consumed the early computers of the 1960s (beginning with the early vacuum tube computers), which resulted in specialty machines in the 1970s that were designed for LISP. In particular, LISP required specialized garbage collection. However, today LISP is able to run on generally available hardware.

Overview of the LISP Language

Let's now dig into the LISP language, and explore some of the core concepts from representing data to representing programs. Note that, as we'll see, data and programs are represented identically. In fact, LISP programs can be combinations of program and data.

Data Representation

As the language's acronym suggests, everything in LISP is a list. The following are examples of data in LISP, from the simple, to more complex representations.

'()	Empty list.
'(())	List containing an empty list.
'(1)	List with a single atom.
'(2 4 8 16 32)	List with multiple atoms.
'((1 3 5 7) (2 4 6 8))	List of lists.
'(LISP (John McCarthy) (MIT) (1958))	List as a structure.

Simple Expressions

Evaluating math expressions in LISP looks very similar to the data representation example, except that math symbols are provided which are known in LISP to be math operations. LISP uses what is called prefix notation, where an operation is specified, followed by the necessary arguments for the operation. Consider the following examples:

(+ 1 3)	Evaluates to 4
(* 5 7)	Evaluates to 35
(* (- 7 5) (- 9 4))	Evaluates to 10
(/ 8 2)	Evaluates to 4

Note above that each of the examples are examples of lists. As LISP evaluates the functions, it identifies the operator symbol, and then applies the subsequent arguments to it.

TIP

It's important to note that every LISP expression returns a value. In fact, a LISP function can return any number of values.

Predicates

LISP also includes predicates that provide the ability of introspection. The atom predicate returns true if the argument is an atom. For example:

(atom 5)	Evaluates to True
(atom ())	Evaluates to False

Variables

LISP also supports variables through a number of means. First, let's look at the setq means of evaluating a symbol. The setq permits binding a value to a symbol of a sequence of values to a sequence of symbols, for example:

(setq score 100)	Evaluates to 100
(setq score-1 95 score-2 100)	Evaluates to 100
(setq thedate '("April" 13 1968))	Evaluates to ("April" 13 1968)

Note in the last example the use of the single quote (or tick) symbol. This tells the LISP evaluator not to evaluate the list that follows. If the quote had not been used, then LISP would attempt to evaluate the list (looking for a function called "April") in order to bind the resulting value to thedate.

LISP also provides a more complex form of variable assignment called the let form. In this form, a number of bindings can be temporarily created. Consider the following example:

```
(let ((x 5)
      (y 7))
  (+ (* x x) (* y y)))          Evaluates to 74
```

Note that in this example x and y have no value once the evaluation is complete. We could bind the result to a variable as follows:
(setq var

```
(let ((x 5) (y 7))
    (+ (* x x) (* y y)))        Evaluates to 74
```

List Processing

Let's now look at how LISP performs list construction and processing. We've already seen the simplest way to create a list, through the use of setq. Now we'll look at two functions that can be used for list construction. The first is called cons, which constructs a list from two arguments (with the second always being an empty list).

(cons 1 ())	Evaluates to (1)
(cons 1 (cons 2 ()))	Evaluates to (1 2)

LISP also provides a simpler way to construct lists, called list. This function is much simpler as shown in the following examples:

(list 1 2 3)	Evaluates to (1 2 3)
(list 1 '(2 3))	Evaluates to (1 (2 3))
(list '(1) '(2))	Evaluates to ((1) (2))

Now that we've explored some ways to construct lists, let's look at a few of the basic list-processing functions provided by LISP. The two basic operations are called car (to retrieve the first element of a list) and cdr (to retrieve the remainder of the list without the first element), for example:

(car '(1 2 3))	Evaluates to 1
(cdr '(1 2 3))	Evaluates to (2 3)

To retrieve the second atom of the list, we can combine the car and cdr functions:

(car (cdr '(1 2 3)))	Evaluates to 2

LISP also provides some simplifications on this theme, by providing functions that combine these primitive functions for list processing. For example, the following two operations are identical:

(car (cdr '(1 2 3)))	Evaluates to 2
(cadr '(1 2 3))	Evaluates to 2

The cadr operation is therefore a combination of car and cdr. There's also a combination of cdr and cdr called cddr. The following two examples are also identical:

(cdr (cdr '(1 2 3 4)))	Evaluates to (3 4)
(cddr '(1 2 3 4))	Evaluates to (3 4)

LISP provides a number of these combination operators, some of which are shown in Table 13.6.

Table 13.6:   LISP operation combinations and their equivalents.

Operation	Equivalent
(cadr x)	(car (cdr x))
(cdar x)	(cdr (car x))
(caar x)	(car (car x))
(cddr x)	(cdr (cdr x))
(caddr x)	(car (cdr (cdr x)))
(caaddr x)	(car (car (cdr (cdr x))))

Finally, we can append to lists using the `append` function. This function takes two lists and puts them together:

(append '(1 2) '(3 4))   Evaluates to (1 2 3 4)

Programs as Data

Recall that program and data are the same. Here's an example that illustrates this. We start by creating a variable called `expr` and loading it with a list. We then use the `eval` function to evaluate the data as a LISP program.

(setq expr '(* 5 5))   Evaluates to (* 5 5)
(eval expr)   Evaluates to 25

Now let's look at how program flow is altered in LISP. We'll start with a review of conditionals in LISP, and then look at function creation and iteration.

Conditions

Controlling the flow of a LISP function can be achieved a number of ways. We'll look at two methods here, cond and if. The first method we'll explore is the if function. The if function is very simple and is made up of a distinct set of expressions. The format for the if function is:

```
(if (expr)
   (print "expr is true")
   (print "expr is false"))
```

A simple example of this form is:

```
(if (> 2 1)
  (print "2 is gt 1")
  (print "1 is gt 2"))
```

The false portion of the form can be omitted if not necessary, as follows:

```
(setq name "Elise")
(if (equal name "Elise")
  (print "Hi Elise"))
```

The cond form is slightly more complicated, but permits greater flexibility in the conditional structure. The cond form can specify as many test clauses as are necessary. The following example illustrates the cond form with four clauses:

```
(setq name "Elise")
(setq salutation
(cond
  ((equal name "Marc") "Hi Marc.")
  ((equal name "Megan") "Hi Megan.")
  ((equal name "Elise") "Hi Elise.")
  ((equal name "Jill") "HI Jill.")
  (t "Hi you.")))
(print salutation)                            Evaluates to "Hi Elise."
```

Note that in the end of the cond form is the 'else' (or default) portion of the conditional. The 't' simply represents TRUE, and as it always represents true, the value "Hi you." is returned if no other conditions are met.

Functions in LISP

A function is created in LISP using the `defun` macro. The format of the `defun` macro is as follows:

```
(defun func-name (parameter*)
  "Optional string to describe function."
  body-form*)
```

The func-name can be a sequence of alphabetic characters (and hyphens), as well as some other special characters. The parameter° represents zero or more parameters, which is followed by a documentation string (used by the documentation function). The body of the function then follows.

Let's look at a simple example of a function. Recall the quadratic discriminant ($b^2 - 4ac$). This can be represented in LISP very simply as:

```
(defun qd(a b c)
  "Calculate the quadratic discriminant"
```

```
(- (* b b) (* 4.0 a c)))
```

An example use of this function is shown as:

```
(setq val (qd 5 4 2))
```

Now let's look at a few examples that demonstrate some of the core features of LISP. We'll build a set of functions that manipulate a very simple database (a list of lists). Let's begin with a definition of our database. Our simple database (db) will represent a list of records, each record being a list containing a name followed by an age. We'll use the defvar function to create our database with an initial set of records (defvar creates a global variable).

```
(defvar *db* '((TIM 41) (JILL 35) (MEGAN 14) (ELISE 9) (MARC 6)))
```

Now let's create three functions that manipulate this database. We'll create LISP functions to return the number of records in the database, emit the names in the database, and add a new record to the database.

Returning the number of records in the database (function num-records) is a great function to explore recursion in LISP. The function num-records takes as its input the database. The first thing that the function does is test for a null list, and if so, it returns 0 (as we've reached the end of the list). Otherwise, it adds one to the result of a recursive call to num-records.

```
(defun num-records (x)
  "Return the number of records in the list."
  (if (null x) 0
    (+ (num-records(cdr x)) 1)))
```

Let's say that our input to the function is a database that contains four records. Figure 13.1 illustrates the recursive call trace along with the return values. Note at the end, the function reaches the null list, and zero is returned. At this point, each function adds one to the return of the value returned by the recursive call.

Recursive Call Trace	Return Value
(num-records `((A 1) (B 2) (C 3) (D 4))	1 + 1 + 1 + 1 + 0
(num-records `((B 2) (C 3) (D 4))	1 + 1 + 1 + 0
(num-records `((C 3) (D 4))	1 + 1 + 0
(num-records `((D 4))	1 + 0
(num-records `()	0

FIGURE 13.1: Illustrating the recursive nature of the num-records function.

Now let's look at another example of a LISP function that is used to emit the names contained in each of the records (emit-names). This will follow the same approach and recursively iterate through the records (sublists) of the database (superlist). This function operates as follows. First, we test to see if the input is an empty list (using the null function). If it is, we return nil (which is the same as '()) and the process is complete. Otherwise, we set the variable name to the first atom of the first sublist. Within the let form, we print this name, and then recursively call emit-names. This recursive call continues until the empty list results, at which point the call chain unwinds and the process is complete.

```
(defun emit-names (x)
  "Emit the name portion of each record in the database."
  (if (null x)
    nil
    (let ((name (caar x)))
    (print name)
    (emit-names (cdr x)))))
```

The final function that we'll provide demonstrates the pure simplicity of LISP's list-handling functions. In this example, we'll demonstrate how to add a new record to the database. This function, add-record, simply appends the new record to the database, and then uses setq to set the database to this new list.

```
(defun add-record (x)
(setq *db* (append *db* x)))
```

Finally, let's look at an example of calling these functions. The following three examples illustrate the use of the three functions (num-records, add-record, and emit-names).

```
;;;
(format t "~%Num records : ~D~%" (num-records *db*))
(format t "Current record list:")
(emit-names *db*)
(format t "~%~%Adding a new record~%")
(add-record '((MADDIE 3)))
(format t "Num records : ~D~%" (num-records *db*))
(format t "~%Record List:")
(emit-names *db*)
```

This LISP program results in the following output:

```
Num records : 5
Current record list:
TIM
JILL
MEGAN
ELISE
MARC
Adding a new record
Num records : 6
Record List:
TIM
JILL
MEGAN
ELISE
MARC
MADDIE
```

LISP Summary

This introduction to LISP provided a tip of the iceberg of the capabilities provided by the LISP language. While LISP may be an ancient language considering the timeline of some of the more recent popular languages, it's well worth learning for the unique concepts and features that it provides.

The Scheme Language

The Scheme language, created during the 1970s at MIT, is a modern dialect of the LISP language. But instead of simply being a functional language, it was designed to support a number of other programming paradigms such as imperative and object-oriented.

History of Scheme

The Scheme language was the result of a series of papers by Gerald Jay Sussman and Guy Steele, Jr. These papers focused on ideas in programming language design, specifically the design of a simple language that was both efficient and unconstrained by arbitrary rules. The language that evolved from these papers illustrated a simple architecture with very few primitive constructs and all other elements implemented as libraries.

The Scheme language is now standardized through an IEEE standard, and also through a formal review process called the RxRS (Revised Report on Scheme). The entire language is described in around 50 pages, with another roughly 100 dedicated to library discussions. [R6RS] From this specification, numerous implementations exist including PLT Scheme, MIT Scheme, Scheme48, and an interactive shell that allows operators to write scripts and interact with an operating system in Scheme called SCSH (Scheme Shell).

Overview of the Scheme Language

Let's now dig into the Scheme language, and explore some of the core concepts. As you'll see, Scheme is a very simple language, and while it's easy to learn the core ideas of programming in scheme, it's very difficult to master. As a dialect of LISP, data and programs are represented identically.

Data Representation

Like LISP, Scheme supports the basic data type of the list. Scheme also supports integer, real, strings and symbol types (among others). Consider these examples that illustrate Scheme's use of lists and atoms.

```
'()                         Empty list
'( () )                     List containing an empty list.
'(1)                        List with a single atom.
'(2 4 8 16 32)              List with multiple atoms.
'( (1 3 5 7) (2 4 6 8))     List of lists.
'(Scheme ((Guy Steele Jr.)(Gerald J Sussman)) (MIT) (1975))
                            List as a structure.
```

Simple Expressions

Evaluating math expressions in Scheme is identical to LISP; math symbols are provided, which are known in Scheme as math operations (primitives). Scheme uses what is called *prefix notation*, where an operation is specified, followed by the necessary arguments for the operation. Consider the following examples:

(+ 1 3)	Evaluates to 4
(* 5 7)	Evaluates to 35
(* (- 7 5) (- 9 4))	Evaluates to 10
(/ 8 2)	Evaluates to 4

Each of the examples are examples of lists. As Scheme evaluates the functions, it identifies the operator symbol, and then applies the subsequent arguments to it.

Scheme requires no operator precedence rules because operators use the prefix notation with fully parenthesized operands.

Predicates

Scheme also includes a variety of predicates, which can be used to determine the type of an object, or the equivalence of two objects. Predicates always return a boolean, true (#t) or false (#t) value. Predicates are defined as the type followed by the '?' symbol.

For example, we can identify if an object is a null (or empty) list using:

(null? '())	Evaluates to #t (true)

We can also identify if an object refers to a procedure with:

(procedure? list)	Evaluates to #t (true)

Finally, we can identify if two objects are equivalent using the eqv? procedure:

(eqv? 5 (+ 2 3))	Evaluates to #t (true)
(eqv? car cdr)	Evaluates to #f (false)

Many other predicates exist, which can be found in the R6RS.

If the desire is to check if two memory objects are identical (refer to the same object in memory), then the eq? equivalence operation can be used.

Variables

Let's look at two examples of variables in Scheme, those that have global scope and those that have local scope. Variables in global scope are created using define. This binds a value to a variable as follows:

(**define** pi 3.1415926)

Variables of local scope can also be created using the let form. This form has the structure:

(**let** (var list) (expr))

Here's a simple example that demonstrates a simple expression with two locally scoped variables:

(**let** ((pi 3.1415926) (r 5))
 (* pi (* r r)))

Note that as multiple variable bindings are possible, we can also perform multiple expressions. Additionally, let forms can be embedded in other expressions (as well as other let forms).

List Processing

Scheme provides a rich set of operations for list processing. Let's begin with a look at Scheme's list construction operations. The two basic list construction procedures are cons and list. The cons procedure takes two objects and joins them together. For example:

(cons 'a '(a b))	Evaluates to (a b c)
(cons '(a b) '(c d))	Evaluates to ((a b) c d)

Another way to think about cons is that the first argument is the car of the result and the second argument is the cdr.

The list procedure is much simpler and simply takes a set of arguments and turns them into a list. For example:

(list 'a 'b 'c)	Evaluates to '(a b c)
(list 'a '(b c))	Evaluates to '(a (b c))
(list 'a '() '(a b c))	Evaluates to '(a () (a b c))

The fundamental list manipulation procedures are the same as LISP, car and cdr. The car procedure returns the first object from a list while cdr returns the tail (all objects except the first). For example:

(car '(a b c))	Evaluates to 'a
(cdr '(a b c))	Evaluates to '(b c)
(car '((a b) (c d)))	Evaluates to '(a b)
(cdr '((a b) (c d)))	Evaluates to '((c d))

Scheme also supports combinations of these operators (such as cadr, for (car (cdr))). See Table 13.6 for more options.

The `length` procedure can be used to identify the number of objects in the list. Note that this refers to the number of objects at the root of the list, and not the members of the sublist. For example:

(length '(a b c d (e f)))	Evaluates to 5
(length '((a b) (c d)))	Evaluates to 2
(length '())	Evaluates to 0
(length '(()()))	Evaluates to 2

Finally, to retrieve a specific object from a list, one could use the car/cdr combinations, or simply use list-ref. This function takes a list and a numeric argument and returns that object (using the numeric argument as the index) from the list. Note that the index is base 0, so 0 represents the first object, etc. For example:

(list-ref '(a b c d) 2)	Evaluates to 'c
(list-ref '((a b) (c d) (e f)) 1)	Evaluates to '(c d)

As was illustrated with the LISP language, Scheme is a powerful language for list processing and manipulation.

Conditions

Scheme supports a number of conditional forms. The two most common are the if form and the cond form. The if form is the simplest, supporting an expression for the `true case` and an expression for the `false case`, as:

```
(if (test-expr)
   (expr-for-true-case)
   (expr-for-false-case))
```

The if form can be demonstrated as follows. The return of the overall expression is the first object of my-list if my-var is zero; otherwise, the return object is the remainder of the my-list:

```
(if (equal? my-var 0)
   (car my-list)
   (cdr my-list))
```

If more complex conditionals are required, the cond form can be used. The cond form permits multiple test-expressions as well as a default case (making this a more flexible version of the switch statement available in many imperative and object-oriented languages).

```
(cond (test-expr-1 expr-1)
    (test-expr-2 expr-2)
...
    (else expr-n))
```

To illustrate the cond form, we implement the sign functionality:

```
(cond
    ((< my-var 0) -1)
    ((> my-var 0)  1)
    (else        0))
```

While the if form is much simpler, the cond functionality is recommended for all but the simplest conditional expressions.

Iteration and Maps

Scheme, as a functional language, can rely on recursion for looping and iteration. But Scheme also provides some other forms for iteration. Let's start with a look at the do loop form that permits iterations similar to the for loop provided in many imperative languages:

```
(do
((variable value update) ...)
(test done-expr ...)
cont-expr ...)
```

In this form, we specify our iteration variable, its initial value, and how we'll update the variable at each loop iteration. At each update, we'll perform our test, and if the test is true, the loop is completed and we perform any done-expressions that are available. If the test is false, the loop continues and any continue-expressions are processed. Let's look at a simple example that illustrates the form:

```
(do ((i 0 (+ i 1)))
    ((equal? i 10) (write "done") (newline))
    (write i) (newline))
```

This example simply iterates, using the i variable, from 0 to 9. During the iteration, the value is emitted, and at the end, the "done" string is emitted and the form is complete.

Iteration is typically performed to operate over an indexed object, or to perform an action some number of times. For cases in which the goal is to perform an action over a set of data, Scheme provides what is called the map operation. This is a common operation in functional languages. Recall that higher-order functions in functional languages support functions as arguments to other functions. The map function is used to apply a user-specified function to every element of a list.

A simple example uses a lambda (or anonymous) function, which is applied to each element of a list:

(map (lambda (x) (* x x)) '(0 1 2 3))   Evaluates to '(0 1 4 9)

Now let's look at an example of a user-defined function used in the context of map. Let's return to our simple database application from the LISP introduction. Our simple database contains a list of names and ages, and our user-defined function (print-names) emits the name from one of the records in the database.

```
(define my-list '((Megan 14) (Elise 9) (Marc 6)))
(define (print-names x)
   (write (car x)) (newline))
```

We can then use map to iterate our database with the print-names function as:

(**map** print-names my-list)

The map function iterates the list, and invokes the user-defined function for each object in the list (which is why we extract the name with car instead of needing to do a caar).

Procedures in Scheme

Scheme provides two types of functions, `primitives` and `procedures`. A primitive is a built-in procedure (fundamental elements of the Scheme environment), where procedures are user-defined (or provided through libraries). Examples of primitives include let, car, and the math operations, such as '+' ,and '-'. Scheme is therefore built from a very basic set of operations, and from these operations, more complex forms are derived.

Creating functions in Scheme is similar to LISP, but the syntax differs slightly:

```
(define (proc parameters* )
   body)
```

An example procedure, `square`, takes a single argument and returns the square of the argument:

```
(define (square x)
   (* x x))
```

Now let's return to our simple database implementation and implement the procedures that allow us to manipulate the records of the database. The simple database (db) represents a list of records, where each record contains a name and an age. We'll use the define primitive to declare the database and its initial set of records.

```
(define db '((TIM 41) (JILL 35) (MEGAN 14) (ELISE 9) (MARC 6)))
```

We'll implement the same set of functions as implemented for LISP, but we'll implement them differently to explore some of Scheme's features.

The first procedure we'll implement will return the number of records in the database (procedure num-records). For LISP, we implemented this as a recursive function. For Scheme, we'll use the length procedure to demonstrate an alternative method to implement this.

```
(define (num-records x)
   (length x))
```

Recall that the length procedure returns the number of objects in the list. Objects in this scenario are the number of sublists (or records in the database).

To implement the emit-names procedure, we'll use the map procedure. This procedure applies a function to each object of a list. For this procedure, we simply emit the first element of each object (which will represent the name for the record).

```
(define (emit-names x)
   (write "Database is") (newline)
```

```
    (map (lambda (y) (write (car y)) (newline)) x)
    (newline))
```

Our final procedure is used to add a new record to our database, called add-record. In this procedure, we're modifying the contents of an existing variable, so we use the set! procedure.

```
(define (add-record x)
    (set! db (append db x)))
```

Finally, let's have a look at how we'd invoke these procedures within a Scheme program. The following Scheme code illustrates the initial creation of the database and invokes each of the defined procedures:

```
(define db '((TIM 41) (JILL 35) (MEGAN 14) (ELISE 9) (MARC 6)))
(display '"Num records : ")
(write (num-records db)) (newline) (newline)
(emit-names db)
(display '"Adding a new record") (newline) (newline)
(add-record '((MADDIE 3)))
(display '"Num records : ")
(write (num-records db)) (newline) (newline)
(emit-names db)
```

This Scheme program results in the following output:
```
Num records : 5
Current Record List:
TIM
JILL
MEGAN
ELISE
MARC
Adding a new record
Num records: 6
Current Record List:
TIM
JILL
MEGAN
ELISE
MARC
MADDIE
```

Scheme Summary

Like LISP, Scheme is a useful language to learn because of the ideas that are expressed. While not explored here, Scheme provides continuations which allow program control to continue at a procedure at any point in the program. Scheme also allows programmers to define new syntactic forms to extend the language. How many languages permit extending the syntax of the core language through the language itself? Scheme is definitely not the simplest language to master, but it's worth the effort to explore.

The POP-11 Language

POP-11 is an interesting multi-paradigm language that shares many characteristics of functional languages. POP-11 is dynamically typed with garbage collection like functional languages, but shares a block structured syntax like many imperative languages. POP-11 is also stack-oriented, sharing a relatively unique feature in language design with the Forth language.

History of POP-11

POP-11 is the result of a series of POP languages developed for research in Artificial Intelligence at Edinburgh University. POP-11 was implemented in the mid-1970s on the PDP 11/40 computer on the UNIX operating system, and was designed as a language specifically for teaching purposes. [Sloman 1996] POP-11 has advanced as the state of the art in language design and now includes not only functional aspects, but also object-oriented features and a graphical library. POP-11 can be found for many operating systems, and while a powerful language, is not widely used for production software development.

Overview of the POP-11 Language

Let's now explore some of the features of the POP-11 language. Due to the size and scope of the language, we'll restrict this discussion to some of the basic features that will help illustrate the language and its uses.

Data Representation

POP-11 includes a variety of data objects, from numbers (integers and decimals) to words, strings, and lists. Sharing a heritage from functional languages, lists can be complex, containing other data objects, and collections of these objects in embedded lists.

41	Integer Number
0.707	Decimal Number
7_/11	Ratio

"Zoe"	Word
'a sample string'	String
[a sample list]	List
[simple [embedded list]]	List containing a list
{POP-11 {{Robin Popplestone}} {Univsersity of Sussex} {1975}}	
	Vector as a Structure

Vector data types include a range of classes of standard operations. Users can further create their own vector classes.

Predicates

POP-11 provides a way to identify the data type given an object. In demonstrating this, we'll also show the print-arrow (=>) of POP-11. This instructs the interpreter to emit the result of the expression. For example:

dataword(5) =>	Evaluates to integer
dataword(1.1) =>	Evaluates to decimal
dataword(1_/2) =>	Evaluates to ratio
dataword("Zoe") =>	Evaluates to word
dataword('test string') =>	Evaluates to string
dataword([a test list]') =>	Evaluates to pair
dataword({a {test vector}}) =>	Evaluates to vector
dataword(dataword) =>	Evaluates to procedure

Simple Expressions

As POP-11 is a multi-paradigm language, expressions can be defined and evaluated in a number of ways. The developer can use infix notation (as commonly used in imperative languages) or the prefix notation (as we've seen demonstrated in functional languages such as Scheme or LISP). There are some differences with infix as we'll see in the following examples:

5 + 7 =>	Evaluates to 12
*(3, 4) =>	Evaluates to 12
10 / 3.0 =>	Evaluates to 3.33333
10 / 3 =>	Evaluates to 10_/3
10 - 7 =>	Evaluates to 3

NOTE ▶ *An interesting aspect of POP-11 is the error-reporting mechanism that it provides. POP-11 provides very detailed explanations of errors when they're encountered, which can be very helpful for beginner developers.*

Variables

We declare variables in POP-11 using the `vars` keyword. This allows us to create any number of variables, comma-delimited, as:

vars x,y;

As variables are dynamically typed, they can be assigned any value, for example:

[a b c] -> x;	Assigns [a b c] to variable x
1.99 -> y;	Assigns 1.99 to variable y

Note here that -> is the assignment operator, and the = sign represents a test of equality.

List Processing

Like the functional languages, POP-11 provides a rich set of procedures for list processing. Let's have a look at some of the important aspects of list processing in POP-11.

First, recall that we can declare a list (and in this case two lists) simply as:

vars clist1 = [a b c d], clist2=[e f g h];

Concatenating lists is performed using the <> operator. We can combine the two lists to a new list as:

clist1 <> clist2 -> comblist;	
pr(comblist);	Evaluates to [a b c d e f g h]

POP-11 also provides a way to merge lists with a little more flexibility than the <> operator allows. For example, we can combine the two previous lists with a few additional elements easily:

[x ^^clist1 y ^^clist2 z] -> newlist;	Evaluates to [x a b c d y e f g h z]
pr(newlist);	

Let's look at one last useful operation that POP-11 provides for list construction. The single arrow operation allows a list to be constructed with values of variables, for example:

```
vars x, y, z;
1 -> x;
2 -> y;
3 -> z;
[^x ^y ^z] -> mylist;
mylist =>                                      Evaluates to [1 2 3]
```

POP-11 provides list-manipulation procedures that mimic those provided by LISP and Scheme. Recall in LISP, the car function returned the first object from the list and cdr returned the list without the first object. In POP-11, these functions are hd (to return the head of the list, like car) and tl (to return the tail of the list, like cdr).

```
hd( [ [a b] [c d] [e f] ] ) =>            Evaluates to [a b]
tl( [ [a b] [c d] [e f] ] ) =>            Evaluates to [ [c d] [e f] ]
hd( hd( tl( [ [a b] [c d] [e f] ] ))) =>  Evaluates to c
```

POP-11 also provides a length function, which identifies the number of objects in a list. This is demonstrated as follows:

```
length( [ [a b] [c d] ] )=>               Evaluates to 2
```

Conditions

Conditionals in POP-11 follow an imperative block-structured model. The basic pattern for a conditional in POP-11 is:

```
if <condition> then
<statements>
endif
```

The condition can be made up of a number of conditions, separated by logical operators (such as and, or). Let's look at a short example of the conditional:

```
if length(mylist) > 0 then
mylist =>
endif
```

This snippet simply tests the length of the list (tests for a non-null list), and if it's not empty, prints the contents of the list. An else can also be supplied.

Iteration and Maps

POP-11 provides many of the looping constructs that are found in the imperative languages. This includes until-do, do-until, repeat, while-do, for, and others. Let's look at a couple of examples.

The while-do loop is one of the simplest and most commonly used iterator. The following example iterates over a list and emits each object. Note that during the loop, we destroy mylist by setting it to its tail as we emit the head.

```
[a b c d e f] -> mylist;
vars num;
0 -> num;
while num < length(mylist) do
hd(mylist) =>
tl(mylist) -> mylist;
endwhile;
```

The `for` loop provides a bit more flexibility, and is only slightly more complicated. The following example illustrates iterating through the objects of a list:

```
[a b c d e f] -> mylist;
for 0->num; step num+1->num;
till num = length(mylist)
do
hd(mylist) =>
tl(mylist) -> mylist;
endfor;
```

You can see the pattern here used in other languages (start, iterator, end). This is less compact than in languages like C, but the semantics are roughly the same.

> *While POP-11 supports a variety of iteration methods, they are fundamentally very similar, and in fact, some are simply syntactic sugar. Syntactic sugar (coined by Peter J. Landin) defines additions to a language, but do not extend the expressiveness of the language.*

As POP-11 supports functional programming, it supports higher-order functions, and the `map` procedure. Recall that the `map` procedure can be used to apply a function over a list. In POP-11, the maplist procedure can be used:
maplist([-7 89 0 -14 3 1], sign) =>   Evaluates to [-1 1 0 -1 1 1]

Pattern Matching

POP-11 provides a nice set of pattern-matching features that can be used for logic programming, or natural-language programming. Let's explore some of the pattern-matching features that are provided by POP-11.

Let's first look at simple matching in POP-11. Let's say that we want to identify if an element exists in a list, and if it does, store a parameter related to that element. For example, if our list is defined as:

```
[ [tim 41] [jill 35] [megan 14] ] => mylist;
```

The matches keyword can be used to find an element in a list, and potentially store an element of that sequence. The snippet:

```
vars age;
mylist matches [ == [jill ?age] == ] =>
```

returns true if the element 'jill' is matched in mylist. Further, the ?age element instructs the matcher to store the following element after the match in the defined variable. If we now emitted age, such as:

```
age =>
```

we'd emit the value 35. The '==' elements indicate that something may begin or end in the list, and to ignore these elements of the list. This pattern matcher can be useful in building natural language systems (for example, the famous Eliza program has been written in POP-11 using the matches pattern-matcher). For example:

```
[I hate you] -> inp_sentence;
if inp_sentence matches [ I ?verb you == ] then
[why do you ^verb me?] =>
endif;
```

The result of this snippet is [why do you hate me ?]. You'll recognize this as a typical response from 'bot' programs, such as Eliza. From this simple snippet, you can see how easy it is to construct natural-language systems with POP-11.

Procedures in POP-11

Defining procedures in POP-11 is what you would expect from a block-structure language (such as C or Pascal). The procedure definition includes a define block, the optional set of arguments that are to be passed in, and any value that is returned. For example, the following procedure implements the square (returns the product of the single argument):

```
define square( num ) -> result;
num * num -> result
enddefine;
```

Demonstrating a call to this function is done very simply as:

```
square(5) =>                         Evaluates to 25
```

Where it's possible to pass multiple arguments to a procedure, it's also possible for a procedure to return multiple results. The following procedure illustrates multiple arguments and multiple returns:

```
define multi( num1, num2 ) -> (result1, result2);
num1 -> result1;
num2 -> result2;
enddefine
```

Calling this procedure as:

```
vars x, y;
multi(3, 7) -> (x, y);
```

results in x being bound to 3 and y being bound to 7.

Let's now return to our simple database application to see how this could be implemented in POP-11. We'll begin with the creation of the database, which is simply a list of lists.

```
[ [TIM 41] [JILL 35] [MEGAN 14] [ELISE 9] [MARC 6] ] -> db;
```

Identifying the number of records in our database can use the length procedure. This returns the number of objects in the list:

```
define numrecords( thelist ) -> result;
length(thelist) -> result;
enddefine;
```

Using our previously defined database, we can call this easily as:

```
numrecords( db ) =>
```

to emit the number of records.

The procedure to emit the names of the records is provided next (emitnames). For this procedure, we've used an imperative style, iterating through the database list for a number of times defined by the length procedure.

```
define emitnames( thelist );
  vars num;
  0 -> num;
  while num < length(thelist) do
  hd(hd(thelist)) =>
  tl(thelist) -> thelist;
endwhile;
enddefine;
```

This function can be called as shown here:

```
emitnames( db );
```

Let's look at our final procedure, to add a new record to our database (addrecord). This procedure simply combines two lists (using the <> operator) and sets the result back to the original database variable (db).

```
define addrecord( record );
db <> record -> db;
enddefine;
```

This procedure is called with a list object (actually a list containing our list record):

```
addrecord( [ [MADDIE 3] ] );
```

Finally, let's look at the complete application (user calls to our database procedures) to see the expected output from the POP-11 interpreter. First, our simple application emits the current names in the database, adds a new record, and then emits the names again. Finally, we emit the number of records in the database.

```
[[TIM 41] [JILL 35] [MEGAN 14] [ELISE 9] [MARC 6] ] -> db;
printf('Current record list\n');
emitnames( db );
printf('Adding a new record\n');
addrecord( [ [MADDIE 3] ] );
printf('Num records: ');
numrecords( db ) =>
printf('\n');
printf('Current record list\n');
emitnames( db );
```

Executing this POP-11 program with our previously defined functions provides:

```
;;; DECLARING VARIABLE db
Current record list
** TIM
** JILL
** MEGAN
** ELISE
** MARC
Adding a new record
Num records: ** 6
Current record list
** TIM
** JILL
** MEGAN
** ELISE
** MARC
** MADDIE
```

POP-11 Summary

POP-11 is an interesting language, first because while old it's still useful, and second because it's an interesting perspective on multi-paradigm programming. POP-11 supports imperative programming, logic programming, and functional programming within a single language. A large task, but POP-11 does it well.

Prolog

Prolog (which stands for "Programming in Logic") is one of the most interesting languages in use today. Prolog is a declarative language that focuses on logic. Programming in Prolog involves specifying rules and facts and allowing Prolog to derive a solution. This differs from typical declarative programming, where a solution is coded. Building a Prolog application typically involves describing the landscape of the problem (using rules and facts), and then using goals to invoke execution.

History of Prolog

Prolog was created around 1972 by Alain Colmerauer and Robert Kowalski as a competitor to the LISP language. LISP was dominant at the time for artificial-intelligence applications, but Prolog then came. Prolog, as the name implies, focuses on logic rather typical sequential programming.

The earliest Prolog applications were in the domain of natural-language programming, as this was the object of research by its creators. Natural-language programming (otherwise known as computational linguistics) is supported by a unique feature of Prolog. Prolog includes a built-in mechanism for parsing context-free grammars, making it ideal for NLP or parsing grammars (such as the Prolog language itself). In fact, like LISP, a Prolog interpreter can be easily implemented in Prolog.

Today, Prolog remains a language used primarily by researchers, but the language has advanced to support multiple programming paradigms. Prolog is ideal for developing knowledge-based systems (such as expert systems) and also systems for research into computer algebra. Prolog's problem-solving capabilities maintain it as an important language for problems in the knowledge domain.

Overview of the Prolog Language

Prolog is comprised of two fundamental elements, the database and the interpreter. The database contains the facts and rules that are used to describe the problem. The interpreter provides the control in the form of a deduction method. From this simple description, it's clear that programming in Prolog differs from programming in other declarative languages. For this reason, we'll sharply focus on the unique features of Prolog for building knowledge-centered systems.

Data Representation

Prolog doesn't include data types, per se, but instead what can be referred to as lexical elements (or sequences of characters in legal combinations). Some of the important lexical elements of Prolog include atoms, numbers, variables, and lists.

An atom is a string made up of characters (lower and upper case), digits, and the underscore. Numbers are simply sequences of digits with an optional preceding minus sign. Variables have the same format as atoms, except that the first character is always capitalized. A list is represented as a comma-delimited set of elements, surrounded by brackets.

person	Atom
f_451	Atom
'A complex atom.'	Atom
86	Number
-451	Number
Person	Variable
A_variable	Variable
[a, simple, list]	List
[a, [list of lists]]	List

List Processing

Like the functional languages we've explored so far, Prolog provides the typical set of list-processing predicates. These allow the construction of lists, manipulation of lists, and also extracting information about lists.

NOTE ▶   *The following Prolog examples will show the dialog with a Prolog interpreter. Commands are shown in bold (following the Prolog command prompt, ?-).*

Constructing a list is performed simply as follows:

```
| ?- [a, b, c, d] = X.
X = [a,b,c,d]
yes
| ?-
```

The X variable refers to the list [a, b, c, d], which is identified by the Prolog interpreter. We can also concatenate two lists using the append predicate. This predicate takes two lists and produces a new list for the variable name defined (third argument).

```
| ?- append( [[a, b], [c, d]], [[e, f]], Y ).
Y = [[a,b],[c,d],[e,f]]
yes
| ?-
```

Prolog can also tell us how many objects are in a list, using the length predicate. The form of this predicate takes two arguments, the first a list, and the second, a variable which will be used to refer to the length:

```
| ?- length( [a, b, c, [d, e]], Length ).
Length = 4
yes
| ?-
```

Prolog also allows matching an object from a list using the member predicate. Using this predicate, we get

```
| ?- member( elise, [marc, jill, megan, elise, marc] ).
true ?
yes
| ?-
```

Finally, Prolog also permits the typical head and tail manipulations of lists. As in LISP and Scheme, the head of a list is the first element, and the tail of a list is the remainder. Prolog can extract both the head and the tail of a list at the same time. In the following example, we create a list, and then extract the head to variable H and the tail to variable T.

```
| ?- [a, b, c, d] = [H | T].
H = a
T = [b,c,d]
yes
| ?-
```

As illustrated here, Prolog provides a rich set of list-processing predicates matching those provided in the functional languages. Let's look now at the features that make the Prolog language unique.

Facts, Rules, and Evaluation

What separates Prolog from all other languages is its built-in ability of deduction. Let's start with a look at facts, and how we can define new facts for the Prolog database. We'll begin a simple example, and then build up to more complex facts.

Let's start with a set of rules describing fruits and vegetables. A fact is known as a predicate, and consists of a head and some number of arguments.

For example, the following facts define the head as the type of product (fruit or vegetable) and the argument is the name of the object.

fruit(pear).
fruit(apple).
fruit(tomato).
vegetable(radish).
vegetable(lettuce).
vegetable(tomato).

Each of these predicates is true, so we can query the Prolog database, such as:

| ?- **fruit(pear).**
yes

for which Prolog would reply with 'yes' (a pear is a fruit). We could also query whether a pear is a vegetable, and Prolog would return 'no' (a pear is not a vegetable).

| ?- **vegetable(pear).**
no

Now let's say we want to know what things are fruits. We could provide a variable to Prolog (as the argument) and get the things that are fruits, such as:

| ?- **fruit(X).**
X = pear
X = apple
X = tomato
yes

You'll also notice that the tomato is both a fruit and a vegetable. Let's call this an oddity, and create a rule to define it as such. What we want to do is tell Prolog that if a thing is both a fruit and a vegetable, then we'll classify it as an oddity. In Prolog, we would create this rule as follows:

oddity(X) :-
fruit(X),
vegetable(X).

With this new rule, we can ask Prolog if any oddities exist, by the following query:

```
| ?- oddity(X).
X = tomato
yes
```

So let's look at our rule in more detail. The oddity rule simply says that an object is an oddity if the object is both a fruit and a vegetable (binding to the variable X). The :- sequence can be read as IF, and ',' can be read as AND.

Finally, let's say that we want to know if a thing is a fruit or a vegetable. We can encode an OR using the semicolon, as follows:

```
fruit_or_vegetable(X) :-
fruit(X);
vegetable(X).
```

Invoking this rule as 'fruit_or_vegetable(X).' results in the list of both fruits and vegetables (with tomato being provided twice).

Let's now look at a more complex example that includes a couple of levels of rules. An interesting example of Prolog's deduction capabilities can be illustrated using genealogy. A simple family tree is shown in Figure 13.2. This tree shows four generations, with parents at the top and great-grand children at the bottom.

In the end, we'll show how to encode rules to deduce the parents of a child, the grandparents of a child, the children of parents or grandparents, and others.

Let's start with facts, and how we'll encode the family tree information in Prolog. First, we encode the gender of the individuals in the tree using the predicate male and female. The following facts encode the gender of a person:

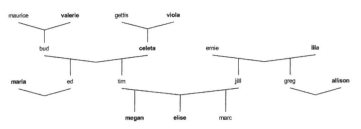

FIGURE 13.2:　**A sample family tree for Prolog deduction.**

male(maurice).
male(gettis).
male(bud).
male(ernie).
male(tim).
male(ed).
male(marc).
male(greg).

female(katherine).
female(viola).
female(celeta).
female(lila).
female(jill).
female(allison).
female(maria).
female(megan).
female(elise).

Next, we identify the members of the tree that are married using the married predicate. This relates a male person and a female person in holy matrimony:

married(maurice, valerie).
married(gettis, viola).
married(bud, celeta).
married(ernie, lila).
married(tim, jill).
married(ed, maria).
married(greg, allison).

The next step is to identify the relationships of the people to one another. The only relationship that's necessary to note is the set of parents for a given individual. From this, we can deduce other relationships, such as grandparent or grandchild (as we'll see later).

father(maurice, bud).
father(gettis, celeta).
father(bud, tim).
father(bud, ed).

father(ernie, jill).
father(ernie, greg).
father(tim, megan).
father(tim, elise).
father(tim, marc).

mother(valerie, bud).
mother(viola, celeta).
mother(celeta, tim).
mother(celeta, ed).
mother(lila, jill).
mother(lila, greg).
mother(jill, megan).
mother(jill, elise).
mother(jill, marc).

The father and mother facts specify the parent followed by the child. The predicate, father or mother, defines their specific relationship.

Now that we've defined our facts, let's create a set of rules that allow us to deduce some additional relationships. First, let's have a look at two rules that can determine the husband or wife of a given person. To be a husband, a person of the male gender is married to a person of the female gender. Similarly, a wife is a female person that is also married to a male person.

husband(Man, Woman) :-
    male(Man), **married**(Man, Woman).
wife(Woman, Man) :-
    female(Woman), **married**(Man, Woman).

The next rule defines whether a person is a parent of a child. In this rule, we use an OR (;) and simply define that a person is a parent of a child, if that person is a mother or father of that child.

parent(Parent, Child) :-
    father(Parent, Child); **mother**(Parent, Child).

We can then use the parent rule to create a new rule for the child test. In this rule, we define that a person is a child of person if that person is the parent of the child (using the parent rule).

child(Child, Parent) :-
    parent(Parent, Child).

With the child rule, we can create two other rules to refine the child relationship. First, we create a son rule, which defines that a son is a male child of a parent. Similarly, a daughter is a female child of a parent.

son(Child, Parent) :-
    male(Child), **child**(Child, Parent).
daughter(Child, Parent) :-
    female(Child), **child**(Child, Parent).

So far, our rules have focused on direct relationships between persons in the database. Now let's look at two rules that define indirect relationships to persons in the database, grandchildren and grandparents. A grandparent can be defined as the parent of the child's parent. Conversely, a grandchild is the child of the grandparent's child. We can look at these both as parent relationships, as defined below:

grandparent(Gparent, Gchild) :-
    parent(Gparent, Parent), **parent**(Parent, Gchild).
grandchild(Gchild, Gparent) :-
    grandparent(Gparent, Gchild).

In the grandparent rule, we match the facts for the grandparent, and find the children (which are referenced by the Parent variable). Then we use the parent rule to identify if the specified Gchild is a child of that Parent. The grandchild rule is then a reverse of the grandparent rule.

    Let's now have a look at this database in action. This is illustrated below using the GNU prolog interpreter (`gprolog`), (see Listing 13.8).

Listing 13.8: Querying the family tree database with `gprolog`.

mtj@camus:~$ **gprolog**
GNU Prolog 1.2.18
By Daniel Diaz
Copyright (C) 1999-2004 Daniel Diaz
| ?- **consult('family.pl').**
compiling /home/mtj/family.pl for byte code...
/home/mtj/family.pl compiled, 71 lines read - 5920 bytes written, 51 ms
(10 ms) yes

```
| ?- grandchild(marc, X).
X = bud
X = ernie
X = celeta
X = lila
no
| ?- married(bud, X).
X = celeta
yes
| ?- daughter(X, jill).
X = megan
X = elise
no
| ?- son(X, maurice).
X = bud
no
| ?- mother(celeta, X).
X = tim
X = ed
yes
| ?- grandparent(X, tim).
X = maurice
X = gettis
X = valerie
X = viola
(20 ms) no
| ?-
```

Also of interest is the trace facility provided by `gprolog`. This allows us to trace the flow of the application of rules for a given query. For example, the following query checks to see if a person is a grandparent of another person. Note here that the variables preceded by underscores are temporary variables created by Prolog during its rule checking. Note also the call/exit pairs which determine the relationships along the ways as needed by the specific rules. As specified above, a grandparent is a person who is the parent of the parent.

Listing 13.9:   Querying the family tree database with `gprolog` with trace enabled.

```
| ?- trace.
The debugger will first creep -- showing everything (trace)
```

```
yes
{trace}
| ?- grandparent(bud, marc).
    1   1  Call: grandparent(bud,marc)
    2   2  Call: parent(bud,_79)
    3   3  Call: father(bud,_103)
    3   3  Exit: father(bud,tim)
    2   2  Exit: parent(bud,tim)
    4   2  Call: parent(tim,marc)
    5   3  Call: father(tim,marc)
    5   3  Exit: father(tim,marc)
    4   2  Exit: parent(tim,marc)
    1   1  Exit: grandparent(bud,marc)
true ?
yes
{trace}
| ?-
```

Prolog can be used for much more complex relationships, but this illustrates the power of deduction provided by the Prolog engine.

Arithmetic Expressions

While Prolog supports the arithmetic operators, their use differs from what you might expect. For example, the following expression is false:

2 * 4 = 8.

This expression is false because '2 * 4' is a compound term and '8' is a number. Arithmetically, they are the same, but Prolog sees this differently. If we're testing the validity of an expression, we instead use the is operator. For example, the following expression is true, as we're checking the validity of the expression using is:

8 is 2 * 4.

We can relate our expression to a variable using the is operator as well. The following final example illustrates the variety of operations that are available.

| ?- X is (6 * 2 + 4 ** 3) / 4.

X = 19.0
yes
| ?-

Finally, let's look at an example that combines arithmetic expressions with logic programming. In this example, we'll maintain facts about the prices of products, and then a rule that can compute the total cost of a product given a quantity (again, encoded as a fact).

First, let's define our initial set of facts that maintain the price list of the available products (in this case, fruits).

```
cost( banana, 0.35 ).
cost( apple, 0.25 ).
cost( orange, 0.45 ).
cost( mango, 1.50 ).
```

These facts relate (or create a mapping between) a fruit to a per-item cost (for example, mangos run around $1.50 each). We can also provide a quantity that we plan to purchase, using another relation for the fruit, for example:

```
qty( mango, 4 ).
```

We can then add a rule that calculates the total cost of an item purchase:

```
total_cost(X,Y) :-
  cost(X, Cost),
  qty(X, Quantity),
  Y is Cost * Quantity.
```

What this rule says is that if we have a product with a cost fact, and a quantity fact, then we can create a relation to the product cost and quantity values for the item. We can invoke this from the Prolog interpreter as:

```
| ?- total_cost( mango, TC ).
TC = 6.0
yes
| ?-
```

This tells us that the total cost for four mangos is $6.00.

Prolog Summary

As we've demonstrated here, Prolog is unique language that offers programming in a semi-traditional imperative paradigm, as well as logic programming based on first-order predicate calculus. While restricted to Horn clauses, Prolog is a powerful language that permits the development of knowledge-based applications. This introduction has only scratched the surface of Prolog, and the resource section provides more information on where to go to learn more.

OTHER LANGUAGES

As illustrated by the many examples in C provided by this book, artificial-intelligence applications are by no means restricted to the traditional languages of AI. Other popular languages provide some of the powerful features that were demonstrated for LISP and Scheme. For example, the Ruby language provides dynamic function creation similar to the lambda function available in LISP and Scheme. In fact, the lambda keyword remains. The following example illustrates the lambda function in Ruby.

```
irb> mulby2 = lambda{ |x| x*2 }
=> #<Proc>
irb> mulby2.call(5)
=> 10
```

Ruby also provides the Procs method, which creates new procedure objects:

```
irb> def mulby(x)
irb>  return Proc.new {|n| n*x }
irb> end
=> nil
irb> mulby2 = mulby(2)
=> #<Proc>
irb> mulby2.call(5)
=> 10
```

The Python language also supports some of the functional features you'll find in LISP or Scheme. Recall the map function which allows a function to be applied to a list of data. Using map, a function is provided (which is to be applied to the list), as well as the list itself. The following example illustrates creating a function that multiples the argument by two, and then applies this function to a list.

```
>>> def mulby2(val):
...         return val*2
...
>>> mylist = [1, 2, 3, 4, 5]
>>> newlist = map(mulby2, mylist )
>>> print newlist
[2, 4, 6, 8, 10]
>>>
```

As these short examples illustrate, functional programming is not restricted solely to functional languages. The newer object-oriented scripting languages, such as Ruby and Python, have borrowed the key features from their ancestors and are bringing them into the future.

CHAPTER SUMMARY

Languages are the vehicles by which developers create solutions to problems. But unfortunately, languages are also religious artifacts that become the centerpieces of heated debates. But ultimately, languages are tools, and each has their strengths and weaknesses. This chapter introduced the major classes of languages for AI, and also discussed four particular languages that are used in AI application development. The chapter concluded with a review of some of the features that started in the older functional languages, but have now been applied to modern domain-specific languages.

REFERENCES

[R6RS] Sperber, Michael, et al "Revised Report on the Algorithm Language Scheme," 9/5/2006.
Available online at http://www.r6r2.org/r6r2_91.pdf
[Sloman 1996] Sloman, Aaron "An Overview of POP-11," Second Edition.
Available online at http://www.cs.bham.ac.uk/research/projects/poplog/primer/

RESOURCES

Dybvig, R. Kent. "The Scheme Programming Language," 2003. The MIT Press.

GNU Prolog

Available online at http://gnu-prolog.inria.fr/

McCarthy, John. "Recursive Functions of Symbolic Expressions and Their Computation by Machine." 1960.

Sloman, Aaron. "Teach Primer – An Overview of POP-11," 1996.

Available online at http://cs.bham.ac.uk/research/projects/poplog/primer/

Steele, Guy and Sussman, Gerald. "The Original Lambda Papers," 1975-1980.

Available online at http://library.readscheme.org/page1.html

EXERCISES

1. Historically, what was the first AI language, and what features made it ideal for AI programming of the day?
2. What does it mean for a language to be Turing complete?
3. Describe the primary features of functional languages, as described in this text.
4. Describe the purpose of the map function, which can be found in the older functional languages, as well as the new domain-specific languages such as Ruby and Python.
5. Describe how first-class functions are important for AI programming.
6. Define the important characteristics of imperative programming.
7. Describe what is meant by polymorphism for object-oriented languages.
8. Define one primary difference of logic programming languages, such as Prolog, to other languages.
9. What feature of LISP introduced the concept of dynamic functions?
10. What is the result of the operation (car (cdr '(a, (b, c), d))) in LISP?
11. What is the result of the operation (cadr '(a, (b, c), d, e))) in LISP?
12. Describe the purpose of the eval function in LISP.
13. Write a function in LISP to return the age given a name for the database functions.
14. Describe some of the primary differences between Scheme and its predecessor, LISP.

15. In Scheme, provide the evaluation for (list '(a b) '(c d) 'd).

16. In Scheme, what is the evaluation of (length '(()))?

17. Provide the result of this Scheme example:

(map (lambda (x) (+ x 1) '(1 2 3 4))

18. Create a Scheme function that emits the Fibonacci sequence for a defined limit.

19. Write a Scheme function that emits the age for a name in the example database.

20. How does POP-11 compare to LISP and also to imperative languages like C?

21. Describe the differences in list processing between Scheme and POP-11.

22. Build a simple conversational program in POP-11 that supports simple English language interactions.

23. Define how the Prolog language is different from other languages discussed in this chapter.

24. Describe the fundamental list-processing operations provided by Prolog.

25. Extend the Prolog family tree example for two new rules, grandson and granddaughter.

A ABOUT THE CD-ROM

- Included on the CD-ROM are simulations, code, videos, figures from the text, third party software, and other files related to topics in artificial intelligence.
- See the "README" files for any specific information/system requirements related to each file folder, but most files will run on Windows 2000 or higher and Linux.

INDEX